Anglo-Saxon Studies 22

FOOD, EATING AND IDENTITY
IN EARLY MEDIEVAL ENGLAND

T0386108

Anglo-Saxon Studies

ISSN 1475-2468

GENERAL EDITORS
John Hines
Catherine Cubitt

'Anglo-Saxon Studies' aims to provide a forum for the best scholarship on the Anglo-Saxon peoples in the period from the end of Roman Britain to the Norman Conquest, including comparative studies involving adjacent populations and periods; both new research and major re-assessments of central topics are welcomed.

Books in the series may be based in any one of the principal disciplines of archaeology, art history, history, language and literature, and inter- or multi-disciplinary studies are encouraged.

Proposals or enquiries may be sent directly to the editors or the publisher at the addresses given below; all submissions will receive prompt and informed consideration.

Professor John Hines, School of History, Archaeology and Religion, Cardiff University, John Percival Building, Colum Drive, Cardiff, Wales, CF10 3EU, UK

Professor Catherine Cubitt, School of History, Faculty of Arts and Humanities, University of East Anglia, Norwich, England, NR4 7TJ, UK

Boydell & Brewer, PO Box 9, Woodbridge, Suffolk, England, IP12 3DF, UK

*Previously published volumes in the series
are listed at the back of this book*

FOOD, EATING AND IDENTITY IN EARLY MEDIEVAL ENGLAND

Allen J. Frantzen

THE BOYDELL PRESS

First published 2014
The Boydell Press, Woodbridge
Paperback edition 2017

ISBN 978 1 84383 908 8 hardback
ISBN 978 1 78327 245 7 paperback

The Boydell Press is an imprint of Boydell & Brewer Ltd
PO Box 9, Woodbridge, Suffolk IP12 3DF, UK
and of Boydell & Brewer Inc.
668 Mount Hope Avenue, Rochester, NY 14620–2731, USA
website: www.boydellandbrewer.com

A CIP catalogue record for this book is available
from the British Library

The publisher has no responsibility for the continued existence or
accuracy of URLs for external or third-party internet websites
referred to in this book, and does not guarantee that any content on
such websites is, or will remain, accurate or appropriate

This publication is printed on acid-free paper

For George R. Paterson

Contents

Illustrations

Acknowledgments

In 2005 I heard Chris Loveluck read a paper on feasting that ranged from Anglo-Saxon calendar illustrations to dolphin bones found at a site in North Lincolnshire called Flixborough, a name I knew from no Anglo-Saxon text. Archaeology had evidently changed since I had last struggled through essays about shield bosses and the complexities of dating them. A few weeks later I visited Loveluck's site in Denmark. I troweled through sandy soil a half inch at a time, hoping something would turn up, a bit of bone or a piece of pottery. At the end of the first day we had nothing but shifted sand and aching backs to show for our labor. Although wet, cold, and unpromising, that experience was a good introduction to archaeology and to the distance between literary history and the material record of the early Middle Ages. That is where this inquiry into food, eating, and identity began.

My thanks to those who have read parts of this project and helped me at various stages: Renata Bauer, Graham Caie, Andrew Donnelly, James Driscoll, Jennifer Frey, Chris Grubbs, Stacy Klein, Christina Lee, Shannon Lewis-Simpson, Michael Mason, Leonard Niedorf, and William Schipper. I am grateful for the kind cooperation of Rose Nicholson, North Lincolnshire Museums Service; Lesley Collett and Christine Kyriacou, York Archaeological Trust; and D. H. Evans, Humber Archaeology. I wish to thank Joyce Wexler, Department of English, Loyola University Chicago, and Loyola's Office of Research Services for support. At Boydell & Brewer, Caroline Palmer, Rohais Haughton, Rob Kinsey, and Rosie Pearce were engaged and helpful at every stage, and Faith Eales was a marvelous copy editor. I am especially grateful to four scholar-teachers who have been generous with their time and talent. Chris Loveluck and John Hines have opened new dimensions of Anglo-Saxon material and textual culture to me. I owe my interest in archaeology to them and to Gareth Davies and Edward Oakley, and to each my warm thanks.

Abbreviations and Citations

ASP	Frantzen, ed., *The Anglo-Saxon Penitentials*
ASPR	Anglo-Saxon Poetic Records
BAR	British Archaeological Reports
BEASE	Lapidge *et al.*, eds., *Blackwell Encyclopaedia of Anglo-Saxon England*
CBA	Council for British Archaeology
CED	Haddan and Stubbs, eds., *Councils and Ecclesiastical Documents*
DOE	Cameron *et al.*, eds., *Dictionary of Old English*
DOEWC	Healey, ed., *Dictionary of Old English Web Corpus*
EETS	Early English Text Society
EHD	Whitelock, ed., *English Historical Documents*, vol. 1
GDA	Liebermann, ed., *Die Gesetze der Angelsachsen*, vol. 3
LEEK	Attenborough, ed. and trans., *The Laws of the Earliest English Kings*
LKE	Robertson, ed. and trans., *The Laws of the Kings of England*
MEL	Wormald, *The Making of English Law*
MHP	McNeill and Gamer, trans., *Medieval Handbooks of Penance*
OE	Old English
OEC	*OE Canons of Theodore* (penitential)
OED	*Oxford English Dictionary*
OEH	*OE Handbook* (penitential)
OEI	*OE Introduction* (penitential)
OEP	*OE Penitential* (penitential)
OES	*OE Scriftboc* (penitential)
PL	Migne, ed., *Patrologiae cursus completus, series latina*
TOE	Roberts *et al.*, eds., *Thesaurus of Old English*

Complete references are given in the Works Cited. First citations of all works, including internet resources, are given in the notes by the author's full name, short title, and page. For URLs, I give the plain English title of the site; all sites included in the Works Cited were viewed on September 1, 2013. Translations of Old English and Latin are mine unless otherwise noted.

References to the Anglo-Saxon penitentials are taken from Allen J. Frantzen, *ASP*, online at http://www.anglo-saxon.net. Please note that newer browsers, such as Firefox or Chrome, tend to provide better functionality for all aspects of this website. Please follow these directions to locate texts on the site. For the sentence from the *Scriftboc* marked X26.08.01, the reference given is Frantzen, *ASP*, *OES*, X26.08.01. To find this canon from the homepage, select Texts, then *Scriftboc*, then Description & Index, then Table 2, which is the Canon Finder. At Table 2, use Ctrl + F to search X26.08.01. You will be taken to the sentence marked X26.08.01; versions of this canon in other manuscripts, Y26.08.01 and S26.08.01, will be available there, along with a translation. The database includes all versions of every canon.

Introduction

The Anglo-Saxons understood material things in a way most people no longer do. Yet their relationship to objects is not entirely beyond our grasp. In the 1950s, when I was a boy, rural life in the United States bore some resemblance to conditions in Anglo-Saxon England. Animals, plants, and the tools needed to manage and process them filled our living space. Cows had to be milked and fed every day, including Thanksgiving, Christmas, and all the other holidays. Family feasts included meat from our own animals – pork sausage in the turkey stuffing, perhaps – and canned or frozen vegetables from the garden. We experienced the relationship between plants and animals and food on the table directly. Although there currently is a trend for restaurants and food businesses to emphasize local produce and stress the connection between what is on the plate and where it was grown, few people butcher their own animals or grow their own food any longer. In my youth this was not the case.

Until the period after World War I, most people in the United States, Canada, and Great Britain lived in the countryside, like my family. The shift from rural to urban was gradual. The US Census Bureau shows that the split was 60 percent to 40 percent in favor of the rural population in 1900. By 1920 the distribution was almost even, 51 percent rural to 49 percent urban. Thereafter the shift was more pronounced: 44 percent to 56 percent in 1940; 30 percent to 70 percent in 1960. By 1990 the United States was 25 percent rural and 75 percent urban. Much of this change, in which over one-third of the country's population was reclassified as urban, happened in the first two decades of the century (when the rural population shrank by nine percentage points) and between 1940 and 1960 (when the rural population declined a further fourteen points). Losses since have been much smaller, in part because rural life itself has changed.[1] Blue collar workers who live in the countryside drive to factory jobs and shop in supermarkets and discount chains. Their habits are more urban than rural. Cities have changed too. Until recently it was common for people in some urban areas to raise their own animals and to have large gardens. Tour the impressive reconstruction of Viking York, or Jorvik, and you will see that ducks, pigs, and cows shared domestic space with the inhabitants, as did animals in the hinterlands. In the developed world, of course, nobody lives like that any more.

---

[1] United States Census Bureau, "Urban and Rural Population" (August 1995).

1

My interest is in rural life one thousand years ago and what it tells us about food culture, by which I mean the relationship of food to objects and words for these objects. The history of rural life is difficult to recover. The Anglo-Saxon countryside was not necessarily remote from document-producing centers of secular and ecclesiastical administration. Every Anglo-Saxonist knows that the cowherd Cædmon needed only the reeve who supervised him to gain an audience with Abbess Hild, who was in charge of the monastery at which Cædmon worked. Monasteries in Bede's time, like the Irish monasteries on which they were at least partly modeled, kept a core of workers near the enclosed precincts. These workers, mixing with working monks, wander through Bede's pages as they must have wandered around Monkwearmouth-Jarrow and other monastic estates. In psychological and ideological terms, however, the distance between the rural population and the academic elite was (and still is) immense.

Texts are only part of the story. Their testimony is more than matched by that of the ordinary objects archaeologists have unearthed. Unlike the texts, the object survivals are democratic. Most Anglo-Saxons never saw a book, but the pots, pans, knives, bones, and leatherwork that surrounded them survive in such great numbers that cataloguing them runs years behind their discovery. In order to access the vast archaeological record, I analyze reports from recent excavations and survey their claims about production, distribution, and consumption. Their inventories of food-related objects, especially those that archaeologists call "small finds," include querns or grinding stones, pottery fragments, parts of iron tools, and objects in wood. Recent reports also incorporate sophisticated analysis of evidence of animal husbandry, fishing, butchery, and other diet-related practices.

By looking at rural life in terms of food objects and processes, I hope to illuminate the everyday food culture of the Anglo-Saxons. Urban or rural, food culture is usually discussed in terms of the feast. I have already alluded to Christmas and Thanksgiving, not as high-points in my family's annual cycle of menus (although they were), but as special events that did not mean a holiday from food-related labor. We might say that feasts are to food as poetry is to history: important but selective evidence that is too stylized to represent daily life. Feasting, like poetry, is rarified and sometimes spectacular. For all that, however, feasting is not more important than the routine events it obscures.

Much has been written about feasting, just as – and not coincidentally – much has been written about *Beowulf*, a feast-rich poem that stands over Anglo-Saxon poetry as the feast stands over Anglo-Saxon food culture. We should study this great epic, by all means, but we should not, as we do so, believe that we are unpacking the worlds of Denmark or England between the sixth and the eleventh centuries. Feasting in *Beowulf* is about making speeches, passing gold cups, and demonstrating how well warriors hold their liquor. To feast is to drink, but any feast, like any poem, can lead to information about the culture that produced it, provided that food can be given a place at the table and food products traced to their roots in the everyday. Such contextualizing activity is more common in the study of poetry than in the study of feasting. Readers of Old English know that poems share ideas with administrative and didactic texts such as laws and homilies, as well as with scriptural exegesis, world history, and scientific and medical writing. Studies of the feast, however, are seldom integrated into studies of food culture. The analysis of feasting ought to include information about what medieval people ate and should encourage awareness of the social mechanisms that contributed to agricultural markets and trade in food objects. Feasts were a product of such systems, not the end of the food chain but rather one of several nodes linked by craft, trade, appetite, and social custom that formed food networks.

My focus is on what the Anglo-Saxons ate and how their diet, their processes, and their food words and objects contributed to their identities. This task resembles descriptions of daily life in the Middle Ages, a kind of inquiry now disdained because it has so often been both insufficiently specialized and undertheorized. The identities in such work are also often imported from modern ideas of the Anglo-Saxons, stereotypes which the evidence, bent along teleological lines, invariably confirms. Readers have enjoyed such accounts at least since 1862, when John Thrupp published *The Anglo-Saxon Home: A History of the Domestic Institutions and Customs of England from the Fifth to the Eleventh Century*. Thrupp did not treat food as a separate category, and there is nothing about agriculture in his book. His chapters on the gentlemanly pursuits of fishing and hunting do not, needless to say, describe subsistence-level activities.[2] In 1864, in the preface to a collection of texts illustrating "the history of science" before the Norman Conquest, Rev. Oswald Cockayne celebrated the "very fair share of comfortable food, and healing medicines, and savoury drinks" that the Anglo-Saxons were able to extract from the land, commending "the supply upon the tables" as "abundant, and not over studious of luxury and refinement," an account, however heartening, drawn from Tacitus, who was not discussing the Anglo-Saxons.[3] In 1871 Thomas Wright situated food in more functional and practical contexts in *The Homes of Other Days: A History of Domestic Manners and Sentiments in England from the Earliest Known Period to Modern Times*. Anglo-Saxon drinking glasses, pots, bowls, and buckets appear in the first chapter, most of them recovered from graves but all of them associated, directly or indirectly, with what Wright envisioned as the Anglo-Saxons' "ordinary dwellings."[4] Both books are still useful, although they and similar studies no longer retain credibility. Mountains of new evidence and shifts in theoretical perspectives have changed the study of material culture and its meaning. Perhaps comprehensive accounts of daily life in the early Middle Ages are now outside the realm of possibility,

---

[2] John Thrupp, *The Anglo-Saxon Home*, pp. vii–ix.
[3] Oswald Cockayne, ed., *Leechdoms, Wortcunning and Starcraft*, 2: ix–ix, quotations from pp. vii and xi, n. 7.
[4] Thomas Wright, *The Homes of Other Days*; see pp. 17–21 for illustrations of the objects mentioned.

although not outside the realm of desirability. A recent entry in the field is Sally Crawford's *Daily Life in Anglo-Saxon England*.[5] As an archaeologist, Crawford is well aware of the importance of information that never before figured into books like hers, including population density and life expectancy, settlement organization, and diet. Her book, limited only by its minimal scholarly apparatus, is a significant advance in popular studies of Anglo-Saxon culture. Along with the pioneering work of Debby Banham and Ann Hagen, Crawford's study bodes well for new views of daily life as it was lived a thousand years ago.[6] Peter Fowler's *Farming in the First Millennium AD* breaks down conventional period divisions, and H. E. M. Cool's *Eating and Drinking in Roman Britain* shows how much can be done to recover the food culture of remote peoples.

Although theoretical ideas about daily life can be hard to find even in recent studies, new work emphasizes the regional and the local, highlighting disciplinary differences that are seldom discussed in earlier studies, which often focus on the national and the diplomatic.[7] Still of great value is Dorothy Whitelock's *The Beginnings of English Society*. Published in 1952, this book outlines the place of agriculture, fishing, and hunting in the Anglo-Saxon world.[8] Whitelock's book is, in a way, the direct descendant of the books by Thrupp and Wright. Whitelock offers a history of the Anglo-Saxons that embraces more than their politics and religion. Objects of a certain class receive their due in David Wilson's *The Anglo-Saxons*, published in 1966; images and objects pertaining to ecclesiastical and aristocratic art and dress predominate, and a few agricultural tools represent the working world.[9]

Taking advantage of strides in archaeology since Whitelock and Wilson wrote, and sharing in the central aims of their work and that of Hagen, Banham, Crawford, Fowler, and Cool, this book balances written and material evidence. It also takes up some of the theoretical issues that make the steady friction between archaeological and textual data productive. The book is divided into three parts, the first exploring theoretical connections between words and things; the second examining archaeological and textual evidence of four important groups of food objects; and the third focusing on connections between ecclesiastical and secular processes that connected food to social life and shaped identities for those who fasted and feasted.

Chapter 1 describes the problems we encounter when we try to locate ordinary objects in the rich library of texts and images from the period. The chapter examines the need to balance texts with material culture, and

[5] Sally Crawford, *Daily Life in Anglo-Saxon England*.
[6] Debby Banham, *Food and Drink in Anglo-Saxon England*; Ann Hagen, *A Handbook of Anglo-Saxon Food and Drink* and *A Second Handbook of Anglo-Saxon Food and Drink*.
[7] See comments in Peter Fowler, *Farming in the First Millennium AD*, pp. 25–27.
[8] Dorothy Whitelock, *The Beginnings of English Society*, pp. 98–104 (agriculture and fishing), pp. 65, 85, 91, 99, 208 (hunting).
[9] David Wilson, *The Anglo-Saxons*, "Figures" and "Plates," pp. 7–10.

critiques the recent phenomenon of textualization, which treats objects as part of textual discourse and implies that objects can be read and decoded as texts are read and decoded. Such ways of reading were not widespread among the Anglo-Saxons, most of whom were not literate, unlike their learned and articulate lay and religious leaders. As an alternative to textualization, this chapter looks at objects in contexts that demonstrate their functions in the working world rather than meanings assigned to the objects within a universe of symbolic meanings.

The second chapter surveys what has been said about food and feasting in the Old English period. Some studies approach the feast as a literary event; others move from the feast to the social space of feasting and to the things needed to prepare and stage the feast. The feast was an occasion for communal rites. It was more than an emblem of heroic culture, for it also framed a stark contrast between scarcity and excess. In place of the implied model of a pyramid in which life at the top, celebrated in the feast, overshadows the productive activity needed to sustain opulence, I develop the concept of food within a network of nodes, some formed by multiple intersections, some by only a few. Networks are connections; no point in a food network, no matter how small or large, is a terminus. Feasts are the densest points in a food network – like market towns, they are points at which large numbers of supply lines converged.

Chapter 3 describes the Anglo-Saxons' kitchen vocabulary and identifies the kinds of texts that comprise the world of food words. I classify the lexical evidence of food culture found in the *Thesaurus of Old English*. The lexical evidence, I show, lends itself to a network model as well. I use food vocabulary to examine genres in which food is written about. Regulatory texts and a few other genres treat food in material rather than symbolic ways that link production to consumption; glosses prove especially useful. References to food in most kinds of poetry are rare and tell us little about the workings of Anglo-Saxon society; riddles and charms are exceptions. I focus on texts that help us learn about food objects and how they were made or used, not what they might have symbolized.

The four chapters of Part II focus on food objects and the words for them. Chapter 4 takes up the quernstone (or hand-mill), examines evidence from a range of Anglo-Saxon settlements, and looks at the textual evidence that describes milling and mills. Chapter 5 examines cooking pots, the largest category of pottery, and related forms. Chapter 6 explores cooking implements made of iron and Chapter 7 examines the rarest of such survivals, objects in wood. Food objects were incorporated into social processes of many kinds, most of them – preparing produce, cooking, eating, for example – leaving few textual traces. We are, however, able to connect some objects through networks joining settlements to geographical regions and beyond. The key in every case is the settlement context in which an object was recovered. The object-focused chapters are organized generally by settlement type, ranging from small, rural, early locations such as West Stow to later, frequently rebuilt sites such as Goltho and

Flixborough. The lives of those who made, sold, traded, and used things related to food at those settlements are, and will probably remain, obscure. But their activities can still be traced through objects. Food things moved from person to person, from maker to user, and also along paths, roads, or rivers. These objects linked the lives of those who created and used them.

Part III moves from things to people and to the processes that shaped identities related to food. Chapter 8 looks at food purity as defined by handbooks of penance and proposes that some food workers served as officers who were responsible for maintaining food purity according to Christian standards. Chapter 9 examines food culture as it exists in law codes and describes new forms of interaction between the Church and the laws in the late Anglo-Saxon period. I also look at the centralization of large estates, a development that gave the Church an opportunity to use the resources of the rural elites. Chapter 10 continues the exploration of fasting, focusing on the role of fish in the fasting diet, with special attention to recent arguments about increases in marine fish in the late Anglo-Saxon period. The eleventh chapter uses a little-discussed poem to imagine a group of Anglo-Saxons gathered to eat as well as to drink – a rare sight in the literature related to food.

I have omitted much, including broader views of data from the many disciplines that contribute to modern archaeological inquiry – paleoecological, paleobotanical, and zooarchaeological studies in particular – although I note that archaeologists themselves sometimes find these data difficult to integrate into comprehensive understandings of settlement life and food culture. Scholars at work in these fields are finding more ways to speak to each other. I hope to enlarge the conversation by linking archaeological investigations to textual data about food culture, eating, and identity. My concern is the function of ordinary things – food things – in daily life. The Anglo-Saxons did not live in a static or unchanging universe, any more than we do. Much evidence that contextualized their daily lives has disappeared, and much that remains – objects retrieved from graves especially – points to ceremonial and symbolic dimensions of culture. But other evidence from excavations points to practical functions. Food waste, for example, creates a rich context for broken or discarded objects, and waste itself is a well-recognized index to diet. I focus on settlements, not on cemeteries, and on ordinary meals rather than feasts. I look at texts that created situational identities and that prompted changes in social life, rather than at classics of Old English poetry and models of identity generated in *Beowulf* or lyric poems that have become indispensable to cultural criticism. The heroic and poetic will always have a greater audience than the ordinary world of food culture, but most of us live simple lives and can learn from the simple sides of life a thousand years ago. Great occasions can teach us much, but so can the little things of daily life.

Part I

Food Words

1

The Symbolic World of Food

Remembering things

Many more objects than words survive from Anglo-Saxon England. The objects reveal more sides of lived experience than do words and texts, but the objects are more difficult to study, or even to see. Some of them, especially those found in the millions, including pottery fragments, coins, nails, broken stones, and bones, have never been photographed. Those that have been photographed are difficult to reproduce if money is an object. In contrast, Anglo-Saxon texts have been cheaply available in editions and translations for decades and can be accessed in electronic form as editions or digital facsimiles, often at no charge. There are good reasons for these disparities, since material culture is expensive to curate and reproduce; words, once printed, are not. One unfortunate consequence is that texts dominate scholarly understanding of the Anglo-Saxon world, while objects – with the exceptions of treasure troves, a few swords and helmets, and, of course, manuscripts – remain in the background. My focus in this chapter is the relationship between words and things as texts present it and as recent theory in archaeology helps us reconceptualize it.

Anyone who wants to explore the connections between words and things must connect both media to lived experience, a process that brings a further consequence of textual dominance. Powerful but unwritten rules determined what would be written about and what would be passed over. Most texts do not describe or discuss ordinary things, and the more extraordinary the text – *Beowulf*, for example, or Wulfstan's *Sermon of the Wolf to the English* – the less likely it is to refer to daily life in any but hyperbolic terms. Ordinary things, including the ordinary things of Anglo-Saxon daily life, might find a wider scholarly audience if they could be accessed more readily. Peter Shillingsburg has called for "knowledge sites," archives of electronic resources rich in both texts and images, to bring us closer to ancient worlds and remote times by telling us about "the things that went without saying." Shillingsburg's phrase, "the things that went without saying," might well include the ordinary objects of Anglo-Saxon England. The phrase describes information available to authors but not to their readers, the kind of information that authors benefited from but did not pass on because they did not anticipate that it would be lost.[1] King Alfred believed that learned works had not been translated into the vernacular because his predecessors did not anticipate a day in which priests could not read Latin.[2] That time was not long in coming. Once things have gone "without saying," they will be lost. That is why readers who want to study daily life in the Middle Ages must find a way to remember, identify, and think about ordinary things. Texts, even when they concern ordinary things, do not help us see them.

A familiar text that both celebrates and yet conceals material culture is Psalm 8, a description of cosmic order that can help us understand how everyday objects and their work have come to be everywhere and nowhere, invisible and yet in plain view. The following version, which includes an Old English gloss, is translated from a twelfth-century psalter written in Canterbury. One Old English version includes a Latin introduction: "Unto the end, for the wine-presses: a psalm of David, voice of the ancient church; he speaks about Christ and the faith."[3] In the Paris Psalter, the psalm reads:

David sang this eighth psalm when he wondered at the wonders of God, who willed all creation. And he also prophesied through this psalm about the glorious birth of Christ. 1. Oh, Lord, our God, how wonderful is your name throughout the earth. 2. For exalted is your greatness over the heavens. Even from the mouths of children who suck milk you are praised. 3. They do that as a reproach to your enemies, because you destroy the enemy and all those who bring unrighteousness, and defend (it). 4. Now I see the work of your fingers, the heavens and the moon and the stars that you have established. 5. What is man that you should be mindful of him or the son of man that you should search him out? 6. You have made him little less than angels and you glorify and honor him and crown him in glory and set him over the work of your hands. 7. All creation you put under his feet and under his power: sheep and all oxen and all the beasts of the field 8. and the birds of the air and fish of the sea that move through the sea paths. 9. Lord, Lord, our God, how wonderful is your name throughout the earth!

Þysne eahteoðan sealm sang Dauid þa he wundrade Godes wundra, se wylt eallum gesceaftum; and eac he witgode on ðam sealme be þære wuldorlican acennednesse Cristes. He cwæð 1. Eala, Drihten, ure God, hu wundorlic þin nama ys geond ealle eorðan. 2. For þam ahefen ys þin myclung ofer heofonas. Ge furðum, of ðæra cilda muðe þe meolc sucað, þu byst hered. 3. Þæt hi doð to bysmore þinum feondum; for ðam þu towyrpest þine fynd and ealle þa þe unrihtwisnesse ladiað and scyldað. 4. Ic ongite nu þæt weorc þinra fingra; þæt synd, heofonas and mona and steorran þa þu astealdest. 5. Drihten, hwæt is se mann þe þu swa myclum amanst, oþþe hwæt is se mannes sunu þe þu oftrædlice neosast? 6. Þu hine gedest lytle læssan þonne englas; þu hine

---

[1] Peter L. Shillingsburg, *From Gutenberg to Google*, p. 69.
[2] Alfred, "Preface" to *Pastoral Care*, in Simon Keynes and Michael Lapidge, eds. and trans., *Alfred the Great*, pp. 124–27, at p. 125.
[3] The Latin introduction is found in James L. Rosier, ed., *The Vitellius Psalter*, p. 12. This introduction is not included in the Paris Psalter (ed. Patrick P. O'Neill, *King Alfred's Old English Prose Translation*, pp. 106–7); *Eadwine's Canterbury Psalter* (ed. Fred Harlsey); or the *Tiberius Psalter* (ed. A. P. Campbell).

gewuldrast and geweorðast, and him sylst heafodgold to mærðe, and þu hine
gesetest ofer þin handgeweorc. 7. Ealle gesceafta þu legst under his fet, and
under his anwald: sceap and hryðera and ealle eorðan nytenu. 8. Fleogende
fuglas; and sæfiscas þa farað geond þa sæwegas. 9. Drihten, Drihten, ure God,
hu wundorlic þin nama ys geond ealle eorðan.[4]

David wonders at the wonders of God. His vision of cosmic order encompasses objects and processes that constitute food culture and form networks of production, distribution, consumption, and communication. In
the first verse, the earth serves as a universal measure of God's praise,
which issues even from the mouths of children nursed on milk (*þe meolc
sucað*, ver. 2), a conceit familiar from the prologue to Chaucer's *Prioress's
Tale*.[5] The nursing babes focus attention on what goes into the mouth as
well as what comes out of it. Everybody has to eat, and for that a food
chain is needed. Some creatures produce food from their bodies (sheep),
others labor with workers in the fields (oxen), and still others feed animals
as well as humans (birds and fish; vers. 8–9). No plants are mentioned, but
they grow in the fields plowed with the oxen's help. The wine-press of
the introduction gestures beyond grapes to the spiritual meaning of this
fruit, which belonged to a sacrificial cycle in which one form of life was
extinguished so that another could be sustained. This hymn in praise of
creation introduces judgment and the sober theme of harvesting rather
than planting, of ends rather than beginnings. The psalm's catalogue of
ordinary things traces a path of nourishment and sustenance that reaches
from birth to death.[6]

The place of ordinary things in Psalm 8 was slow to be recognized, as
readings produced over some 1,500 years show. The first commentator was
St. Paul, who focused on the hierarchy that positions Christ between God
and his people. Paul quoted the psalm in Ephesians 1:20–22 to support his
claim that God "has put all things under [Christ's] feet and has made him
the head over all things for the church."[7] Paul's concern with the order
of creation left no room for commentary on things or the work they do,
but later writers did sometimes illuminate the food processes implicit in
the text. Augustine of Hippo (d. 430) observed that the Scriptures "often
convey one and the same idea under many and various symbols." He saw
such likenesses in the psalm's references to food and framed them with
themes of sacrifice and judgment. "The text of this psalm tells us nothing
whatever about these wine-presses from which it takes its title," Augustine
noted. He himself compared the wine-presses to the threshing-floor: "In

[4] My translation of Psalm 8 is based on the Paris Psalter, ed. O'Neill, *King Alfred's Old English
Prose Translation*, pp. 106–7; see the commentary, pp. 177–78.
[5] Geoffrey Chaucer, prologue to "The Prioress's Tale," *The Riverside Chaucer*, ed. Larry D.
Benson, p. 209, ll. 453–59.
[6] Walter Brueggemann, *The Message of the Psalms*, pp. 28 and 36. See also Willem A. Vangemeren,
who identifies the form of the psalm as "creation praise" (*Psalms*, pp. 62 and 137) and notes
that all creatures "are subject to human authority and may at their will be used for food"
(p. 142).
[7] Paul quoted the psalm several times; see I Corinthians 15:27–28 and Hebrews 2:7.

fact, both on the threshing-floor and in the wine-press, the produce is merely cleared of its coverings, necessary as they were for the formation, growth and ripening of the harvest or vintage." He likened the separation of wheat and chaff to the separation of the good from the bad. "The time will come, however, for the grain to be separated and stored in barns and the wine in cellars." The wheat will be gathered up "but the chaff he will burn with unquenchable fire" (Luke 3:17).[8]

Turning to the psalm itself, Augustine compared the milk drunk by nursing babies to the meat eaten by adults, distinguishing more mature believers who are ready for perfect knowledge from those who are not. The psalm's reference to fish and the "paths of the sea" suggested nets "in which were enclosed good fish and bad [and] Noah's ark, which held both clean and unclean animals." Augustine prayed that God would "separate the pure wine from the skins. Let us, on our part, strive to become the wine and to rank with the sheep or oxen, not the grapeskins or the beasts of the field, the birds of the air or the fishes that pass through the paths of the sea."[9] The food objects of the psalm served as points of departure for Augustine's complex similitudes, husk to be discarded so that the kernel of truth could be revealed. Later commentators, including Cassiodorus (d. c. 585), repeated Augustine's figurative understanding of such objects as the wine-press and its work of separating the flesh from its covering.[10] Augustine's influence on early medieval thought is clear in a commentary on Psalm 8 once assigned to the Venerable Bede (d. 735).[11] In *De universo libri viginti duo*, written between 842 and 846, Hrabanus Maurus also relied on figurative meanings such as those suggested by Augustine.[12]

About four hundred years after Hrabanus, Thomas Aquinas (d. 1274) brought Psalm 8 somewhat closer to the materiality of food culture. His commentary, based on Augustine's, connects the psalm to a celebration known as the feast of booths (Deuteronomy 16), a major feast held during the grape harvest. The feast commemorated "the divine bounty, because God led the sons of Israel out of Egypt in booths, and led them into the land of promise where there were fruits to enjoy." To enjoy "the finest fruits" the sons of Israel needed wine-presses," Aquinas wrote, and when, therefore, "he said for the presses, this [was] meant literally." Aquinas buttressed his reading with agricultural references, including Isaiah 5 ("And he fenced it in, and picked the stones out of it") and Matthew 21 ("There was a man, a householder, who planted a vineyard . . . and dug in it a press"). Aquinas saw the Church as a wine-press because "in the church the good are separated from the evil by the work of the ministers," just as lees are separated from wine. What matters is the hierarchy and how it expresses the order

---

[8] Augustine, *St. Augustine on the Psalms*, 1: 96–97.
[9] Augustine, *St. Augustine on the Psalms*, 1: 107–9.
[10] See *Cassiodorus: Explanation of the Psalms*, trans. Peter J. Walsh, 1: 7–8, 109–10.
[11] Bede, *De Psalmorum libro exegesis*, in Migne, ed., *PL* 93, col. 524d–529a.
[12] Hrabanus, *De universo libri viginti duo*, ch. 8, "De pecoribus et jumentis," in J.-P. Migne, ed., *PL* 111, col. 201a.

of creation. Aquinas manifests the same concern as Paul and Augustine: symbolic meaning triumphs over materiality.

The food culture of Psalm 8 seems to have escaped symbolic confines first in the work of John Calvin, who, in 1563, wrote, "There is no man of a mind so dull and stupid but may see if he will be at the trouble to open his eyes, that it is by the wonderful providence of God that horses and oxen yield their service to men, – that sheep produce wool to clothe them – and that all sorts of animals supply them with food for their nourishment and support, even from their own flesh." The more clearly we see this dominion, the more should we "be affected with a sense of the goodness and grace of our God as often as we either eat food, or enjoy any of the other comforts of life." For Calvin, the psalm was a "mirror in which we may behold and contemplate the dominion over the works of his hands, with which God has honored man."[13] This commentary looks at the food in the text rather than beyond it. Calvin captured the spirit of God's renewed promise of human domain over the earth, a promise first made in the Garden. "Into your power they are delivered," God said to Noah of all the animals. "Every creature that is alive shall be yours to eat; I give them all to you as I did the green plants" (Genesis 9:3). Despite a reputation for austerity, Calvin was among the few to do justice both to the "comforts of life" that the psalmist describes and to the food culture on which those comforts depend.[14]

These commentaries outline three phases of the visibility of food culture. The complex relations between texts and objects, between words and things, become clearer with each phase. Objects were less important to Paul and Augustine than to Aquinas, and processes related to food production were less important to Aquinas than to Calvin. This difference in the authors' positioning of food reflects their audiences' expectations. Augustine and Aquinas wrote for the learned. They stand together against Calvin, who used the psalms to teach preachers but also to illustrate sermons for the laity. Calvin wrote about the material world itself, not the similitudes it pointed to. Reflecting on Psalm 8, he thought that those who could be "at the trouble to open [their] eyes" should be able to grasp God's providence in the form of horses, oxen, sheep, and other animals that supply the faithful with food, "even from [the animals'] own flesh."[15]

Yet the materiality and actuality of the things in Psalm 8 remains implicit. Audiences did not need to be told about the objects necessary to convert grapes into wine, or wheat into flour, or animal flesh into stew. If they did, they would not have looked for this information in Calvin's sermons, for it had been available in texts such as herbals and recipes at least since the

---

[13] John Calvin, *Commentary on the Book of Psalms*, pp. 107–8.
[14] On Calvin's humanism, and his underappreciated approval of food and drink, see William Bouwsma, *John Calvin*, pp. 135–36. For commentary on the psalms in the Reformation contexts, see Marjorie O'Rourke Boyle, "For Peasants, Psalms."
[15] Wulfert de Greef, *The Writings of John Calvin*, p. 88.

Old English period.[16] Food objects are often mentioned in these plain and practical texts, if seldom described there; they are rarely mentioned in other kinds of writing, most of it dealing with things in incidental rather than central ways. Augustine and Aquinas seem to have assumed that the objects of Psalm 8 were present to the mind's eye and did not need explicit recognition. As a result, ordinary things remain submerged, their presence unarticulated and their force in the world of ideas obscure.

Objects in the world

The Norwegian archaeologist Bjørnar Olsen has asked "why things were forgotten" in the records of medieval civilization, an important question for anyone concerned about food culture and its traces in texts or objects.[17] The answer involves both the role of objects in everyday life and the role of writing. Olsen did not need to ask why some objects were remembered in discourse from which most others had been banished. Important objects were written about; swords, helmets, crosses, brooches, grave goods, and similar materials appear in both medieval texts and the archaeological record. Scholars in all disciplines have long favored such objects, which abound in graves and hence in museums, art history books, and popular representations of medieval culture. Olsen is asking about everything else.

Why ordinary things were forgotten is not a mystery if we consider the relationship of writing – and not only of literary texts – to material reality. It is not so much a matter of writing but of what kinds of writing a culture employs. In *Eating and Drinking in Roman Britain*, H. E. M. Cool has shown that some five hundred years of the history of eating and drinking in Roman Britain are comparatively well documented. If texts from the period are not as numerous or forthcoming as we would like, they are much more informative about ordinary things than texts from the next five hundred years of that history. The Romans wrote everything down in forms that have survived. The same cannot be said for the Anglo-Saxons, who recorded little that has survived, apart from what is religious and royal. Cool cites shopping lists, notes written on amphorae and tiles, letters about food, and other forms of textual commentary outside the category of "literature" by any standard. In the history of Romans in Britain, she shows, things were remembered often and well. Old Irish evidence is also impressive, as one can see in Fergus Kelly's *Early Irish Farming*, which looks to Bronze Age, Iron Age, and Roman food evidence as well as that of early Ireland. The eighth-century law tract called *Críth Gablach* ("branched purchase") sets out a hierarchy of farmers and indicates which tools and animals each is expected to have. This and other Irish legal texts name

[16] From the later medieval period there are cookbooks and detailed descriptions of feasts; see Stephen Mennell, *All Manners of Food.*
[17] Bjørnar Olsen, "Material Culture after Text," p. 90.

a variety of foods and their social significance, specifying, for example, which cuts of meat are appropriate to which ranks.[18]

One response to Olsen's question, then, is that in some times and places – early Ireland and Roman Britain among them – things were not forgotten. Rather, they were remembered in textual forms that can be used for many purposes, including reconstructing the daily diet of ordinary people – soldiers and slaves included – if not for constructing visions of heroic and courtly culture.[19] The gap between words and things in the Anglo-Saxon period, the half millennium that follows the period Cool studies, is particular to the Anglo-Saxons and their record-keeping habits and technologies. Archaeologists are more inclined now than previously to allow for continuity between Iron Age Britain, Roman Britain, and the early Anglo-Saxon period. They hypothesize that early Anglo-Saxon settlers were acquainted with some late Roman ironwork and pottery, for example, although the settlers did not benefit from "a continuing Roman-derived material culture suite." It has long been understood that the architectural ruins of Roman Britain made a powerful impression on later occupants. But the occupiers were in flux; by the fourth century Roman building types were becoming less distinctive.[20]

The predispositions of those who recover the culture's material are also a factor in what is remembered. Cool mentions working on a dig after "a highly enthusiastic fish bone specialist" addressed the crew, which then began finding fish bones, which "had rarely appeared in the preceding weeks" in the finds trays.[21] When the expert remembered the bones, archaeologists began to find them. Some objects seem more important that others, inevitably, but the order of precedence does not well serve the archaeology of daily life. For the Anglo-Saxon period, we can say, in answer to Olsen, that ordinary things were forgotten because, in their necessary but routine functions in the workplace and the home, they did not seem important. That is, they did not seem to mean anything in terms of status or social standing. Augustine and other allegorists might have remembered ordinary things in order to create similitudes of interest for a handful of learned readers, but for them the similitudes, not the things that suggested them, were what mattered. Ordinary objects communicate status no less effectively than exceptional ones, but their power to do so was not commented on. That power must be inferred from the objects themselves and from contexts that can be reconstructed for the objects. Who owned the object? Who used it? Who transferred it to a new owner?

[18] Fergus Kelly, *Early Irish Farming*, p. 358 on cuts of meat, pp. 316–59 on diet and cooking, and pp. 463–503 on tools and technology.

[19] A slave at Vindolanda is known to have bought radishes for an important festival. See H. E. M. Cool, *Eating and Drinking in Roman Britain*, p. 126; on Roman armies' supply practices, see pp. 132–36. Kelly notes that even bound slaves were entitled to feast (*Early Irish Farming*, p. 359).

[20] Simon Esmonde Cleary, "The Ending(s) of Roman Britain," p. 18. On Roman architecture, see pp. 15–17.

[21] Cool, *Eating and Drinking in Roman Britain*, p. 104.

Ordinary things generated meaning through those human relationships, none of them requiring texts or even witnesses apart from the two or three people involved in them.

Material culture, James C. Barrett has written, is "an active participant in the construction of the social system, and its meaning is internal to that system."

> Material culture in all its forms – artefact production and use, settlement location, food selection, burial mode and so on – is the result of actions which are at once *both* articulated through social relationships, and are also the means by which those social relationships are constructed. The social being exists through action which is formulated and reflected upon within a culturally modified material world. Material culture is thus an active participant in the construction of the social system, and its meaning is internal to that system.[22]

The material world is modified by the relationships that surround it. Those relationships ("social forms") constitute a network in which objects are enmeshed. Barrett writes about "food selection" rather than food, with an emphasis on the process related to the object rather than the object itself. The food acquires significance from the process of selection, significance that depends on the people involved, their needs, and their means of satisfying them. In turn, the food lends significance to those who select it, underscoring their power to act on behalf of others in food matters. In later chapters, I will call these people "food officers," those whose responsibilities included power over food and its purity. Their identity in their communities derived in part from their power over food; food flowed along the lines these people directed.

Two theoretical concepts can help us understand how ordinary things participate in the processes that create identity. They are Pierre Bourdieu's theory of the *habitus*, which has been situated within Anglo-Saxon archaeology by Paul Blinkhorn and Chris Cumberpatch, and William O. Frazer's concept of social identity as it is worked out in terms of early medieval culture. The *habitus* is not in and of itself a satisfactory way to study material culture as opposed to the behavior that explains how objects were seen and used. The *habitus* was defined by Bourdieu as a set of "principles which generate and organise practice," "classificatory schemes" that establish the "regularities of the social world for which and through which there is a social world." It has been described as "a set of dispositions which generates practices and perceptions."[23] In the *habitus*, objects meet the customs governing their manufacture and use.[24] According to Randal Johnson, the *habitus* structures practices and representations, making them regular "without being in any way the product of obedience to rules."[25] I take

---

[22] James C. Barrett, "Aspects of the Iron Age in Atlantic Scotland," p. 206.

[23] Randal Johnson, "Editor's Introduction," in Pierre Bourdieu, *The Field of Cultural Production*, p. 5.

[24] Pierre Bourdieu, *The Logic of Practice*, p. 140, quoted in C. G. Cumberpatch, "Towards a Phenomenological Approach to the Study of Medieval Pottery," pp. 125–26.

[25] Johnson, "Editor's Introduction," p. 5.

this to mean that the *habitus* operates in the silence of cultural consensus. When a community must change, either from internal or external pressure, "rules" become explicit – as, in the case of Anglo-Saxon England, when Christian missionaries arrived to convert pagan populations. The *habitus* becomes visible when practices change. In contemporary culture we are more aware of practices than the dispositions behind them. A change in parking regulations might prompt us to ask how the old regulations came to be and what attitudes (i.e., disposition) lay behind their particular form. Until the practice was changed, drivers hardly thought about the disposition behind certain parking regulations. Perhaps the same was true in the Anglo-Saxon period. When a change in diet was ordered (to keep a fast day, for example), those involved might wonder, for the first time, about the old custom as well as the new one.

Blinkhorn and Cumberpatch have given the *habitus* and its silent operations practical meaning by using them to account for changes in cooking pots and other ceramic forms. They emphasize the practices as lenses on the "dispositions" that might have been behind them. Potters' practices were not "the product of obedience to rules" (where obedience is a disposition: one follows orders) but rather what Blinkhorn, borrowing a metaphor from Bourdieu, describes as "conductorless orchestration," the operation of prevailing customs that structured craft production and that perpetuated certain techniques and styles from parents to children and on.[26] The disposition behind such continuity is simply the desire or need to acquire the skills that inform practices in use. One potter is like another because the second one learns from the first one, not because they both obeyed the same rules.

Blinkhorn uses Bourdieu to discuss pottery shapes and the locations of handles on cooking pots. He shows that through these features ordinary objects, no less than decorated ones, represented relationships, and hence social meaning and identity, to those who used and looked at them. Blinkhorn associates identity with the communication of information about one person to another person, often through the mediation of objects. He writes that such objects as cooking pots could "broadcast information about the user that was related to their age [and] gendered social station." The objects did so through their fabric, shape, and functional features, not only through ornamentation or decoration. Commenting on funerary pottery, Blinkhorn argues that if certain shapes of pot were considered appropriate to hold the ashes of the dead, those shapes might well have broadcast the same information when those people were alive.[27] Pots in the grave communicated information that, in life, the deceased themselves communicated in other ways – by being associated with the pots, for example, or by wearing such objects as brooches or carrying tools on their person.

---

[26] Paul Blinkhorn, "Habitus, Social Identity and Anglo-Saxon Pottery," p. 115.
[27] Blinkhorn, "Habitus," p. 122.

Blinkhorn and Cumberpatch resist the tendency to treat decoration as the most important information on a pot. They regard that assumption as inviting a bias against simple, undecorated pots – and, I might add, against other ordinary objects that, like many forms of pottery, would have been "extremely visible" in the hall and a possible source of cultural information to all who beheld them.[28] The claims Blinkhorn and Cumberpatch make for the silent, unobserved, but pervasive power of the *habitus* can and should, I believe, be extended to many food objects. Just as pots would have been made in a characteristic way by one Germanic tribe and would have encoded identity for those who used them, so too knife handles, wooden objects, and many others would have taken shape under the unseen guidance of the *habitus* and its power to preserve forms of identity by ensuring the persistence of traditional forms for ordinary things.

Frazer's approach to identity also uses representation to connect social processes to material culture in ways that can change according to circumstances. For Frazer, identity is less about race, sex, or political affiliation than about how people present themselves to others (and to themselves).[29] Personal identity is usually inferred from material evidence and hence seems stable or fixed. Persons of high status have traditionally been favored in early medieval studies of identity, especially those studies based on burials. Heinrich Härke has noted that archaeology emphasizes "the material expression of status" in terms of household, gender, and age. He writes that "virtually the only archaeological indicator used to infer [social] complexity has been burial wealth, measured by a quantitative analysis of grave goods."[30] This evidence is static, Frazer argues, and operates as though it were a collection of archaeological "artefact 'kits'" containing bones, food implements, and other objects that signify status. Frazer describes identity based on objects as "the coming together of pre-formed 'selves.'" He points out that grave goods express one's status in death, which is only one of many phases that make a "storied" life.[31] Frazer encourages a focus on personal identities that encompasses change over the course of a lifetime. He sees objects and artifacts, like settlements and the landscape itself, as keys to more than fixed and unchanging identities.

To accommodate the concept of dynamic identity, Frazer describes a person's "second nature," which consists of acquired tendencies brought out in certain situations and consciously, deliberately manipulated.[32] This is a fruitful suggestion, although it seems better to avoid the term "second nature," which implies a stable or fixed identity. That is to say, a "second nature," like a "first nature," could be seen as residing in the

---

[28] Blinkhorn, "Habitus," p. 123.
[29] William O. Frazer, "Introduction," pp. 3–4.
[30] Heinrich Härke, "Early Anglo-Saxon Social Structure," p. 151.
[31] Frazer, "Introduction," pp. 3–4.
[32] Frazer, "Introduction," pp. 2–3.

human subject as an essential and perhaps unchanging property.[33] Instead of Frazer's "social identity" (all identity is "social," after all, the self in relation to others, if only another self) I prefer "situational identity," a term I use to describe identity formation that can be linked to specific events and occasions. Those events and occasions evoke changes because the people who participate in them adopt new kinds of behavior, thus altering public perceptions of who they are. For example, a cook might have had to exert his or her authority over the food supply during Lent and thus would have been seen as someone who rationed food as well as prepared it. The cook had an occupational, social identity as one who prepared food; the occasion of the Lenten fast caused the cook to call upon a situational identity as a food officer who directed the flow of food to others. Situational identity (as opposed to "occasional identity," which suggests irregularity) is a temporary mode of behavior that is partly within one's control and partly not. Situational identity is object oriented, site specific, and relational. It involves objects that one uses and perhaps owns; it varies from place to place, with terrain; and it expresses human relationships at varying levels. Such identity helps us see how the objects and processes of food culture helped to connect the people engaged with things and to create public impressions of who they were.

We can see that objects can be related to identity in traditional ways in which the object marks status, and also in terms of more recent formulations in which objects create meaning within social systems and, at the same time, acquire meaning from them. How do textual sources contribute to our understanding of identity as it is related to objects? Even in relation to high-status objects this is not a simple matter. In the course of listing Old English words associated with the finds of Sutton Hoo, Jane Roberts commented that it was "notoriously hard to match the words that remain to the artefacts removed from the earth." She found it easier to move from objects found in the earth to words for them than to move from words to things, and I believe that most scholars who have tried to work in either direction would agree with her.[34] On the theoretical level, Barbara J. Little and Bill Brown have made influential arguments about material culture and words, and Christopher Loveluck, Peter Fowler, and John Hines have sharpened the focus within Anglo-Saxon studies.

Loveluck notes that archaeological research has often been carried out in the context of "grand narratives" that divided history into "the long eighth century," "Mid Saxon" (650–850), or "Late Saxon" (850–1100) phases. These "narratives," he believes, erase many signs of local or regional character. "Local changes can be ignored as 'exceptions' to otherwise grand schemes of interpretation," Loveluck writes. "Regional" might be so broad as to include "the countries bordering on the North Sea as a whole," for

---

[33] The use of "the subject" rather than "the individual" de-centers traditional assumptions about consciousness and identity as inherent properties of the self.

[34] Jane Roberts, "Anglo-Saxon Vocabulary," pp. 185–86 and pp. 193–202 (the list).

example. Without denying "the reality of local and micro-regional trajectories of development," scholars seem to prefer "synthetic interpretation" that, combined with limited funding for excavations, promotes "a lack of desire to discuss the effects of local and regional complexities" and the dynamism inherent in them.[35] Such "narratives" are common in the work of historians and literary scholars, who use broad divisions among Bede (d. 735), Alfred (d. 899), and Ælfric (d. 1010) to define the major periods of Anglo-Saxon history and culture. Almost all vernacular writing comes from the late period, the corpus of which does not yield insight into the eighth century or the ninth. Sarah Foot has stressed the lack of uniformity at just about every level in monastic life before 900, and T. A. Shippey has made similar observations.[36] Scholars who imagine a single culture, religious or otherwise, for the Anglo-Saxons will be inclined to use textual evidence to confirm their view.

Contributing to the synthesizing force of grand narratives is textually based research, which, in the case of Anglo-Saxon England, focuses on historical narratives such as the *Anglo-Saxon Chronicle* and Bede's *Ecclesiastical History of the English People*, and on homilies and poems. Apart from the laws, administrative texts seem to be of less interest, although, as Cool has shown in her work with Roman Britain and Kelly in his with Irish law, they are more likely to engage ordinary objects. Loveluck has written about the ways in which textual references not only led archaeologists to specific (monastic) sites but helped to determine what they would find in them. In Anglo-Saxon studies the classic example is Bede's *Ecclesiastical History*. With the help of this work, archaeologists "located excavations at the sites of documented settlements, with a view to gaining the first insights into the nature of Anglo-Saxon society as reflected in the physical remains below the modern ground surface. All of the settlements targeted for excavation were associated with textual labels, and in many cases with Anglo-Saxon descriptions of buildings, events and activities at specific sites."[37] Sites with textual connections form a small but important percentage of those included in Philip Rahtz's 1976 gazetteer, in that they are said to hold "definite evidence of domestic settlement."[38]

Anders Andrén points to the disparity between texts and archaeological evidence. Texts record "a partly different 'version' of the past from the one preserved in material culture." Therefore artifact and text are not "equivalent semiotic signs" or commensurate systems for communicating cultural meaning.[39] Andrén reacts against Peter Sawyer's notorious observation

---

[35] Christopher Loveluck, "Changing Lifestyles, Interpretation of Settlement Character and Wider Perspectives," pp. 145–46.
[36] T. A. Shippey, "Old English Poetry: The Prospects for Literary History." Sarah Foot, *Monastic Life in Anglo-Saxon England*, stresses the danger of reading early monastic culture through the lenses of the tenth century; see pp. 5–10 and pp. 186–91.
[37] Christopher Loveluck, "Cædmon's World," p. 153.
[38] Philip Rahtz, "Gazetteer of Anglo-Saxon Domestic Settlement Sites" and "Buildings and Rural Settlements."
[39] Anders Andrén, *Between Artifacts and Texts*, p. 4.

that archaeology can become "an expensive way of telling us what we know already."[40] Andrén believes that "research in archaeology is traditionally text-bound and thematized according to the self-understanding of the Middle Ages – for example, the doctrine of the four estates (or three) of society – in studies concerning the countryside, the towns, the churches, and the castles." He stresses that archaeology promotes inquiry into "areas that are rarely or never mentioned in written sources, such as technology, economy, social conditions, and everyday life."[41]

The dispute between textual and archaeological knowledge bases has been pursued "passionately but wastefully," Peter Fowler points out in his lucid summary, since the evidence exceeds the capacity of any one discipline to explain it.[42] A more recent form of text-based analysis has reframed the discussion with the postmodern trope of "textualization," which attempts to turn ordinary objects into texts to be "read." Barbara J. Little objects to "reading" the archaeological record as if it were writing. This trope should be distinguished from what Fowler has in mind when he refers to land that "speaks," an idea about which he is dubious, and "reading" the land, a trope he endorses.[43] Nor is the analogy to language, I believe, what archaeologists mean by such terms as "settlement morphology."[44] Rather, Little writes about a movement that became popular in the 1990s as part of "post-processualism."[45] Processualism itself represented a shift from describing cultures as historically constituted wholes to explaining cultural change and seeing culture in terms of various processes, including rituals. Post-processual archaeology, or social archaeology, describes work in the discipline subsequent to this (by no means universally observed) shift.[46] Social archaeology reacted against dependence on textual models, especially historical narratives that could be used to frame archaeological data. Archaeologists have proposed various ways to limit the "cult of authority" that surrounds written sources and to seek a better balance between material and textual records.[47] In part they emphasize the processes that left no trace, the web of relations and practices that were not recorded but that contextualized objects and those who used them (a description evocative of Bourdieu's *habitus*).

Since processual archaeologists have reacted against the prioritizing of text over object, it is ironic that the dominant model to emerge from their work should have been "reading" the archaeological record. Influential

[40] Peter Sawyer, quoted by Philip Rahtz, "New Approaches to Medieval Archaeology," p. 15, cited in Andrén, *Between Artifacts and Texts*, p. 3.
[41] Andrén, *Between Artifacts and Texts*, p. 31. The estates more commonly include those who fight, those who pray, and those who work.
[42] Peter Fowler, *Farming in the First Millennium AD*, p. 29.
[43] Fowler, *Farming in the First Millennium AD*, p. 23 (speaking), p. 41 (reading).
[44] See, for example, Tom Saunders, "Class, Space and 'Feudal' Identities in Early Medieval England," p. 218.
[45] Barbara J. Little, "Texts, Images, Material Culture."
[46] See Christopher Scull, "Urban Centres in Pre-Viking England?", pp. 269–70.
[47] Larry McKee, Victor P. Hood, and Sharon Macpherson, "Reinterpreting the Construction History of the Service Area of the Hermitage Mansion," p. 161.

works in this movement include Ian Hodder's *Reading the Past* (1986); *Re-Constructing Archaeology*, by Michael Shanks and Christopher Tilley (1987); and Tilley's *Reading Material Culture* (1990).[48] J. D. Richards's discussion of symbolism and early Anglo-Saxon cemeteries, written a decade after Tilley's *Reading Material Culture*, is an example of this approach. Drawing on Bourdieu, Richards asserts that symbolism is an "abbreviated form of communication." He cites Barrett's view (seen above) that material culture is "an active participant in the construction of the social system, and its meaning is internal to that system.[49] Richards also discusses Edmund Leach's view that "all the various non-verbal dimensions of culture, such as styles in clothing, village lay-out, architecture, furniture, food, cooking," and others, "are organized in patterned sets so as to incorporate coded information in a manner analogous to the sounds and words and sentences of a natural language."[50] Thus pottery decoration can "represent concepts" and "in societies with a strong oral tradition, material culture is frequently used to store and pass on information, and, given its relative permanence, it may be used as an alternative to writing."[51] If one wants an example of how material culture is textualized, one could do no better than this.

It comes as a relief to be reminded by Richards that "much material culture is not obviously representational and has little figurative or iconic content."[52] Richards, however, uses this observation to assert the ambiguity of material culture and its dependence on context. Drawing on Leach's work, Richards asserts that all non-verbal forms encode (i.e., represent) information. If "much material culture is not obviously representational," how do we conceptualize its informational value? Food that does not encode information analogous to language is not representational; surely all food does not have semiotic significance, although some food does (a roasted boar, a wedding cake). I suggest instead that the information coded in cooking and food comes not from any possibly symbolic content of the objects but from the processes in which they are enmeshed. Richards writes that such processes are "analogous to the sounds and words and sentences of a natural language."[53] One might reply that there is no reason to assume (and many reasons not to assume) the Anglo-Saxons knew of only *one* way to eat or cook. The practices of food culture, like language itself, presumably varied with social and economic status. Nor is there a

---

[48] Ian Hodder, *Reading the Past* (now revised, with Scott Hutson); Michael Shanks and Christopher Tilley, *Re-Constructing Archaeology*; Tilley, *Reading Material Culture*.

[49] J. D. Richards, "Anglo-Saxon Symbolism," p. 134, citing Barrett, "Aspects of the Iron Age in Atlantic Scotland," p. 206.

[50] Richards, "Anglo-Saxon Symbolism," p. 132, quoting Edmund Leach, *Culture and Communication*, p. 10.

[51] Richards, "Anglo-Saxon Symbolism," p. 132.

[52] Richards, "Anglo-Saxon Symbolism," p. 133, citing Ian Hodder, "Post-modernism, Post-structuralism and Post-processual Archaeology," in Hodder, ed., *The Meanings of Things*, pp. 64–78.

[53] Richards, "Anglo-Saxon Symbolism," p. 132.

way to know to which of the "natural" languages spoken in a region the organization of such processes could be analogous.

Richards acknowledges some of these points but alternates between claims about symbols on one hand and arguments about "the symbolic power" of artifacts on the other. Richards admits one difficulty, which is that speech and writing are linear, while material culture is not.[54] Even so, processualists seem to believe that both objects and social formations can be decoded as if they were written texts. These scholars seem to entertain an idea of "text" that reinscribes a textual model into their analysis. For example, Shanks and Tilley write that "objects depend on being incorporated into texts; they are internally constituted by the changing script of social relations into which they fit." As Little points out, such a view supports the celebrated if unhelpful Derridean claim that everything is text and participates in a process of "textual conversion."[55] The word "script" used this way seems arbitrary and conveniently figurative. Social relations are ephemeral and are not easily figured as script, which is, after all, permanent. The "script" of social relations may be "changing," but once it is recorded it becomes a template into which objects, in Shanks and Tilley's revealing word, "fit."

Little regards "textual conversion" as a form of presentism – seeing ancient works in terms of modern cultures – since text is "a natural and obvious category with which to organize the world because we are literate." She warns that so long as text "constitutes the basis of our authority and the metaphor for our understanding, material culture, seen as much more ambiguous, will remain secondary, reflective, and supportive, rather than informative."[56] She adds that "[a]rchaeologists need to think not only about interpreting material culture as text, but also about interpreting text and other discourse as material culture. We need a way to turn around the primacy of texts and to see material culture as a principal informant."[57] Little does not go far enough in making this point. Turning around the "primacy" of texts as sources for archaeological paradigms, as Loveluck and others have stressed, is imperative. In order to see material culture as a "principal informant," we need to understand how objects and processes together constitute the material, as Barrett proposes.

Little's solution is to shift the terms of the discussion from text and object to image. For Little, images "exist in the material world, fulfill some function or functions, react to what already exists, respond to other images, respond to real and perceived needs, and further create the material world that forms the context of images, representations, things, and their interrelationships." The image becomes "a general notion" that holds the world together with "figures of knowledge," an expression that Little

[54] Richards, "Anglo-Saxon Symbolism," p. 133.
[55] Shanks and Tilley, *Re-constructing Archaeology*, p. 21, quoted by Little, "Texts, Images, Material Culture," p. 217.
[56] Little, "Texts, Images, Material Culture," pp. 217–18.
[57] Little, "Texts, Images, Material Culture," p. 217.

draws from W. J. T. Mitchell.[58] Tellingly, in my view, Mitchell borrowed the idea from Michel Foucault's *The Order of Things*, a book about early modern attempts to impose layers of connected meanings over things and join those meanings into a coherent system.[59] Little also finds support in John Berger's assertion that images offer "direct testimony about the world which surrounded other people at other times" and are therefore "more precise and richer than literature." Little defines "image" to include more than two-dimensional art, so that what Berger calls "relics" – i.e., objects – can be understood as images.[60] But there are problems with these views. An image is a representation and an interpretation of reality, not "direct testimony" of it, and it is not clear that images are "more precise" than literature if objects can be understood as images. The claim that ordinary things like spoons or fish hooks are "more precise and richer than literature" is suspect. Unless they are decorated in some way, as are painted pots or engraved sword hilts, such objects do not encode or represent abstract meaning, which, in any case, is rarely "precise," however "rich" it might be. The bone spoon on the cover of this book (Figure 1) has distinct aesthetic appeal but hardly seems elaborately decorated or symbolic. What abstract meaning might it encode, if any? Is it "rich" or "precise"? If so, in what way?

Words and ordinary things

Berger and others who explore the relationship of objects to words concentrate on literary sources. That is understandable, perhaps, but literary texts are not the only written forms that need to be taken into consideration in a discussion of words and things. John Hines has demonstrated fruitful ways to study relationships between words and things. Hines notes that high-status objects (swords, helmets, brooches, etc.) use "straightforward symbolism" to denote "group-association or identity." That is why they were placed in graves and why they are often mentioned in texts.[61] Hines writes that "an obvious way to start to correlate the literary records and the archaeology of Anglo-Saxon England with one another is to look for specific correspondences between the two: to identify features and objects in archaeological reports or museum collections for which we also have textual references," the kind of work commented on by Roberts in relation to words and the finds from Sutton Hoo.[62] Hines agrees on the limitations afforded by specific and limited comparisons. He links the decorated helmet from Sutton Hoo to *Beowulf* and relates burial practices to funerary

---

[58] Little, "Texts, Images, Material Culture," p. 219, quoting W. J. T. Mitchell, *Iconology*, p. 11.
[59] Michel Foucault, *The Order of Things*, p. 19.
[60] Little, "Texts, Images, Material Culture," p. 219, quoting John Berger, *Ways of Seeing*, p. 10, and Pierre Bourdieu, *Distinction: A Social Critique of the Judgement of Taste*, p. 173.
[61] John Hines, *Voices in the Past*, p. 11.
[62] Hines, "Literary Sources and Archaeology," p. 972; Roberts, "Anglo-Saxon Vocabulary," pp. 185–86.

imagery in "The Wife's Lament," *Andreas*, and other texts. Hines argues that, with the exception of the Old English riddles, few texts are realistic in handling natural or "manufactured components" of the world in which they circulated. Rather, textual accounts are "individual, reflective, and often quite imaginative," a view that challenges Berger's claim that objects are "more precise and richer than literature."[63] For Hines, textual accounts are *too* precise to be correlated with objects.

Moving beyond text-object comparisons, Hines proposes that "ultimately the most rewarding approach to the correspondences between literature and archaeology is to relate both modes of expression – whether, superficially, they coincide or not – to a deeper level of structure and practice." This level of "structure and practice" can be accessed through any academic discipline; one who wants to link words and things must use several approaches. The understanding of human behavior requires an interdisciplinary approach, Hines writes, because "interdisciplinarity is *the* precondition for a history of culture that overrides and is in fact indifferent to the modal divisions between the types of evidence that are reflected in the disciplinary specializations of history, textual and literary criticism, art history," and other areas. Texts are one kind of evidence; historians, literary critics, and archaeologists read them differently. Objects are another kind of evidence; archaeologists with different specializations read them differently, while those in most other disciplines do not read them at all. The structures and practices with which Hines is concerned can be detected by any of these approaches in the search for signs of "deep-seated and persistent attempts in the Anglo-Saxon past to define and realize ideals and objectives."[64] As an example, Hines connects the use of material artifacts in *Beowulf* to early Anglo-Saxon burial practices, not to compare objects in two settings but rather to study the purpose these sources share. Beowulf, Hines notes, wears his helmet all through the feasting at Heorot. The hero's body armor has been one of his tools for constructing identity; his armor is not just a status symbol but rather "an embodiment of that constructed identity." Later, when Beowulf wants to compete with Grendel as a cultural equal (i.e., unarmed), the hero strips and thereby acquires a new identity (which I would call his situational rather than his social identity).[65]

Among the comparatively few attempts to link words to things one can find in Anglo-Saxon studies, Hines's arguments are among the most effective, although their usefulness in the study of ordinary rather than symbolic and representational objects is limited. Both contexts in the example above are symbolic; the text is literary, a mode Hines defines as "art in the medium of language," and the objects are high status.[66] Hence both sources are likely to focus on the ideals and objectives Hines describes, occasional art that celebrates the manipulation of masculine identity.

---

[63] Hines, "Literary Sources and Archaeology," p. 973.
[64] Hines, "Literary Sources and Archaeology," pp. 974–75.
[65] Hines, "Literary Sources and Archaeology," pp. 976–77.
[66] Hines, "Literary Sources and Archaeology," p. 970.

What about texts and artifacts with lesser aims? The material objects and texts about which Hines writes are laden with significance. Armor and weapons, whether worn on the hero's body or buried in his grave, signify in and of themselves. They represent gifts or booty and the identities they construct are public, highly labile, and understandably the focus of attention at the highest levels of culture, as befits the bodies associated with them. The poems are likewise imbued with the portentous: mournful, heroic, ominous, they are memorable to the extent they are not ordinary. What is ordinary in them – anything suggestive of routine behavior or routine events – is easily ignored.

Hines writes that riddles offer "glimpses of real life" that we "do not have in any other form."[67] I agree, but I would note that many prose works address material reality in non-symbolic ways, including laws, handbooks of penance, many homilies, and some poems, such as "The Seasons for Fasting," "An Exhortation to Christian Living," and others. These works are not invested in symbolic occasions as are "The Seafarer," *Beowulf*, "The Dream of the Rood," and others; they are devoid of the irony and playfulness of the riddles. They manipulate materiality in non-symbolic ways, sententiously and ponderously, but not symbolically. There is also plenty of non-symbolic materiality in the artful works Hines discusses. Helmets might be decorated, but ornamentation could only be applied to a solidly constructed piece. It is easy to see how identity is manipulated when a man puts on or takes off armor, or when he hoists a shield, or when he mounts a horse. It is less obvious to see how non-symbolic texts express identity when people do simple, necessary things: stir the porridge, fetch the dead mouse out of the water barrel, pull the bread from the oven. We read about the spoon in medical texts, the rodent in the handbook of penance, the baked bread in a saint's life. How do these texts and the ordinary objects they refer to construct identity?

In such texts, humans interact with material objects, although not to "define and realize ideals and objectives." Spoons, barrels, and bread ovens were not treasured for their situational symbolism. Like cooking pots, they could be inserted into symbolic settings. Pots were included in burials, for example, and have been found inverted on women's bodies and buried with men, surely for a reason. But in order to understand how non-literary texts and ordinary things helped to construct and manipulate identity, it is necessary to leave behind the semiosis of such cultural theaters as the cemetery and great events such as the crises in the mead hall or on the battlefield. There seems to be little "potential for interpretation," to quote Hines, in grinding grain, although literary Anglo-Saxons, like their predecessors, found some.[68] The quern recalled the rotation of the heavens; the fish hook recalled the devil's deceit. The "potential for interpretation" in stirring broth with a spoon or cutting bread with a knife was not exploited.

[67] Hines, "Literary Sources and Archaeology," p. 974.
[68] Hines, "Literary Sources and Archaeology," p. 979.

But this does not mean that those activities did not contribute to social or situational identity, or both.

In part our grasp of the capacities of ordinary things depends not so much on our ability to remember them (to recall Olsen), but on our willingness to remember them as parts of identity-generating processes. It might seem that all we need to do is to remember them as things, but that, it turns out, is not so simple. For Bill Brown, things are holders of the "thingness" of things. In "Thing Theory," an invitation to a "new materialism," Brown claims to be writing about things, but in my view he writes about imaginative qualities that adumbrate them. In a key statement he claims that "we begin to confront the thingness of objects when they stop working for us" – that is, when they become something other than that thing which they are. That a tool expresses its "thingness" when it no longer works is a witty deconstructive insight (a tool is most a thing when it is no longer a tool) but not a useful one. Brown's work should really be called "things theory," because he is more interested in the ambiguity of "things" than in any one thing. "The word *things*" is ambiguous because it "denotes a massive generality as well as particularities, even your particularly prized possessions," he writes, and "thing" itself "designates the concrete yet ambiguous within the everyday." We say, "Give me that thing," meaning just one object, even though we do not give it a name.[69] Brown does not linger on the everyday; his work with things has the quality of romance found in the photographs that illustrate his article, all of them remarkable, all of them showing things out of context, odd, even unrecognizable because they have stopped "working for us" as that which they are. Once tools, they are now visual and thoroughly literary artifacts.

Brown does comment on how things interact with people in ways that, I think, produce identity. When he writes about "what work [things] perform," he does not mean grinding grain or churning butter or any other activity that illustrates the subject-object dichotomy, but rather cultural work related to "private and public affection," a masterfully mystifying phrase. When Brown began thinking about things, someone reminded him that Russian Constructivists of the 1920s were engaged in rethinking things. "Constructivist materialism sought to recognize objects as participants in the reshaping of the world," Brown notes. "'Our things in our hands,' Aleksandr Rodcheko claimed, 'must be equals, comrades.'" The subject-object dichotomy that the Constructivists were seeking to break down was, many believe, not part of medieval thought before Christianity. Sounding like a Russian Constructivist himself, Olsen proposes that we conceive of "a symmetrical archaeology founded on the premise that things, all those physical entities we refer to as material culture, are beings in the world alongside other beings, such as humans, plants and animals." Olsen sees the object as a "silent thing" and as "a new and unknown actor"

---

[69] Bill Brown, "Thing Theory," p. 4. See further Brown, *A Sense of Things*.

in partnership with human agency.[70] At first this sounds suspiciously New Age, not of a piece with Constructivist thought. "One thousand years ago the Vikings ascribed personality, intention, and social identity to their swords," Olsen writes. By naming their weapons the Vikings bridged what we see as separate human and non-human worlds, as did reindeer herders who "hugged and greeted pine trees" and "had long conversations with drums and stones."[71]

These relations are not good indices for the social life of everyday things because they mystify ordinary objects and elevate them above their everyday functions to something that recalls Brown's "private and public affection." The pine tree signifies something other trees do not; the drums and stones likewise support specific cultural symbolism. To modern ways of thinking, Olsen writes, Viking warriors and reindeer herders did not understand "where reality ends and its metaphorical representation begins." They did not regard things as symbols or metaphors but rather as their partners, leading to what Olsen calls an "appalling mixture of people and things."[72] Unlike the medieval folk Olsen describes, modern readers intuitively acknowledge the "Great Divide" described by Bruno Latour in *We Have Never Been Modern*: on the one side, thinking subjects; on the other, unthinking objects.[73] Bede and his contemporaries also seem to have objected to that "appalling mixture of people and things" and set out not only to discredit the pagans' amulets and auguries – the aim of many miracles in the *History* – but to replace the mixture with a pattern of subject-object relations that supported the Christian perspective of the material world.[74]

A Russian, but no Constructivist, medieval historian Aron Gurevich has elaborated the subject-object dichotomy. The pagans Bede opposed grasped "the relationship of men and natural phenomena" as a tie "of interaction or even as mutual aid," Gurevich writes. "The natural forces can help or harm man, who in turn is able to influence them in ways that are advantageous for him." In a system characterized by "archaic beliefs" such as these, Gurevich claims, "men think of themselves in the same categories as the rest of the world, not isolating themselves from it and construing an 'object-subject' dichotomy." Gurevich, like Olsen, describes "an ultimate unity" predicated on a "reciprocal penetration of nature and humankind, organically connected with each other and magically interactive."[75] The Church disapproved of pagan "identification of man

[70] Olsen, "Material Culture after Text," pp. 88–89.

[71] Olsen, "Material Culture after Text," p. 95.

[72] Olsen notes that modern people do, however, "fall in love" with things like jackets, cars, and gadgets and "mourn them when they fall to pieces – when they die." See "Material Culture after Text," p. 95.

[73] Bruno Latour, *We Have Never Been Modern*, p. 13, cited by Olsen, "Material Culture after Text," p. 95.

[74] I give some examples in "All Created Things," pp. 116–18, from which this and some of the following material is adapted.

[75] Aron Gurevich, *Medieval Popular Culture*, p. 81.

and nature" and attempted "to tear people away from it, for the only cleri-cally approved contact with a higher power was in and through the church of God."[76] Humans can then be seen as alienated from nature so that "the link between them ceases to be organic and becomes symbolic." Objects in the pre-Christian world needed to be brought into a proper relation-ship with their Christian masters and the "natural forces" that "can help or harm man" had to be seen as expressions of God's favor or disfavor.[77] Psalm 8 presents them that way and commentators on it, as we have seen, stressed the role of things as expressions of God's goodness to his people.

In order to study food objects, I believe, we have to leave behind much that has been written about things, whether as texts or images, and their thingness, and reconsider the subject-object dichotomy that con-temporary theory, no less effectively than medieval Christianity, mysti-fies. Archaeologists are associated with objects, rather than texts, in this discussion, so it might come as a surprise to find Fowler writing that "most archaeological evidence from the first millennium is redundant" for purposes of studying farming. He regards this material as "secondary or tertiary evidence in that the overwhelming majority of the objects and materials were produced by or for agrarian societies." Objects "can say something about their contemporary society," he writes, but the "main contribution" of archaeology is the study of "settlement and other human sites of this millennium, that is the places where people lived, worked and worshipped."[78] We can call this landscape rather than land – land as humans reshape and use it. I endorse Fowler's view insofar as he is studying farming rather than farmers. My focus on identity requires that objects be seen as primary and as part of the human imprint that makes a place a settlement, a house a home. I propose that we look at objects within the context of ordinary interactions that make humans recognizable to each other. That is how food objects contribute to the formation of social identity.

When reading texts that refer to these objects, we should consider inter-actions, and models of identity based on them, that the texts might be engaging or trying to shape. One such relationship is pedagogy. A fish hook, for example, was a tool that required technology to be learned and mastered. The identity of those involved in that process was closely con-nected to the object and to its manufacture and use. The hook had to be connected not simply to a general idea of fishing but to marine or fresh-water fishing. The hook was designed to catch particular kinds of fish, suited to its weight, and to be used with other equipment (string, pole, net, etc.). Fishing was linked to local resources and to technology developed to exploit them. It was site specific. Seen as a "principal informant," in Little's terms, the hook might also have communicated in an interpersonal way.

---

[76] Gurevich, *Medieval Popular Culture*, p. 97.
[77] Gurevich, *Medieval Popular Culture*, p. 96.
[78] Fowler, *Farming in the First Millennium AD*, p. 36.

For example, a father who passed fishing equipment to his son might have taught the child to use it and to make similar objects. However informal such training might have been, it was centered on transferring skill in the use of the objects involved. It was, then, relational, part of a network of personal contact through which instruction was imparted. The process of transferring the object and associated skills endowed the object with meaning that constructed identities for the participants. The object itself made this process possible, as Barrett points out – even necessary. Skills and the tools they required had to be transferred to a new generation. Objects mediated social relations and created social communication for people who did not have access to texts, who had little or no contact with law, and who seldom were exposed to elite images (whether carved stone, manuscripts, or ornamented objects).

We are familiar with such communication in other Anglo-Saxon contexts. No one doubts the messages that were created by the hereditary weapons seen in *Beowulf*, for example, if only because the poet himself calls our attention to them. Sometimes such "messages" are even engraved on the weapons themselves, as on the sword hilt Hrothgar decodes in that poem.[79] The relationships that formed around ordinary things were as conceptual as was writing or images on sword hilts. Capable human beings think about what they do, whether their thoughts are conventional or original, public or private. Ordinary objects exist within a system of signs and ideas. That system was not a written one; it was structured differently from text and understood differently from text. The content communicated through that system would have been primarily social (i.e., interpersonal and immediate) but would also have been abstract to some degree (everyone has an idea of a teacher and an idea of a student, unless he or she has never taught or learned anything, which is unlikely). Even in societies in which literacy was not widespread, objects were closely tied to ideas, practices, and traditions associated with them. For example, a cauldron or the iron chain on which it was suspended might communicate ownership and patrimony. Likewise, the value of the skill required to make or use an object could form part of the message the object transmitted. Such data support Little's claim that "much of the communication involved in material culture is about interpersonal relationships." Such relationships "are real but not necessarily visual," and can be communicated "through messages of the created environment."[80] The object itself, I believe, could be the agent of such communication and could make it visible. The object could communicate as an object – that is to say, as itself.

For modern people who live deep inside a world of verbal signs it is difficult to know anything about how object-centered acts of communication and interpretation worked a millennium ago. We cannot be sure what

---

[79] *Beowulf*, in R. D. Fulk, Robert E. Bjork, and John D. Niles, eds., *Klaeber's* Beowulf, p. 57, ll. 1687–98.
[80] Little, "Texts, Images, Material Culture," p. 219.

it meant for someone who was not literate to look at a book or at an object inscribed with text or with an image that he or she was not able to decode. Nor, in terms of performance and public events, can we be sure how those who did not read might have interpreted the complex cultural messages of ritual, especially those that were text based (e.g., the liturgy). In comparison, the cultural messages of ordinary objects required no elaborate interpretation. No interpretation was required to assert a pattern of inheritance implied in handing on a tool from father or mother to son or daughter, for example, or a set of expectations of skill regarding use of that tool. Words – but not written words – would have been part of such exchanges. Even without speech, the meaning of the transfer would have been clear. Wulf Schiefenhövel has written that "there is probably no society that does not assign some status value to different kinds of food."[81] I suggest that there is probably no society that does not also assign value to different kinds of food objects, although that value might not be apparent to us.

Unlike texts and images, ordinary objects do not exist primarily to communicate meaning symbolically. They communicate cultural meaning that is encoded in objects by the process of their creation, possession, and transfer to new owners. There is no need to resort to the apparatus of visualization and textualization, with its roots in the work of Derrida and other post-structuralists and their semiotic gymnastics. Textualization will not help us understand social communication undertaken by those who did not read texts or images in the way we do, those who sent and received cultural messages through ordinary things and the practices joined to them. Textualization turns objects into images and then incorporates them into discourse, into an abstract system that privileges symbolic meaning that is shared visually and that inevitably dematerializes the material.

And there is the answer to Olsen's question. "Things were forgotten" because they were dematerialized in the modern era, swallowed up by discourse and severed from the practices attached to them, just as Brown's gallery of photographs severs its ordinary things from the social relations that made those things useful to somebody. Written words leave things behind, replacing them with images of things that discourse can manipulate. Olsen asserts that "material culture" has become "a contradictory term for reaching a culture that is not material."[82] In cultural studies, he writes, life seems to be nothing more than discursive practice in a world "held together almost solely by human cognition." The phrase is a silent echo of Foucault's claim, in *The Order of Things*, that the image "holds the world together with 'figures of knowledge,'" as good a description of discourse as one can imagine.[83] Foucault's assessment of things in the world

---

[81] Wulf Schiefenhövel, "Preface," in Polly Wiessner and Schiefenhövel, eds., *Food and the Status Quest: An Interdisciplinary Perspective*, p. viii.

[82] Olsen, "Material Culture after Text," p. 90.

[83] Olsen, "Material Culture after Text," pp. 88–89; Little, "Texts, Images, Material Culture," p. 219, quoting Mitchell, *Iconology*, p. 11, where Mitchell refers to Foucault, "The Prose of the World," the second chapter of *The Order of Things*, pp. 17–45.

before the Renaissance operates entirely within the realm of representation; it is a matter of discourse and another instance of textualization.[84] Things in such a world are important chiefly because, as signs, metaphors, and symbols, they reveal social and cultural meanings shaped by human consciousness. In Little's terms, that is one way in which they form parts of systems of communication. But in Olsen's view, the things integral to such processes as harvesting or preparing food for the table need to be understood in the context of what they were made to do, not in the context of what they could be made to mean.

Olsen brings us back to objects themselves in the context of other objects and the processes that link these things in networks of human activity. When he describes archaeology as "the discipline of things *par excellence*," he encourages a focus on things as they function in the working world, not as images that form part of discourses and symbolic systems. He thinks of archaeology as a discipline focused on materiality, on ordinary objects in the working world, not symbolic objects framed by texts. Even a simple spoon might contain some decoration – if not enough to suggest that it was a ceremonial object that could be raised to public importance, perhaps enough to contribute to the social identity of those who were associated with it. We can return to the spoon on the cover of this book for an example (Figure 1). Carved from bone, the spoon features a "leaf-shaped 'knop' terminal" that might echo Roman design; the "tiny feature on the back rib" is said to "recall sculpted ninth-century animal heads" from Deerhurst.[85] Such decoration on a spoon has meaning. It is evidence that care was taken in making the object, or a sign that this spoon is to be used differently from others. To decorate does not, in such cases, necessarily mean to infuse with symbolic meaning – at least not with symbolic meaning modern scholars recognize and perhaps not part of public sign systems at the time the spoon was made.

The care taken to make simple things is an invitation to pause, to look for interpersonal and private meaning, and to acknowledge that this meaning exists alongside the meanings associated with ceremonial objects in such public spaces as the church or the hall. Because every cross was made by hand, it had meaning as craftwork as well as meaning as a symbolic object that could be read by those learned enough to decode it. Modern construction workers might not understand the significance of large art objects their labor is needed to create, but their labor and participation invest those objects with a kind of meaning that the artist might never have considered. The same was surely true in the Anglo-Saxon world of any made thing, whether a carved wooden bowl or a carved cross.

We are not inclined to look at, much less look through, the ordinary objects that were central to the food culture of the Anglo-Saxons, or to

[84] See Foucault's discussion of similitudes in *The Order of Things*, pp. 17–23.
[85] See D. H. Evans and Christopher Loveluck, eds., *Life and Economy at Early Medieval Flixborough*, pp. 231–33 (no. 2316, fig. 5.35 and plate 5.9). The spoon is dated to the mid-eighth to early ninth century (p. 231).

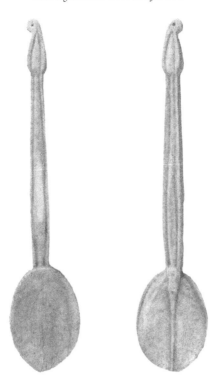

Figure 1. Bone spoon with leaf-shaped handle, Flixborough; no. 2316, RF 4135.

sketch the networks that gave the objects meaning as tools and as vehicles of interpersonal and social communication. We are limited by the habit of thinking about food objects in the context of feasting. At the feast, as texts recall it, mundane things and practices went without saying so that more important objects and rituals, including speeches and toasts, could be remembered. With those things in mind, I turn now to the feast and its milieu.

2

Food Knowledge: Texts, Feasts, and Objects

Picturing food: pyramids and networks

Everyone who has read Old English literature knows about Cædmon and his gift of song. The cowherd of Whitby abandoned a feast at which he was about to be called on to sing, retired to watch the cattle, and in his sleep was visited by a messenger who commanded him to sing, which Cædmon then did. This remarkable event, seen as the invention of Christian poetry in English, took place because Cædmon declined to sing at the *gebeorscipe*, a "carousal" according to the *Dictionary of Old English*, or what Bede, in the *Ecclesiastical History*, calls a *convivium*, a feast. He went "to the cattle byre," where "it was his turn to take charge of [the animals] that night" (*ad stabula iumentorum, quorum ei custodia nocte illa erat delegata*). Duty paired with shyness to motivate self-imposed exile.[1]

Stephen Pollington defines a *gebeorscipe* as a "drinking party" and contrasts it to the *symbel*, a "heavily symbolic" event, and to other words for "high-status feasting." This distinction might not be so clear, however. Bede elsewhere uses *convivium* to describe a celebration in a village. A visitor arrives there, and, according to the translator of the Old English version of the *Ecclesiastical History*, finds that "all the hamlet was assembled for a feast" (*þæt ham eall to symble gesomnad wæs*).[2] Those participating in this *symbel* readily welcome the stranger; they do not sound at all like aristocrats caught up in formalities. Bede himself associates Cædmon with the *symbel* when saying that, when it was his turn to sing, "he then arose out of shame from the feast and went home to his house" (*þonne aras he for forscome from þæm symble & ham eode to his huse*).[3] The translator seems to have treated the *symbel* and the *gebeorscipe* as interchangeable. If so, we should consider the possibility that Cædmon's feast was not the only celebration at Whitby that night. If it were a feast day, monks

---

[1] Thomas Miller, ed., *The Old English Version of Bede's Ecclesiastical History*, book 4, ch. 24, pp. 342–43. For the Latin, see *Bede's Ecclesiastical History*, ed. Colgrave and Mynors, book 4, ch. 24, pp. 416–17.

[2] Miller, ed., *The Old English Version of Bede's Ecclesiastical History*, book 3, ch. 8, pp. 180–81 (forms of *symbel* occur three times in this passage).

[3] Miller, ed., *The Old English Version of Bede's Ecclesiastical History*, book 4, ch. 24, pp. 342–43.

and nuns would have gathered not too far away to celebrate as well. Around one table the men and women feasted on simple food from simple vessels and drank beer. Abbess Hild and her peers enjoyed wine and food removed by many stages from its point of origin, just as their tableware, some of which no doubt was imported, was far from its place of manufacture. They were also spared the reek of animals. For Cædmon and his friends, on the other hand, the distance between production and consumption was short. Indeed, they feasted within shouting distance of the barn.

Social structure is often configured as a pyramid, an approach that makes sense if we focus on consumption rather than production, on literary examples rather than recipes, and on high-status objects and their display rather than on the ordinary things used to prepare food and drink. At the peak of the Anglo-Saxon social pyramid, the feast is always seen as an occasion for the few and their treasures. It was much more than that. Hild's feast, like many others, was made possible by large numbers of well-equipped workers, most of them operating invisibly at lower levels. Lower still were the animals who had to die so that their flesh could be eaten, and beneath the beasts were the plants that fed humans and animals alike – in other words, the order of creation as we have seen it in Psalm 8.

Cædmon's feast cannot be satisfactorily imagined as a pyramid, and neither can the feasts enjoyed by most other Anglo-Saxons, men and women who had more in common with him than with the abbess. Hild's place in the pyramid depends on the mystique that accrues to power when it is insulated from its source. We see the finger-wagging president at a podium, not the entourage, or the security force, the flock of handlers, the drivers, police officers, and others who must be mobilized every time this august figure moves from rally to rally. Likewise in Bede's narrative, we would be aware of the abbess but not of the workers in attendance – if only Bede had mentioned her feast. At Cædmon's table, we can imagine the cowherd among his peers, those who worked with animals as Cædmon did, including the butcher, the cook, and those who grew the vegetables and brewed the beer. They produced and then consumed the fruits of their and the animals' labor. Some of them made the pots, others the hooks that pulled the meat from the broth; some carved the cups, threshed the grain, and so on. Nothing is disguised at a table at which workers feast on their own fare. Ideology's power is restrained, not neutralized; among the workers, as among their betters, some are more important, older, and richer than others. Cædmon's feast does not so much expose its own workings (although one can imagine a fashionable deconstruction along those lines) as express them.

The workers gathered in the spirit of Thomas Hardy's country folk, who, in *Far from the Madding Crowd*, shear the sheep and then celebrate by eating mutton and washing it down with beer. They are content to let Bathsheba and Gabriel dine in the big house. They have their own meat and ale sent down to Warren's Malthouse.[4] Like Bathsheba and Gabriel, Hild occupied the center of a network that grew denser as it neared her. More hands were required to serve her food and drink, to set her table, and to supply her pantry, than to furnish the workers' feast. The amazing thing is that Hild seems to be surrounded by nothing at all. That is the magic of the pyramid so often used to imagine social structure. It also points to a flaw in the pyramid as a model, which is that it conceals density. The higher the social space, the fewer are the people and things visible within it. The *Old English Heptateuch* illustrates this isolating principle in a representation of Isaac's weaning (Genesis 21:8): "As was the custom, Abraham gave a great feast for the pleasure of his people on that day that the child was removed from nursing."[5] This *micelne gebeorscipe*, "great feast," includes Abraham and Sarah, Isaac, and the feasters, but no attendants. The celebrants in this *gebeorscipe* gather on one side of a table covered with plates, knives, a ladle, and various trays; many of the drinkers hold cups. The table seems to typify feasting in late Anglo-Saxon England.[6] We see the peak of the social pyramid but not the food network that supplied its demands. So tidy is the scene that things to eat, to say nothing of the work required to produce them, have themselves been banished.

Cædmon's feast, like Hardy's, points to the connection between workers and their sustenance. It is not an image of stratification, such as that represented by the pyramid, but of links and exchanges. I see Cædmon's feast as a figure for the world of food, a series of connected points distributed on a single plane. I imagine that network as a map of Anglo-Saxon England: settlements of various sizes are joined by paths, roads, streams, and rivers, some nodes formed by multiple intersections, some by a few; no point in the network is a terminus. The larger the settlement, the more paths lead to and from it, and the busier those paths will be with food, food objects, and those who produced and managed them. Every settlement, however, belongs to the network. My aim in this chapter is to consider what previous writers have said about the feast and to situate it in the context (and concept) of a food network rather than a food pyramid, the paradigm that many of these studies implicitly engage. The network makes the density of power evident. I imagine networks growing from the center out, as one food worker connects with others who reach out to still others. Pyramids must be built from the ground up, yet their foundational elements – workers in the field, grain threshers, carters, millers, bakers, and others – are never the focus, which is always life at the top.

[4] Thomas Hardy, *Far from the Madding Crowd*, ch. 7, p. 57.
[5] London, British Library, MS Cotton Claudius B.iv. *Abraham worhte, swa swa heora gewuna wæs, micelne gebeorscipe to blisse his mannum on þone dæg, þe man þæt cild fram gesoce ateah.* S. J. Crawford, ed., *The Old English Version of the Heptateuch*, p. 138, para. 8 (my translation).
[6] See Benjamin C. Withers, *The Illustrated Old English Hexateuch*, p. 93. The image is also reproduced in Carole A. Morris, *Wood and Woodworking in Anglo-Scandinavian and Medieval York*, p. 2183.

The workplaces of Cædmon and his peers formed nodes through which dairy and other products passed on their way to the abbess's table. Every step that separated Hild from Cædmon can be seen as a node that gathers interconnecting lines from the periphery and leads to the center. When Cædmon retreats to the cattle shed, he reminds us of others who may have been gathered at feasts farther from the center of power than he was. The Anglo-Saxons knew that they lived in a social pyramid (they were aware of social difference) but also understood their lives as situated within networks that linked them to other peoples and places. What Chris Loveluck writes of Flixborough, a Lincolnshire settlement continuously occupied from the seventh to the eleventh centuries, can be said of countless other settlements, small or large. "At no point within the occupational history of the Anglo-Saxon settlement did the inhabitants support themselves as an isolated, self-sufficient community," he writes. Instead the residents of Flixborough were in contact with nearby and distant peoples and settlements. Those who inhabited small settlements also depended on contact with outside locations for some things they could not do without. "Objects and commodities were procured or supplied to support the patterns of production and consumption which regulated life within the settlement," Loveluck writes.[7] Such patterns included agriculture, artisanal activity, religious observances, and other forms of social and economic exchange that moved along the food network's lines of supply and distribution. Those links were especially busy when feasts were being prepared, but the inhabitants depended on such connections for many basic things. Ann Hagen stresses that "Anglo-Saxon populations were not static, locked into small, totally self-sufficient communities they never left."[8] Ordinary people did not travel as extensively as their betters, but they too were aware of their connections to other settlements and sources.

Literary studies focus on the hall and the feast because *Beowulf* points to them. But the heroic world was linked to rural life, to small, agricultural settlements such as West Stow or Mucking. Food culture at those places, it is assumed, would have been a matter of subsistence rather than of specialized production and trade. At West Stow (Sussex), for example, only a few lines would have met to form a network. Those who planted, tended, and harvested crops and raised and killed animals did so primarily for their own sustenance rather than for that of their overlords. Huts at West Stow were clustered around halls, with some clusters possibly focused on specific activities such as weaving.[9] The settlement raised its own grain and livestock and, for its most basic food – ground meal – depended on hand-mills or querns that would have been in near-constant use. Each activity at the site – baking, milling, carving, smithing – fed the hall at the center, the node at which these activities met and were integrated. Those living at

[7] See Chris Loveluck, "Introduction," in Loveluck, Keith Dobney, and James Barrett, "Trade and Exchange," p. 112.
[8] Ann Hagen, *A Second Handbook of Anglo-Saxon Food and Drink*, p. 326.
[9] See the description by Stanley West, *West Stow Revisited*, pp. 24–48.

small settlements could produce much but not all of the food and equipment that they needed. The settlement might have had its own potter, and perhaps its own smith and woodworkers, although itinerant workers might have filled the latter functions. Specialized forms of pottery and ironwork would have come from elsewhere. Quernstones used for grinding grain came from remote sites; only a few locations for lava or granite have been found for the querns that appear so often in the archaeological record (see Chapter 4).

Some smaller settlements were, already in the early eighth century, caught up in complex networks that suggest central economic planning. Eighth-century Ipswich had developed a large-scale pottery industry. It has been suggested that it was provisioned by smaller, nearby sites that grew grain or raised livestock for the town, their production having been converted from mixed agriculture to a single purpose.[10] Thus lines joining production to consumption were not limited to short paths from field to preparation area to kitchen, as we think of them at Mucking or West Stow. Meat might have arrived at larger settlements on the hoof in order to be prepared for consumption. Labor expended on converting raw substances such as grain into finished products might have been performed where the substances were grown, and the products then shipped to settlements where industrial or commercial activities, rather than provisioning, were the focus. Different models operated elsewhere, as at Hamwic, for example. Hamwic was an important eighth-century market, which, apparently because of its geography, was not part of a provisioning network similar to the one hypothesized for Ipswich, even though cattle were the main meat animal there as at Ipswich.[11] The question, then, is to explain how Hamwic was provisioned, a matter, Mark Brisbane has pointed out, that depends on a more integrated approach to urban and rural archaeological studies, linking urban and rural in a network.[12]

Sometimes, as at large rural estates, the food network's literal structure can be seen in the settlement's design. Rosamond Faith describes the "directly exploited core area" of large estates as *inland* or an "inner estate" inhabited by peasants who were charged with providing the landlord with supplies. Living close to the manor or lord's house, they comprised an indispensable, mixed labor force "of people of notably dependent and low social status." Their chief duty, Faith stresses, was to ensure "regular supplies of foodstuffs."[13] This pattern of settlement also characterized monasteries, which in all periods were surrounded by their own agricultural communities. Faith traces this organization to the *familia* referred

[10] For a discussion of Ipswich, see Keith Wade, "Ipswich."
[11] See Chris Wickham, *Framing the Early Middle Ages*, pp. 682–88, who comments on Hamwic's "lack of an elaborated relationship with its West Saxon hinterland," p. 686. See also Helena Hamerow, *Early Medieval Settlements*, pp. 122–23.
[12] Mark Brisbane, "Hamwic (Saxon Southampton)," p. 107.
[13] See Rosamond Faith, *The English Peasantry*, p. 58, for the definition of *inland*, and for the reference to foodstuffs, see p. 16.

to in Irish monastic records.[14] Monastic estates, Sarah Foot's "minsters," were organized along hierarchical patterns, and their food culture is documented through hagiographies especially, sources not available for most rural settlements. These estates were often small, and although the minster and living quarters were isolated, food culture inevitably brought those who worked the land into contact with those who prayed more than they worked (although the pious also often labored).[15] Manual labor was undertaken for the monks under the supervision of intermediaries, managers who interposed nodes between the center and the outer areas.

Even in the inner area, access to power was mediated as well as direct. In Bede's *Ecclesiastical History*, the monk Owine, a skilled laborer, communicated directly with Chad, the bishop, while Cædmon, an unskilled worker, approached his superiors through the reeve. After Cædmon had his vision and composed his famous verses, he reported the event to the steward or reeve, *ad uilicum*.[16] The latter's job was not to carry messages from cowherds to the monastery's leaders, but to carry commands from the leaders to the workers. Cædmon and Owine were part of the monastic *inland* (or its equivalent); most workers were not and occupied settlements far removed from Cædmon's feast, not to mention Hild's. It is worth remembering that monastic estates were also domestic settlements and that land management was as important for them as it was for secular estates. Like secular estates, monastic estates seem to have been managed by overseers or reeves and worked by those who might have been known, as was Hadwald, a shepherd at Whitby, as *frater*, meaning that "he was the minster's tenant."[17] Workers like Hadwald (remembered only because an abbess had a vision of his death) participated in short-range food networks around their living and working areas. They also contributed to long-distance networks that were created to provision specialized settlements that the workers themselves never visited. The model of the network, with its multiple centers and connecting nodes, requires us to account for these people's presence and their labor. The model of the pyramid does not.

Feasting in poetry

Food networks are not the focus of the studies of feasting and food culture that I discuss here. The authors seem to be thinking of pyramids, especially of life at the top, but the objects and institutions they describe functioned within networks of many kinds, whether those that formed around the hearth in a rural hut or those that reached across the sea to

---

[14] Faith, *The English Peasantry*, p. 35, and see pp. 16–18. In continental monasteries, Faith notes, *familia* included "the workers on the monastic inland" (p. 35).

[15] Sarah Foot, *Monastic Life in Anglo-Saxon England*, pp. 97–99; on her use of "minster" to define a monastic household, see pp. 5–10.

[16] *Bede's Ecclesiastical History*, ed. Colgrave and Mynors, book 4, ch. 24, pp. 416–17. Both Owine and Cædmon are discussed in Allen J. Frantzen, "All Created Things," pp. 128–39.

[17] Foot, *Monastic Life in Anglo-Saxon England*, pp. 179–80.

manufacturing sites that produced fine pottery and glass. I examine elements of the network in Anglo-Saxon scholarship on feasting, the hall, and the grave, by Hugh Magennis, Stephen Pollington, and Christina Lee. Contributions by Ann Hagen and Debby Banham move to the kitchen and field. I also refer to recent studies by H. E. M. Cool and Peter Fowler. Some of Hagen's views about feasting and fasting raise questions about subsistence and surplus, and farms and cities. I link those questions to work by Richard Hodges and Chris Wickham, who have studied markets, trade, and exchange. The farther all this research stands from texts about the feast, we will see, the closer it comes to the materiality of food networks.

Literary scholarship has traditionally said little about the material world of feasting. Representing the best of the tradition is Alvin Lee's *The Guest-Hall of Eden* (1972), which focuses on the literary meaning of the hall rather than on the building itself. The book's title is a fascinating attempt to imagine the natural space of a garden as a hall. Heaven is commonly seen as a guest hall in Old English texts, but that is a different analogy, since ideas of heaven and the hall as places of congregation and celebration are compatible; the garden would seem to serve a different purpose. To see the feast through poetry is the most exclusive approach possible; materiality is left to one side, largely a matter of background. A more contemporary approach is taken by Hugh Magennis in *Images of Community in Old English Poetry* (1996) and *Anglo-Saxon Appetites: Food and Drink and Their Consumption in Old English and Related Literature* (1999). Three chapters of *Images of Community* concern *Beowulf* and the culture of heroic celebration. The focus is less on the feast itself than on communal institutions associated with feasting and the hall.

Readers will remember that in *Beowulf* humans do not eat but are eaten, supplying the principal food of that poem. Food "is never so much as mentioned in feasting images in Old English poetry," Magennis notes.[18] *Anglo-Saxon Appetites* seems to begin with the question arising from that observation, which is to say, why "food is not mentioned with reference to feasting in Old English poetry."[19] Magennis proposes several answers. One is that the act of eating might too readily have demonstrated the "materiality of the body" (a phrase he borrows from Mikhail Bakhtin). Eating was "not a positive symbol" because it awkwardly juxtaposed elite social bonding to the animal function of nourishment.[20] Hence we see little eating at feasts. So long as knives and especially forks were used to prepare food but not to eat it, humans and animals would resemble each other when they ate but not when they drank. Most surviving forks from the Anglo-Saxon period are large meat forks, not tools for getting food into the mouth, although a few of the latter survive, forming one end of a

---

[18] Hugh Magennis, *Images of Community in Old English Poetry*, chapters 2, 3, and 4; see p. 45 for the quote.

[19] Magennis, *Anglo-Saxon Appetites*, p. 11.

[20] Magennis, *Anglo-Saxon Appetites*, pp. 61–65.

combination utensil with a spoon bowl at the other.[21] Given the elaborate feasting ware known to the Anglo-Saxons, it was easier to represent drinking with ceremony and pomp. In accounts of the feast, much is made of cups and goblets. Some animals can be trained to drink the way humans do, but few hold cups or bowls. Drinking vessels, which survive in many forms, offered more opportunity for display of design than the knife or spoon, the most common eating tools of the Middle Ages. As Magennis shows, scenes featuring the passing of drinking cups, horns, and other ostentatious drinking gear are common in heroic literature.[22]

Magennis notes that food had other liabilities, especially its association with gluttony. He describes two Old English poems, "Soul and Body I" and "Soul and Body II," that link the materiality of the body to the display of feasting (they are two versions of one work).[23] The rotting body of the damned soul provides "a feast for worms," *wyrmum to wiste* (l. 25), a phrase that occurs in both versions here and in a later description of the decay of the damned soul's body (l. 122). The *Vercelli* text also employs the phrase in reference to the decay of the good soul's body (l. 155). In both versions, the damned soul's body is said to have been proud in feasting (*wiste wlanc*, l. 39).[24] The closest this poet came to portraying indulgent Anglo-Saxons at their meat is the image of worms feasting on the dead.

Spiritual symbolism was another factor inhibiting the representation of eating (rather than drinking). Magennis points out that Old English sources represent the Eucharist in both carnal and spiritual guises.[25] Although the Mass in Anglo-Saxon times involved the consecration of both wine and bread, the Eucharistic meal was centered on an act of eating and was associated with the Body of Christ. In his Easter homily, Ælfric compared the Israelites' eating of the Paschal lamb to Christians' spiritual eating of Christ's body and drinking his blood: "Now we eat the spiritual body of Christ and drink his blood when we receive the sacred bread with true belief" (*We ðicgað nu gastlice cristes lichaman. and his blod drincað. þonne we mid soðum geleafan þæt halige husel ðicgað*). Once consecrated, the host signified the body Christ offered and the blood he shed (*Witodlice þis husel ðe nu bið gehalgod æt godes weofode is gemynd cristes lichaman. þe he for us geoffrode. and his blodes þe he for us ageat*).[26] Ælfric's stress on "spiritual" (*gastlice*) consumption addresses possible anxiety about cannibalism. Magennis suggests that Anglo-Saxon poets were careful to separate actual meals from echoes of the Last Supper or references to "heavenly bread," and to keep

---

[21] For examples from Brandon, Suffolk; Sevington, Hampshire; and Southampton, see Leslie Webster and Janet Backhouse, eds., *The Making of England*, p. 86, item 66 (p).

[22] The cups he discusses are cups of death; see Magennis, *Anglo-Saxon Appetites*, pp. 132–34.

[23] Magennis, *Anglo-Saxon Appetites*, p. 121.

[24] Douglas Moffat, ed. and trans., *The Old English "Soul and Body,"* pp. 50–63 (parallel texts of the *Exeter Book* and *Vercelli Book* versions).

[25] Magennis, *Anglo-Saxon Appetites*, pp. 160–65.

[26] Malcolm Godden, ed., *Ælfric's Catholic Homilies*, pp. 150–60. Quotations from pp. 151–52, ll. 61–63, and p. 156, l. 217.

the act of eating and the process of spiritual nourishment in different categories.[27]

One of the successes of *Anglo-Saxon Appetites* is to demonstrate the Anglo-Saxons' acute need to isolate the feast from the ordinary. Designed to stand above and apart from humble associations, the feast was all too clearly connected to processes that threatened its aura of exclusivity and privilege. The decorum that governed the feast, illustrated by Pollington, was one way of ensuring the feast's status as a ritual and exclusive event. But so too was the tradition that kept poets from referring to food and to eating. The textual network proves to be preoccupied with isolating various meanings of the feast and ensuring that its enormously important spiritual significance was not compromised by material aspects of either food or drink. Pollington has commented on the threat of disorder posed by drinking. "In the light of the large quantities of alcohol available in the hall," he writes, "the conclusion seems inescapable that some feasts must have ended in arguments, brawling and all-out fighting."[28] In fact, we can be sure that such disruptions took place. The ordered processes of culture were at risk when violence broke out, as it did, to judge from the law codes, even in the king's presence. "If the king is feasting in anyone's house," the laws of Æthelberht (d. 616) declare, "and any sort of offence is committed there, twofold compensation shall be paid." The laws of Hlothhere and Eadric do likewise (c. 685), and the laws of Alfred (d. 899), like those of Ine (d. 726), suggest that such a crime could be punishable by death.[29]

However ceremonious it was, feasting was a time of excess and drunkenness. It is striking that by far the longest chapter in Hagen's study of food production deals with fermented drinks.[30] As to drunkenness itself, Hagen notes that the offense is mentioned in monastic rules that were translated into Old English from the Latin and also mentioned in the penitentials.[31] The monastic rules are not good guides to lay behavior, however. They say much more about food than most other texts because life in spiritual communities was much more highly regulated than life in the settlements around them. In the penitentials there is remarkably little that addresses drunken behavior (see Chapter 8). For obvious reasons, then, poets isolated heavenly feasts such as the one alluded to at the end of "The Dream of the Rood" from the celebrations of heroic legend. According to Magennis, homiletic literature and admonitory works use feasting and drinking "to represent the carnal appetite and worldly orientation that lead the soul to destruction," portraying pleasures as symbolic of the *deadne life* (dead life)

---

[27] See the discussion of eating of bodies in Magennis's analysis of *Andreas* (*Anglo-Saxon Appetites*, pp. 143–47). For Ælfric's views, see Magennis, *Anglo-Saxon Appetites*, pp. 166–70.
[28] Stephen Pollington, *The Mead-Hall*, p. 118.
[29] For Æthelberht 3, see F. L. Attenborough, *LEEK*, pp. 4–5; in F. Liebermann, *GDA*, p. 3. For Hlothhere and Eadric 12–14, see Attenborough, *LEEK*, pp. 20–21; in Liebermann, *GDA*, p.11. For Ine 6–6.5, see Attenborough, *LEEK*, pp. 38–39; in Liebermann, *GDA*, p. 92. For Alfred 7–7.1, see Attenborough, *LEEK*, pp. 68–69; in Liebermann, *GDA*, pp. 52–54.
[30] Hagen, *A Second Handbook*, pp. 204–58.
[31] Hagen, *A Second Handbook*, pp. 249–50.

of earthly existence, a phrase from "The Seafarer."[32] Such warnings did little, however, to dim the glamour of the feast. Evidence of the importance of feasting grows stronger in later (i.e., early eleventh-century) law codes, probably the most important texts for helping us assess the Anglo-Saxons' cultural institutions (see Chapter 9).

Whether as a pyramid or network, any connection between feasting and eating would have demolished the mystique of the feast. That anxiety, which clouds all forms of exclusiveness, is made especially apparent when life at the top is isolated from the social forms that make it possible. Drinking had to be kept separate from eating and one kind of eating kept separate from another. When undisciplined adults at the table are disparaged by the author of "The Seasons for Fasting," one of the poems Magennis writes about, they are compared to dogs and wolves.[33] The Anglo-Saxons struggled to isolate the feast from contamination by ideas and traditions associated with eating. This struggle was not concerned with food purity (which I discuss in Chapter 9) but with the ideological purity of the feast. The evidence in Magennis's book on feasting shows how difficult it was to suppress the reality of the networks connecting the feast to food as well as to the disorder drink could bring about. Some voices in the culture glorified the hall and the feast; others portrayed those same institutions as forms of living death; still others used them as images of heaven, the one guest hall they could think of in which no one needed to worry about drunken disorder or running out of wine.

Feasting and material culture

Pollington's representation of the feast also favors the model of the pyramid, creating a study rich in images of elite wares and rare objects, including musical instruments, menus, and a program for the evening's events. Pollington animates life in the hall with social concepts of gift giving and exchange, even making the vertical nature of the pyramid explicit in a diagram showing that service went up the line and favors came down it. Reciprocity lends itself to vertical rather than horizontal representations of power.[34] His diagram does not say so, but those of higher status also exchanged gifts among themselves, as did their inferiors, forming horizontal as well as vertical bonds. Pollington explores the rooms in which feasts were held and the splendid objects on display. He moves from prestigious tableware to the demands that lordly feasts placed on the estates associated with their governing center. Those objects include large cauldrons and other containers such as those unearthed in ceremonial burials at Sutton Hoo and Taplow. Impressive works, they point beyond food-function to symbolic value and to the social status of

---

[32] Magennis, *Anglo-Saxon Appetites*, p. 121, and p. 128, quoting "The Seafarer," l. 65.

[33] Magennis, *Anglo-Saxon Appetites*, p. 87 (stanzas 27–29). See Chapter 11, below, for an extended discussion of "The Seasons of Fasting."

[34] Pollington, *The Mead-Hall*, p. 52.

the owner, with whom the object, a symbol of his or her power as a provider, was buried. One of the few examples of a bronze cauldron found north of the Humber was discovered in a famous double grave at Sewerby (East Yorkshire), in a coffin containing the body of a young woman of great wealth. Among many other grave goods found with her were a cauldron, a knife, and some animal ribs, the latter a possible food offering.[35] Feasting cauldrons symbolize the power of the wealthy to provide for their dependants but also point to material aspects of the hall. Chains found with the cauldron from Sutton Hoo, as reconstructed, suggest that the beam from which the bronze kettle hung must have been less than five meters high, about two meters more than the chain from Flixborough reproduced in this book (see Figure 2). The cauldron had a capacity of nearly 100 liters. Pollington suggests that a small drinking vessel might have held half a pint (0.3 liter), so it is possible that the large vessel might have held 200 to 300 servings.[36] Iron fittings were used to suspend the cauldron, which also had iron handles. The cauldron was probably too thin (at just 1.2 mm) to have been used for preparing the drink, a task demanding larger and sturdier wares and thus pointing to an unseen node in the food network, the site at which the contents, along with other elements for the feast, were prepared. Just as its thinness suggests that the cauldron held drink prepared elsewhere in a stronger vessel, its iron handles remind us that the container had to be carried into the hall, hung, filled, and later taken down and cleaned. For the *Beowulf* poet and others who comment on drinking in the hall, such work went without saying, as do the contributions of numerous craft workers in the feasting network, whether they prepared cups and cauldrons or meat. A network of skilled labor and materials comes into view when Pollington comments that a cauldron from Taplow could have "come from the same workshop" as the one from Sutton Hoo.[37] These impressive objects had to be made to order and created by skilled workers. The potential to link feasting sites to places of manufacture is a practical side to evidence of feasting. That network of skilled labor was created by those who demanded objects of exceptional size and ornateness. The paths along which such objects eventually moved was first traversed by the elites who were conscious of the value of display.

Because Pollington is concerned with materiality in many senses, his book points to more ordinary forms of the food network, from the paths of animals raised on farms and "driven to town for sale and slaughter" to domestic life "centred round the hearth." He identifies some of the nodes connecting the farm to the feast where its produce and livestock were consumed. Pollington cites a mid-ninth-century charter listing food rents paid to Christ Church, Canterbury, from an estate at "Burnam." This unidentified Kentish location had to supply 240 loaves of bread, as well as cheese,

---

[35] Susan M. Hirst, *An Anglo-Saxon Inhumation Cemetery at Sewerby*, pp. 39–40 and 92–94.
[36] Pollington, *The Mead-Hall*, pp. 161 and 164.
[37] Pollington, *The Mead-Hall*, p. 166.

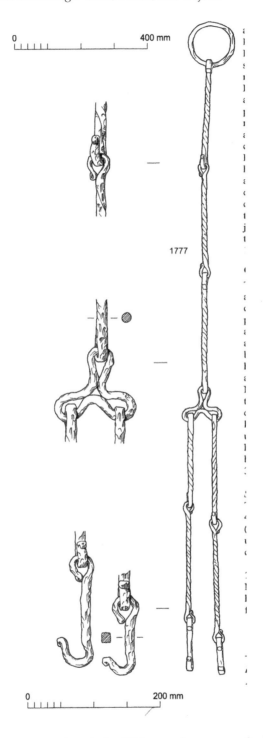

0   400 mm

1777

0   200 mm

Figure 2. Iron cauldron suspension chain, Flixborough; no. 1777. Scale 1:8.

ale, and animals.[38] Pollington compares these figures to those found in the poem known as the "Dialogue of Solomon and Saturn," which refers to a contribution of 720 loaves per year to one's serving man, suggesting an allotment of two loaves per day (assuming that 720 is an error for 730, or twice 365).[39] Although 240 loaves sounds like a lot, at the rate of two per person per day, it would, using Pollington's calculations, be enough to feed a servant for only four months (or 120 days).

Like these loaves, every other item on the estate list had to be processed in order to move up the pyramid, or, as I see it, closer to the center of the network. The animals had to be raised, delivered live to a central point, and kept there until slaughtered. Food renders had to be staggered to keep the estate's central stores from being overloaded. The rents from estates attached to a location such as a cathedral or a manor had to be organized to accommodate and regulate the flow of both preserved and perishable items. The demands of such rents also had to be factored into the management of the estate's resources and its own food needs. Provisions for feasts were complicated by the same concerns for transportation, storage, and preparation. These material aspects of the food network, especially transportation, are not obvious when the feast is seen in a pyramid. But when we see the feast as a central node drawing on distant centers of supply, themselves fed by more remote points, the advantage of the network becomes clear.

Pollington briefly discusses the custom of "funeral feasting," a ritual meal at the graveside showing that the Anglo-Saxons prepared feasts for the dead.[40] Cool describes remnants of such feasts in Roman Britain.[41] This kind of food network is the subject of Lee's *Feasting the Dead*, which shows how feasting joined the dead and the living in a food network. Lee demonstrates the various ways in which food culture reached into the grave and ways in which archaeologists are able to use these things, some of the most prestigious food objects yet recovered, to study settlement life, a practice known as chorology. Grave goods, as Claus Kjeld Jensen and Karen Høilund Nielsen have shown, can suggest how these objects functioned amid the routines of the living.[42] Food objects found in graves have three advantages over those found in settlements. First, objects buried with cremated or inhumed remains were more likely to survive so long as the grave remained undisturbed. Second, the objects included in a burial, and their disposition in relation to the body, might reflect deliberate choices and point to identities associated with the dead. Third, feasting required

---

[38] Pollington, *The Mead-Hall*, pp. 119–80. For the charter, found in London, British Library, MS Cotton Augustus ii.52, see Pollington, *The Mead-Hall*, pp. 122–23, and P. H. Sawyer, *Anglo-Saxon Charters*, no. 1195, p. 351.

[39] Pollington, *The Mead-Hall*, pp. 122–23. See James E. Cross and Thomas D. Hill, eds., *The Prose Solomon and Saturn* and *Adrian and Ritheus*, p. 34, c. 59 and notes, pp. 123–34.

[40] Pollington, *The Mead-Hall*, pp. 62–64.

[41] H. E. M. Cool, *Eating and Drinking in Roman Britain*, pp. 52–53.

[42] Claus Kjeld Jensen and Karen Høilund Nielsen, "Burial Data and Correspondence Analysis," pp. 30–32.

food preparation, traces of which remain in and around burial contexts in cemeteries. Lee has argued that remnants from burial feasts might have been mixed into the backfill of the grave.[43] This possibility shows the risk of confusion between what was selected for burial with the dead and what was used to fill in the grave. But it also offers occasional opportunities to observe the remains of a real feast, a kind of evidence not to be hoped for in other contexts.

Cooking objects point to networks in other ways. Objects found in graves may point to the deceased person's occupation. The dead were sometimes buried in the garments they wore when they worked, for example. At West Heslerton a series of female graves contained vessels, interpreted as cooking pots, that were positioned over the abdomens of the bodies. Perhaps this gesture reflects the association of these women with food preparation. Lee describes other ordinary vessels recovered from inhumations, including pots with traces of sooting suggesting that they were used for cooking.[44] Not all pottery found in graves is decorated, and some was buried in fragmentary condition, the part representing the whole.[45] These objects may "give us some indication who this person was," Lee writes, and tell us "how they were seen by those who buried them."[46] Her use of sight lines is suggestive. In a discussion that complements Lee's, J. D. Richards has used lines of sight to link burial objects to their function among the living. We need to think of mourners standing around a grave as they ate and drank and perhaps saw some wares in the grave that they were used to seeing at the hearth. Richards believes that decoration on a pot would have been visible only when viewed from above, once the pot was placed in the grave. So positioned, the pot would be viewed as it had been when placed on a trivet over a fire. Richards regards symbols on pots as a form of burial inscription and compares them to the way in which brooches would have been decoded when worn on the clothing of the living.[47] This and other evidence shows how food objects found in graves document a dead person's association with particular phases of food production in settlement life and thereby point to the node he or she occupied in the local food network.

Outside the feast: day-to-day food culture

Both Hagen and Banham anchor their descriptions of diet and food preparation in agriculture, animal husbandry, and social routines. Banham begins *Food and Drink in Anglo-Saxon England* by recalling that, as a student, she listened to lectures on kings and bishops and wondered what they ate for

---

[43] Christina Lee, *Feasting the Dead*, p. 87.
[44] Lee, *Feasting the Dead*, pp. 83–85.
[45] Lee, *Feasting the Dead*, p. 79.
[46] Lee, *Feasting the Dead*, p. 76.
[47] J. D. Richards, *The Significance of Form and Decoration of Anglo-Saxon Cremation Urns*, pp. 148–54, and "Anglo-Saxon Symbolism," pp. 141–42.

breakfast. In other words, she imagined the king enmeshed in networks of supply and demand associated with daily needs, not seated atop a pyramid. Her catalogue of resources reveals why her book is exceptionally useful in creating mundane contexts: archaeological evidence, including artifacts and food remains; place-name evidence; words for Old English plants and foods; and the visual arts.[48] Banham organizes her discussion according to food groups (bread, fruit and vegetables, meat) and centers her work on the household. She stresses the seasonality of food and modifications to the diet to accommodate sickness and other special conditions.

Banham makes recommendations for recreating an Anglo-Saxon feast, something I would wager few scholars have attempted. It is not necessary for a modern cook to shell and grind corn in order to make *briw*, a one-dish meal based on ground grain and flavored with vegetables, herbs, and perhaps a little bacon, but Banham herself has ground grain at a quern, and writes: "My own experiments suggest that the average modern person would not last half an hour at such work, and would have produced enough flour for a couple of rolls."[49] Modern visitors to Firkat, a reconstructed Viking settlement in Denmark, can try it, using a quern at waist height, not one embedded into the floor, as ancient querns were. If we take two rolls as a small loaf, we can see that it would take a modern worker an hour to make two small loaves. The daily allotment in "The Dialogue of Solomon and Saturn" is two such loaves for a serving man. Thus each serving person would have required one hour of grinding for his or her daily bread. It easy to see why Banham came to the conclusion that bread was not the daily necessity for the Anglo-Saxons that we sometimes think it was.[50]

Banham sketches two other kinds of networks related to food. Her extensive documentation includes photographs of modern animals considered close to the stock that roamed Anglo-Saxon pastures. Banham also describes modern food processes that resemble those of the ancient world. Such documentation links past to present in the way that woodworkers or potters do when they reconstruct ancient processes, as does the woodworker Carole A. Morris.[51] A second kind of network, lexical and verbal, is to be found in Banham's edition and translation of the *Monasteriales Indicia*. This work describes the sign language used by monks when speech was forbidden, a document that I will analyze in the next chapter. Monks used sign language when they talked about food; most Anglo-Saxons created an audible conversational network when they ate and drank, a form of communication seen when elite members of one community became aware of

---

[48] Debby Banham, *Food and Drink in Anglo-Saxon England*, pp. 7–12.

[49] Banham, *Food and Drink*, pp. 18 and 71–77.

[50] Banham, *Food and Drink*, pp. 24–25. Compare Cool, *Eating and Drinking in Roman Britain*, pp. 73–74. See also Chapter 4, p. 94, below, for further discussion of Banham's findings in relation to querns.

[51] Morris, *Wood and Woodworking*.

and acquired for themselves elegant wares such as cauldrons that they had seen elsewhere.

Hagen produced a two-volume handbook of Anglo-Saxon food and drink. She uses both textual and archaeological sources to trace four major food-related activities: production, distribution, processing, and consumption, the latter being the category that, as we have seen, dominates other studies. The first volume concerns processing and consumption, and describes drying kilns and milling before explaining how bread was baked. Chapters on dairying, butchery, and food preservation lead up to her account of cooking itself. The second volume, which concerns production and distribution, describes how food was measured and how food supplies were organized and administered in Anglo-Saxon settlements. Archaeological data up to 1986 are integrated into every chapter.[52] Hagen's books are the best and most practical guides to Anglo-Saxon food culture available and are frequently cited in both literary studies and site reports. Rich in textual information, these works demonstrate numerous ways in which food culture was organized into networks that connected production to sites of consumption. Sometimes Hagen makes the links literal, as in her discussion of laws regulating food use. She includes such seldom-considered matters as how people – for example, clerics who attended synods – traveled with food. Her account of production and distribution includes growing crops and raising animals; some fifteen chapters describe nearly everything the Anglo-Saxons were known to have eaten. Hagen deals with differences in urban and rural diet and with limitations on food production in towns. She describes food hospitality and the role of food in charity, both matters that required a surplus of food.[53] These books are effective, in part, because they do not advance a thesis about either a food pyramid or a food network. Rather, Hagen focuses on summarizing what is known about food processing and consumption, a topic that begins with the ordinary and moves up the scale to feasting. Problems are inevitable in a study so broad; they include the use of outdated editions and translations, and the use of texts translated from Latin continental sources as direct evidence of Anglo-Saxon food culture.[54]

Books by Cool and Fowler integrate food into historically based studies of production. Cool's *Eating and Drinking in Roman Britain* concerns the period immediately before the Anglo-Saxon age, but anyone interested in food culture, archaeology, and texts should consult it. Like Banham, Cool is engaged with food in both modern and ancient modern modes, and often refers to the chemistry of cooking. Cool took as her model "classic

[52] Ann Hagen, *A Handbook of Anglo-Saxon Food and Drink; A Second Handbook of Anglo-Saxon Food and Drink*.
[53] Hagen, *A Second Handbook*, pp. 326–52.
[54] For example, a poisonous plant mentioned in a homily about St. Martin, who lived in the fourth century, written by Sulpicius Severus (who died c. 425) might not be the same plant known to the Anglo-Saxons. See Hagen, *A Handbook*, p. 140, and, for the reference to *hellebore* in the life of Martin, Walter W. Skeat, ed., *Ælfric's Lives of Saints*, 2: 232–33. Hellebore was known for its purgative properties and was not always poisonous. See pp. 66–67 below.

works" that "explore the cuisine of particular parts of the world." She cites Marcella Hazan and Elizabeth David as examples, an appropriate gesture for a book that superbly illustrates what pioneers in the provinces made of their rich Roman tradition.[55] Spanning Roman Britain and the Anglo-Saxon age, Fowler's *Farming in the First Millennium AD* reaches from the broad environmental concerns of agrarian history to agricultural implements and details of food preparation. Of particular interest is a chapter on foods other than those gathered from "mainstream agrarian activities" and on feasting, which is seen as a "broad-based social activity."[56] Both books contextualize food in terms of settlements that are more than sites, a distinction I draw from Fowler, who contrasts "sites *per se*" to settlements, which are contexts "containing numerous aspects of human behavior."[57] A settlement is a node in a network comprised of other nodes and the human interactions that power them.

Settlements and markets

Food studies can begin at the bottom, where Banham and Hagen start, or with the view from the top, where Hodges starts. We will see that Hodges and Hagen sometimes hardly seem to be talking about the same food world. If we look at their arguments within the context of a network, however, we can understand and even mediate their points of difference. Hagen's attention is concentrated on the kitchen, the garden, and the farm, but her concern with distribution links her work to that of historians who connect markets to political developments that span borders and boundaries. They include Hodges, Wickham, and John Moreland. I will contrast the picture of food culture that emerges from Hagen's work to that created by Hodges and then assess some responses to his work from Hodges's critics.

Hagen's summary view of Anglo-Saxon food culture is pessimistic, even grim, and it contrasts in useful ways to Hodges's views and ideas about market structures. In any age, including ours, many go hungry. In Hagen's view, the Anglo-Saxons, even when eating, were not necessarily well-off. There is no disputing her account of smoke in poorly ventilated rooms, which produced chronic sinusitis, or of fungi, lead poisoning, and worms.[58] Cemetery evidence leaves no doubt of these and other ailments. Pollington also cites grave evidence suggesting that "all individuals seem to have been exposed to the risk of malnutrition."[59] Such memorable

---

[55] Cool, *Eating and Drinking in Roman Britain*, pp. 6–7.
[56] Peter Fowler, *Farming in the First Millennium AD*, pp. xi–xii and 240–56, quotation from p. 240.
[57] Fowler, *Farming in the First Millennium AD*, p. 41.
[58] Hagen, *A Handbook*, pp. 140–43. The reference to worms is found in the translation of Boethius attributed to King Alfred's court (late ninth century); both the Latin source and the translation describe worms that live inside bodies, but the translation suggests that they are visible on the outside. For the Old English, see Malcolm Godden and Susan Irvine, eds., *The Old English Boethius*, 1: 273, and, for translation 2: 23 (book 2, prose 6, is chapter 16 of this edition).
[59] Pollington, *The Mead-Hall*, p. 122.

details bear on Hagen's view of the feast and its role in Anglo-Saxon culture. "References to feasting in the literature are so emotionally loaded as to make one realise that such indulgence in food and drink probably took place against a background of deprivation," she writes. She suggests that the "gratification of the moment" that the Anglo-Saxons experienced in times of plenty might have conflicted with "the need to eke out food during the winter months" and in times of crop failure. The Church's approval of feasts "made it possible to indulge without guilt and to endure periods of fasting."[60] I myself doubt that the Church ever allowed its members to "indulge without guilt." As Pollington and Magennis show, there is very little Christian discourse about feasting that is not shadowed with warnings about sinful excess.

Hagen's observations pair well with her general view of food in the context of scarcity and abundance, and the Anglo-Saxon life as seesawing between the threat of starvation and inconvenient surpluses. Hodges at one point contrasts "organic" to "rational" models of agricultural production.[61] Hodges's use of "organic" points to the kind of rural and indeed personal food world of Hagen's books and Banham's book as well, a world in which it is easy to imagine workers at their supper in low-ceilinged and smoky quarters. In such a world feast or famine seem to be unavoidable alternatives; peasants engaged in subsistence farming could never be sure from one season to the next how well they would do (a drawback to modern agricultural life as well). Hagen's food world begins at the local level, the level of subsistence, and works from the bottom up: a settlement produced enough for its own survival then built a surplus that could be traded. Hagen associates feasts with times of plenty and describes feasting as the consumption of surplus to prevent spoiling. Pollington agrees that "an English *gegadorwiste* [feast] was a group of people who assembled for the purpose of consuming their food surplus in as agreeable a manner as possible."[62]

There, I think, we see the limits of the "organic" view of food culture, to use Hodges's language, and some advantages of the "rational" view behind his own much-debated theories. It is not realistic to assume, with Hagen, that feasts fattened up the faithful so they could "endure periods of fasting." Fasts of forty days were not the only times the Anglo-Saxons had to tolerate a restricted diet, since fasting could be required without the reward of a feast in sight. Her view seems to limit the feast to matters of supply and demand. Surely those factors affected what could be eaten and when, but they also imply that feasting was an entirely localized phenomenon determined by the supplies of a settlement, which is seen as a terminus of consumption rather than a way station. We know from the size of food renders, such as those Hagen describes, that large quantities of

---

[60] Hagen, *A Handbook*, p. 146, and *A Second Handbook*, pp. 357–58.
[61] For comments on rational and organic approaches, see Richard Hodges, "*Dark Age Economics* Revisited," ch. 4 in *Goodbye to the Vikings?*, p. 71.
[62] Pollington, *The Mead-Hall*, pp. 20–21. He refers only to "Hagen, 1992."

food had to be shipped and stored, and that the food supply was "rationalized" in this way, meaning that surplus was stored against the possibility of scarcity. That was not everywhere the case. It was not uniformly, as Hodges demonstrates, a hand-to-mouth world. Support for his view comes from Faith's reference to the *inland* as a source of "regular supplies of foodstuffs."[63] Feasts at estates were possible because the *inland* stored foodstuffs as well as grew them. At large estates, feasts would have been comprised of foodstuffs acquired from outlying areas and stored to be used as needed. In difficult times perhaps those in outlying areas did not observe feasts so that their betters might. I see such a hypothesis, which is supported by Faith's work, as an example of a "rational" rather than "organic" model because it links the feast both to a network and to a central power structure able to assert its prerogatives at the expense of smaller centers. It is hard to imagine that all levels of Anglo-Saxon society feasted equally often; surely nobody imagines that they feasted equally well. In some instances the feast would have been a grand event that depended on transportation to supply special foods and ordinary foods in large quantities. Such feasting would not have been possible outside a food network that involved multiple settlements and points of supply.

Hodges's early works introduce several arguments about tiered market systems and their role in managing production and distribution from port to pantry. In *Dark Age Economics: The Origins of Town and Trade A.D. 600–1000* (1982) and in *The Anglo-Saxon Achievement* (1989), Hodges integrates field systems and settlement planning into discussions of the political economies that emerged in the Anglo-Saxon period. Hodges's food world is one in which administrative centers were created to serve the highest levels of demand and then became the end points of systems of supply and production organized to meet their needs (hence a rationalized system). These centers were accompanied by regional markets, "the major centres, the initial nodes in the competitive marketing system ultimately derived from administrative foci."[64] Hodges reasserts this top-down perspective in his later work and stresses the role of politics in shaping trade patterns. The "gateway" communities he discusses, including Dorestad (Netherlands), Ribe (Denmark), and Hamwic (Hampshire), were "political entities predominantly intended to serve their regions." The long-range trade they supported was "of signal symbolic importance for prestige goods exchange, whereas the greater part of the settlement was involved in agrarian and craft production." Such locations were not only ports of trade but regional centers, and were centers with their own subsistence economies.[65]

Hodges's vision of Anglo-Saxon agriculture and subsistence differs from the view of Hagen and many others and, in its many iterations, has

[63] Faith, *The English Peasantry*, p. 16.
[64] Hodges, *Dark Age Economics*, p. 177.
[65] Hodges, *Goodbye to the Vikings?*, p. 68.

often been challenged. Whereas I find Hagen's view too dark, others have found Hodges's views too optimistic. Using late seventh-century laws about land holdings and cultivation, and moving on to the great emporia of the eighth century, Hodges argues that "the Anglo-Saxon villagers were quite affluent" (although many, incidentally, would challenge his reference to "villagers"). Farmers "apparently enjoyed unprecedented wealth as a result of environmental resources, a modest population level and a socio-political climate that gave every ceorl a stake in the future of his kingdom." These workers "were not the exploited, overworked peasants who suffered the hardships so vividly described by cultural anthropologists."[66] Hodges believes that the consolidation of smaller settlements into larger ones and the central planning or nucleation of settlements came about as the consequence of developing emporia and towns in the eighth century and after.[67] Ipswich would seem to provide a good example of such a development. Centralization, brought about by powerful political figures, created the need for "the apparent food-mountains" produced by Anglo-Saxon farmers. Always seen as a buffer against hard times and poor crop-years, surpluses were also necessary to feed "the emergent institutions" of the market.[68]

Hodges views Anglo-Saxon food culture in terms of complex economic models and focuses on many parts of the food network, ranging from salt on the table to large agricultural and urban developments. He describes the food world seen by others as a redistributive system operating under various leveling mechanisms (gift exchange, for example) that would "counteract the accumulation of wealth by a central person." His own model posits "the recruitment of goods and services for the benefit of an elite." For Hodges, trade replaces exchange and depends on networks built up of other networks.[69] Hodges describes a tiered system that ranges from regional markets (the largest), to central markets spaced between regional markets, and down to what are called standard or third-tier markets. These markets are thought to have developed from the top down, not the bottom up; the smallest markets, which Hodges calls "green vegetable" markets, were the last to develop.[70]

Hodges envisions estates surrounded by settlements that supplied them. He posits a transition from conspicuous consumption, made possible by provisioning for the estate's lord by smaller settlements around it, to new functions, including storage of surplus required by markets. At Wicken Bonhunt, a high-status estate center from the mid-Saxon period, Hodges points to a line of timber buildings and ditches crammed with refuse. These remains suggest a meat production site or perhaps granaries

---

[66] Hodges, *Dark Age Economics*, pp. 137–38.
[67] See David Hall, "The Late Saxon Countryside"; J. G. Hurst, "The Changing Medieval Village in England"; and, more generally, Della Hooke, *Medieval Villages*.
[68] Hodges, *Dark Age Economics*, p. 139.
[69] Hodges, *Dark Age Economics*, pp. 15–16.
[70] Hodges, *Dark Age Economics*, pp. 15–17 and 177–78.

needed for storage.[71] The settlement's great hall, which would have been the center of gift exchange and displays of feasting, was eclipsed by storage barns, a symbolic transformation if ever there was one. Hodges interprets that change as a shift away from display and conspicuous consumption that was based on a shift from a gift economy to trade. In reference to buildings perhaps intended for servile laborers, located far from the great family's dwelling, he writes, "These buildings must represent a new ethos in Anglo-Saxon society, marking a growing shift from conspicuous consumption to increased production for storage and exchange."[72] If he is right, Wicken Bonhunt had undergone a shift in what Chris Loveluck might describe as its "settlement biography," acquiring a new role as a center for storage that complemented a new role as a trading center.[73] The domestic – understood to include the hall, the site of feasting and other centralized functions – would have given way as the site became a pass-through point that served larger centers. The old model is the one we see in Hagen, driven by subsistence and dedicated to supplying food renders to the estate center and to the Church. The new one, which we see in Hodges's work, encompasses a much larger network centered on powerful administrators acting at royal command who organized supplies from outlying areas into storage centers that could meet the demands of society's most important and powerful figures. His work emphasizes "the intervention of master-planners" working for kings, "place-makers" who founded market centers such as Dorestad, Ribe, and Hamwic.[74] In his view these master-planners were masters of the food culture network, which they reshaped to serve royal prerogatives.

Some historians have reservations about Hodges's claims, among them Blinkhorn, Wickham, and Moreland. Blinkhorn has challenged Hodges's optimism, seen in Hodges's estimate of the abundance produced by early Anglo-Saxon farmers. Blinkhorn points out that the estimate is based on a single list of food rents that cannot be generalized to describe production across all of Anglo-Saxon England.[75] Taking a pan-European view of markets and hence food culture, Wickham disagrees with Hodges's view that "Charlemagne consciously developed the market to buttress the state in Francia." Wickham questions the existence of "this form of economic consciousness" in the period and proposes that both the market and the state were already thriving by 800. He regards integrated market systems as a guide to local levels of aristocratic dominance and centralization; he envisions smaller networks than those proposed by Hodges. Wickham also doubts that gift-exchange systems were transformed into markets. In his

[71] Dating and site description for Wicken Bonhunt is taken from Keith Dobney, Deborah Jacques, James Barrett and Cluny Johnstone, "Zooarchaeological Evidence," p. 223. See also Pam J. Crabtree, "Animal Exploitation in East Anglian Villages."
[72] Hodges, *The Anglo-Saxon Achievement*, pp. 136–39.
[73] Chris Loveluck, "Cædmon's World," pp. 152–53.
[74] Hodges, *Goodbye to the Vikings?*, p. 71.
[75] Paul Blinkhorn, "Of Cabbages and Kings," p. 7.

view, tribute, gifts, warfare, and fines were all sources of wealth for kings such as Offa (Hodges's Anglo-Saxon counterpart to Charlemagne), but collectively they mattered less than economic control of land, resources, and peasant labor. "That feudal power, of lords over peasants, was essential for lasting royal wealth and dominance," he writes.[76] It is worth noting that Faith's view of the *inland* – which, ironically, rests in part on an earlier essay by Wickham – is that "these early core areas represented a transition between an economy based purely on tribute and the manorial system."[77] As does Blinkhorn, Wickham argues that agricultural surplus was unlikely in the early period. Peasants could not count on trade to supply their needs, he suggests, because trade networks would be unreliable. Instead, peasants had to produce what they needed, including most of their tools and food objects. Although removed from prestigious exchange networks, they were nonetheless embedded in networks of rural production and distribution. The basic needs of the wealthy, in contrast, were satisfied by their own provisioning networks, although their need for markers of status could not be satisfied that way and so required imports.

Criticism from another direction comes from Moreland, who casts doubt on Hodges's thesis about the relationship of markets to the needs of secular elites. In Moreland's view, Hodges did not sufficiently emphasize the role of non-royal forces in the development of emporia and long-range trading networks. Moreland has argued that the "hidden hand" seeking control over production and distribution of food and goods in the countryside belonged to both ecclesiastical and secular elites. Moreland especially stresses the early role of Church leaders in bringing about centralized settlements, seeing this development already in the seventh and early eighth centuries. Ecclesiastical centers were monastic and required intensified production for their large populations. To this end, the Church partnered with secular authority, which would have been necessary to manage labor and production on a new scale.[78] He finds support for his arguments in John Blair's view that "commercial activity" in the late seventh century was directly linked to the development of minster churches.[79]

Moreland sketches a hierarchy of settlements, with major secular and ecclesiastical sites such as Flixborough and Brandon at the top. More modest settlements, perhaps rural centers (e.g., Wharram Percy, Barnham), shared in some of the material benefits of the exchange networks developed for the major sites. Further down were sites that participated in exchange networks to a degree but owed more to rural production, and beneath them "archaeologically invisible" centers that supplied richer settlements

---

[76] Wickham, *Framing the Early Middle Ages,* pp. 378–79
[77] Faith, *The English Peasantry,* p. 16, citing among others Wickham, "The Other Transition: From the Ancient World to Feudalism," pp. 31–32, and Sir Frank Stenton, *Anglo-Saxon England,* p. 477.
[78] John Moreland, "The Significance of Production in Eighth-Century England." For comments on Moreland, see Hodges, *Goodbye to the Vikings?,* p. 71.
[79] Moreland, "The Significance of Production," p. 103, citing John Blair, "Minster Churches in the Landscape," p. 38, and Blair, "Ecclesiastical Organization and Pastoral Care."

but did not reap the benefits of the networks to which they contributed.[80] Moreland's model, also evident in the structure of sites around Ipswich seen by Blinkhorn and others, makes a clearer statement when seen as a network. The closer to the center of the network, the richer the site, fed by supply and distribution lines that grow thicker as they accumulate resources from outlying areas and transfer them to the center of power. The farther from the center a settlement was, the poorer it was likely to be.

Moreland also argues against the claim that an economy of exchange developed into a trade system. He proposes that the two systems coexisted and calls Hodges's view of a transition from one system to another "an exercise in unreality."[81] Moreland's pyramid of sites, together with the network I would fashion from it, modifies Hodges's thesis without contradicting it. Production and consumption, as seen by Moreland, were driven by the needs of powerful elites, secular or ecclesiastical. Food networks were not created from the margins but from centers that had needs their own provisioning networks could not meet. This was especially the case for Anglo-Saxons who, through travel and contact with foreigners, had become aware of standards of living elsewhere. Whereas Hodges sees these figures as people attached to royal households and centers, Moreland and Blair emphasize the role of Church officials in promoting the control of production and distribution. Bede's *Ecclesiastical History* shows that, in the early eighth century, ecclesiastical figures such as Benedict Biscop frequently traveled to the Continent to obtain books, vessels, and paintings for Anglo-Saxon churches.[82] It would not have been possible to pursue those goals without trade networks and the ships required for them. If we prefer exercises of reality to those of "unreality," we should embrace the ways in which a network represents rivers, waterways, and roads, the paths along which objects and those who made and used them traveled.

The material network of Anglo-Saxon food culture is seen in objects that survive from the Anglo-Saxon world: millions of animal bones, sherds of pottery, fragments of iron and other metalwork, glass, worked stone, and more. It is a difficult network to study, for, unlike the textual database, it is constantly expanding. The "basic source of information" in archaeology, John Hines writes, is "constantly changing and growing: new finds are made at a faster rate than most archaeologists can cope with."[83] The textual network – the corpus of Anglo-Saxon words and documents – is not expanding, however, and is therefore, for all its size, easier to grasp. It is also, unfortunately, more limited than the material evidence in what it reveals about food culture, however rich it is in presenting symbolic practices such as the feast.

---

[80] Moreland, "The Significance of Production," p. 96. See Gustav Milne and Julian D. Richards, *Wharram: A Study of Settlement on the Yorkshire Wolds.*

[81] Moreland, "The Significance of Production," pp. 75–76.

[82] Benedict Biscop himself made six journeys to Rome; see Michael Lapidge, "Benedict Biscop."

[83] John Hines, *Voices in the Past*, p. 19; see also Hamerow, who refers to "an abundance of new information regarding early medieval settlements" (*Early Medieval Settlements*, p. 4).

Figure 3. Cant stave from cask head, showing cooper's mark, an incised cross with the end of each arm cut by a semicircle, York, Coppergate watching brief site; no. 9170. Top and bottom semicircles are visible left of center.

Food words and food objects form a single network that has two levels. On its textual level, the network contains many gaps. We can assume that much of the practical writing of the Anglo-Saxons – lists of things, records of administrative transactions, and so on – has disappeared, including that which took form as notches on sticks or marks on pots or barrel tops. Such evidence is seen in Figure 3, a cask head from York, which bears what is probably a maker's mark. In its material form the network is often fragmentary. Millions of food objects survive only as partial forms, few of them in contexts that yield unambiguous information about how the objects were used. These deficiencies notwithstanding, we can trace food culture on both levels, one level telling us what was thought about objects and those who worked with them (what was said about millers, for example), the other level giving us an idea of how particular objects, such as various kinds and sizes of grinding stones, figured into that labor, and at what level of production – whether the household, the craft shop, or the industrial scale of Ipswich. Connecting the nodes of both networks were workers, the people whose energy brought the objects and the words to life. The workers' energy disappeared even before they did. In a book on medieval households, David Herlihy observed that "even archaeology, the one true frontier of early medieval history, does little to illuminate the softer aspects of culture, such as human relations or domestic ties."[84] This is true enough, but Herlihy might have added that texts, literary or otherwise, are even less effective than archaeology at illuminating the Anglo-Saxon everyday. In the next chapter we will see many reasons why this is so.

[84] David Herlihy, *Medieval Households*, p. 29 (quoted, to quite different effect, by Hamerow, *Early Medieval Settlements*, p. 4, who argues that archaeology does a great deal to illuminate social life).

3

Food Words and Old English Genres

Texts are much easier to study than are things, since texts are more readily available and finite. Objects from the Anglo-Saxon world will continue to be discovered so long as humans dig into the soil, whether the objects are removed from it or, as may soon become possible, thoroughly examined without being extracted. It is very rare indeed that new words are discovered, although the meanings of some words long known will long be debated. How close texts can bring us to the material world of eating in early medieval England depends on the food vocabulary and its disposition within the surviving genres of Old English.

Food networks in the Thesaurus of Old English

I begin my exploration in the abstract, examining food words as they stand in a modern source, the *Thesaurus of Old English* (*TOE*). Both a "treasury" and a "storehouse of knowledge" (which is how the *OED* defines "thesaurus"), the *TOE* aims to include every word in the lexicon. Its entries are organized into "strings of words" that share "a component of meaning." These strings are "embedded within an inclusive conceptual scheme" of eighteen categories of meaning that were derived from English dictionaries.[1] I treat these categories as nodes, each radiating outward to conceptual subdivisions that are themselves divided into dozens of words. I propose to use the *TOE* as a lexical form of the food network.

The *TOE* creates a fresh view of Old English. Unlike its cousin, the *Dictionary of Old English* (*DOE*), the *TOE* is not alphabetically organized, although the editors have wisely provided an alphabetical index. They describe the *TOE* as an "inside-out dictionary" but acknowledge that it resembles a real dictionary because it "incorporates information about word meaning" that native speakers would not need but that readers today cannot do without – although some words in the *TOE* would also have left many native speakers scratching their heads.[2] Because words in

---

[1] Jane Roberts and Christian Kay, with Lynne Grundy, eds., *Thesaurus of Old English* (hereafter *TOE*), p. xv. See also Roberts, "Anglo-Saxon Vocabulary," pp. 192–93.

[2] *TOE*, p. v.

the *TOE* have no context but other words with similar or related meanings, the thesaurus, like a dictionary, can be said to atomize the genres of Old English. In the *TOE* it does not matter in what kind of text a word occurs. What matters is the word's meaning in the context of the "strings of words" to which the word belongs. By grouping word strings into "conceptual categories," the *TOE* reconstructs in one way what it fragments in another. It is up to readers to use the context-creating concepts of genre to assess how the word works in texts.

Two of the *TOE*'s eighteen categories include food: "Material Needs" and "Work." "Material Needs" is described as "Consumption of Food/Drink" (category 04), a slightly misleading designation since three of the six divisions do not address food or drink. Three divisions contain most of the language's references to food: "Digestion" (04.01), "Farm" (04.02), and "Hunting" (04.03). Those not related to food are "Weaving" (04.04), "Building-construction" (04.05), and "Salubrity" (04.06).[3] The *TOE* also engages food culture in "Work" (category 17), which is described as "Work, Doings, Actions, Labour." The subdivisions include "Strenuous effort" (17.01), "Work, Occupation, Employment" (17.02), "Implements, Tools" (17.03), "Materials" (17.04), and "Fuel, Fire, Lighting" (17.05). The latter three groups contain many words essential to food and farming.[4] Enormous though categories 04 and 17 are, they are not the largest. The list for "Existence" (05) extends for over one hundred pages; the list for "Law and Order" (14), at twenty-three pages, is one of the shortest.[5]

In order to see the food networks outlined in the *TOE*, we can visualize "Consumption of Food/Drink" (04) as a node with six extensions, each having extensions of its own. The longer the extension, measured by decimal places, the more specific the reference to food culture. For example, "Digestion" (04.01) has three extensions of its own: "Eating" (04.01.01), "Means of Subsistence" (04.01.02) and "Drinking" (04.01.03). "Eating" (04.01.01) has eight subdivisions, ranging from "Chewing" (04.01.01.01) to "the grounds of the mead hall," the last of the eating places listed (04.01.01.08). Not surprisingly, most references to the mead hall (*beorsele, meduseld*, and others) are found in poetry.[6] The second extension of "Digestion," "Means of Subsistence" (04.01.02), is the largest; its entries cover thirteen pages. Subdivisions include "food" (04.01.02.01), a term for which there are over thirty Old English words, which extend six decimals out, the last being places for quartering officials, of which there are three: *hus be wege, inn*, and *tocirhus* (04.01.02.04.05.01.01).[7] The third extension of "Digestion" is "Drinking" (04.01.03), which ranges from *þurst* (thirst)

---

[3] *TOE*, p. v.
[4] They concern tools (17.03) and cooking implements related to fire (17.05), such as an oven-rake and a trivet or andiron (all forms of the latter two words found only in glosses, 17.05.02, p. 710).
[5] For category 5 ("Existence") see *TOE*, pp. 248–355; for category 14 ("Law and Order"), see pp. 613–35.
[6] *TOE* entries 04.01.01 to 04.01.01.08, pp. 185–88.
[7] *TOE* entries 04.01.02 and following for *bileofa*, pp. 188–201.

(04.01.03.01), to *hlædfæt* (04.01.03.05.04.03), a bucket or pail for drawing water.[8] The main category, "Consumption of Food/Drink" (04), has two more complex extensions, "Farm" (04.02) and "Hunting" (04.03), the category to which both fowling (04.03.04) and fishing (04.03.05) belong.[9] In this lexical network, every point – every concept and every word – functions as a node, and every node can be the starting point for an inquiry that could, in theory, reach any other point in the network, passing through many nodes on the way, each created by the agency of food workers.[10]

The *TOE* leads us to food words much more efficiently than would reading the entire Old English corpus. Having located hundreds of relevant words, however, we have to assess their value as evidence of food culture and try to determine what kinds of context they create for food. Every entry in the *TOE* is already contextualized by the word string to which it belongs. To reach material contexts – to get to sites of agency – through words is another matter. The word "context" is overused, and such expressions as "social context" and "historical context" are seldom explained. The context I seek to establish is the daily experience of social exchange, the life of food workers (whether growers, producers, shippers, craft workers, or others) and of food officers, as I think of them – those who make decisions about food use for others. These people used objects and words related to food to care for themselves and to communicate with others. I want to know what words and objects related to food can tell us about agency and its consequences for creating food-related identities.

Context for archaeologists is, in the field, concrete and three-dimensional. Archaeologists document the sites in which objects are found by sketching small finds (objects, fragments of objects) in situ before removing them. Their drawings measure depth in layers defined by changes in soil color or texture; the layers constitute a chronology within the broad limits of the site (for example, early, mid, or late Saxon). Objects are also located in horizontal grids defined by the Ordnance Survey National Grid reference system.[11] Dating of objects can sometimes be established within narrow limits. Wood can be dated using dendrochronology; sherds of pottery can be connected to centers of production of which the fabric sequences have been dated.[12] Archaeologists can be sure that their finds engaged human hands at many points, from the creation of objects to their use and disposal.

We cannot say the same about contexts for words or about the capacity of words to illuminate the workings of food culture. Anyone concerned with the meaning of a food word needs to know something about the

---

[8] *TOE* entries for *(ge)drenc* (drink), 04.01.03 to 04.01.03.05.04.03, pp. 201–5.

[9] The three sections omitted include "Weaving," "Fulling," and "Building."

[10] Both animals and plants are included as subdivisions of category 2, "Life and Death." It was impractical to assess the relevance of each occurrence of plant or animal words to the food network. Not every plant or animal mentioned was used for food.

[11] *Ordnance Survey* (online resource).

[12] See James Graham-Campbell and Magdalena Valor, eds., *The Archaeology of Medieval Europe*, pp. 38–39.

word itself and about the genre of the text in which the word appears. Texts have audiences and act on them. Texts themselves can be deployed as agents through which some people seek to do something – change, inform, reform, instruct, reprove – to others. Dictionaries, fortunately, say more about words than what words mean. If the word is in the *DOE* (in progress, published through G) we know how frequently the word occurs and what its variant spellings are – that is, we know all the forms in which the word is found. Readers can find this information for words not yet published in the *DOE* by cautiously using the *Dictionary of Old English Web Corpus* (DOEWC), which includes every Old English word in its context.[13] For words with a high-frequency count, tracking use accurately is difficult. Many words are spelled alike, and the *Web Corpus* does not lemmatize them (i.e., group them under headwords); all the inflected forms of one word will not necessarily come up in the same search.[14]

The editors of the *TOE* note that the corpus is "probably skewed in its representation of Anglo-Saxon vocabulary," which is to say that the words recorded in texts do not necessarily represent words that were used in speech.[15] Certain words survived and others did not; certain speech patterns were recorded and others were not. Place-name studies have recovered some words that were lost because they were never written down or, if written, were recorded in texts that have not survived.[16] Rare words have to be cited with caution, although a word that occurs just once might be highly informative – for example, a word in a medical text that suggests how a remedy was prepared. At the same time, a word found many times in a narrative genre might not be useful if it refers to a biblical episode or to conditions removed by centuries from early medieval food culture. There are other difficulties. We know that dialects of Old English cause certain vocabulary to be found, for example, only in Anglian texts and not in West Saxon texts. We can be sure that then, as now, there was regional variation in names for things.

When we move from words to texts we also move to genre. The reader has to assess the genre in which the word is documented. In the case of poetry and glosses, as I show below, the *TOE* offers helpful advice. The goal is to link the word to the objects associated with it and also to human agents who were active in the food network. In order to do this, we need to understand the relationship of textual genres to lived life. To determine if such a relationship is possible is itself a challenge. A homily based on a Latin source might, even if discussing an everyday food process, be transmitting information about the world of the Bible, not early England. Bishop Asser's life of King Alfred, on the other hand, might well be assumed to

[13] Antonette diPaulo Healey, ed., *Dictionary of Old English Web Corpus* (online resource).
[14] Attested spellings of strong verbs are especially numerous; forms of *etan* (to eat) in the *DOE* take up a full double-spaced page.
[15] *TOE*, pp. xxi–xxxi.
[16] Carole Hough, "Place-name Evidence for an Anglo-Saxon Animal Name," pp. 1–2.

describe objects from the king's world (e.g., Alfred's famous lantern).[17] There was, however, no King Alfred of food culture, and the king's own food failed to draw the interest of his biographer. Poetry is especially problematic. Poetic subjects can either be vague about the material (a soul addresses its body) or grand (a dragon sleeps in a cave); either context is difficult to imagine in concrete ways. Poems, with the exception of some works agreed to be early (including *Genesis A*, *Exodus*, and others), are difficult to date.[18] Dating prose is sometimes easier, since it may be tied to events and circumstances. The problems of context are exacerbated by the modern tendency to favor late dates for most poems, which complements the late date – that is, a full century after Alfred's reign – for much of the most influential Old English prose (such as that by Ælfric and Wulfstan). Work by R. Vleeskruyer on pre-Alfredian prose, from the mid-twentieth century, still has much to teach us about the world of Old English texts before Alfred.[19]

The textual forms most closely linked to lived life are administrative, including laws (a name attached to many kinds of texts), charters, and wills. These texts address matters of personal property, rights, restitution, and others that pertain to animal husbandry, agriculture, and the food supply. Historians have drawn on these sources for decades to document the value of livestock, pasturing rights, food rent owed to lords, and similar concerns. Also valuable are herbals and medical texts, which were sometimes translated from Latin sources. (My emphasis is on vernacular texts, but food culture was regulated and recorded in two languages, not one.) Ecclesiastical regulations, including handbooks of penance and laws for priests, are also valuable non-narrative sources. Among poems, the riddles frequently focus on the domestic world and mention food objects and processes, including churning and baking (although often only to make sexual jokes about them).

Poems and glosses as contexts for food words

Words from two genres, poetry and glosses, struck the editors of the *TOE* as needing special treatment. They use one-letter "flags" for words of limited distribution: "p" for words found only or chiefly in poetry, "op" those found only once in poetry; "g" for those found only in glosses, "og" for those found only once in a gloss. "O" marks words found only once in the corpus in other genres, and "q" signals words that survive in uncertain or "queried" forms. These flags are not uniformly distributed in the *TOE*'s categories. There are some three thousand words related to food culture in Old English, a figure that excludes the vocabulary for plants and animals.

---

[17] David Pratt, *The Political Thought of King Alfred the Great*, pp. 185–92.
[18] Ashley Crandell Amos, *Linguistic Means of Determining the Dates of Old English Literary Texts*. See also R. D. Fulk and Christopher Cain, *A History of Old English Literature*, pp. 5–6, 12–23, and 38–40.
[19] R. Vleeskruyer, *The Life of St. Chad*, pp. 38–62.

In "Digestion" (o4), over a third of the words occur in flagged forms. Of the flagged forms over half are found in glosses or only in glosses; less than 10 percent of the forms are found in poetry or only in poetry.[20] I have not determined if this is a higher percentage than one would find for other categories (e.g., prayer, writing, thought). However, as one moves out from the center to the edges of the network, from general to particular, the number of flagged forms rises. Only 15 percent of general terms for "Work" are flagged, but in particular categories of tool or task up to 40 percent are flagged.[21]

The problems of poetry as a context for food words include a tendency to memorialize drinking rather than eating, a consequence of the focus on heroic culture; the use of ancient sources (such as books of the Hebrew Testament), which address food cultures remote from the early Middle Ages; and Christian moralizing that associates consumption with excess and sin. The exceptional poems are riddles, especially those exploiting analogies between food objects and sex acts. The dominant genres, heroic and lyric in particular, are useful in studying feasting but less useful in studying food networks.[22] Glosses too are limited sources, but they prove much more rewarding to the investigation of food culture than poems. Glosses account for a significant percentage of words in some food categories and also for the largest number of flagged terms. There are, for example, some 330 words related to farming and hence to food production and agriculture. Of these words, 129 – nearly 40 percent – are found primarily in glosses or are found only once in a glossed text. Many words – about 45 percent of 330, some 147 of them – are found only once in the corpus in any genre. Glosses functioned chiefly in the classroom, and it seems unlikely that an academic form would tell us much about food culture outside those precincts. If a word survives only in glosses, especially in only one gloss, we must wonder if the word was used anywhere else. Yet glosses have their uses for contextualizing food culture. Glosses rendered Latin into Old English but did not always do so directly. Sometimes glosses were used to clarify the morphology of the Latin word or its semantic structure, in which cases the Old English word imitates the Latin word. Mechthild Gretsch offers the example of *inscribtione*, rendered as Old English *inwriting*. "It is often difficult to estimate to what extent such neologisms were coined for permanent incorporation into the Old English lexicon," she writes.[23] Neither *inwriting* nor *inwritere* is found outside a glossed text.

Glossing was indispensable to the project of translating Latin into the vernacular. This process required a system of lexical equivalence, lists of

---

[20] The percentage of flagged words in all of category o4 is 38 percent (of 2,248 words, 862 flagged). Many more flagged words are found in glosses than in poetry.

[21] My count, derived from *TOE* category 17.

[22] Hugh Magennis finds a few poems that discuss gluttony, including "The Seafarer," "The Seasons for Fasting," and "Soul and Body"; see *Anglo-Saxon Appetites*, pp. 85–128. See also John Hines, "Literary Sources and Archaeology," p. 974.

[23] Mechthild Gretsch, "Glosses," pp. 209–10. *Inwritere* glosses *antigraphus* (scribe or copyist) in an Old English manuscript of Abbo of St. Germain, *Bella Parisiacae Urbis III*, pp. 103–12.

synonyms as well as commentaries on words and ideas (called *scholia*). Glossaries took two forms. In classroom glossaries, words were entered into the space between lines or in the margins. Old English glosses were sometimes written only over occasional words. Sometimes the glosses were continuous, accounting for every word. In a second form, glosses were collected from texts and reproduced as Latin lists with Old English synonyms (*glossae collectae*), creating a rudimentary dictionary that grouped glosses according to the Latin word glossed (the *lemma*). When they were grouped by subject or "semantic sphere," collected glosses were usually not alphabetized beyond the first two letters.[24] The *TOE* can be seen as a modern reflex of the collected gloss, its words pulled from their context and grouped into "word strings" and "conceptual categories."

Glosses swelled numbers of words in many food categories, preserving forms helpful for linguistic and lexical purposes but of dubious value in documenting food culture. For example, glossators deployed terms for a common food reference, the granary, that were not used elsewhere. *Bere-ern*, the root of modern English "barn," means "a covered building for storage of grain" and other "produce of the earth" (*OED*). This word is found sixty times in Old English, in glossaries, homilies, and other prose texts, including charters and a charm. *Bere-ern* (also spelled *bern*, and *bearn*) was the preferred Old English word outside and inside the classroom. It also translates Latin *area*, threshing floor, as do two other words, *bere-flor* and *bere-tun*, both meaning "barn area." *Bere-tun* (literally, "grain enclosure") is attested four times, twice in homilies, once in a charter, and once in a gloss. *Bere-flor* is found in two glosses. Another term for granary, *bern-hus*, is found just once, in a translation of the *Dialogi* of Gregory the Great (manuscript variants include *byrene* and *berne*).[25] The *TOE* lists two other words for barn, *bere-ærn* and *melu-hudern* (the latter found only once, meaning "meal store-house")[26] and two forms found only in glosses, each only once: *cornhus* (corn house) and *meluhus* (meal house).[27] But the *TOE* also lists *bere-brytta* (barn-keeper); *corn-hwicce* (corn bin); *hieg-hus* (hay-store); and *æppel-hus* (fruit store). The latter two are found only in glosses.

Glossators also produced numerous words for another common food object, the water pitcher. *Wæter-fæt* occurs twelve times in prose, most often in texts attributed to Ælfric, including his *Glossary*.[28] Many other words for similar objects occur, however. *Wæter-crog* and *wæter-cruce* each occur just once, also in glosses. *Wæter-flæsc* is found in a medical text. *Wæter-buc* occurs in translations of the Book of Judges and Luke 22:10.

---

[24] My summary follows Fulk and Cain, *A History of Old English Literature*, pp. 39–40.

[25] The manuscript of Gregory's *Dialogi* is Cambridge, Corpus Christi College, MS 322. See *DOE*, *bern-hus*; Hans Hecht, ed., *Bischof Waerferths von Worcester Übersetzung der Dialoge Gregors des Grossen*, book 1, ch. 9, p. 68, l. 22.

[26] As translated by Michael Swanton, *Anglo-Saxon Prose*, p. 32. The word is defined as "meal store-house" in Bosworth and Toller, *An Anglo-Saxon Dictionary, Supplement*.

[27] *Cornhus* glosses Latin *granarium* (granary) in L. Kindschi, "The Latin-Old English Glossaries in Plantin-Moretus MS. 32," line 636.

[28] I report results of a *DOEWC* search.

Wæter-flax appears in a translation of Mark (the same episode is found in Luke).[29] As with the element *–hus* above, the second element of these compounds shows wider distribution. *Crog* means "a vessel, pitcher, or crock" and occurs only in glosses. *Buc* is "a vessel of some sort, earthen pot, flask, bottle" (*DOE*), a definition that merges several kinds of container. Two examples of these *wæter-* compounds are from the Old English translation of the Book of Judges, two from glossaries, and one is from a tract called *Concerning the Discriminating Reeve* (sometimes known as *Gerefa*, "the reeve"), which, as we will soon see, was partly drawn from a collected gloss (*DOE, buc, crog*). *Flæsc* (also *flax*) occurs in prose, chiefly in the Old English translation of the *Dialogi* of Gregory the Great. Glossators had to differentiate among kinds of objects named in their Latin texts. For an object as common as the water pitcher or bottle they seem to have invented many options, few of which can be linked to other texts or to objects. Firm conclusions, however, are unwise. The excavation of Anglo-Saxon watermills in the 1960s and 1970s produced "physical evidence which might enable us to recognize the meaning of some Old English words" that were known to be related to milling but that had remained "more or less obscure" until the evidence emerged.[30]

Glosses show that some Anglo-Saxons had access to multiple terms for food objects. But Ælfric, himself a glossator, did not use them when translating Latin texts that referred to food and food objects from cultures remote from the Anglo-Saxons, a situation in which one might expect rarified terms to be applied. An example is *cytel*, which means iron kettle, cauldron, or cooking vessel. The word is found about forty times (*DOE*). In Ælfric's life of St. Margaret, the holy woman is to be put into a cauldron, *ænne cytel*, once it comes to the boil (*innen þone weallende cetel gesetton*).[31] In the glossaries, Old English *cytel* has various Latin equivalents: *olla aenea*, a bronze cooking pot (Roman); *caccabos* (cooking pot); *sartaginis* (frying pan, baking pan); *lebes, lebetes* (bronze cauldron); and still others.[32] A word with such a wide semantic range in the vernacular (compare *buc* above) has limited value as evidence of the food network, since it might refer to the famous hanging cauldron from Mound 1 at Sutton Hoo (see Chapter 2) or an ordinary frying pan. The gloss indicates the variety of vessels to which *cytel* refers and enables the reader to see the difference in size that would distinguish them as objects. Ælfric relied on context to inform his audience of the size of the vessel in question, which probably had no equivalent in their world.

Another example concerns the herb hellebore. Although food varied greatly from Roman to Anglo-Saxon times, some species of plant

---

[29] *TOE*, entries 04.01.03.05.04 (*crog*) and 04.01.03.05.04 (*wæter-crog*), p. 203.
[30] See Philip Rahtz and Donald Bullough, "The Parts of an Anglo-Saxon Mill," and Philip Rahtz and Robert Meeson, *An Anglo-Saxon Watermill at Tamworth*.
[31] Mary Clayton and Hugh Magennis, *The Old English Lives of St. Margaret*, p. 166.
[32] The *DOE* reports forty occurrences of *cytel*, including eight in glosses and seven in medical texts.

introduced by the Romans continued to flourish in Britain after the Romans left.[33] Plant names can be confusing even without problems of translation involving Latin sources and vernacular authors. In her discussion of poison plants, for example, Ann Hagen writes that St. Martin, a fourth-century saint in Tours, ingested hellebore, which she identifies as a poisonous plant that might be eaten accidently.[34] Her source is Ælfric: "Martin at this time had eaten a poisonous herb that is called *hellebore* in his food, and the poison soon so endangered him that he nearly died" (*Martinus þa on þære tide on his mete þigde þa ættrian wyrt, þe elleborum hatte, and þæt attor sona hine swiðe þreade fornean to deaðe*).[35] *Hellebore* is mentioned eighteen times in Old English, but this is its only narrative context. Six examples are found in medical texts; the others are glosses, which refer to this herb as both medicinal and poisonous.[36] There were several species of hellebore, which was known for its purgative properties. Once again there are several Old English equivalents for a single term. Black hellebore was known as *ceasteræsc* (possibly not true hellebore); *ceasterwyrt* (hellebore or a similar plant); and *hamorwyrt*. White hellebore was known as *tunsingwyrt* (*elleborum album*) or *wedeberge*, the name for a plant used to cure madness.[37] Hellebore is also called *þung*, an Old English word that also translates Latin *aconitum* (monkhood), *mandragina* (nightshade), and *toxa* (poisonous plant). One gloss conflates the last two meanings of *elebore* (*eleborus þung woedeberge*), but most glosses differentiate forms of the herb.[38] It might be that Martin did not ingest a poisonous form of the herb at all but might have taken it as a purgative. If he were in a weakened condition (i.e., if he had been fasting), the plant might have had a near-deadly effect. Ælfric seems to have relied on the popular definition of *hellebore* as poisonous, even though glossators offered a more precise vocabulary. Glosses show us that authors had access to specialized vocabulary that they did not always put into practice.

A more practical aspect of glosses is seen in texts based on glossed terms. Old English authors sometimes extracted topical glosses from texts concerned with conduct appropriate to professions, ranks, and social classes, topics of a genre I will designate as estates literature. In this chapter I will discuss examples associated with glosses; in Chapter 9 I will show how estates literature overlaps with legal codes to such an extent that estates texts are sometimes referred to as legal tracts, although they have nothing to do with law. Estates literature is a form of satire best

[33] Marijke van der Veen, Alexandra Livarda, and Alistair Hill, "New Plant Foods in Roman Britain."
[34] See Ann Hagen, *A Handbook of Anglo-Saxon Food and Drink*, p. 140. For alternate translations and uses of the word, see *OED*, "hellebore," etymology.
[35] Walter W. Skeat, ed., *Ælfric's Lives of Saints*, 2: 232–33.
[36] *DOEWC* search; *hellebore* is treated as a Latin word and is not in the *TOE*, or in Joseph Bosworth and T. Northcote Toller, *An Anglo-Saxon Dictionary*, or the *Supplement* .
[37] Both words for white hellebore are found in Bosworth and Toller, *An Anglo-Saxon Dictionary*.
[38] For the Corpus Glossary, section 5, l. 120, see Jan Hendrik Hessels, *An Eighth-Century Latin-Anglo-Saxon Glossary*, pp. 9–122.

known through William Langland's *Piers Plowman* and Geoffrey Chaucer's *Canterbury Tales*.[39] The archetype is the *Hermeneumata pseudo-Dositheana*, a Latin-Greek teaching instrument that incorporated colloquies (written dialogues) and word lists for teaching purposes. Scott Gwara has examined topics according to which the *Hermeneumata pseudo-Dositheana* and its descendants were organized. They include religion, entertainments, food and refreshments, animals, metal objects, and others, topics about which one could know and enumerate things – categories that could be populated to create knowledge.[40] This is an ancient and, it seems, now nearly lost category of educational discourse. At one level, it seems to be information for its own sake, data with which nothing is done. Forms of this teaching instrument survived for centuries and can be seen in the much-derided tradition (however unfairly it is now regarded) that required school children to memorize the names and lengths of rivers, the capitals of states and provinces, and other facts. Who now can reproduce such object-based knowledge without recourse to an electronic device? Yet facts have their uses, as anybody who knows a few will attest, and texts based on glosses show how important thing-based knowledge was in the medieval educational world.[41] To see how glosses came to be connected to estates literature, which seems remote from glossing, it is necessary to know something about the uses of writing outside the monastic classroom, where we seldom think it operated.

Forms of writing in which food culture, including objects and processes, was the subject have all but disappeared. It is often assumed that practical matters of food preparation and distribution were not the focus of writing in cultures that reserved writing for ecclesiastical and legal purposes. However, this view is losing its hold. In ancient cultures, information about the contents and weight of shipping containers was sometimes written on the containers themselves. An example from the Anglo-Saxon period can be seen in Figure 3, a photograph of a wooden cask head from York, which bears a cross-shaped design that may be a maker's mark. Fragments of amphorae used to ship olive oil and wine from Spain to Rome and elsewhere in the Mediterranean survive in huge numbers. An estimated 25 million amphorae are thought have been piled up to form Monte Testaccio in Rome. Some amphorae bear the names of the amphora manufacturer, the producer of the oil that the jar contained, and weights of the amphora both empty and full.[42] Writing for informational purposes of this kind might be seen as less prestigious than discursive prose or poetry,

[39] See Jill Mann, *Chaucer and Medieval Estates Satire*, pp. 1–16.
[40] Scott Gwara, *Latin Colloquies from Pre-Conquest Britain*, p. 12; see also Gwara and David W. Porter, eds., *Anglo-Saxon Conversations*, pp. 16–17.
[41] On the development of intelligence based on hypotheticals and visual images versus concrete data (people in this century, compared to those of previous centuries), see James R. Flynn, *Are We Getting Smarter?*
[42] On commercial amphorae, see Graham-Campbell and Valor, *The Archaeology of Medieval Europe*, pp. 290–92. See also Jarrett A. Lobell, "Trash Talk," and Simon Keay, "The Amphora Project" (online resource).

but it is more important than either as evidence of the link between record-keeping and literacy.

Evidence of writing outside of learned contexts has begun to emerge in Anglo-Saxon archaeology. The presence of styli at settlements that either were not monastic, or were not continuously ecclesiastical, suggests that writing implements and writing were in use for administrative and commercial purposes. Susan Kelly has emphasized the importance of writing as a means of storing information rather than developing ideas, the latter being the usual frame of reference for writing in Anglo-Saxon culture. Kings and wealthy landowners, like occupants of great monasteries, used texts to keep track of their affairs, not only to manage their image for succeeding generations. Monastic houses had scriptoria, trained scribes, and all the necessary materials needed to create and preserve documents. Since some houses occasionally forged documents to support their claims to wealth, they had multiple motives for keeping written records. Secular records were more difficult to retain, especially at lower levels and in media other than parchment (e.g., wax or wood). Monasteries might preserve charters recording transfers of ownership of land, but other secular documents, in Kelly's words, had "no chance of direct survival."[43]

Evidence of writing may be thin, but the list of sites with impressive regional trading contacts is growing, and with it the assessment of administrative sophistication needed to manage these sites. Tim Pestell has stressed the role of writing in non-ecclesiastical estates and compiled an extensive analysis of styli at Flixborough (Lincolnshire), emphasizing the link between ecclesiastical authorities and scribes working on secular estates.[44] At Ipswich, Pestell notes, one grave containing a stylus might be that of a book-keeper.[45] John Moreland has surveyed evidence from several secular centers. He takes the view that there was "a set of integrated regional economies" that included emporia (i.e., market places) but extended far outside those settlements and that depended on writing for "recording the product of the land and the renders due" to ecclesiastical centers (presumably to other centers as well). He believes it is no accident that evidence for the "secularisation of literacy" is associated with so-called productive sites.[46] We can assume that the Anglo-Saxons and their trading partners kept track of vital information regarding trade, taxes, and finances, among others. Perhaps using wood and wax as media, which are more likely to disappear than stone or pottery, their book-keepers wrote food culture, even though they did not write about it in ways familiar to us from other authors.

---

[43] Susan Kelly, "Anglo-Saxon Lay Society and the Written Word," p. 51.
[44] Tim Pestell, *Landscapes of Monastic Foundation*, pp. 38–48. For styli at Flixborough, see Pestell, "Writing and Literacy-Related Items," pp. 123–38.
[45] Pestell, "Writing and Literacy-Related Items," p. 130.
[46] John Moreland, "The Significance of Production in Eighth-Century England," pp. 95–96. Note that "productive site" is sometimes used to refer only to sites known for or through ironwork.

Kelly's observation about "direct survival" is important, since a few estate texts have survived in a form adapting them to different purposes. The most important example is a text composed for the estates of St. Peter's, a property-owning minster church in Bath. This tenth-century record survives in late (i.e., eleventh-century) adapted form as *Rectitudines Singularum Personarum* (Rights [or Duties] of Individuals), a work which, as its title suggests, embraces a range of occupations up and down the social scale. This text is seldom cited when archaeologists or historians refer to the textual evidence of food culture. Instead they turn to two works, *The Colloquy* and *Concerning the Discriminating Reeve*, of much more limited value to this enterprise but highly useful to understand how glosses were combined with other discursive forms in the Old English period. I will discuss these two works and their indebtedness to glosses before taking a brief look at *Rectitudines*, which does not seem to be indebted to the classroom tradition.

Glosses in context: The Colloquy *and* Concerning the Discriminating Reeve

Both *The Colloquy* and *Concerning the Discriminating Reeve* (*Be gesceadwisan gerefan*) are eleventh-century texts incorporating food word glossaries. *The Colloquy* is a dialogue between a monastic master and pupils who impersonate workers at levels ranging from a plowboy to the king's own hunter. *Concerning the Discriminating Reeve* outlines the duties of the reeve and lists equipment the reeve is to look for on the estates he supervises. This text lacks the overt didacticism of *The Colloquy* and avoids the dialogue's patronizing tone, but, like that text, merges the enumerative function of the *Hermeneumata pseudo-Dositheana* with exhortations to good conduct.

Often associated with Ælfric, *The Colloquy* was written in Latin and was given a continuous Old English gloss by someone else (but probably not his student, Ælfric Bata).[47] The aim of the text was to teach Latin to schoolboys, both as vocabulary and as grammar, through use of the Old English words and constructions. The sequence of topics is artificial and seems to have been designed to move pupils through a vocabulary organized by topic.[48] G. N. Garmonsway calls *The Colloquy* "a natural sequel" to Ælfric's *Grammar* and *Glossary*.[49] *The Colloquy* moves from occupation to occupation, shifting between terse interrogation and sententiousness. It covers topics ranging from the daily routine of boys in a monastic school to skilled and unskilled work, and its relative importance in maintaining society. The first list occurs when the master asks the monk what his "friends" do. The monk replies, "Some are plowmen, some shepherds,

---

[47] Errors in the Old English gloss have often been pointed out and the general conclusion seems to be that Ælfric himself is not responsible for them. See G. N. Garmonsway, ed., *Ælfric's Colloquy*, p. 11.

[48] Garmonsway, *Ælfric's Colloquy*, p. 1.

[49] Garmonsway, *Ælfric's Colloquy*, p. 7.

some ox herds, also some are hunters, some fishermen, some fowlers, some merchants, some leather workers, some salters, and some bakers." The Old English reads: *Sume synt yrþlincgas, sume scephyrdas, sume oxanhyrdas, sume eac swylce huntan, sume fisceras, sume fugeleras, sume cypmenn, sume scewyrhtan, sealteras, bæceras.* Those phrases gloss the following: *Alii sunt aratores, alii opiliones, quidam bubulci, quidam etiam uenatores, alii piscatores, alii aucupes, quidam mercatores, quidam sutores, quidam salinatores, quidam pistores, coci.* The Master then turns to these workers, beginning with the plowman, speaking to them in constructions notable for their lack of complexity: *Quid dicis tu, arator? Quomodo exerces opus tuum?* This is glossed, in Old English: *Hwæt sægest þu, yrþlingc? Hu begæst þu weorc þin?* ("What say you, plowman? How do you perform your work?") The student taking the plowman's part replies, *O, mi domine, nimium laboro,* which is glossed as *Eala, leof hlaford, þearle ic deorfe* ("O, my lord, I work very hard").[50] One can see the relationship of these constructions to entries in Ælfric's *Glossary*: *noster piscator est* (*ure fiscere he is* ["he is our fisher"]); *nostri piscatoris rete* (*ures fisceres nett* ["our fisher's net"]); *nostro piscatori do nauem* (*urum fiscere ic gyfe scip* ["to our fisher I give a boat"]).[51]

Two further lists appear when the fisher is asked what he catches in freshwater. He answers: *Ælas & hacodas, mynas & æleputan, sceotan & lampredan, & swa wylce swa on wætere swymmaþ, sprote* ("eels and pike, minnows and eel-pout [burbot?], trout and lampreys, and others that swim in [fresh] water"). This glosses the Latin: *Anguillas et lucios, menas et capitones, <tructas> et murenas, et qualescumque in amne natant, saliu.* He is also asked what he catches in the sea, and replies, *Hærincgas & leaxas, mereswyn & stirian, ostran & crabban, muslan, winewinclan, sæcoccas, fagc & floc, & lopystran & fela swylces* ("Herrings and salmon, dolphins and sturgeons, oysters and crabs, mussels, periwinkles, shellfish, plaice and flounder, and lobsters and many things like that"). The list in Latin is: *Alleces et isicios, delfinos et sturias, ostreas et cancros, musculas, torniculi, neptigalli, platesia et platissa et polipodes et similia.*

Some words in these lists occur rarely if at all outside of glossaries. *Hacod* is found only here and in glossaries; *æleputa* (eel-pout) elsewhere just twice, both glossaries; and *lamprede* (lamprey) only here and in glossaries. From the second list, *sæcoccas* (shellfish) and *lopystran* (lobsters) occur only here; *fagc* (plaice) is found only twice. Although *floc* (fluke or flounder) is found twelve times and *leax* (lox) nearly twenty times, half of those examples occur in glosses. *Mereswyn* (dolphins) is found seven times, five times in glosses, once in the Old English translation of Bede's *Ecclesiastical History* and once in a charter.[52] *Crabba* (crab) is found seven times, but only once outside of glosses and Ælfric's *Grammar*. The kinds of fish named in *The Colloquy* seldom seem to have been referred to

---

[50] Garmonsway, *Ælfric's Colloquy*, p. 20, ll. 18–22.
[51] Julius Zupitza, *Ælfrics Grammatik und Glossar*, p. 105, l. 11.
[52] Garmonsway, *Ælfric's Colloquy*, pp. 27–29, ll. 101–8.

outside of glossaries. One can imagine a list of fish to be sold in a market at given prices, or valued at a certain rate for exchange, even though such a list has long since vanished. But it would be difficult to imagine using such lists as these to document claims about fish caught in Anglo-Saxon times, given that the sources of these lists are Latin texts quite probably written in other climates and in earlier times. If there were texts that listed fish the Anglo-Saxons caught and ate, those records have disappeared. The children being educated by *The Colloquy* are learning about Latin grammar and vocabulary, not about marine or freshwater methods of fishing.

A fourth list is recited when the master asks the monk to list his "good and very necessary" companions. The monk replies: "I have blacksmiths, ironsmiths, a goldsmith, a silversmith, a coppersmith, a carpenter, and workers of many other crafts" (*Ic hæbbe smiþas, isene smiþas, goldsmiþ, seolo-forsmiþ, arsmiþ, treowwyrhtan & manegra oþre mistlicra cræfta biggenceras*). In the Latin this is: *Habeo fabros, ferrarios, aurificem, argentarium, ęrarium, lignarium et multos alios uariarum artium operatores.*[53] This list is also dominated by terms found only in glosses. Five words use the root element *–smiþ*, which is more common. The words themselves are surprisingly infrequent. *Goldsmiþ* occurs just five times, *isensmiþ* and *seoloforsmiþ* only here. *Treowwyrhta* appears only here and in two glosses, including Ælfric's (*DOEWC*).

Even more obviously than *The Colloquy, Concerning the Discriminating Reeve* (*Gerefa*) is a composite, comprised of two lists of farm implements that follow a discussion of how estates are to be managed. Although it is sometimes misleadingly called a legal tract, *Gerefa* does not concern itself with the law in any way, as we will see by comparing it to *Geþyncðu* (see below). Like *The Colloquy, Gerefa* incorporates word lists into a document with an ideological imperative. The reeve's reputation for corruption is memorably seen in the reeves created by Chaucer and Langland. The problem existed in Anglo-Saxon England as well. Wulfstan denounced corrupt reeves in *The Institutes of Polity*, in which he wrote that reeves ought to be shepherds but were in fact robbers.[54] Any work on the stewardship expected of the reeve would, after Wulfstan's time, have had the moralizing cast associated with estates literature.[55] We know that reeves played a key role in managing the local food network. They operated at many social levels, from royal reeves to sheriffs, and could be known as *heah-gerefa*, *scir-gerefa*, or *wic-gerefa* (high-ranking, parish- or shire-, or market-reeve).[56] The reeve's office, like that of the steward (*gewicnera*), was subject to corruption, no doubt one reason why the priest was not allowed

[53] Garmonsway, *Ælfric's Colloquy*, p. 38, ll. 205–7.
[54] See Mann, *Chaucer and Medieval Estates Satire*, pp. 163–64. On Wulfstan and reeves, see Patrick Wormald, *The Making of English Law* (hereafter *MEL*), pp. 388–89.
[55] On this aspect of Wulfstan's work, see Wormald, *MEL*, pp. 388–89.
[56] Pauline Stafford, "Reeve."

to hold either.[57] These officials worked together. One of Æthelred's laws instructs the reeve to support the temporal needs of abbots and to ensure that the rights of the abbot's stewards (his *wicneran*) are protected.[58]

Concerning the Discriminating Reeve has been taken at face value as evidence of Anglo-Saxon food culture. At best, however, the text portrays an imaginary food world created in part from glosses. The text is concerned with only one profession but implies a world of orderly obedience which is determined, in the first instance, by the weather. There are three sections. The first concerns "efficient management and the direction of the workers on the lord's farm," in Mark Gardiner's words, and the second emphasizes that work is to be undertaken at the proper time.[59] The third contains two often-cited lists of farm implements.

The first section addresses the reeve's duties broadly. He has to be sure that work on the estate is performed when needed, that he always look to his lord's advantage, and that he keeps workers subordinate to him and hence to his lord. Conditions on estates are not everywhere the same. Plowing, mowing, and pasturing happen earlier on some than others. The reeve must do as the weather directs him (*ðe hine weder wisað*).[60] One section sets out duties in a pattern of pairs: lesser and greater, more and less important, as in "the manor and on the down, in the woods and in the water, in field and fold" (*ge on tune ge on dune, ge on wuda ge on wætere, ge on felda ge on falde*). This conspicuous device suggests the hand of a writer influenced by Wulfstan, whose prose frequently exploits alliterative patterns and internal rhyme.[61] However effective the style, it does not help to define a practical focus or communicate essential information.

The second section is also concerned with weather and timeliness, addressing labor appropriate to seasons of the year. The reeve's chief duty is to see to cultivation of the soil at the proper time (*ðæt he asece, hu he yrde mæge fyrme geforþian ðone ðæs time sy*). He is told that, if he does his job well, he will never run out of work. The influence of the glossing tradition emerges in this section, which contains a list-like summary of seasonal labors the reeve is to supervise from May to November. May and June are for shearing sheep, building, weeding, making sheepfolds, and building

---

[57] Frantzen, *ASP, OEP*, Y43.08.01: "It is not permitted to any masspriest or deacon that they be a reeve or steward, nor be occupied with any of the world's business except that to which they are nominated" (*Nis nanum mæssepreoste alyfed ne diacone þæt hy gerefan beon ne wicneras. ne ymbe nane worldbisgunge abisgod. butan mid þære þe hy to getitolode beoð*).

[58] For VIII Æthelred 32, see Robertson, *LKE*, pp. 126–27: "And the king enjoins upon all his reeves in every locality: you shall support the abbots in all their temporal needs as you best can, and if you desire to have God's favour and mine, help their stewards everywhere to obtain their rights so that they themselves may constantly remain secure in their monasteries and live according to their rule" (*And se cyngc beodeð eallum his gerefan on æghwilcere stowe, þæt ge þam abbodan æt eallum worldneodum beorgan, swa ge betst magon, & be þam þe gewillan Godes oððe minne freondscipe habban, filstan heora wicneran æghwar to rihte, þæt heo sylfe magan þe oftor on mynstrum fæste gewunian & regollice libban*) (Roberston's translation).

[59] Mark Gardiner, "Implements and Utensils in *Gerefa*," p. 261.

[60] For *Gerefa*, see F. Liebermann, *GDA*, p. 453, para. 2.

[61] See Liebermann, *GDA*, p. 453, para. 3.

fishing weirs and a mill. Months from August through October are for mowing, cutting wood, gathering crops, thatching, and preparing winter quarters for pastured animals. The author does not name months after October but specifies work during "hard frosts," which includes planting winter crops, digging ditches, and more. He concludes with the work of spring (again without naming months), especially plowing and planting. Although the text outlines the labors of the entire year, it does so in an inconsistent fashion that suggests more than one source was used and that the author made no effort to adopt one approach (i.e., naming all the months) to the information. The contrast to legal style, with its formulaic clauses and uniform point of view, is important; *Gerefa* lacks the hallmarks of legal writing.

The third section begins with another reference to the timeliness of the reeve's work but follows no chronology. It comprises two lists of tools the reeve's workers must have on hand. Some readers have assumed that the lists are guides to equipment needed to farm and to manage estates and have used the lists to authenticate certain archaeological finds as essential pieces of farm equipment. While the text has value for study of the food network, it is not journalism or administrative prose, and the integrity of these lists as indices to implements used on Anglo-Saxon farms has been challenged. Patrick Wormald, for example, skeptically refers to "the ideal reeve's fabulously stocked tool shed."[62] *Gerefa* lists agricultural implements of many kinds. There are two lists, one a list of "implements for the buildings," including:

> axe, adze, bill, awl, plane, saw, spoke-shave [tool used for shaping spokes], tie hook, auger, mattock, crow-bar, share, coulter, and also goad-iron, scythe, sickle, hoe, spade, shovel, woad-trowel, barrow, broom, mallet, rake, fork, ladder, curry-comb and shears, fire-tongs, steelyard . . . .

> æcse, adsan, bil, byrse, scafan, sage, cimbiren, tigehoc, næfebor, mattuc, ippin-giren, scear, culter & eac gadiren, siðe, sicol, weodhoc, spade, scofle, wadspi-tel, bærwan, besman, bytel, race, geafle, hlædre, horscamb & sceara, fyrtange, wæipundern . . . .

A list of cloth-working tools follows, and the reeve is then told that he must assist other specialized workers (*smeawyrhtan*) with their tools as well, including the miller, the shoemaker, and the lead-founder. A second list follows, mentioning "all the tools one must have":

> One is to have a wagon-cover, plowing tackle, harrowing tackle, and many things that I am not now able to name, and also a measure, a fork (or hook), and, for the threshing floor, a flail, and many implements: a pot (bowl), a leaden cauldron, a kettle, a ladle, pans, a crock, a gridiron [a trivet supporting a kettle over fire], dishes, a handled vessel, a large jar for liquids, a tub, a churn, a cheese-vat, a pouch or basket, . . .

---

[62] Wormald, "Archbishop Wulfstan and the Holiness of Society," in Wormald, *Legal Culture in the Early Medieval West*, p. 249.

Man sceal habban wængewædu, sulhgesidu, egeðgetigu & fela ðinga, ðe ic nu genæmnian ne can, ge eac mete, awel & to odene fligel & andlamena fela: hwer, lead, cytel, hlædel, pannan, crocca, brandiren, dixas, stelmelas, cyfa, cyflas, cyrne, cysfæt, ceodan, . . .[63]

Parts of the first list were written to alliterate. For example, *siðe, sicol, weodhoc, spade, scofle, wadspitel, bærwan, besman, bytel* (scythe, sickle, hoe, spade, shovel, woad-trowel, barrow, broom, mallet). The first two sets of three words seem parallel (*siðe, sicol, weodhoc, spade, scofle, wadspitel*), Gardiner notes, and they are followed by an alliterative group.[64] John Hines argues that the two lists "were not composed by the same person on the same occasion" but came from "different sources." All fifty nouns in List A are in the accusative plural, while those in the second List B vary between singular and plural. The author might have been the first to bring together two "glossary-type alphabetical lists" but little time was spent revising the lists to make them grammatically consistent.[65]

Many words in *Concerning the Discriminating Reeve*, like many in *The Colloquy*, occur elsewhere chiefly or only in glosses. *Cimbiren, tigehoc, næfebor, wadspitel*, and *bærwan* are named nowhere else but in List A, and *byrse, culter, weodhoc*, and *horscamb* occur only in List A and in glosses. *Mattuc* (pickaxe) is found in glosses, once in a homily by Ælfric, and once in the Old English translation of the *World History* of Orosius (*DOEWC*). *Sicol* (sickle) is found in glosses and a translation of Mark 4:29 (Bosworth-Toller; *DOEWC*). *Geafle* (pitchfork) occurs elsewhere three times, once used by Ælfric and twice in glosses (*DOE gafol*). Although hardly conclusive, this evidence associates *Gerefa* more closely with the classroom than the working world of the farm. Gardiner suggests that the list was formed along the model of a glossary but "without any didactic intent."[66] Depending on how one understands "didactic intent," this view, as I will show later, is open to question.

The Colloquy and *Gerefa* are far more limited sources for the study of food culture than some writers assume. Even so, there is a great gap between them and poems, homilies, and other, more familiar texts. I suggest that there is an inverse relationship between lists of things found in glosses and the representation of social relations found in these other textual forms. Narrative texts of even the most conventional kind (i.e., hagiography) illuminate social relations, if only through the crude exercise of power such as that subjugating saints to their torturers. Objects named in narratives are contextualized by plot and the circumstances of the agents using the

---

[63] *Gerefa*, ed. Liebermann, *GDA*, pp. 453–55. For commentary, see Wormald, *MEL*, pp. 387–89. Both texts are also translated by Swanton, *Anglo-Saxon Prose*, pp. 26–33. The manuscript is Cambridge, Corpus Christi College, MS 383.

[64] Gardiner, "Implements and Utensils in *Gerefa*," p. 262. See also Christine Fell, "Some Domestic Problems," cited by Gardiner, p. 262, nn. 59, 61.

[65] John Hines, "Gerefa §§15 and 17."

[66] Gardiner, "Implements and Utensils in *Gerefa*," p. 264.

objects – a torturer, a victim, a saint. The text is focused on the development of the plot in which the kettle or the herb is merely an instrument.

In comparison, glossaries are mere lists or lists with brief commentaries on words. *The Colloquy* and *Gerefa* are obviously more informative of
food culture than the glossaries on which they are, in part, based. They
create opportunities for commenting on ordinary elements of food culture,
whatever the point of view. When an author sets such a list into a didactic
context – for example, the master's need to teach boys Latin, or someone's
need to outline the duties of a reeve – the objects themselves become the
subject and the texts become what we might think of as fictions without
plot. The first two parts of *Concerning the Discriminating Reeve* idealize the
relationship between the reeve and his lord, and the reeve and his hired
workers as one of unquestioning obedience. He governs within *folcrihte*
(customary law), and if those whom he should govern instead govern
him, he should lose his job (*gyf hine magan wyldan ða ðe he scolde wealdan*).
Similar in significance – and tone – is *The Colloquy*'s injunction that "he
who neglects his craft . . . is by his craft forsaken" (*forþam se þe cræft his
forlæt, he byþ forlæten fram þam cræfte*).[67] These two texts round out the
illusion of verbal completeness with social completeness: they surround
orderly words with an orderly world. In them, each object is associated
with a task that describe the labor in which the object plays a part and, in
some cases, the social good that results. No doubt part of the value of *The
Colloquy* and *Gerefa* is that, as modern readers, we resemble the author's
target audience, which was assumed to need instruction and exhortation
that occasioned fundamental observations about things and their uses.
This information does not, however, qualify as expertise in the intricacies
of the Anglo-Saxon food network.

The Colloquy and *Gerefa* seem almost equally to be works for school children, although the latter lacks the pedagogical apparatus formalized in
the dialogue. Both works transcend the limitations of the glossary list, the
purpose of which is to abstract selected elements from the material world.
But they do so only to set the objects they list into a pedagogical context.
There is no need for pedagogy about these matters outside the classroom.
Hence the texts lapse into fiction. No one who supervised an agricultural
estate needed a list of tools. No one who fished needed to be told about the
dangers of whaling. No plowman's boy needed to explain his suffering,
for it is safe to say that anyone familiar with his work knew the hardships
that came with it and that anyone unfamiliar with his work would not
care. Workers at certain levels needed to keep records, but they did not do
so in textual forms that survived. The texts that do survive manage only to
create artificial, fictional contexts for the objects and tasks they enumerate,
subjecting the food culture network to a kind of textual and intellectual
control that would not have credibility outside the classroom.

---

[67] For *Gerefa* 7, see Liebermann, *GDA*, p. 454; Garmonsway, *Ælfric's Colloquy*, p. 41, ll. 240–41.

In Chapter 9 we will look closely at *Rectitudines Singularum Personarum* (Rights [or Duties] of Individuals), mentioned above in association with Bath, an important example of estates literature. For the sake of contrast with the classroom agenda of *The Colloquy* and *Concerning the Discriminating Reeve*, however, it is useful to look at *Rectitudines* here. The text is organized by categories of rank that can be confirmed in other sources, and descriptions of food-related tasks are complex rather than, as they are in the other two texts, simplistic, even naive. *Rectitudines* also lacks the universalized, moralized point of view found in *Gerefa* and some sections of *The Colloquy*. One cannot imagine that craft workers ever heard the dialogues of *The Colloquy*. *Rectitudines* strikes a different note, even when taking a pedagogical tone. "As I said before, estate laws [*landlaga*] are various," the author writes. "Nor do we apply these regulations, which we have previously spoken, about in all districts. But we tell what the custom is where it is known to us. If we learn better, we will readily delight in and maintain it, according to the custom of the people among whom we then live."[68] Laws vary; those outlined in this text do not apply everywhere. That concession to history and tradition is lacking in the other two texts, where one example stands for all.

Food and food objects in monastic contexts

We can see just how artificial *The Colloquy* and *Gerefa* are when we compare them to the *Monasteriales Indicia*, which illustrates the gestures to be used by monks when speech was forbidden. This is a text for adults, not children, although it shares a monastic provenance with *The Colloquy*. Debby Banham, who edited and translated this text, believes that the Old English list of foods that it contains was based in part on Latin directions brought from the Continent during the reform of monasticism in the tenth century, but also allows for the possibility that there were also English directions for the use of signs. Surviving examples from the Continent are all later than the manuscript containing the Old English *Monasteriales Indicia* (London, British Library, MS Cotton Tiberius A.iii).[69]

Eating is an important subject in the text, and the refectory is a prominent space. Here we meet food culture in a new way, at the daily table rather than at the feast. Nearly one-third of the signs pertain to food and food objects, ranging from fish to nuts and bowls to skewers. Some signs illuminate details about food – for example, an oval shape meant a loaf of bread. Some signs suggest the properties of food; the sign for the leek, for example, was to hold one's nose "as if you were smelling something." Other signs suggest the use of equipment. Pepper seems to have been shaken out of a horn, while salt was sprinkled on food by the fingers.[70]

---

[68] Swanton, *Anglo-Saxon Prose*, pp. 28–30.
[69] Debby Banham, ed. and trans., *Monasteriales Indicia*, pp. 8–10.
[70] Banham, *Monasteriales Indicia*, bread (no. 54), p. 31; leeks (no. 59), p. 33; pepper (no. 61) and salt (no. 68), p. 33.

Many but not all of these signs are shared with comparable lists. No other list has a sign for oysters or raw vegetables. Other lists differentiate various kinds of fish, but the Old English list does not.[71] Rather surprisingly, the *Indicia* lists only oysters and eels rather than various kinds of fish, as do other such lists, perhaps because oysters and eels do not look like fish and needed separate signs.[72] But this might also be a sign that the monks ate less fish than some suppose (a matter discussed in Chapter 10).

The text is an important and little-noticed companion to the frequently cited *Colloquy*. Both the dialogue and the *Monasteriales Indicia* had a pedagogical function. They supply details about diet, the prestige of certain foods and drinks, and the expectations about food and drink in religious houses, which were denser nodes in the food culture network (that is, better supplied) than most Anglo-Saxon kitchens. Both texts also furnish some discourse about food culture that centers on food and expectations associated with it, writing of a sort rare in the period. But the *Monasteriales Indicia* is not indebted to the glossing tradition, and it lacks an ideological perspective. Its representation of the food world is not pressured by a need to teach beliefs; its focus is a form of communication useful to those in a community of belief. *The Colloquy* memorializes and defines status, while the *Monasteriales Indicia* educates and informs. Ideology brings order to texts because it compels its audience to choose one point of view among others. The *Monasteriales Indicia* does not compel choice, an imperative easily avoided when belief is not at stake.

The pressure of ideology turns both *The Colloquy* and *Gerefa* into fictions based on a pyramid of power. Both works articulate food culture through hierarchies of power and distribution. They seek to transform the horizontal, interdependent networks of food production and consumption into a vertical structure, at the peak of which sit the speaker and his comrades. The texts focus on duties, not on rights, because their objective is to inculcate a sense of duty rather than to describe the exchange of labor and goods that create food networks. Peaks communicate power more effectively than centers, it seems. If we can describe Anglo-Saxon political culture (understood broadly) as an authoritarian world in which ecclesiastical prerogatives take precedence, then few texts mold food culture to political culture as clearly as does *The Colloquy*. *Concerning the Discriminating Reeve* is not a text about religion, but it too articulates political culture. The reeve must know "the lord's rights respecting the estate and the rights of the people" as they were decided by "councillors of olden days." There are no assertions of the people's rights, however, only their duties. The reeve is to ensure that the estate is managed to "the

---

[71] There are 127 signs; 38 of them, or about 30 percent, pertain to the refectory. See Banham, *Monasteriales Indicia*, pp. 31–37. On the oyster, see p. 63, n. 72; on raw vegetables, p. 71, n. 58; on fish, p. 63, n. 70.

[72] Banham, *Food and Drink in Anglo-Saxon England*, p. 65, and Banham, *Monasteriales Indicia*, p. 63, nn. 70–72.

lord's advantage," and the imperatives that follow presumably pursue that single objective.[73]

Conclusion

As glosses and forms of estates literature indebted to glosses show, words are easy to manipulate, things less so. Glosses gave common objects names that existed nowhere else and, perhaps, also gave names to objects that did not exist. Texts with allegiance to intellectual and rhetorical constructs can easily be used to create food culture as a pyramid. Texts with allegiance to the material workings of food culture create networks. It is difficult to move from ideological pyramids to food culture because, in reality, food moved through and along networks powered by humans and animals, not up and down social scales. Texts that allow us glimpses of human agents, including *Rectitudines Singularum Personarum* and *Monasteriales Indicia*, show us food, food objects, and food processes in action in ways that help us imagine daily life in the period. The key to a network is interdependence. Small nodes sustain larger ones; if a small node disappears, lines that passed through it must be rerouted. If the lines of support that feed it disappear, the node will vanish. Texts that illustrate both the firmness and the fragility of points of connection best represent the workings of the food culture network. Those that fictionalize the network as a pyramid, as do *The Colloquy* and poems about feasting, sustain the illusion, necessary to the maintenance of power and to representations of the heroic world, that such occasions as feasts did not have costs or require labor and that cooking as an ordinary daily activity did not require skill.

Ordinary things dominate the following four chapters, each concerned with a different food object (the quern) or medium in which food objects were created (pottery, iron, wood). In each I turn first to objects, searching sites and settlements for examples of querns, cooking pots, hooks, bowls, and cups. Then I examine the lexicon for words associated with these objects, including words that refer to the people who used them. Some of these people were food workers, as were many of those named in *The Colloquy*: plowmen, shepherds, oxherds, hunters, fishermen, fowlers, merchants, leatherworkers, salters, bakers, and others. Some of these people were not only food workers but what I call food officers, men and women whose judgments determined who could eat what and when. Some food officers were officially designated. Reeves and *discþegns* (stewards), for example, were charged with direct responsibility for food supplies. But there must have been dozens of others, cooks especially, who decided if meat and other supplies were edible, how foodstuffs would be apportioned, and what would be eaten during frequent periods of fasting. In Chapters 8 and 9 I cull handbooks of penance and laws for references to

---

[73] *Gerefa*, ed. Liebermann, *GDA*, p. 453, para. 1–2.1.

food officers, those whose identities were as closely connected to food as were the identities of those who grew or raised it.

I will seek to associate the objects with processes that help to determine the social contexts for these things and will also look at textual evidence to see what it might add to the material contexts. In most cases it will be difficult to see how the matter of the object, its material form and its purposes, might affect the way we read the text. Thus I explore food words in as many textual forms and contexts as possible, seeking to broaden the basis for future studies of food culture by pointing to these references, many of them unnoticed. We can link objects to social processes that create the broadest categories of meaning only by concentrating on the human agents whose labor and skill put the objects – the tools – to work. Food culture created occupational and occasional identities for food workers and food officers. By understanding their roles, we can begin to understand ways in which food culture, in both its textual and material aspects, was used to shape identity. First, however, we need to see the tools they grasped when they worked with food.

Part II

Food Objects

4

The Quernstone

Most objects essential to food networks – pots for cooking and storage, and iron tools – had to be readily obtainable and easily replaced. Hence they would have been produced in many small settlements and would not appear in long-range trading networks. Among such objects, the quernstone, a hand-mill for grinding grain, is an exception. Although found in nearly every settlement, this implement was not usually produced locally. Most quernstones excavated at Anglo-Saxon sites came from the Rhine Valley, although some were quarried in England. Imported quernstones had penetrated the hinterlands already in the ninth century. Quernstones were large objects, approximately fifteen to sixteen inches wide, and between three and four inches thick.[1] Querns usually survive as fragments, but the site in York known as Fishergate 46–54 yielded the rare find of both parts of one sandstone quern. Both parts are illustrated in Figure 4. The two stones measure 400–420 mm across, with holes in the top stone for two handles and a perforation with a flange or rim on the upper side, the funnel through which grain was poured.[2] The lower stone had a finer grain and a convex surface, matching the concave surface of the top stone.

Querns and burials

Querns sometimes resurface in mysterious contexts. The most written-about Anglo-Saxon quernstone is a fragment found in a sixth-century grave at Sewerby, East Yorkshire. The grave was shared by two women who were interred separately. One of them, the younger, was given a "richly furnished burial," facing up in a wooden coffin, something rarely found, with a bronze cauldron near her head and many grave goods (grave 41). Not long after her death, an older woman was buried over her, face down, her contorted body oriented in the opposite direction from that of the woman under her (and from that of most graves in the cemetery). Found on her back was a quernstone fragment (grave 49).

---

[1] Measurements taken from Tom Freshwater, "A Lava Quern Workshop," p. 42.
[2] This find is fully described by Nicola S. H. Rogers, *Anglian and Other Finds*, pp. 1322–28.

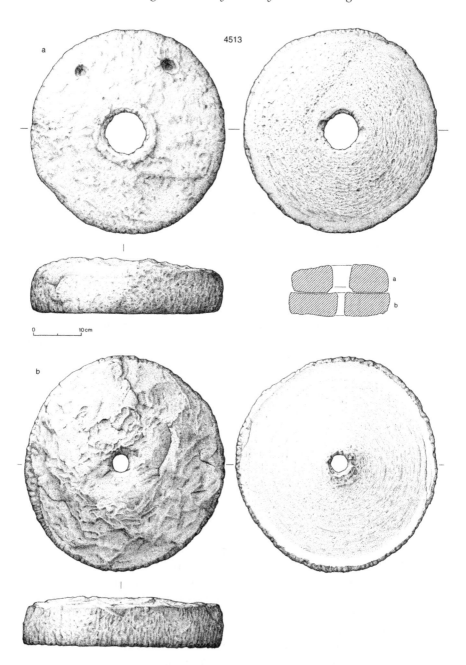

Figure 4. Sandstone quernstones forming a complete rotary quern, York; no. 4513, 46–54 Fishergate. Scale 1:4.

Susan Hirst, who excavated the site, suggests that the upper burial took place while the woman was alive.[3] Lloyd Laing and Jennifer Laing describe the body as "weighed down with a piece of quernstone for grinding grain, no doubt to keep her from climbing out of her grave."[4] Robin Fleming has created a sensational account of this woman's death, asserting that she was pushed into the grave from behind and that the quernstone fragment was thrown on her with enough force to fracture her pelvis. She was, Fleming believes, thought to have been responsible for the younger woman's death.[5] There is other evidence of live burial, perhaps punitive, in the period.[6] Howard Williams, however, has cast doubt on dramatic interpretations of the Sewerby burials. He sees the second burial as a symbolic response to the first one, a "bad" death (perhaps caused by trauma, distorting the limbs) over a "good" one (which was elaborately commemorated). For him, the quernstone was "an attempt to prevent the cadaver from literally rising out of its grave" (the cadaver, that is, not the woman while still alive, which was Hirst's hypothesis). Williams suggests that precautions were taken to ensure that, with her misfortunes, she would not come back to harm the living. Other stones were placed over her grave after it was closed.[7]

The role of the quernstone in either of these interpretations is significant. It possibly had neither symbolic nor functional attachment to grinding grain and was merely a heavy object used either to keep an exhausted victim from escaping the grave or to mark the corpse for another unknown reason. On the other hand, the quernstone might have been included to signal connections to settlement life. Perhaps the older woman was a slave whose main task was to grind grain and who was buried over her mistress.[8] Alternatively, she might have been a free woman whose association with grain and bread was salubrious, or perhaps she was in charge of the grinding slaves. In that case the quernstone would have been used to evoke an honorable occupation. Evidence so striking, ripe for competing interpretations, is one reason why more cemeteries than settlements have been excavated.

The links of graves to nearby settlements are suggestive but confusing, since sites were often built over. Buildings and other graves were cut into older burial sites already in the Anglo-Saxon period, and graves were robbed, meaning that some burial evidence might have been disturbed soon after it was deposited.[9] Even where this was not the case, as in the burial at Sewerby, it is difficult to determine how an object from a grave relates to the dead person's life. All we can be sure of is that it was no longer fulfilling the purpose for which it was made.

[3] Susan M. Hirst, *An Anglo-Saxon Inhumation Cemetery at Sewerby*, pp. 33–40.
[4] Lloyd Laing and Jennifer Laing, *Anglo-Saxon England*, pp. 81–83.
[5] See Robin Fleming, *Britain after Rome*, pp. 245–49.
[6] See Andrew Reynolds, *Anglo-Saxon Deviant Burial Customs*.
[7] Howard Williams, *Death and Memory in Early Medieval Britain*, pp. 96–100.
[8] Laing and Laing, *Anglo-Saxon England*, p. 82.
[9] See Helena Hamerow, "Communities of the Living and the Dead."

Querns in the making

Anglo-Saxon trade networks reached from England to Asia Minor, although most imports came from northwestern Europe. Drinking glasses and pottery from the Rhineland reached London through intermediate ports at Dorestad (now in the Netherlands) or Quentovic (Normandy), locations which have been partially excavated. Quernstones also moved up the Rhine to Dorestad, where there was a large industry given over to finishing the stones, as there was at Hedeby in Denmark and at London.[10] Common along the eastern coast of England and in settlements served by good river transport, quernstones from the Eifel region, in northwest Germany (near the cities of Koblenz and Mayen), are found at numerous sites in England.[11] Heavy, bulk-quantity items, quernstones have been recovered from loading areas and even from sunken ships. Not all the quernstones recovered were transported in Anglo-Saxon times. The Romans imported quernstones from this region "into Britain throughout the Roman period" before the Anglo-Saxons and other peoples arrived.[12] Before this time the quern had undergone a change. The beehive-shaped quern of the Iron Age was replaced by the flat rotary quern, comprised of two horizontal stones, that the Romans brought from Germany. A less common form also used by the Anglo-Saxons was the saddle quern, in which the upper stone slid back and forth rather than rotated over the lower. H. E. M. Cool notes that some querns made in Britain followed the beehive model, which was still in use in the third century.[13]

Like pots, querns can be subjected to petrological analysis, making it possible to know where they were produced and how far they had to travel to the site where they were used and, centuries later, recovered. Imported quernstones were shipped as blanks, as they are sometimes called, meaning that they were already cut into a roughly circular shape.[14] Quern fragments found at London and Winchester suggest that the stones arrived there unworked and generated a local finishing industry.[15] The Thames Exchange site, dated to the late tenth or eleventh century, has been called a "trans-shipment centre," the first facility of this kind to have been found in London. By this date the workshops at Hedeby and Dorestad no longer functioned. According to Tom Freshwater, "The importing of such querns is one aspect of the developing trade which London saw in this period, when the beach markets were gradually giving way to a more formalized system of quayside warehouses and market places."[16] The

[10] Rogers, *Anglian and Other Finds*, p. 1329.
[11] For maps of distribution of quernstone finds, see Ulf Näsman, "Exchange and Politics," pp. 50–51.
[12] Nina Crummy, "Small Finds," p. 189.
[13] H. E. M. Cool, *Eating and Drinking in Roman Britain*, pp. 71–72.
[14] See Jonathan Parkhouse, "The Distribution and Exchange of Mayen Lava Quernstones," for boat finds from 1957 and 1964, both continental and early medieval.
[15] Martin Biddle and D. Smith, "The Querns."
[16] Freshwater, "A Lava Quern Workshop," p. 45.

London Exchange site seems to mark "the re-emergence of foreign trade in the City after a period of contraction." Other London sites have produced quern fragments similar to those found at the Exchange site.[17] Quernstones shipped from London were transported up the Thames and have been recovered from "rural settlements as far upriver as Oxfordshire."[18]

One of the earliest quernstones (found in fragments only) comes from Shakenoak (Oxfordshire), from a pit deposit, possibly seventh century. The excavation report is vague about provenance, suggesting Northern Ireland, or the Inner Hebrides, or "various Continental sites."[19] Most quernstones are considerably later. Large numbers of lava quernstones are found from the Middle Saxon period, sometimes included among "luxury imported commodities," as they are in reports on the excavations at Flixborough.[20] Quernstones from Germany became widely available in the ninth century and were preferred for nearly two centuries. Ship finds help us trace the networks along which quernstones moved. Best known is the Graveney boat, which was found off the north Kent coast and dated to c. 930.[21] This ship is thought to have contained up to 280 querns, 28 in each of ten framed spaces, with a combined shipping weight of approximately seven tons. Jonathan Parkhouse ventures to compare the weight of a single shipment to that of the entire surviving corpus of Anglo-Saxon quernstones, which amounts to less than the Graveney boat could have brought on a single voyage.[22] The Graveney boat also included hops and other kinds of stone, including salvaged Roman tiles. This boat had a shallow draught and was suited to coastal movement and small waterways, although the quernstone cargo suggests that the boat also crossed the English Channel.[23] James Lang suggests that "even the upper reaches of the river Ouse system in Yorkshire would have been accessible to stone" carried in a ship with a draught of .65 meters or less.[24] The shallow draught of the Graveney boat means that such cargo could have penetrated far inland via small rivers and streams.

Helena Hamerow contrasts quernstones with the merchandise for which they provided ships' ballast, noting that some of the oldest pottery in early medieval northwest Europe comes from the Eifel region, along the middle and lower reaches of the Rhine, as do so many querns.[25] She comments that quernstones were "widely distributed within mid Saxon England, indeed

---

[17] Freshwater, "A Lava Quern Workshop," pp. 44–45.

[18] Helena Hamerow, "Agrarian Production," p. 226.

[19] The fragment measures 3 ½" x 2 ¾" x 7/8" and is of basaltic, vesicular lava. See A. C. C. Brodribb, A. R. Hands, and D. R. Walker, *Excavations at Shakenoak Farm*, p. 48.

[20] Keith Dobney, Deborah Jacques, James Barrett, and Cluny Johnstone, eds., *Farmers, Monks and Aristocrats*, p. 4.

[21] W. A. Oddy and P. C. Van Geersdaele, "The Recovery of the Graveney Boat."

[22] Parkhouse, "The Distribution and Exchange of Mayen Lava Quernstones."

[23] Mark Gardiner, "Hythes, Small Ports, and Other Landing Places," p. 108.

[24] James Lang, *Corpus of Anglo-Saxon Stone Sculpture*, p. 19. He estimates the Graveney boat "would have had a carrying capacity of over 7 tonnes and a draught of only 0.65 metres."

[25] See Helena Hamerow, *Early Medieval Settlements*, p. 182.

much more widely than imported pottery."[26] For Chris Wickham, quernstones point to prestige imports, which would include glass and pottery. He groups quernstones with glass and pottery from northern France as evidence of continental influence on Anglo-Saxon trade and of developing urbanism. Wickham compares the emporia of Dorestad, Ribe (Denmark), and Hamwic, three centers of commercial rather than political power, the contacts of which are traced partly through the presence of quernstones from the Eifel region.[27] As Hamerow notes, there was a difference in distribution for glass and other prestige imports, and querns. When the ships were unloaded, high-value objects would have been sent to the few courts and estate centers that had ordered them. Quernstones went to workshops for finishing and were eventually distributed more widely and deeply into the hinterlands than the prestige imports. Unlike a fork, knife, or pot, a quernstone had but a single use and might have been the only imported object at a small settlement. Archaeologists often associate querns with luxury consumption, but querns were more widely distributed than other imported objects.

Querns became more fragile and hence more valuable as they neared their destinations. Edges of stones found at the Exchange site show stress that was incurred "possibly as a result of upright storage or transport," as they might have been stored in the Graveney boat and similar vessels. Processing the stones, especially drilling central holes, also weakened them. The final stage of production took place, according to Freshwater, "shortly before use," when two final features were added. First was the rynd chase or seating for the rynd, the fitting that supported the upper stone on a spindle. Then came the hole for the handle that would be used to power the upper stone.[28] Finishing the stones demanded skill; the upper stone of both types, rotary and saddle quern, required a concave grinding surface and the lower stone a slightly convex one. At its final destination, someone with experience would have set up the tool and adjusted it for use.

Querns in settlement contexts

Querns have been recovered from Anglo-Saxon sites in all periods. I describe two models, the small site of short duration that seems to have been largely self-sustaining, and the larger site with many links to trade and transportation. Early settlements, such as Mucking and West Stow, exemplify the former; York and Flixborough are examples of the latter. West Stow and Mucking have been referred to as "unstructured," meaning that they show no signs of domination by a stable, elite population, although cemeteries associated with unstructured settlements sometimes

[26] Hamerow, "Agrarian Production," p. 226. See also Freshwater, "A Lava Quern Workshop."
[27] Chris Wickham, *Framing the Middle Ages*, pp. 683–87.
[28] Freshwater, "A Lava Quern Workshop," pp. 42–43.

suggest the existence of an elite social class. It has recently been suggested that Mucking served as a market and meeting place, giving it a more complex profile attributable to its location in the Lower Thames basin.[29] The complexity of a settlement seems to have determined how its artifact basis survived. The more diverse the settlement's probable network was, the richer the surviving artifact base is likely to be. The less structured a settlement was, the more likely its artifacts are to have been scattered in the topsoil rather than disposed of in one place, i.e., in a ditch or refuse pit.[30] Refuse pits tended to remain in use over long periods and were sometimes sealed at various levels (e.g., by blowing sand) and so were stratified. Domination by a stable elite meant an organized settlement able to participate in regional and perhaps long-distance trade that contributed to the settlement's artifact base. The wealthy, including ecclesiastical leaders in search of prestige for their establishments and their patrons, needed trade to supply those markers of social distinction – glass vessels, certain styles of jewelry, and others – that were otherwise unavailable. Expensive and rare objects had greater chances of survival than ordinary things. But the exceptional and the ordinary were linked. Just as ships that brought glass and fine pottery also brought quernstones, the wine trade, which served the elite, provided the means for trade in textiles and metalwork.[31]

Abandoned by the early eighth century, West Stow was a small, early site that shows possible reuse of Roman quernstones. Stanley West proposed that the settlement had been organized into seven large hall groups, with a total of seventy sunken-featured buildings (SFBs) excavated. Twenty huts produced fragments of quernstones, thirteen of them lava quernstones that might have been reused Roman stone. These huts were found in five of the seven groups. West suggested that the other two hall groups were less associated with grinding. West Stow, like other settlements, was periodically rebuilt, and these hall groups are not contemporary. There was some shifting of buildings over time. Grinding might not have taken place at every hut where fragments were found; not every fragment represents a complete quern.[32] West's model suggests that the village was organized into two or three hut groups at any one time, with grinding huts accommodating the needs of a hall group rather than the entire settlement. Given the limited capacity of one quern to supply the needs of a given population, such a model seems plausible.

The mid-Saxon trading center of Hamwic was occupied continuously from the early eighth century, a date suggested by a coin from the reign of Aldfirth of Northumbria (685–705). From about 850 on the site shows decline, especially seen in the lack of new structures from approximately the mid-century to the end of the century, coinciding with a decline in

[29] Susan M. Hirst, "Mucking/East Tilbury: Lower Thames Meeting Place and Mart in the Early and Middle Saxon Periods?"
[30] Wickham, *Framing the Middle Ages*, pp. 502–3.
[31] Wickham, *Framing the Middle Ages*, p. 802.
[32] Stanley West, *West Stow Revisited*, p. 35.

long-range trade and a shift of the settlement to "higher, more defensi-
ble ground." Excavations at Hamwic yielded numerous quernstone fragments, many of them imported. The evidence suggested to Mark Brisbane
that "grinding corn went on throughout the town, presumably on a house-
by-house basis," although it is not certain that each house ground its own
grain.[33] Quern fragments might be a sign of whole querns or, as at West
Stow and many other places, might be refuse that was put to another
purpose. Hamwic hosted a wide variety of crafts and might have been
a point for finishing a variety of goods for export, rather than a point of
entry and exit for finished goods. When it came to provisioning, however,
Hamwic required a local, short-range food network similar to the networks found in smaller settlements. If we accept the view that grain was
ground on a "house-to-house" basis, some important similarities emerge
to liken grand Hamwic to West Stow, its humble rural cousin. Evidence of
quernstones attests to the organization of communities around an essential
element of the food supply. Whatever its significance as a site of industry
and finishing of goods produced elsewhere (not quernstones, however),
Hamwic seems to be a collection of small units organized around the food
supply. The settlement has not yielded evidence of extensive supply links
to surrounding communities, or what Brisbane calls the "spatial relationship of this central place to its rural hinterland." He continues, "Indeed
even defining the extent of that hinterland is full of problems," since the
surrounding area of "scrub and heath" was not settled earlier. Hamwic
seems to have no history linking it to earlier settlements out of which the
center developed. We can easily imagine West Stow as we know it having
emerged from a smaller settlement. Hamwic, by contrast, seems to have
been created by royal order, part of what Richard Hodges calls "a radically
new political polity for Saxon England."[34]

Both West Stow and Hamwic were settlements of relatively short duration. Settlements at York and Flixborough were very long-lived. Querns
found at the latter two sites were both imported and domestic, with the
latter appearing chiefly in the records of the tenth century and after.
Imported querns (from the Eifel region) seem to have been used exclusively in the late eighth and ninth centuries. Fragments of a lava quernstone dated to the eighth century, i.e., to pre-Viking York, have been found
with other eighth-century deposits in a refuse pit near the end of some
post-built structures. The other eighth-century deposits include coins,
glass, lava quernstone fragments, and debris from the manufacture of
antler and bone tools. According to Terence O'Connor, York was a trading
site at that time, described by Alcuin as an *emporium*, although we do not
know exactly what the term meant to him.[35]

[33] Mark Brisbane, "Hamwic (Saxon Southampton)," p. 104.
[34] Brisbane, "Hamwic (Saxon Southampton)," p. 107, citing Richard Hodges, *The Hamwih Pottery*, ch. 1.
[35] Terence O'Connor, "8th–11th Century Economy and Environment in York," p. 137.

York was occupied by Scandinavian settlers after the early, Anglian period. Around 935 the settlement at Coppergate was rebuilt; the later Anglo-Scandinavian period saw more rebuilding. Contexts were disturbed many times, making it impossible to comment on such matters as the distribution of querns, which at West Stow and Hamwic was comparatively clear. However, because of the waterlogged conditions at Coppergate, which O'Connor has described as a "squalid" and "densely settled" part of Jorvik, a great deal of organic food matter has been preserved, bone material much more abundantly than plant material.[36] Quern fragments were found in both eighth- to ninth-century and later contexts. The earlier fragments were imported, perhaps indicating trade with the Continent. Domestic (sandstone) querns have been found at York only in the new settlement established there in the late tenth century, and (residually) in subsequent contexts.[37] The preference for local querns in the later period does not mean that trading did not take place then as well. Rather, it might mean that querns were no longer associated with prestige, or that local quernstones had become less expensive and were preferred for that reason.

The sandstone quernstones seen in Figure 4 from Fishergate 46–54 are dated from the eleventh to the twelfth centuries and were found in a riverside pit in the largest Anglian settlement in York, a site first settled from 700 to c. 850 and reoccupied in the eleventh century. The quern's origin is the "Millstone Grit sequence of the Pennines," perhaps Thorner or Follifoot (closer to York than other outcroppings, but river transport means that the more distant locations are also plausible).[38] The complete rotary quern was associated with over one hundred quern fragments, almost all of them vesicular lava, quarried in Germany; the complete quern is not earlier than the late tenth to early eleventh centuries.[39] The survival of a whole quern is most unusual and suggests some cause other than wear and tear for discarding it. This is important late evidence of the continued use of imported querns in a period in which many believe that they were being phased out. An obvious explanation is the expanded use of water-mills to grind grain, as we will see below. Also of interest is a fragment of an upper quernstone fitted with a thong to rotate the upper stone; the lower stone shows deep grooves that are perhaps signs of "attempts to renew its roughness." This quern might be earlier than the tenth century, like so many that have been found.[40]

Both imported and domestic quernstone fragments were also found at Flixborough (Lincolnshire). The stones are probable evidence of changes in site identity. A posthole at Building 18 was described as holding "a

---

[36] O'Connor, "8th–11th Century Economy and Environment in York," pp. 139, 143.
[37] Rogers, *Anglian and Other Finds*, p. 1329; see p. 1206 for a description of period contexts at the site.
[38] For the quern, see Rogers, *Anglian and Other Finds*, p. 1326, no. 4513. See also Gaunt's comments on the place of origin, p. 1329.
[39] Rogers, *Anglian and Other Finds*, pp. 1321–29.
[40] Rogers, *Anglian and Other Finds*, p. 1323 for the quern powered by the thong (object no. 4508) and p. 1322 for the quern that was renewed.

large collection of rotary quern fragments – many imported from the Eiffel region of Germany."[41] Lava quernstone fragments far outnumber those made of sandstone, there being only 11 of the latter but some 229 of the former. All the Flixborough quernstones are fragments and, as at York and elsewhere, none was found in a context that suggests food preparation or storage. The lava fragments are concentrated in tenth-century contexts, either in ditches or refuse pits and with discarded material. They are not found with evidence of use or exchange, such as coins or glass, those being "exotic luxuries or high value items" and the settlement's best evidence of trade relations with the Continent.[42] Lisa M. Wastling and Patrick Ottaway nevertheless suggest that lava quernstones were perhaps preferred at Flixborough as a sign of prestige, even though there were "more locally available" querns.[43] Christopher Loveluck, Keith Dobney, and James Barrett observe that "commodities such as the Eifel querns and pottery vessels are likely to have travelled as bulk commodities or ballast, and were probably exchanged as important everyday or novelty items of less value."[44] This observation suggests that residents distinguished imported from domestic querns. Perhaps those finished at import depots differed in some functional way from querns of domestic origin, possibly in details of their finishing. In the end, querns at York and Flixborough reveal less about daily food preparation for the inhabitants than about the connections between these settlements and their trading partners, and the kinds of prestige goods they exchanged. The mixture of domestic and imported querns suggests that the inhabitants were conscious of the quern's origin, and that ownership of the objects communicated information about the identity and status of the households that owned them.

Once situated, a quern might have lasted for many years, inviting the possibility that accounts of ancestral identity could have been associated with a quern by storytellers who preserved a settlement's history. If so, the stones would not have been the interchangeable and indistinguishable objects we take them to be. Those seeing and hearing querns in use might have thought of them as ancient properties of the settlement and therefore as an identity-forming link to ancestral culture. Conversely, new querns might have been interpreted as a sign of wealth. Quernstones could have acquired attributes and inflections of local culture such as are associated with pottery, much of which might have been made for a settlement within the settlement's precincts. A quernstone might have become a marker of *habitus*, Pierre Bourdieu's term for the prevailing customs that structure crafts and that perpetuate technique and style across generations.[45] Did

[41] Chris Loveluck, "A High-status Anglo-Saxon Settlement at Flixborough," p. 156.
[42] Lisa M. Wastling and Patrick Ottaway, "Cultivation, Crop Processing and Food Procurement," pp. 246–48.
[43] Wastling and Ottaway, "Cultivation, Crop Processing and Food Procurement," p. 246.
[44] Christopher Loveluck, Keith Dobney, and James Barrett, "Trade and Exchange," p. 116.
[45] Pierre Bourdieu, *The Logic of Practice*, p. 140, quoted in C. G. Cumberpatch, "Towards a Phenomenological Approach to the Study of Medieval Pottery," pp. 125–26.

those who performed this taxing labor have the energy to talk or sing as they worked? Surely it is possible to imagine a social network forming around that kind of work; such networks, we know, form around field work in the modern period.

The assembled quern would have been set in a location near the facility used for grain storage, and also near the kitchen and bakehouse, the central places where ground grain would be processed into bread or porridge – and perhaps gathering places for workers as well. Both the site of grinding grain and the site of food preparation were centered on stones, and hence seemingly built to last. But archaeologists have had little success in reconstructing the contexts in which quernstones functioned. Fixed structures such as hearths and ovens were among the most stable remnants of food culture. Locations in which food was stored and prepared do not survive except as traces of stone foundations or marked by holes for posts used to support buildings. Many fragments of the settlement's life were preserved only because they had been discarded in the topsoil and used to backfill postholes.[46]

When pottery, grains, bones, or other food objects are found near hearths and ovens, we have contexts that suggest food preparation. But such evidence is rare. Hearths are sometimes known only because of charcoal fragments or burn marks in the soil or on stones – stones that sometimes include quernstone fragments. Food itself, including grains and plants, was highly perishable in most contexts. Some grain survives, as does pollen, if it was carbonized. Four small, round, carbonized loaves of bread have survived from an eleventh-century context in Ipswich.[47] Plants survive only in traces. Both fish and mammal bones, found in large numbers, have been used to establish the proportion of cattle to pigs and sheep in the diet, the age at which animals were slaughtered and consumed, and even the manner of butchering (seen in marks on the bones).[48] When this evidence occurs in assemblages of pottery, the remains of hearths, or other data related to food preparation, we can see how different parts of the food network converge. Such patterns are clear for larger settlements, which were likely to leave more evidence of planning – for example, in boundary ditches and paths – and richer finds that accumulated through far-flung food networks.

Paradoxical though it seems, fragmented and repurposed quernstones might constitute better – at least more direct – evidence of food culture than the few whole querns that survive. At Flixborough sandstone quern fragments were used to form hearth bases; six of eleven quern fragments showed burn marks. Another fragment was reused as a hone for sharpening tools.[49] At Pudding Lane, London, the use of imported quern fragments

---

[46] For a description of methods, see James Graham-Campbell and Magdalena Valor, eds., *The Archaeology of Medieval Europe*, pp. 30–43.

[47] Debby Banham, *Food and Drink in Anglo-Saxon England*, p. 22, and plate 5.

[48] See, for example, Jennifer Bourdillon, "The Animal Provisioning of Saxon Southampton."

[49] Wastling and Ottaway, "Cultivation, Crop Processing and Food Procurement," p. 246.

as bedding foundations for timber was taken as a sign of the owner's wealth.[50] Christopher Scull has contrasted the form in which fragments are unearthed to the social life they witnessed, which, in the archaeological context, has become only "the detritus of human activity."[51] The most difficult function to document is their primary purpose, since surviving stones reveal nothing about how they were used or by whom.

We tend to think of querns in terms of what they produced, rather than in terms of what it took to make them work. Grinding grain was laborious, not a task assigned to those inclined to reflect on the heritage of their working tools. The research of Debby Banham suggests even small settlements would have needed more than one quern. She estimates that some thirty minutes of grinding today would produce enough flour for "a couple of rolls."[52] Experienced grinders at the time would have been more productive. Cool uses estimates based on the productivity of skilled quern operators in modern Algeria to suggest that up to three kilograms of flour an hour could be produced. A unit of about thirty Roman soldiers was issued between five and six units (*modii*) weighing four kilograms each as a day's ration, or about twenty to twenty-four kilograms. The Algerian worker would have to work ten to twelve hours to produce that amount. Cool notes that querns had to be embedded in the floor, not conveniently positioned at waist height, as they are in museums, adding to the labor of this work.[53] An Anglo-Saxon settlement of one hundred persons would require three grinders working ten-hour days for a comparable supply. Some experts on early medieval diet assume that bread was a staple, but it is not clear how querns could have produced enough flour to meet the assumed need. For this reason, Banham argues that bread was not, in fact, a common food, and that instead peasants ate boiled grain or porridge that did not have to be finely ground before it was consumed.[54] Yet even if boiled, grain had to be broken down and coarsely ground first. Querns were necessary for the latter process as well as for the former.

Texts and querns

Texts offer only indirect help in situating querns in settlement contexts. For example, the work known as *Rectitudines Singularum Personarum* (Rights [or Duties] of Individuals) refers to the duties of many workers on an estate, including the granary-keeper, who was allowed to take corn spilled at the granary door at harvest time.[55] We need to imagine the tasks that were related to the granary-keeper's duties, since they are not enumerated.

---

[50] Brian Hobley, "Lundenwic and Lundenburgh," pp. 79–80. Hobley identifies quernstones as Offa's "black stones," p. 73.

[51] Christopher Scull, "Urban Centres in Pre-Viking England?", p. 269.

[52] Banham, *Food and Drink*, p. 18. See also Chapter 2, p. 48, above.

[53] Cool, *Eating and Drinking in Roman Britain*, p. 73.

[54] Banham, *Food and Drink*, pp. 24–25.

[55] *Rectitudines* is edited by F. Liebermann, *GDA*, pp. 444–53, and translated by Michael Swanton, *Anglo-Saxon Prose*, pp. 26–30.

Grain had to be brought to the quern hut or stored nearby for grinding and the ground meal or flour transferred to jars or bags and carried to the kitchen, where the precious commodity had to be protected against insects and rodents. Grinding sheds might have been closer to the storage sheds than to food preparation and eating zones. Such a location was more likely if those doing the grinding were of lesser status and were required to eat and sleep in quarters remote from the hall. We also have to imagine noise, sweat, dust, exhausting labor, and the tedium associated with operating the quern and handling both grain and meal. The *Rectitudines* does not mention querns, and texts that do mention them do little to help us imagine the networks to which querns belonged.

Cweorn (*cwyrn*, *cwern*) is found just twenty-five times in Old English texts (*DOE*). Compounds are few; they include *cweorn-bill* (stonecutter's axe); *cweorn-burna* (millstream); *cweorn-stan* (quernstone); *cweorn-toþ* (molar [tooth]); *eosol-cweorn* (millstone turned by an ass); and *hand-cweorn* (hand-mill). *Cweorn-bill* and *cweorn-toþ* are found only in glosses. *Cweorn-burna* is found only in a charter of 962 by King Edgar; *eosol-cweorn* is found four times, twice in prose, twice in glosses. *Cweorn-stan*, found thirteen times, has a varied distribution, including four glosses, a medical text (where the stone is a source of heat), and homilies referring to scripture (*DOE*). Examples of *hand-cweorn* include a translation of the Book of Judges and a recipe (one about grinding and drying herbs).[56]

The quernstone is an ancient object and appears in several biblical contexts, some translated into Old English. The object was given figurative meaning as well. Books of the Hebrew Testament are straightforward in representing the hand-mill in daily use. An Old English translation of Numbers 11:8 found in a Canterbury manuscript describes how the Israelites gathered and prepared manna in the desert: "They gathered that [manna] and ground [it] in mills or crushed and boiled [it] in cooking pots and made loaves out of it: they were like those that were baked in oil" (*þæt hi gaderodon & grundon on cwyrne oððe brytton & sudon on croccan & worhton hlafas ðærof: þa wæron swylce hi wæron elebacene*).[57] The Anglo-Saxons might have seen the similarity between food preparation in ancient times and their own, since the Anglo-Saxons themselves prepared grain both as flour for baking and as meal for boiling, although they did not bake bread in oil (*DOE, elebacene*).

The quern was linked to servitude. Moses warns that all firstborn sons will die, including the "firstborn son of the servant who is sitting at the mill": *oð þære wylne frumcennedan sunu þe sit æt ðære cweornan* (Exodus 11:5).[58] The blinded Sampson is said to have been forced to work *æt hire handcwyrne*, "at [his enemy's] hand-mill," although he is usually seen performing the work of the grinding ass at a mill, not that of a grinding slave

---

[56] Arthur S. Napier, "Altenglische Miscellen," pp. 325–26.
[57] S. J. Crawford, ed., *The Old English Version of the Heptateuch*, p. 310.
[58] For Exodus 11:5, see Crawford, *The Old English Version of the Heptateuch*, p. 242.

at a quern (Judges 16:21).[59] In an example not found in Old English, a proud woman, "the virgin daughter of Babylon," is humbled and told to "take the millstones and grind meal" (Isaiah 47:2, *NRSV*). The mill was also, for two reasons, a symbol of life. First, given the association of the object with grinding and crushing grains for bread and porridge, the quernstone served as a synecdoche for daily life. Second, its rotary motion suggested the revolutions of time. In the Book of Jeremiah the Lord threatens ruin and vows to banish "the grinding of the millstones and the light of the lamp" (Jeremiah 25:10). The plural form suggests that settlements in the ancient world (and probably those in Anglo-Saxon England) required several querns to satisfy the community's need for grain. The grinding of the millstones was as basic to the life Jeremiah described as lamplight – not food and light themselves, but the human labor of preparing food and the human device for lighting darkness, perhaps so that grinding could continue when there was no more daylight.

References in the Gospels complement the use of the quern to invoke fundamental properties of communal life but also imminent death and judgment. The quern is a common sight used to illustrate the sudden and arbitrary nature of death. Both Matthew and Luke report Christ's warning about the unexpected coming of the kingdom, which will find two women grinding at the mill, one of whom will be taken and one not (Matthew 24:41; Luke 17:35). This passage is cited in Boniface's letter to Eadburga: "he saw, here in this world, a maiden grinding at a quern" (*he geseage grindan her on worulde an mægden on anre cweorne*).[60] More famous is Christ's use of the quernstone as an instrument of punishment. Matthew 18:6, Mark 9:42, and Luke 17:2 include the episode in which Christ declared that anyone who corrupted other followers, including children, would better have had a millstone (*cweornstan*) tied around his neck and been cast into the sea.[61] This reference appears in the seventh-century Latin *Penitential* of Theodore; the canon, which was translated into Old English, concerns one who creates scandal by not keeping an appointed fast.[62] The word *eosol-cweorn* (millstone turned by an ass) is used in the Old English version of the *Cura Pastoralis* to point to the "circuit of this world" and of human life, and also to humanity's toil and final judgment; the word is also used in a gloss.[63] There is grim irony in the use of a tool that produced food for

[59] Crawford, *The Old English Version of the Heptateuch*, p. 413.

[60] Kenneth Sisam, *Studies in the History of Old English Literature*, p. 221, l. 179.

[61] Walter W. Skeat, ed., *The Holy Gospels in Anglo-Saxon*, see Mark 9:42, p. 74, and Luke 17:2, p. 166.

[62] *Penitential* of Theodore, book 1, ch. 11, c. 5, ed. A. W. Haddan and W. Stubbs, *CED*, p. 186. For Oxford, Bodleian Library, MS Laud Misc. 482, fol. 28a, see Allen J. Frantzen, *ASP*, *OEC*, Y81.01.03. "If anyone scorns a commanded fast among God's people and against the decree of the witan or the confessor, he is to fast 40 days, not counting the ordained fasts and the Lenten fast. If he does it often and it is customary for him, he is to be driven from God's church as the Lord himself said: 'If any man seduces one of these, it would be better for him that a millstone were tied around his neck and he were thrown into the sea.'"

[63] Henry Sweet, ed., *King Alfred's West-Saxon Version of Gregory's Pastoral Care*, book 1, ch. 2, pp. 30–31.

the living as an instrument of execution, but the warning has a practical side nonetheless, since the millstone would have a hole in the middle and so could more readily be adapted to this purpose than many other stones.

The juxtaposition of life and death through the millstone also appears in Revelation. An angel stands before an audience of sailors and shipmasters and casts a great millstone into the sea to show how Babylon will be "thrown down with violence." Then the sound of the millstone – like other sounds of the great city – will be heard no more and "the light of the lamp" shall shine there no more (Revelation 18:21–22), linking the quern and the lamp, as did Jeremiah (25:10). The angel's list of city sounds includes the grinding of grain. The other sounds – music, and the voices of bride and groom – seem more urban to modern ears. But the grain imported by ancient cities had to be prepared for baking somewhere convenient; hence the angel's portrait of urban life includes it. Old English authors, so far as I am aware, do not comment, as various books of the Bible do, on the sound of the quern. But the biblical references help to animate this unspoken aspect of grinding grain, which is that querns made a distinctive sound that would have been audible throughout the day – the white noise of their time and a reminder of the pressing demand for food that necessitated the continuous, if not endless, revolutions of one stone over another.

It is easy, then, to see why Anglo-Saxon authors used the quern as an image of continuous time and the burdens of daily life. In "Sermo de die judicii," Ælfric exploited the shape as well as the weight of the millstone: "And worldly care is compared to the millstone, that ever goes about many thoughts and various deeds that people require, and about heavy labors, as you yourself know" (*And seo woruldcaru is þære cwyrne wiðmeten, þe æfre gæð abutan ymbe fela geþohtas and mislicum dædum þe menn behofiað, and hefegum geswincum, swa swa ge sylfe witon*).[64] A similar comment is found in the *Pastoral Care*: "Through the millstone is signified the revolution of the world and also of a person's life and his or her labor" (*Þurh ða cweorne is getacnod se ymbhwyrft ðisse worolde & eac monna lifes & hira geswinces*).[65] Both Alfred and Ælfric connected the millstone to labor, although not to the labor of grinding corn. Ælfric and Gregory used the quern to suggest the weight of the world and its cares, a burden perhaps symbolized in the second burial at Sewerby (see above). These figurative references incorporate material aspects of the labor of grinding corn in a network that links the Book of Numbers, from the sixth or fifth century BC, to Gregory the Great (d. 604), King Alfred (d. 899), Ælfric (d. c. 1010), and the post-Conquest period. In that span of 1,500 years the function of the quern changed little if at all.[66]

The quern appears in practical contexts in a few Old English works, one of which suggests that the quern was not the only tool available for

---

[64] John C. Pope, ed., *Homilies of Ælfric*, 2: 595, ll. 115–18.
[65] Sweet, *King Alfred's West-Saxon Version of Gregory's Pastoral Care*, pp. 30–31.
[66] James S. Ackerman, "Numbers," pp. 87–91.

grinding. A recipe calls for grinding spring or winter barley: "take clean winter barley and grind it in a hand-mill" (*nime þonne clænne lengtenbere & grinde on handcwyrna*).[67] Another calls for grinding pepper: "take six unweighed peppercorns and grind them to dust and add two egg-shells full of wine" (*VI pipercorn unwegen & grind ealle to duste & do win twa ægscille fulle*).[68] The first calls for use of a hand-mill appropriate for grinding grain. The second recipe calls for a mortar and pestle, since it would not have been efficient to use a quern for small quantities of grain, peppercorns, or other costly spices. *Grindan*, the verb used here, is found thirty-five times and is especially frequent in medicinal recipes, although it is used both for querns or hand-mills and for water-mills; *agrindan*, to grind up, is found just once.[69] An anonymous homily, part of the "Sunday letter" tradition of apocryphal texts outlining proper observance of the Lord's Day, links grinding and baking. The text forbids milling on Sunday and sets milling on a level with legal business and commerce: "On Sunday nobody may hold an assembly nor give judgments or make oaths or swear, or mill or bake loaves or buy or sell on the holy Sunday" (*On sunnandæg nan man ne healde gemot ne ne demon domas ne aðas ne swerion ne grindan ne hlafas bacan ne bicgan ne syllon on þone halgan sunnandæg*).[70] If this stricture were applied to the use of hand-mills, Christian households would have to have a store of flour or meal to use on Sunday.

A prognostic from an eleventh-century manuscript also puts the quern into the context of commerce: "It is good on the fourth night of the moon that the plowman take out his plow and the miller his quern, and a merchant to begin selling his merchandise" (*Se IIII nihta mona se byð god þæm ergendan hys sul ut to done, & þem grindere his cweorn, & þem cipemen hys cipinge to anginnane*).[71] The noun *grindere* for the miller occurs only here (*DOEWC*). It is curious that the miller's work would begin at this particular point, since one assumes that mills were in constant use, unlike plows, which were used for seasonal labor. The same concern applies to the merchant's work. The prognostic places the quern in a strategic context linking two objects to what might be the first two of three stages of food-related labor: production (plowing), preparation (milling), and exchange (trading or selling). All three workers were to begin their labors on the same day, their independent processes seemingly synchronized in the author's mind.[72]

[67] Napier, "Altenglische Miscellen," pp. 325–26, para. 4.3.
[68] Oswald Cockayne, ed., *Leechdoms, Wortcunning and Starcraft*, 1: 374–78.
[69] In a remedy for pocks and scabs on sheep; see "Lacnunga," ed. J. H. G. Grattan and Charles Singer, *Anglo-Saxon Magic and Medicine*, pp. 178–79, c. cxliv. Also related is *for-grindan*, which does not refer to grinding but is used figuratively to describe crushing or destroying, as in "grinding down one's enemies," i.e., destroying them (*DOE*).
[70] Robert Priebsch, "The Chief Sources of Some Anglo-Saxon Homilies," pp. 135–38. See Clare A. Lees, "The 'Sunday Letter' and the 'Sunday Lists.'"
[71] For the text from London, British Library, MS Cotton Tiberius A.iii, see R. M. Liuzza, ed. and trans, *Anglo-Saxon Prognostics*, p. 190 (no. 4). See also Max Förster, "Beiträge zur mittelalterlichen Volkskunde VIII," pp. 16–49, cc. 43–45.
[72] Förster, "Beiträge zur mittelalterlichen Volkskunde VIII," pp. 43–45.

Labor to power querns and mills varied. It is assumed that most large mills were powered by water; neither material nor textual evidence has been found for a mill powered by beasts.[73] The labor for querns was, of course, human. The seventh-century laws of Æthelberht of Kent link the labor of grinding to a female slave. This association has been generalized as a condition throughout the Anglo-Saxon period. Intercourse with the king's grinding slave, the *grindende þeowe* (an intermediate class of slave), was punished with a fine of twenty-five shillings. Intercourse with a slave of higher status, the king's slave, entailed a fine of fifty shillings and intercourse with a lesser slave twelve shillings.[74] This is, however, the only reference to a grinding slave in the laws, and it cannot be assumed that the only people who used querns were female slaves. A text attributed to Wulfstan II of Worcester refers to a place "to which some of the nuns used to come to do their grinding" (*Þærto sume þara munecena comon to grindanne*), although the probability of nuns doing this work has been queried, and the reference might be instead to members of the household, not slaves.[75] Those people might have inhabited the space Rosamond Faith describes as the "directly exploited core area" of an estate, the *inland* occupied by workers who provided foodstuffs to the landlord.[76] The *grindere* of the prognostic is male, as, most probably, were operators of water-mills.

The sex of food workers does not follow modern expectations, as we also see in the vocabulary for baking. There are eighteen occurrences of the word for male baker, *bæcere*, and two occurrences of *bæceste*, only one of which is clearly assigned to a woman.[77] The Exeter Book riddle about kneading dough is, according to Christine Fell, the "only indication we have of a woman specifically involved in this range of domestic work." Fell also makes the encompassing point that whatever texts might say or imply about the distribution of labor according to sex, on small estates and settlements it was probable that tasks were assigned to those who could perform them and that "men and women shared generally in many tasks as they need to be done."[78] Hand-mills were indispensable but limited in usefulness. We have seen Banham's estimate of the output of an hour's grinding. Those who could not afford to have their grain ground would have to do it themselves. It is likely that people in small estates baked bread when they could, but relied for their daily diet on boiled crushed grain, as Ann Hagen also suggests.[79] One result, Banham believes, is that,

---

[73] Philip Rahtz, "Mills," p. 314.
[74] See Liebermann, *GDA*, pp. 3–4, and F. L. Attenborough, *LEEK*, pp. 4–5. See also Lisi Oliver, *The Beginnings of English Law*, pp. 64–65.
[75] Benjamin Thorpe, ed., *Diplomatarium Anglicum*, p. 445. Christine Fell, *Women in Anglo-Saxon England*, p. 47.
[76] Rosamond Faith, *The English Peasantry*, p. 58; for the definition of *inland*, and reference to foodstuffs, p. 16.
[77] This example comes from Gregory the Great, *Dialogi*, ed. Hans Hecht, *Bischof Waerferths von Worcester Übersetzung der Dialoge Gregors des Grossen*, book 3, ch. 37, p. 251, l. 24.
[78] Fell, *Women in Anglo-Saxon England*, p. 49 (concerning baking), and p. 48 (on general labor).
[79] Ann Hagen, *A Handbook of Anglo-Saxon Food and Drink*, pp. 12–13.

as we have seen above, and contrary to the general view, bread was not necessarily a staple food everywhere.[80]

Banham points out that bread lost status in the Anglo-Saxon period. *Hlaf* ("loaf") forms part of three important compounds: *hlaford*, lord, a term widely distributed throughout the corpus, early and late; *hlafdige* or "bread-kneader," the lady alongside the *hlaford*; and *hlafæta*, literally "bread-eater," or dependant, a term found only once, in the seventh-century laws of Æthelberht of Kent: "If a man slays the dependent of a commoner, he shall pay [the commoner] six shillings compensation" (*Gif man ceorlæs hlafætan ofslæhð, VI scillingum gebete*).[81] *Hlafweard*, "bread-keeper," is found only in the verse translation of Psalm 104 in the Paris Psalter.[82] Both *hlaford* and *hlafdige* were influential terms, the latter the root of modern English "lady."[83] The term is not widely used in Old English, but a reference from the Old English translation of Bede's *Ecclesiastical History* shows that it meant "lady" in the ninth century (*æfter þære hlafdigan forðfore*, "after the death of that lady").[84] *Hlaford* means "lord," but the term might have been applied to women of high social standing as well as to men.[85] Banham suggests that these words were more common in the early period; except for *hlaford*, they are rare in surviving texts. This is true of *hlafæta* and *hlafweard* especially; *hlafdige* is not well attested, not a surprise in a corpus in which women are mentioned less often than men. *Hlaford*, on the other hand, is extremely common, with some 1,162 occurrences in prose, 101 in glosses, and 63 in verse. *Hlafdigan* occurs in four glosses (*domina, matrone*), once in the Old English translation of Bede's *Ecclesiastical History*, once in a charm, once in a marginal note to the Gospel of St. John, and in the *Anglo-Saxon Chronicle*. It does not occur at all in verse (*DOEWC* searches). It seems reasonable to conclude with Banham that *hlaford* and *hlafdige* lost their associations with bread; people no longer thought of relationships in terms of loaves.

Hand-powered querns would not have been adequate for producing the hundreds of loaves of bread that would have been consumed in a week at a major estate, or supplying the large numbers of loaves mentioned in some food renders cited by Banham and Hagen.[86] The size of these payments

---

80 Banham, *Food and Drink*, p. 18.
81 Banham, *Food and Drink*, p. 17. For Æthelberht 25, see Liebermann, *GDA*, p. 4, and Attenborough, *LEEK*, pp. 6–7.
82 George Philip Krapp, ed., *The Paris Psalter*, Psalm 104, p. 81, l. 17.
83 See the etymology for "lord" in the *OED*: "In its primary sense the word (which is absent from the other Germanic languages) denotes the head of a household in his relation to the servants and dependants who 'eat his bread' (compare Old English *hláf-æta*, lit. 'bread-eater', a servant); but it had already acquired a wider application before the literary period of Old English." The *OED* entry for "lady": "The semantic development of LADY *n*. is much influenced by Anglo-Norman and Old French, Middle French, French *dame* . . . (and its parallels in other Romance languages) and its etymon classical Latin *domina* . . . which the English word frequently translates (compare discussion at LORD *n*.)."
84 Thomas Miller, ed., *The Old English Version of Bede's Ecclesiastical History*, book 4, ch. 12; see 2: 290, l. 6.
85 Fell, *Women in Anglo-Saxon England*, p. 40.
86 See, for example, Ann Hagen, *A Second Handbook of Anglo-Saxon Food and Drink*, pp. 165–66.

should prompt us to consider how much grain in the period could have been ground by hand. For example, according to a provision dated to the laws of Ine (r. 688–726), ten hides were to render three hundred loaves. Hagen cites a ninth-century will that requires 270 loaves of various kinds to be given as an annual charity. She notes that such contributions obviously had to be produced over and above what an estate or family required for its own use. Later charters required even greater numbers of loaves for monasteries: for example, some 1,300 annually to Bury St. Edmunds.[87] The large quantities of flour needed to meet the impressive renders mentioned in early charters and other documents could only have been satisfied by the use of water-mills.

Hand-mills and water-mills

Querns coexisted with the water-mill throughout the Old English period, as Old English texts indicate. The Domesday Book lists over 5,624 mills, most of them water-powered, with a horizontal wheel, a figure that some regard as too low. The Domesday commissioners were concerned with the revenue generated by mills and assessed them in those terms.[88] Most of those water-mills were built before 1066, although records of them in Old English texts are rare. Only in the tenth century does lexical evidence suggest that water-mills were spreading in Anglo-Saxon England (most texts date from this and later periods).[89] Hand-mills were outlawed in the twelfth century, when water-mills were protected by legislation requiring their use.[90] This development no doubt resulted in discarding hand-mills (or, more likely, their destruction and repurposing).

Mills were an old invention, not an innovation. The technology was well established by the eleventh century, although it was not uniformly spread throughout the territories the Domesday commissioners surveyed.[91] Carolingian capitularies of the early ninth century refer to the importance of working water-mills. At Tamworth, a royal residence in Mercia, the water-mill dates from the late eighth century, when the technology required for water-mills was adopted on royal estates where both waterpower and labor were available. The mill sequence at Tamworth is from the ninth and tenth centuries. The mill at Old Windsor is from the late seventh century, and mills from Barking Abbey and Corbridge are both eighth century.[92] The recent find of a large multiple water-mill at Corbridge has been dated eighth to tenth century.[93] Some locations had multiple mills. Blackley had twelve, shared with Ditchford and Icomb, and in 1086 Minchinhampton

---

[87] Hagen, *A Handbook*, p, 19.
[88] H. R. Loyn, *Anglo-Saxon England and the Norman Conquest*, p. 359.
[89] Philip Rahtz and Donald Bullough, "The Parts of an Anglo-Saxon Mill," pp. 18–19.
[90] Biddle and Smith, "The Querns," pp. 881–90.
[91] Loyn, *Anglo-Saxon England and the Norman Conquest*, p. 357.
[92] See Rahtz, "Mills," p. 314.
[93] "Anglo-Saxon Watermill Found in Tyne" (online resource).

had eight working mills. Philip Rahtz estimates that a water-mill such as that found at Tamworth, powered by a leat diverted from the river Anker, would have made sixty revolutions a minute. This mill could be adjusted and the distance between the millstones narrowed or widened to accommodate different kinds of grinding.[94] This technology had developed over a long period and was necessary to support renders of the scale Hagen and Banham describe.

The lexical evidence of the mill is much more revealing than that for the quern. There are numerous compounds including Old English *mylen*, ranging from *mylen-broc* ("millbrook"), to *mylen-wer* ("millpond"). The vast majority of these references appear in charters, testifying to the physical presence of the mill and its apparatus and their association with distinctive land features. Vernacular evidence for the mill comes chiefly from boundary clauses, as in the charter of 962 from the reign of Edgar, which refers to the *cweorn-burna*, the millstream.[95] As to the mill itself, only a few of its working parts are named.[96] Ælfric makes one of a handful of references to the mill wheel, using it as a figure for the rotation of the heavens, which "turn around us swifter than any mill wheel" (*heo æfre tyrnð onbuton us swyftre ðonne ænig mylenhweowul*).[97] The same expression occurs in the *Enchiridion* of Byrhtferth of Ramsey.[98] Textual references to the mill (*mylen*) focus on the physical situation of the plant and the role of this dominating structure in defining boundaries. Forty-two of fifty-one uses of *mylen-* and its compounds are found in charters or boundary clauses, and five in glosses.[99] The words appear once in the *Rule* of St. Benedict (which says that a monastery should be located near water and a mill).[100] There is a rare poetic reference in "The Battle of Brunanburh," in which the swords of the men of Wessex are described as "mill-stone sharp" (*mecum mylenscearpa*).[101]

Mills leave textual traces because they were landmarks, querns because they were known to ancient cultures reflected in books of the Bible and translated into Old English. Writers of non-legal discourse looked to texts, not to the world around them, for material. What they wrote about querns was, in most cases, what they had read about them. There is a temptation to argue for an exception concerning recipes and prognostics, since we associate them with folk culture. But these forms, R. M. Liuzza observes, are not popular or folk texts but rather examples of literary genres with ancient roots.[102] The world of querns in Old English is the world of the

[94] Rahtz, "Mills," p. 314.
[95] P. H. Sawyer, *Anglo-Saxon Charters*, no. 703, p. 231.
[96] Rahtz and Bullough, "The Parts of an Anglo-Saxon Mill," p. 21.
[97] Heinrich Henel, ed., *Ælfric's De temporibus anni*, p. 4; see also Martin Blake, ed. and trans., *Ælfric's De Temporibus Anni*.
[98] Peter S. Baker and Michael Lapidge, eds., *Byrhtferth's Enchiridion*, part 2, ch. 1, ll. 251–52.
[99] See Rahtz and Bullough, "The Parts of an Anglo-Saxon Mill," pp. 22–26, for a discussion of these compounds.
[100] Arnold Schröer, ed., *The Rule of St. Benedict*, ch. 66, p. 127.
[101] "The Battle of Brunanburh," ed. Elliot van Kirk Dobbie, *The Anglo-Saxon Minor Poems*, p. 17, l. 24.
[102] Liuzza, *Anglo-Saxon Prognostics*, pp. 59–77.

Bible and patristic authors whose sights and sounds became, through translation, the sights and sounds of the Anglo-Saxons.

The social relations that formed networks around the water-mill and the large-scale baking equipment that was associated with immense food renders differed from the social world of the quern and the small settlements where it was seen, such as West Stow. We think of small Anglo-Saxon settlements with grinding slaves working in their sheds, the sound of their querns clear to all passersby by day and into the night. Grinders at work were easily seen and heard since they worked within settlement precincts, as we see at Hamwic and West Stow. Querns were scaled to the human body and powered by human energy. Hence textual references to the quern focus on the grinding process and its results or on the figurative associations of the stone, its weight and its rotation. The proximity of quernstones to the general population was also true of earlier civilizations, which is why the quernstone became a synecdoche of daily life.

None of these points applied to mills. These devices were of ancient origin but did not lend themselves to analogy or observations in the way quernstones did. Anglo-Saxons were doubtless familiar with the sights and sounds of the water-mill and with its function as a major node in the food network. The mill was connected to several settlements by roads and paths along which carts moved grain in one direction and bags or jars of flour in the other. That these were different networks from those formed around querns is attested both by textual evidence and by the physical evidence, fully set out by Rahtz and Donald Bullough in their analysis of the mill excavated at Tamworth.[103] The water-mill was built to a scale that we would think of as industrial, not located within a settlement but at a point near water, which inhabitants would either have to travel to or access through the services of a carter. It was a shared facility in some cases, not a mill exclusive to one estate. A tidal water-mill found at Greenwich in 2009 had foundations measuring more than thirty by thirty-six feet at the foundations with a waterwheel more than twenty feet in diameter (timbers from which were felled in 1194).[104] The Tamworth mill was much smaller, to judge by the reconstruction Rahtz and Bullough sketch, with foundations perhaps half the size of the tidal mill. The millstone itself was less than a meter in diameter, perhaps twenty-eight inches, much larger than a typical quernstone with its diameter of fifteen to sixteen inches. The horizontal wheel of the Tamworth mill was considered to be "relatively small," 1.2 meters in diameter. Vertical wheels were generally larger; a typical small waterwheel might measure 2.5 meters in diameter, larger examples perhaps 4–6 meters.[105] The roar of such equipment must have been audible across the countryside.

---

[103] Rahtz and Bullough, "The Parts of an Anglo-Saxon Mill."
[104] Louise Jury, "Uncovered: Archaeologists Unearth Remnants of a Giant Medieval Watermill" (online resource).
[105] Magnus Alexander, *Mills* (online resource).

Water-mills and hand-mills performed comparable functions but did not produce comparable products. Hand-mills, whether rotary or saddle querns, were all the same: they shared a single design and function. But their products were different and individual, as were their operators. When settlements began depending on mills, they began using flour and meal prepared to general specifications, not those of their own quern operators. The water-mill could be adjusted to grind to various levels of fineness. At the same time, because it was mechanized, the water-mill introduced uniformity in ground grain that did not exist before. The mill was a large machine able to produce many times what a crew of grinders could do working with querns. Mills and querns operated simultaneously. Comparisons between these two forms of performing one task must have been inevitable, with the small-scale settlement depending on its grinding slaves and larger estates on their mills. Production scaled to querns could not withstand forces that centralized the economy. Millers paid for and asserted their rights to grind grain in a given area, a custom later known as *thirlage*, according to which those who provided an expensive service (the mill) had the right to force others to pay for it. The feudal aspect of this arrangement, visible in Chaucer's *Reeve's Tale*, with its cunning miller and his complicit household, had yet to emerge in the Old English period, although, as discussed in Chapter 3, the reeve's temptation to dishonesty was manifest to Wulfstan and others, and one of the Old English penitentials forbade priests from service as reeves.[106]

Texts referring to querns and mills are found throughout the range of writing in Old English, not surprising since both objects were common in the late as well as the early period. The narrative of progress invites us to think of mills replacing hand querns, but that development did not take place until the end of the Old English period. Quernstones continued to function in the hinterlands and in markets, in such places as Hamwic and West Stow, but also in York and other urban settlements. Some querns found at York date from the eleventh century. The London Exchange site and others show that the shipping and processing of querns continued later in the Anglo-Saxon period. The two forms of this food object functioned simultaneously, with settlement size and location determining whether quernstones or mills were the chief means of grinding grain.

The mill provides a striking example of human and mechanical power performing the same task, a single device created in two different scales. It is one of few food objects that could be adapted in this way. The oven was another, variable in both size and capacity, and the pottery wheel was a third. The introduction and wide acceptance of certain designs and fabric of pots from Ipswich in particular introduced a similar change. Pots, knives, and wooden bowls would continue to be made one at a time, although quality and design would change as the tools for making them

---

[106] Chaucer, "The Reeve's Tale," *The Riverside Chaucer*, ed. Larry D. Benson, pp. 77–84. See Chapter 3, pp. 72–73 and n. 57, above.

changed. Creating flour or meal from grain was different. In the Anglo-Saxon period two workers, depending on their tools, could produce vastly different quantities of flour. There is no evidence that the skilled technology replaced the unskilled technology until perhaps the twelfth century. But there is evidence that the older, slower, human-scaled process made a deeper imprint on observers and on creators of textual culture than its swifter, more complex successor. Psychological and conceptual associations with the quernstone are deep and various, while those with the mill are difficult to document. This contrast resonates with personal identity deriving from work with food. But it also constitutes an early example of the power of technology to distance people, including writers, from food culture. This is a distance modern consumers take for granted and a gap that also went unnoticed in Anglo-Saxon sources. Pottery, as we will now see, also presented the Anglo-Saxons with a contrast between slow and long-established practices and a swift new technology in the form of another spinning circle, the potter's wheel.

5

Pots for Cooking and Storage

An object with a single but essential purpose, the quern acquired its final form before it became a fixture of Anglo-Saxon settlements. Quernstones varied only slightly from one period of Anglo-Saxon history to the next or from region to region. They broke – most survive only as fragments – but not so often as objects made of clay, wood, or iron. Querns could be repurposed, but they could not be repaired. This was true of pottery as well. Imported pottery followed the same international trade routes as querns, but in most other respects pots form a contrast to quernstones. Most pottery was domestic and moved through distribution points that linked settlements both to markets and to manufacturing sites. Themselves bulk commodities, pots served as containers for bulk goods such as wine and oil. Pots were produced with successively new techniques using soils that can be tracked geographically and chronologically. Not surprisingly, pottery fragments comprise a body of evidence that has grown in significance as the dating and localizing of ceramics has become more precise. Remnants are numerous and often site specific. As a result, ceramic evidence has become crucial to the economic analysis of many ancient and early medieval cultures, Anglo-Saxon England among them.[1]

Pottery also illuminates food networks within settlements, including those that trace the preparation and serving of food. Food remains are sometimes preserved on sherds – for example, baked onto the inner surface of a cooking pot. Such evidence connects cookware to diet and to a settlement's resources. A single sherd might bear witness both to a pot's place of manufacture and to the food cooked in the pot. We see, then, that pots – and cups, pitchers, and associated ceramic forms – involve more parts of the food network than do querns or most other food objects. After exploring ways in which pottery has been used to document social identity, I will examine the trajectory of pottery at a variety of Anglo-Saxon settlements, from early to late.

---

[1] See Chris Wickham, *Framing the Early Middle Ages*, pp. 692–824, for analysis of systems of exchange in which ceramic evidence plays a central role.

Pottery and social identity

Whether imported or locally made, pots illustrate distinctions between elite and ordinary consumers. Pots can also be used to explore more subtle aspects of social identity. The emphasis usually falls on decorated ceramics, feeding the impression that other wares did not communicate information about those who made and used them. We will see that even cooking pots, the most common form of pottery that survives, reveal social identity. The familiar parallel between imported and domestic objects, and decorative and practical applications is not always reliable. Use matters. Imported wares were sometimes put to humble uses, including cooking, and sometimes imports were used by the people who imported them, including traders and artisans whose lives otherwise little resembled those of their customers. Locally produced wares also served as markers of identity for those who knew and cared about their manufacture and ownership history. Social identity, in short, is not a matter of elite preference for imports.

According to J. G. Hurst, it had long been the view that all Anglo-Saxon pottery postdated c. 450, the so-called *Adventus Saxonum*. The possibility of earlier imports was discounted, along with continuities between Anglo-Saxon and earlier forms of pottery. Recent studies allow for multiple influences on Anglo-Saxon styles and manufacturing techniques, thus widening the range of social identities and multiplying ways of associating them with ceramic evidence, such as linking early pottery to Iron Age wares. According to Hurst, wheel-thrown pots and industrial-scale production ceased after the Romans withdrew in the late fourth century. For the next three centuries, the Early Saxon period (350–650), pots were handmade (that is, not thrown on a wheel); these wares are often referred to as "domestic" or "household" pottery. The Middle Saxon period (650–850) is known for Ipswich ware (partly handmade) and Thetford ware. The Late Saxon period (850–1100) saw new types, including Stamford ware.[2] Pots produced on slow wheels date from the seventh century in East Anglia, Northumbria, Norfolk, and Yorkshire. A point of change emerges early in the eighth century with the introduction of Ipswich ware, the name given to wheel-thrown pots finished in kilns large enough for mass production.[3] Also important is the mid-ninth-century transition from Ipswich ware to Thetford ware, which was produced on a faster wheel and which, as a result, had a thinner profile.[4]

One function of networks is to promote change by making the distribution of new forms possible across as well as within regions. Changes in the manufacture of ordinary pots seem to support a narrative of progress in which ever-better wares replaced older forms. There is much evidence to

[2] This typology, proposed by J. G. Hurst over thirty-five years ago, has been used, with some adaptation, in many site reports. See Hurst, "The Pottery," pp. 284–85.
[3] Hurst, "The Pottery," pp. 283–84.
[4] Stanley West, "Excavations at Cox Lane," pp. 285–86.

support that narrative. However, site reports also document the continued use of older ceramic forms alongside the newer wares. Paul Blinkhorn has used evidence of persisting older forms to challenge the narrative and, at the same time, to make a compelling case for the power of ordinary objects to contribute to social identity. The kinds of wares Blinkhorn discusses were once dismissed as "crude domestic utensils." Lacking marks that conveyed status, they were not seen as contributing to the study of identity even though they might have been valued at one time because they preserved information about the inhabitants' origins.[5] Blinkhorn argues that decorated wares are often emphasized at the expense of ordinary wares. He notes that meaningful statements about some 50,000 sherds of pottery from West Stow were confined to those which bore some decoration. They amounted to only two percent of the total. The rest are said to have "yielded no useful information."[6]

But ordinary pots elsewhere have yielded so much information that archaeologists have found the data difficult to synthesize. Ordinary objects have been used to construct pottery fabric sequences that are determined by microscopic analysis of the clays from which pots were made. Site reports sometimes outline multiple categories of fabric groups defined by differences in soil and sand, setting out types, sub-types, and even finer divisions. In Blinkhorn's view, data refined in this way do not lead to meaningful conclusions about sites, pots, or the people who made and used them. Tellingly, fabric analysts themselves sometimes seem unsure what their numerous, finely graded categories might mean.[7] Blinkhorn emphasizes instead observable formal differences in pots, such as tempering techniques and shape. In his view inhabitants of settlements during the early and mid-Saxon periods clung "with determination" to remnants of identity associated with their origins. Their preferences are documented in the persistence of certain shapes and techniques, not in the fabric of their wares. He proposes that we look at "the social standing and cultural origins" of those who used vessels as well as at the composition or fabric of vessels.[8] Likewise, Karen I. Meadows stresses that vessel form and function are "integral to the study of consumption" and also notes that fine wares were sometimes used in cooking. An "emphasis on the social context of consumption" requires "the integration of various types of 'data,'" Meadows writes, but such integration "does not necessarily fit with the original intentions of the excavation, the specialists and the resulting publication."[9] H. E. M. Cool also criticizes the way in which site reports are assembled. "In some areas the reports appear to be written

[5] Paul Blinkhorn, "Habitus, Social Identity and Anglo-Saxon Pottery," quoting J. N. L. Myres, *Anglo-Saxon Pottery*, p. 120.

[6] Blinkhorn, "Habitus," p. 120.

[7] Blinkhorn, "Habitus," p. 122. He points out that archaeologists themselves are frequently not persuaded that their categories are distinct and that they sometimes prefer broad classes of fabic; see p. 118 for examples.

[8] Blinkhorn, "Habitus," pp. 123–24.

[9] Karen I. Meadows, "Much Ado about Nothing," pp. 24–26.

mainly for the handful of fellow specialists who work in the field, blithely ignoring the fact that the ultimate aim must be to enable the integration of their information with all the rest of the data from the site."[10] Cool hopes to inspire archaeologists of Roman Britain to mend their ways; Anglo-Saxon archaeologists would do well to heed Blinkhorn, Meadows, and others who have made the same point about their field. It is not only other specialists who need useful data but also humanists whose concerns about material contexts lead them to reports even archaeologists find intractable.

Those who argue for broader interpretive frameworks for pottery would like to change the way settlement pottery preferences are interpreted. Blinkhorn and C. G. Cumberpatch have used pottery to contest the narrative of progress, a common-sense assumption that has silently shaped the history of pottery in Anglo-Saxon England. According to this principle, new wares perform better and hence replace old ones. The narrative is premised on functionality and pragmatism. Taking an alternative view, Blinkhorn regards functionality as an ideological construct, not as common sense.[11] Blinkhorn thinks other factors, especially ties to ancestry and tradition, are equally important in explaining why ceramic forms and fabrics change. His critique, like that offered by Cumberpatch, borrows from processual archaeology and anthropology (see Chapter 1) and is guided by Pierre Bourdieu's concept of the *habitus*, with its "classificatory schemes" that, in Bourdieu's words, establish the "regularities of the social world for which and through which there *is* a social world."[12] Putting this concept to the test, Blinkhorn discusses two sites just thirty kilometers apart, Pennyland (Buckinghamshire, early to mid-Saxon) and Raunds (Northamptonshire, also early to mid-Saxon). Potters' practices there were not "the product of obedience to rules" but were instead what Blinkhorn (after Bourdieu) describes as examples of "conductorless orchestration." This means that the practices were prevailing customs that structured craft production and perpetuated technique and style across generations.[13] At both sites, however, a conductor did take charge in the mid-Saxon period, changing the "orchestration" of the site and its *habitus* along with it.

At North Raunds (Northamptonshire), cooking wares tempered with crushed rock were replaced by those tempered with sand. Those tempered by sand would have been quicker to produce, so this technique represents a "triumph of functionality," in Blinkhorn's words. At Pennyland, however, tempering with crushed rock became more common, not less, indicating that the technique supposedly considered less functional at North Raunds was preferred at Pennyland. Blinkhorn believes that

---

[10] H. E. M. Cool, *Eating and Drinking in Roman Britain*, p. 3.

[11] Blinkhorn, "Habitus," p. 121.

[12] Pierre Bourdieu, *The Logic of Practice*, p. 140, quoted in C. G. Cumberpatch, "Towards a Phenomenological Approach to the Study of Medieval Pottery," pp. 125–26 (emphasis in Bourdieu).

[13] Blinkhorn, "Habitus," p. 115. Cumberpatch repeats Bourdieu's image of a "conductorless" social body in "Towards a Phenomenological Approach to the Study of Medieval Pottery," pp. 125–26.

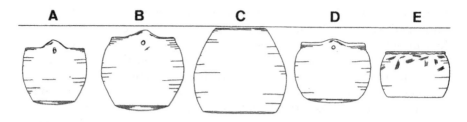

Figure 5. The Flixborough Early to Middle Saxon type series and pottery sequence, Type 1.

the inhabitants had different cultural origins and that they "continued their traditional practices through time and across generations" because they valued cultural form more than function.[14] Evidence at Mucking was comparable. Differences in finish between two categories of pot suggest different origins for those who produced them. Chaff-tempered pots formed less than 10 percent of the finds at Pennyland and Raunds, but 90 percent at Mucking, where chaff-tempering was more common in one part of the site than in others. Blinkhorn argues that the occupants of most parts of Mucking had different backgrounds and persisted in techniques that were familiar to them even though "other, and arguably more efficient, possibilities" were available. He connects this difference in technique to a difference in bowl shapes that also spoke to ethnic origins.[15] The narrative of progress does not explain the potters' decisions.

Blinkhorn does not focus on slight differentiations in fabric but on evidence of form and manufacture. He shows the significance of details such as finish and the location of lugs, the ear-like extensions that, when pierced, could be used to suspend pots over a flame. Both details might have been cultural markers and conveyed "social information" because some pots would have been prominent and "extremely visible." Lugs are seen on three pots in Figure 5, which shows a pottery sequence from Flixborough.[16] Blinkhorn reminds us that ordinary vessels and containers, storage pots and cooking pots alike, were seen by some people all the time. They formed part of the household's identity and visibly registered its participation in the heritage of the settlement. It is customary to associate pots with cooking rather than with storage, but the latter function was also routine. Foods such as grains, spices, and sauces, for example, were always at hand, and would have been kept in pottery vessels or in leather and wooden containers. Not all the containers stayed in the cooking area; some would have been dug into the earth or kept in outbuildings, as we

[14] Blinkhorn, "Habitus," p. 119.
[15] Blinkhorn, "Habitus," pp. 119–20.
[16] Blinkhorn, "Habitus," p. 123.

see in the reconstructed huts at West Stow. Although these displays cannot be regarded as archaeological evidence, they give a concrete impression of how ordinary things might have been displayed. Part of the visual environment, the various shapes and forms of pots might have recalled ancestral identity and local customs.

Pots conserved cultural information as well as foodstuffs because potters wanted them to do so. Richard Hodges describes potters as conservative, "loath to deviate from the wares that were their staple."[17] This claim addresses the effect but not its possible causes in the *habitus*, which include ancestral identity and technical limitations. Innovation took place slowly, no doubt, and changes in the production of pottery would, over time, have forced potters to change their ways. Methods of manufacture were one way in which pottery preserved and transmitted social meaning. As methods for making it changed, so too did the meaning of pottery as a cultural marker. Pots thrown by hand on a slow wheel would have been subject to variation in many details. At West Stow, for example, one can see many irregularities in funeral urns. Although similar in size, some pots are more symmetrical than others, and there are diverse approaches to decoration. Those pots communicated not only cultural identity but also the distinguishing features of a particular potter's work, difficult for us to recognize but not so for the potter's contemporaries. Decoration on this pottery was highly distinctive across many sites in Norfolk and Suffolk in the sixth century and must have been readily identifiable.

In a study of stamps used to mark pots, C. J. Arnold refers to "rules" that potters followed, regimes in which he found differences between the work from West Stow and that from other settlements.[18] Rules such as those Arnold refers to are the heart of the *habitus* (not a concept Arnold uses). To discuss pottery in terms of the *habitus* is to see it within the settlement, where it served as a marker of tradition and continuity. But this function seems to have eroded over time as new forms became available and reached settlements through the channels of the food network; at that point new forms encountered traditional forms. Starting in the eighth century with the spread of Ipswich ware, there must have been periodic collisions between old forms of cooking pots and new ones. At larger sites such clashes would have been more common, since markets would have brought new wares such as Ipswich jars and pitchers along with the commodities they contained.

The most important points to be learned from a survey of ceramic forms, it seems to me, are: first, that the functionalist premise according to which newer is better distorts the evidence; and, second, that the conservatism partly created by the power of pots to evoke origins and ancestry is stronger at some sites than others, and at early- rather than

[17] Richard Hodges, *The Hamwih Pottery*, p. 59.
[18] See C. J. Arnold, "Early Pottery of the Illington-Lackford Type," pp. 358–59.

late-dated settlements. We will see that on large estates as well as small ones, pottery made elsewhere did not completely replace wares that were locally made. Local wares might have been preferred for cultural as well as economic reasons if they affirmed a traditional identity. Pots from outside the site also signified identity, however, which might have stemmed from their novelty and their method of manufacture. If functionalists are right, the new forms won out because they outperformed the older ones. Alternatively, scholars who believe in the power of the *habitus* will be inclined to believe that older forms persisted because they spoke to established concepts of identity. The evidence invites us to consider the site in the broad context of its food networks and look at larger, external factors that, as they shaped and reshaped the economy and the landscape, also reshaped pots.

Cooking pots and early settlement contexts

I will discuss cooking pots from a range of sites, including the small, early agricultural settlements of Shakenoak and West Stow, and two different market sites. The first is Ipswich, the most important site for Middle Saxon pottery, and, in association with it, the nearby settlements of Riby Crossroads, North Raunds, Pennyland, Barham, and Coddenham. The second is Southampton (Hamwic), an emporium that lacked extended relations with its surrounding area. Then I turn to Flixborough and Goltho, both with long histories. All these sites experienced changes in pottery fabric over time. At some of them old forms and fabrics continued to be used even as newer forms became available. If we associate identity with difference, it should be clear that pottery from these sites registered meaningful changes in identity.

A few general observations will be useful. As is true of most food objects, cooking pots are seldom found in contexts that suggest their domestic uses, such as proximity to charcoal from a hearth or stones with burn marks. When found, such assemblies must be regarded as fortuitous rather than as certain evidence of food preparation a thousand years ago. Cooking pots have distinctive features, including a wide mouth and an outward-turned (or everted) rim. Pots used for cooking tend to be small and squat, while those used for storage and shipping are generally taller and larger. Pots survive mostly in fragments (or sherds), but in rare cases enough pieces remain so that a vessel can be reassembled in near-complete form. An example is a whole cooking pot, with an everted rim, found at Coppergate, York, and dated between 975 and early to mid-eleventh century; it measures 125 mm in height (Figure 6).[19] Burn marks show that some pots were set or hung over flame. Other vessels, which were used

[19] For discussion, see A. J. Mainman, *Anglo-Scandinavian Pottery from 16–22 Coppergate*, plate XXVII, shown actual size. For other whole vessels, see Richard Hodges, *Dark Age Economics*, p. 146 (three examples of Ipswich ware).

Figure 6. Torksey-type ware cooking pot, York; no. 2057, 16–22 Coppergate. Scale approximately 1:1.

either for cooking or for storage, also retain food traces, sometimes carbonized. Various residues, including wax to seal food deposits, appear on pottery fragments. Pottery lacking burn marks or cooked residue inside is assumed to have been used for storage; those containers are described here as crocks rather than as cooking pots. The pottery described below might have been used in cooking, in storage, or in shipping. In addition, some vessels from the earlier period, such as those from West Stow, served ceremonial purposes in burials.

Early sites: Shakenoak and West Stow

Pots from the sixth and seventh centuries were made by hand at or near the sites of their discovery. Several were found at Shakenoak, Oxfordshire, a site dated from the mid-fifth century to the seventh century, which was no longer occupied after the middle of the eighth century.[20] A locally made pot found in a ditch was made in the fifth century, its fragments forming the upper part of a vessel with two upstanding, pierced lugs and shallow pouches, the feature important to Blinkhorn's discussion of how ceramic forms encode cultural information. Sometimes called cups, the pouches were thought to have protected the knotted ends of cord used to hang the pot over fire.[21] According to A. C. C. Brodribb, such pots were typical in the fifth to sixth centuries but rarer in the seventh century. Other pots at the site resembled this one, and similar cooking pots are known from Sutton Courtenay. There were said to be no earlier parallels "in this country."[22] The lug was not a feature exclusive to early pots but it is more often found on early rather than late wares.

Lugs persisted. A second, later collection of sherds from Shakenoak, seventh or perhaps eighth century, includes one with an upstanding, pierced lug and remains of a shallow pouch, fragments of a crudely made, upright-walled vessel. Cooking pots with pierced holes intended for thongs were also found at Hamwic.[23] A pot with a similar pouch was found at New Winties Farm, Eynsham, and has been dated to the late sixth century or after.[24] Other early sites producing similar pots include West Stow and Bromeswell, located near Sutton Hoo, an early Saxon settlement clearly associated with the remains of an earlier Roman settlement.[25] Field walking by the Suffolk Archaeological Unit and surface plowing at Bromeswell turned up scattered early Anglo-Saxon sherds along with Ipswich- and Thetford-type ware. Pottery wasters (i.e., defective pieces) and kiln debris, evidence of pottery making at the site, include a pierced upright lug.[26] Fragments with pierced lugs have been found at many other sites, including Thetford and Ipswich (Cox Lane). Examples of such lugs have also been found on larger pots from the Late Saxon period, including some from Flixborough (see below).[27] The upright lug, with or without pouches, was not a standard feature of cooking pots. Many pots seem either to have been set directly on embers or rested on trivet-like bases rather than hung over coals.

The lug might be more important as a marker of origin than of function. Some lugs and cups have been seen as copies of the "ears" on bronze bowls from the Iron Age, a kind of continuity once thought unlikely. An

---

[20] A. C. C. Brodribb, A. R. Hands, and D. R. Walker, *Excavations at Shakenoak Farm*, p. 29.

[21] Brodribb, Hands, and Walker, *Excavations at Shakenoak Farm*, p. 61, no. 399; 5th century, Period F.3.

[22] Brodribb, Hands, and Walker, *Excavations at Shakenoak Farm*, p. 58; they note that cooking pots numbered 399 and 400 are similar. At Sutton Courtenay, they refer to evidence from houses XXIII and XXIV.

[23] Hodges, *The Hamwih Pottery*, p. 7.

[24] Brodribb, Hands, and Walker, *Excavations at Shakenoak Farm*, p. 148.

[25] Stanley West, *A Corpus of Anglo-Saxon Material from Suffolk*, p. 13.

[26] Tom Williamson, *Sutton Hoo and its Landscape*, pp. 68–69, notes that the church at Bromeswell is some 200 meters from the Roman site; other churches are as close as 50 meters to Roman sites.

[27] G. C. Dunning, J. G. Hurst, J. N. L. Myres, and F. Tischler, *Anglo-Saxon Pottery*, pp. 16–17.

example is a hanging bronze (copper-alloy) bowl from Brightwell cemetery, a globular vessel with two triangular upright pierced lugs.[28] Lugs are also believed to have been copied from continental models. Hurst suggested that "peaked lugs" link early Saxon wares to Frisian pots, an idea that Blinkhorn has recently revived.[29] Blinkhorn studied this feature in connection with another, the footring, which is seldom found on pots without lugs. He comments that pots with footrings were more subject to thermal shock than those without them. A preference for lugged vessels with footrings, even though they did not perform well, suggests to Blinkhorn that these features retained "some sort of social or cultural significance." Blinkhorn writes that footed lugged vessels are found in various locations on the Continent but "are extremely rare in the Jutish region," which potentially makes them a marker of identity.[30] This feature becomes rarer at Anglo-Saxon sites. Such a sign of origin or ancestry (and hence identity) would weaken over time, especially as forms made elsewhere began to mix with the settlement's traditional wares. However, locally made pots were sometimes preferred to newer styles, as site reports show.

At West Stow, occupied from the fifth to the seventh centuries, most pottery was locally made. Stanley West found no evidence of firing places, suggesting to him that "firing was probably done in small quantities in surface bonfires." Because no wasters were found, he hypothesizes that pottery at the site "was of an on-demand craft rather than an organized industry producing great quantities of pottery beyond local needs."[31] The potter at West Stow would have had other work and would have used his skill as a potter only occasionally and probably seasonally. The earliest pottery from the site consists of sherds of "corrugated" or grooved ware and "faceted-angled" ware, both from the fifth century. Most pottery from the site is the form called the Illington-Lackford type, found in both Norfolk (Illington) and Suffolk (Lackford) in the sixth century.[32] This pottery was widely distributed across these areas. There is a gap between the late sixth- and early seventh-century evidence from the site. In the final phase of the settlement, which West dates to the seventh century, with some late sixth-century objects, Ipswich ware begins to appear.[33] West believes that "it is difficult to stretch the West Stow evidence to accommodate settlement continuity to 650–750," especially since Ipswich ware would have taken some time to penetrate "into the rural areas." He raises the possibility that Ipswich ware might have been introduced in a manure spread from off the site during an agricultural phase; this is probable, since the site was used

---

[28] This bowl was intended to be suspended but not evidently over a fire; found in a grave, it contained cremated bones. West, *A Corpus of Anglo-Saxon Material from Suffolk*, p. 13 and p. 127 (illustration). Probable date: sixth or seventh century, p. 13.
[29] Hurst, "The Pottery," p. 303.
[30] Blinkhorn, "Habitus," p. 123.
[31] West, *West Stow Revisited*, p. 35.
[32] Arnold, "Early Anglo-Saxon Pottery of the 'Illington-Lackford' Type."
[33] West, *West Stow Revisited*, p. 25, table 15.

for agriculture after it was abandoned.[34] West's charting of developments over two centuries suggests that little changed in the function of West Stow as a settlement. That would seem to have been the case at Shakenoak as well. Such stability would make it more likely that pots, and other food objects too, would preserve cultural capital.

Ipswich and its settlement network

Ipswich and Hamwic, which I discuss below, were both centers of economic power. The settlement history of Ipswich reaches into the Middle Saxon period and shows the *habitus* operating differently from what we see at West Stow or Shakenoak. By the early eighth century Ipswich was a manufacturing center for the pottery that would become known by the settlement's name. This ware was fashioned on a slow wheel, possibly turned by hand, resulting in vessels with thick sides that were fired at high temperatures in a kiln.[35] Hodges has suggested that pottery making in Ipswich goes back to the Early Saxon period and may have its origins in the production of high-status funerary ware. Blinkhorn has proposed the second quarter of the eighth century as the beginning of greatly increased production at the site.[36] The mass production of Ipswich ware meant that the settlement had been transformed into a specialized industrial site, a center with lines to supporting settlements nearby. Ipswich ware spread across many regions, usually because of what was contained in the jars and pitchers made there rather than because of the pots themselves. Hodges hypothesizes that social identity played a central role in creating the pottery industry in Ipswich – not the identity of potters, however, but that of secular or ecclesiastical leaders who were aware of continental pottery forms and who wanted them copied by local artisans. This demand was met, Hodges argues, by "the apparent centralization of the East Anglian pottery industry in Ipswich" in the late seventh century. At this point, and perhaps not by coincidence, pagan funerary rites were suppressed, underscoring the role of patronage, either royal or ecclesiastical, in shaping the economy at Ipswich. Hodges suggests that the earliest stages of the regional economy centered at Ipswich might have been "connected with the kind of kingship witnessed at Sutton Hoo," which many date to the same period.[37] If so, changes in pottery at Ipswich would have been part of large-scale factors reshaping the economy and food-related social identities along with it.

[34] West, *West Stow Revisited*, pp. 31–32.
[35] This description of Ipswich ware is taken from Hurst, "The Pottery," pp. 299–300, with dating from Helena Hamerow, *Early Medieval Settlements*, pp. 122–23.
[36] John Moreland, "The Significance of Production in Eighth-Century England," p. 78, citing Blinkhorn on the *Ipswich Ware Project*. See Paul Blinkhorn, "Of Cabbages and Kings." Blinkhorn bases his dating on the greatly increased use of coins at Ipswich starting at this time, and the arrival of Ipswich ware in London at this time.
[37] Hodges, *The Hamwih Pottery*, p. 60.

Blinkhorn offers a competing suggestion for the development of distinctive ware at Ipswich. Ipswich might logically seem to be a point of innovation, since it was the point of origin for new forms. In Blinkhorn's view, however, Ipswich was a point of adaptation and continuity, not innovation. Before the development of Ipswich ware, he points out, pottery at the settlement did not differ from the traditions "of the other major middle Saxon settlements." Ipswich ware was new everywhere, including to Ipswich, because, according to Blinkhorn, it was modeled on Frisian pottery. He suggests that in the late seventh century and early eighth century the site was dominated by "a large Frisian presence." He believes that "the basic shape, upright rim, peaked lugs, stamp-decoration and range of functional types" in Ipswich ware all "can be paralleled on contemporary Frisian pottery" and that such features were enough to make Ipswich ware what he calls "culturally 'correct'" to the dominant population.[38]

One immediate consequence of the industrial focus of Ipswich would have been the transformation of nearby settlements into supply sites. At two sites within ten kilometers of Ipswich, Barham and Coddenham, large quantities of coins and metalwork have been found by metal detection (the sites have not been excavated). Imports that predate the industrialization of pottery at Ipswich have been found at both of the smaller sites, and metalwork found at both sites suggests that they were centers for production.[39] Trading activity at these two sites points to networks of trade and exchange that might have fostered the establishment of a manufacturing center at Ipswich. More evidence of the network taking shape around Ipswich comes from three nearby sites, two already mentioned: Riby Crossroads, Pennyland, and North Raunds. Blinkhorn suggests that these settlements had become specialized in the mid-Saxon period, each with a focus on supplying food for export, and that each site was in contact with Ipswich. North Raunds, he notes, was "extremely active in trade" and was "practising specialized commodity production by the mid-eighth century." It would seem that North Raunds concentrated on production of a single cereal crop (an unusual specialization) and that Riby Crossroads and Pennyland were centers for raising cattle. Ipswich ware and lava querns at these sites, according to Blinkhorn, suggest both "contact with a redistribution center and a trade in surplus stock."[40] Ipswich had "an exchange relationship with its local hinterland," in Chris Wickham's words, a system of bulk exchange within East Anglia involving high-status sites (but not exclusive to them) and directed by market rather than political forces.[41] At both Riby Crossroads and Pennyland, dispersed settlement structures were replaced, in the early eighth century, by new domestic dwellings, new enclosures, and, at the former, drove ways. Blinkhorn sees such changes to settlement plans as indicative of a new

[38] Blinkhorn, "Habitus," p. 121. See also Paul Blinkhorn, "Stranger in a Strange Land."
[39] Hamerow, *Early Medieval Settlements*, pp. 186–88.
[40] Blinkhorn, "Of Cabbages and Kings," p. 10.
[41] Wickham, *Framing the Early Middle Ages*, pp. 686 and 810.

purpose for the sites, a change "from broad-based agriculture to intensive cattle-ranching," with the change explained by the establishment of a production center at Ipswich.[42] The planned specialization of large sites such as Ipswich and Hamwic (see below) forced the specialization of smaller settlements nearby, using them to meet increased needs brought about by the growth of a new industry.[43]

The functional premise would suggest that, as new wares spread from elite locations, part-time potters at West Stow and similar small sites found that their skills had become obsolete. Yet locally produced pots continued to be used even as new wares appeared. The new processes would not necessarily render older methods obsolete, because new processes went along with new forms, and new forms with new purposes. Shipping and storage are chief among those new purposes in the case of Ipswich ware, those being the chief functions of Ipswich ware pitchers. Most Ipswich ware found outside Ipswich takes the form of jars, including pitchers, assumed to have been used specifically for storage and transport. Widely distributed in Norfolk and Suffolk, Ipswich ware has also been found at Brixworth and Trapston (Northamptonshire) and Wicken Bonhunt (Essex). The most northerly finds of Ipswich ware to date are from Wharram Percy (Yorkshire).[44] The size and thickness of Ipswich ware vessels found there suggested to A. M. Slowikowski that they were associated with the wine trade, since Ipswich ware was the only native pottery found there that included pitchers.[45]

What about pottery within Ipswich? Of the pots found in Ipswich, according to Hurst, the "basic form" was "a small squat cooking pot," with an approximate diameter of four to six inches and a height of five to seven inches.[46] Of the forms catalogued by West, 83 percent were cooking pots between four and eight inches in diameter; three-quarters were between four and one-half and six and one-half inches in diameter. Those over eight inches in diameter West thought could have been used either for cooking or for storage.[47] Imports account for some 15 percent of the wares excavated from Middle Saxon Ipswich, wares chiefly from the Mayen area of northwest Germany, with Flanders and northern France also represented. Although pitchers and amphorae dominate the assemblages, some cooking pots were also included, suggesting that some imported pottery was for trade and some for the traders' own use. Imports, chiefly Badorf ware from the middle Rhineland and dated 800–850, are found in pits with

[42] Blinkhorn, "Of Cabbages and Kings," and Susan Oosthuizen, "Medieval Field Systems," pp. 120–22.
[43] On planned settlements and an eighth-century "takeoff" of the economy, see Wickham, *Framing the Early Middle Ages*, pp. 682–88, and Hamerow, *Early Medieval Settlements*, pp. 122–23.
[44] Hurst, "The Pottery," p. 303.
[45] A. M. Slowikowski, P. Blinkhorn, A. Mainman, A. Vince, and A. Wood, "The Anglo-Saxon and Medieval Pottery," pp. 69–70.
[46] Hurst, "The Pottery," p. 300, citing Stanley West, "Excavations at Cox Lane."
[47] West, "Excavations at Cox Lane," pp. 247–48.

both Ipswich ware and Thetford ware, confirming the mid-ninth century as the period of changeover from the former to the latter.[48]

Domestic and some imported vessels were put to similar uses at Ipswich, and this fact has implications for identity. It seems that traders brought their own pots with them, and there is evidence of this custom from Hamwic as well, suggesting an association of traders with the food objects of their own cultures. Their *habitus* was, in this sense, portable if not exportable. Foreign wares in their imported setting (i.e., in Ipswich or Hamwic) created a point of difference in ordinary cookware. The contrast between domestic objects and those brought by the traders could either have stabilized identity, making those who used either one type or the other more conscious of their ways, or undercut the identity-making power of older pottery by encouraging the use of something new. In an assessment of imported wares at Hamwic, however, D. H. Brown doubts that imports are invariably distinctive and highly valued. Brown challenges the view that imported pottery in Hamwic had special significance. He suggests that imports were not clearly intended to serve any one class of resident and that an imported pot was often "just a pot."[49]

Hamwic and its pottery

At Hamwic (Southampton), as at Ipswich, pottery evidence points to both the extent of trading activity and to the domestic needs of the traders and their suppliers. Again, as at Ipswich, the function of the *habitus* needs to be seen in relation to the networks created by the site's function as a trading center. A site created for commercial exchange no doubt had older roots of some kind, but given the extensive planning that was necessary to create these large, carefully planned sites, links to the past would have been remote. Hodges thinks that Hamwic was established by royal order, a market town of some 45 hectares (about 111 acres), complete with metalled roads and street grid, and occupied by perhaps four thousand people.[50] It seems that traders brought their own pots with them, suggesting a strong association of traders with the food objects of their own cultures. The traders, Hodges writes, found local pottery to be "culturally unacceptable" and chiefly used the pots they imported.[51] If so, Hamwic would resemble Ipswich in this matter. In both locations, according to this hypothesis, traders identified with their own cooking and storage pots, and often avoided those of local manufacture. Hodges notes that traders at Hamwic sometimes used local wares. The difference is that at Hamwic the potters did not begin making pitchers and bowls, "unlike their counterparts in Ipswich, who must have been greatly influenced by the utensils in the baggage of the aliens." The traders at Hamwic did not use their own

---

[48] West, "Excavations at Cox Lane," pp. 285–86.
[49] Duncan H. Brown, "The Social Significance of Imported Medieval Pottery," pp. 108–11.
[50] Richard Hodges, *Good-bye to the Vikings?*, p. 166.
[51] Hodges, *The Hamwih Pottery*, p. 93. See also *Dark Age Economics*, pp. 91–92.

wares exclusively, he notes, "for the two types of pottery always occur in association."[52]

Cultural preference might not be the only factor, since at Hamwic, according to Brown, the imported wares were distinctly superior to (i.e., more functional than) those made locally.[53] Can the traders' preference have been based on function, meaning that their own pots were more efficient than wares available locally? Some sense of identity rooted in their home communities was communicated through the inanimate objects the traders carried, we can be sure, and Anglo-Saxon residents cannot have failed to notice that traders brought pottery with them. It is significant that potters at Hamwic did not feel compelled to produce wares like those brought by the traders. Hamwic was a collection and distribution point, perhaps a finishing point, but not a center of production like Ipswich. Since local and imported wares were used "in association," it might have been the case that the Anglo-Saxon residents used imported wares just as the traders used local wares. The point is that the presence of new types of pot did not move the locals to imitate them. Hodges suggests that local wares were "culturally unacceptable" to traders, an ambiguous remark. Were local wares poorly made? Did the traders' own wares perform better? The phrase "culturally unacceptable" confuses terms Blinkhorn is at pains to separate: that is, cultural acceptability does not depend on function but on traditional associations of forms with a given people's history. What made some pots valuable, Brown seems to be saying, was not that they denoted heritage but that they functioned better than others. (It is safe to say that users from any culture would reject pots that could not withstand heat.) It is logical for people to prefer what is familiar to them, especially if the familiar (i.e., to the traders) is thought to function better than what they find elsewhere (i.e., in foreign emporia). Locals who noted the traders' preference might well have understood it and have made the same choice for themselves in a similar situation. It is not impossible that, like the traders, craft workers who moved to Hamwic for a season brought pots from their own regions with them. Wickham has noted that the type of pottery made at Hamwic, which he describes as "fairly utilitarian," was not widely circulated in the areas around the settlement, another sign of weak links between Hamwic and its surroundings.[54] Archaeologists have commented on the homogeneity of Hamwic, created by strong control from outside and seen in the remarkable degree of uniformity at the site.[55] In a closely regulated and densely settled area, pottery and other food objects might have functioned effectively as registers of identity.

Cooking pots are prominent among the pottery finds at Hamwic and have been found in all classes of Middle Saxon pottery there. They include

---

[52] Hodges, *The Hamwih Pottery*, p. 93.
[53] Brown, "The Social Significance of Imported Medieval Pottery," p. 111.
[54] Wickham, *Framing the Early Middle Ages*, p. 810.
[55] On homogeneity, see Mark Brisbane, "Hamwic (Saxon Southampton)," pp. 101 and 104, and Jennifer Bourdillon, "The Animal Provisioning of Saxon Southampton," pp. 122–23.

grass-tempered, chalk-tempered, sand-tempered, shell-tempered, and other wares. Pots included in the first and third categories are what Hodges describes as "large cooking pots."[56] J. Timby and P. Andrews describe some "simple hand-made cooking pots" from Hamwic that could have been "quite easily produced by individual households." The production of these forms points to "a continuity of style" regarded as "a common feature of the local Hamwic assemblage," an echo of the stylistic conservatism Hodges attributes to potters and possibly an implication that Hamwic existed long enough to develop locally made pots of its own. The decoration of some pots, Timby and Andrews believe, might indicate a second stage, "the emergence of a more specialised mode of production."[57] Timby and Andrews suggest that specialist craft workers chose to work at sites that facilitated the manufacture and distribution of products. However, at Hamwic neither the potters making traditional wares nor the specialists who perhaps (Timby and Andrews are tentative) produced more sophisticated wares were responsive to imported forms, which they did not copy. As a further sign of conservatism at both levels, neither specialists nor potters making traditional wares adopted the potter's wheel.[58] This decision might seem to reinforce traditions of social and cultural identity and to support the operation of the occupants within the *habitus*. But residents of market sites – who might have occupied those sites only seasonally – and residents of permanent sites would have experienced the stabilizing powers of the *habitus* in different ways.

Extended settlement contexts: Flixborough and Goltho

Sites discussed so far offer limited opportunity to examine an extended sequence of pottery in which tension between function and local tradition might have developed. Early hinterland sites such as West Stow were abandoned. Activity at Hamwic seems to have peaked in the Middle Saxon period. The detailed pottery sequences at both Flixborough (North Lincolnshire) and Goltho (Lincolnshire) extend through the Middle Saxon period into the later period. The latter two sites both show a diminishing role for pottery as a marker of identity in the later period, when pottery types were more varied.

Chris Loveluck has shown that Flixborough moved through several identities as a settlement. He condenses them into four phases. His account begins with an aristocratic *habitus* and culture marked by feasting and hunting in the eighth century (which, in the site report, is designated as Period 3 of the occupation sequence), a prosperity to which the site

---

[56] Hodges, *The Hamwih Pottery*, pp. 6–9.
[57] J. Timby and P. Andrews, "The Pottery," p. 209. Decorated cooking pots have been found elsewhere, including Portchester and Whitby. See Barry Cunliffe, *Excavations at Portchester Castle*, p. 187, and Charles Peers and C. A. Ralegh Radford, "The Saxon Monastery of Whitby," pp. 79–80.
[58] Timby and Andrews, "The Pottery," pp. 207–9.

returned in the tenth century. This was followed, in the early to mid-ninth century, by an artisanal culture of specialist crafts. There was some use of writing at this point and it is possible that the site supported an ecclesiastical center, perhaps monastic.[59] The third phase, starting in the late ninth century, marks a decline in the material culture of Flixborough, its *habitus* described by Loveluck as "diminished production on a 'low-status' settlement" (the end of Period 4 and Period 5). Reduced status is evident in declining animal resources and shrunken connections with other centers in the region. "Conspicuous consumption" returned in the tenth century, the fourth phase, with the appearance of a rural elite (Period 6). By that point, Flixborough hosted a manorial center that was eventually supported by the construction of a stone church.[60]

There is a marked change in the *habitus* of the two periods of prosperity. One would expect luxury imports such as glass, seen in the first of these periods, to reappear in the second. However, Loveluck observes that the return to hunting, feasting, and conspicuous consumption in the tenth century was not substantiated by what he calls "portable, intrinsically valuable glass vessels, metalwork and other imported luxuries."[61] Rather than emphasize the "props" of conspicuous consumption, settlement leaders built large buildings, which Loveluck calls "theatres" for those objects.[62] Loveluck suggests that in this period Flixborough was a center of decidedly rural character. Imported wares were not as significant as they had been in the eighth century. If so, this would indicate a shift in the role of pottery as an indicator of social identity, and indeed that is what archaeologists found.

Jane Young and Alan Vince have coordinated the phases of Flixborough's settlement history with a series of pottery horizons. In the early period (650–750) settlements in the East Midlands experienced "considerable contact" crossing natural barriers, ensuring the spread of similar pottery fabrics throughout the region. In the middle of this period (i.e., late seventh century) shelly ware (made from clay with traces of fossil) came into use, and by the end of this period (mid-eighth century) it had replaced what Vince and Young call "locally-produced wares." In addition to a change of fabric, there was a change in the shape of vessels. The spread of these new wares enabled Vince and Young to trace the economic networks including Flixborough and their limits. The River Trent was a "barrier to contact," since wares of the new type, called Maxey wares, seldom crossed the river in the eighth century.[63] At the end of the Early Saxon period, however, Flixborough's pottery shared features with that of many other sites in the

---

[59] See Sarah Foot, *Monastic Life in Anglo-Saxon England*, pp. 97, 118, and especially 225, where she comments on craft production at the site.

[60] Christopher Loveluck, *Rural Settlement*, pp. 8–30 and 148–57. The excavators also outlined two further, later phases.

[61] See Vera I. Evison, Catherine Mortimer, Nicola Rogers, and Susan M. Youngs, "Consumption of Luxuries: The Glass and Copper Alloy Vessels."

[62] Loveluck, "Changing Lifestyles," pp. 149 and 155–57.

[63] Jane Young and Alan Vince, "The Anglo-Saxon Pottery," pp. 395–97.

region. The central location of Lincoln as a distribution point seems to explain the circulation of pottery over land rather than by water.[64]

Significantly, the number of vessels declined from the ninth century onward, when ceramic equipment was replaced with wood or metal, "suggesting a change in cooking practices or the status of the site."[65] There is a useful parallel to North Elmham (Norfolk), an eighth- and ninth-century episcopal center well within the region penetrated by Ipswich ware. But at North Elmham only fifty sherds have been identified from the Middle Saxon period (650–850), "a remarkably small number" that suggests "an almost aceramic phase" at this time.[66] Although there were imports found at this site, they too were, in Hodges's view, "surprisingly small in view of the ecclesiastical importance of North Elmham and the extensive excavations which have been undertaken." The number of imported objects has been seen by others as congruent with what we would expect of a high-status site "in contact with Frankish merchants as well as with Frisian merchants who handled the Rhenish trade."[67] Of forty-four sherds of imported continental pottery found in Norfolk, twenty-six come from North Elmham, which yielded less than 3 percent of the pottery used in the Ipswich ware Project, but nearly 60 percent of the imported pieces.[68] Many imported pieces once formed large burnished jars used to transport wine, suggesting that the evidence from North Elmham is related to consumption of wine, a luxury that only monasteries and other wealthy sites could afford.[69] The pottery finds from this site are uneven, which is understandable given the site's complex history. Danish raids resulted in the death of King Edmund at or near Hoxne (Suffolk) in 869.[70] The bishopric of Elmham, held by Humbert, had been abandoned several years earlier, and perhaps before 854.[71] Excavators are unable to explain the lack of pottery finds from this period except to say that, in the late Middle Saxon period, "more use was made of wooden vessels." Blinkhorn suggested that vessels were made of metal: "the recyclable nature of metal means that such vessels are rarely found in the archaeological record."[72] This would hold for the wares of the bishop and his household, but not for the wares of the many who worked to supply the few. The change from ceramic to

---

[64] Young and Vince, "The Anglo-Saxon Pottery," pp. 393 and 401.

[65] Young and Vince, "The Anglo-Saxon Pottery," p. 373.

[66] Peter Wade-Martins, *Excavations in North Elmham Park 1967–1972*, 1:120; see also 2:423.

[67] Richard Hodges, "Characterisation and Discussion of Identified Imported Sherds," p. 426. See also Hodges, *The Hamwih Pottery*, p. 42.

[68] The Ipswich ware Project was funded by English Heritage to document ceramics known by this name. See Blinkhorn, "Of Cabbages and Kings."

[69] Young and Vince, "The Anglo-Saxon Pottery," p. 360.

[70] Wade-Martins, *Excavations in North Elmham Park*, 2: 423, 427. Coins from Edmund's reign refer to "Eadmund rex," but coins dated within twenty years of his martyrdom refer to him as St. Edmund. See Marco Mostert, "St. Edmund." For an account of Edmund's death, see Ælfric, "St. Edmund," in Walter W. Skeat, ed., *Ælfric's Lives of Saints*, 2: 316–40.

[71] The *floruit* of the settlement is given by Oosthuizen as c. 720–830, based on Wade-Martins, who is not so precise in the pages Oosthuizen cites; see "Medieval Field Systems," p. 120.

[72] Paul Blinkhorn, "Anglo-Saxon Pottery," p. 10.

wood at Flixborough is thought to indicate more probably a loss rather than a gain in status, a point that might strengthen Blinkhorn's suggestion concerning use of metal objects rather than wood at the site.

Finds at Flixborough are unusually rich in evidence of cooking and storage vessels in use. Most types of pot analyzed by Young and Vince contained at least some exterior sooting normally associated with vessels placed either directly over fire or on a trivet placed over flame.[73] Pots dated to the tenth century had a higher percentage showing carbonized deposits or soot, suggesting "that they were used for cooking, or the heating of food or liquids."[74] Residues included beeswax, possible fish oil, dairy fats, and fats traced to cattle, sheep, and pigs. This evidence is consistent with the use of vessels as both crocks and cooking pots. These finds are richer in information about diet than that from many sites.[75] Flixborough finds are also rich in Ipswich ware that is thought to have traveled not "as pottery in its own right" but rather "as containers for traded goods." The lipids found as residue in the Ipswich ware were similar to those just described, although lipids were found in higher concentrations in Ipswich ware. Most Flixborough pottery came from the early tenth century and later, most of it residual, meaning that it was used in earlier periods and excavated from spoils, fills, and other post-use or waste contexts.[76] Locally made wares predominated in the storage and preparation of food. Imported pottery seems to have played a very small role in cooking and was apparently reserved for table display. Young and Vince note that "imported pottery is rare on the Flixborough site," with only fifty-one sherds out of a total of over five thousand. Imported wares did not show signs of use, whether sooting or internal residue.[77] Imported pottery does not seem to have been important for expressing social identity for the wealthy, and this seems to be true of pottery in general there. In its wealthy phases, the inhabitants were able to build grand structures and to supply their tables with what they considered to be the best wares. But the rural elite either could not or chose not to display at their rural homes "the imported luxuries more evident" among the urban elite.[78] Pottery and associated wares were not, for these people, important markers of social status.

Another long-term site, Goltho, is better known than Flixborough. When excavated, the earthworks of the early Norman castle disclosed a fortified enclosure from about 1000 AD, and, beneath it, signs of earlier fortification and a Middle Saxon settlement (early ninth century) that

[73] Sooting is not always unambiguous. At Wharram black residue was found in some pots that had no signs of exterior sooting. Perhaps the contents were burned in the vessels, or the pots were heated but not directly over flame. See P. A. Stamper and R. A. Croft, eds., *Wharram: A Study,* p. 28.

[74] Young and Vince, "The Anglo-Saxon Pottery," p. 373.

[75] Young and Vince, "The Anglo-Saxon Pottery," p. 356.

[76] Young and Vince, "The Anglo-Saxon Pottery," p. 372.

[77] Paul Blinkhorn, "Ipswich Ware," p. 364.

[78] Loveluck, *Rural Settlement,* p. 157.

included hut circles from the first and second centuries.[79] Throughout much of the Saxon period the pottery sequence at Goltho resembles that of other mid- to late Saxon sites. The forms are dominated by cooking pots. Stamford ware is featured in pitchers and tableware. At Goltho in the eleventh century, however, there was a dramatic change from grey sandy ware to "an orange, oxidised fabric" that was, in turn, replaced by splash-glazed ware. Guy Beresford sees a "rapid decline of cooking pots and perhaps also of bowls at the end of the [Anglo-Saxon pottery] series." Splash-glazed ware is seen only after the Conquest, suggesting that pottery at Goltho indexes major events that reshaped the settlement.[80]

In addition to its value in dating the changes at Goltho, pottery offers insight into the contrast between wares for display and those for daily use. Local wares continued to be produced even when other forms were available. Beresford notes that "the range of vessels in harsh shell-tempered ware is limited to cooking-pots and bowls, without the specialist forms produced in Lincoln throughout the late Saxon period." The quantities of "inferior vessels," Beresford's description of Goltho's locally produced pottery, would suggest that "it served local needs better than the utility wares intended for an urban market," so much so that "the whole pottery sequence from the site is indicative of kitchen rather than table wares." At the same time, Beresford stresses that an estate of this size "did not depend on the potter alone for its utility and table wares," meaning that pottery was brought to the site for both purposes. "The pottery described here was ancillary to the products of the cooper, turner, and metal smith, and was chosen for its function rather than its aesthetic appeal."[81] Beresford may be right that the pottery was valued for function rather than "aesthetic appeal," a common-sense judgment that also favors the functionalist premise. It could also have been true that some of the pots were important for other than aesthetic reasons. Not everything that communicates cultural heritage has to be beautiful. Accessible for centuries, the fabric Beresford discusses (coarse shell-tempered ware) became prominent only in the late ninth century, when the first long hall was constructed. It replaced other shell-tempered ware during the tenth century and continued to be used into the eleventh century. Other wares, also local, were used at the table, Beresford notes. That the use of coarse shell-tempered ware was confined to cooking pots may further contribute to the traditional statement this fabric seems to make.

That this ware dominated other wares, and also that cooking pots and bowls dominated other forms in the ceramic finds at Goltho, are valuable facts. However humble it was, coarse shell-tempered ware was the daily stuff of Goltho's cooks and kitchen staff for perhaps two centuries. This evidence suggests an extended *habitus*, a sharp contrast to Flixborough. It

[79] For a summary of the site, see Guy Beresford *et al.*, *Goltho*, pp. 1–14.
[80] Beresford *et al.*, *Goltho*, p. 167.
[81] Beresford *et al.*, *Goltho*, p. 166.

might seem easy to dismiss these objects as routine or common, but their sheer numbers and longevity speak to their value as markers of persistent identity. Cooking pots, the most common of the 1,549 vessels from the site that have been analyzed, reveal more about the food culture at Goltho than do display and prestige wares.[82] The same might be said for one phase of life at tenth-century Flixborough, with its many surviving pots and their residues. It is also possible that at Goltho, as at Flixborough in its late, high-status phase, pottery was not a significant index to social status for those at the top. Other features mattered more at both settlements, including large-scale buildings that implied the ascent of lords as they expanded their power and social standing, a development we will see affecting food culture (in Chapter 9). One must suppose that those wealthy enough to construct large buildings had access to any kind of tableware they would have liked. Loveluck suggests that those at Flixborough did not display luxury imports at their rural estates. It is possible that Goltho presents another example of a similar preference. There is also the possibility that other factors restrained the choice of tableware, such as a desire not to overemphasize newly achieved status, although this is not the behavior we expect of the modern *nouveau riche* or of their medieval counterparts.

Cooking pots: the textual and lexical evidence

The lexicon for quernstones in Old English is very limited; that for table wares and cooking wares is extensive. There are over sixty-five terms for "food receptacle" in the *Thesaurus of Old English* and another eighteen terms for "cooking vessel / pot." Half of the terms I identified, some thirty-three of them, are found only or primarily in glossaries; others occur in contexts that hint at social identity.[83] Among the words occurring frequently outside of glosses are *amber* (a vessel, pitcher, flask, but also a unit of measure), about fifty times; *bledu* (cup or bowl), twenty-seven times; *bolla/bolle* (cup or bowl), over seventy times; *cuppe* (cup), thirty-five times; *disc* (dish), about eighty times; and others.[84] Many of these objects could have been made of ceramic, but some common terms such as *hwer* (kettle, pot, cooking vessel), *panne* (pan), *cytel* (kettle), and such compounds as *brædepanne* and *cocor-panne* might describe either ceramics or objects made of non-ferrous metal. Many words translated as bowl, dish, pot, vessel, crock, cup, platter, plate, jug, flask, and ladle, among others, might refer to objects made by potters, clearly limiting the value of this lexical evidence as a tool for studying identity.

Bolla, found fourteen times in glosses and fifty-three times in medical texts or recipes, is an exception. This distribution constitutes persuasive

[82] Beresford *et al.*, *Goltho*, p. 165, charts top left and bottom right.
[83] *TOE* 1:196–97, heading numbers 04.01.02.02.06.03 to 04.01.02.02.06.05.05. I included "ladle" as a possible container but not spoon (there are three words for ladle).
[84] These approximate counts are based on *DOE* entries for the words in question.

evidence that this term served as a standard reference, although the object to which it referred might have varied in both size and shape. Also well attested is *bledu*, a cup, goblet, bowl, or dish (about one-third of occurrences are in glosses), usually indicating a vessel from which one drank but also a dish or bowl (*DOE*). Writing in the late tenth century, Ælfric uses *bledu* to describe a vessel from which a king drinks.[85] A *bledu* was prestigious enough to be left in the will of Æthelflæd, along with a brooch (*preon*), a wall hanging (*wahrift*), four robes, four cups, four vessels, and four horses (*IIII pellas & IIII cuppan & IIII bleda & IIII hors*).[86] In medicinal texts, the object serves as a measure of how much is to be drunk, i.e., *gode blede fulle*, "a good cupful."[87] Context helps to differentiate dishes, bowls, and cups made of metal (e.g., presumably those left in wills) from vessels used in preparing recipes. The word could refer to both ceremonial and practical containers. *Ceac*, "bowl, basin, water jar, laver; vessel for water or another liquid," is a good example, found twenty-eight times in very different contexts. It is used to refer to a ceremonial vessel in the *Pastoral Care*.[88]

In a medical recipe for an eye salve, however, the *ceac* is a cup or small bowl: "Afterward let the brass vessel, cup, or bowl be cleaned on the bottom so that it is all shining, (then) smear the shining (surface) lightly with drops of honey" (*Sy syþþan æren fæt læfel oþþe cec nyþewerd abywed þæt he eall scine, besmyra eall þæt scinende mid hunigteare leohtlice*).[89] There are three names for the vessel to be used: the *fæt*, usually a storage vessel, although not in this case (discussed below); the *læfel*, a cup or bowl; and the *ceac*. Only the first would certainly have been made of metal (all three might have been, however). We might translate the instruction as "clean [the vessel]," meaning that the one preparing the recipe is to do it; or it might be read as "have [the vessel] cleaned," meaning that another person would do it. The vessel had to be spotless, i.e., "all shining" (*he eall scine*), and then "lightly" (*leohtlice*) coated with honey. Honey smeared on the vessel was infused with the herbs soaking in a crock over which the vessel was suspended. With a wet finger one then removed the honey from the vessel into a *læfel*, another small bowl, and used the honey as a salve. Medical texts such as this one often refer to copper or brass containers (*æren fæt*), as does the example from the *Pastoral Care* cited above.[90] Another example is the *alfæt*, a generic vessel referred to in two glosses and the formula for an ordeal which involves heating water in "a vessel of iron or brass, lead, or made

[85] Ælfric, "St. Martin, Bishop and Confessor," in Skeat, *Ælfric's Lives of Saints*, 2: 258–59.
[86] For the will of Æthelflæd, see Dorothy Whitelock, ed. and trans., *Anglo-Saxon Wills*, no. 14, pp. 38–42, and P. H. Sawyer, *Anglo-Saxon Charters*, no. 1494, p. 418.
[87] *Bald's Leechbook*, Book I, ch. xlvii, 2, ed. Cockayne, *Leechdoms*, 2: 118–19.
[88] The word describes a brass (or bronze) basin (*æren ceac*) in which the faithful wash before they enter the temple. See Henry Sweet, ed., *King Alfred's West-Saxon Version of Gregory's Pastoral Care*, ch. 16, pp. 104–5.
[89] For this recipe, see Cockayne, *Leechdoms*, 3: 292–93.
[90] For an example, see *Bald's Leechbook*, Book I, ch. ii, 14, ed. Cockayne, *Leechdoms*, 2: 32–33: in a brass or copper vessel (*on æren fæt oððe cyperen*).

of clay" (*alfæt isen oððe æren, leaden oððe læmen*).[91] Brass or copper vessels, *arfæt*, are found in medical recipes (eight occurrences), many of which involve cooking processes such as boiling and heating liquids.

Texts do not distinguish cooking pots from crocks in which food was stored. *Crocca* (*chroca*) designated a crock used for mixing, preparing, or storing food or remedies.[92] *Crocca* is also used for a cooking pot. There are some thirty-five occurrences of *crocca* in Old English, a count made without differentiating a crock meant for storage only from a cooking pot. *Crog*, also meaning crock or "vessel for liquids," is found only in glossaries (*DOE*). Generally speaking, textual references to cooking pots are of two kinds: recipes, including herbals or medicinal texts, and narratives based on the Bible. Most references come from medical texts, which are specific to the use of cooking pots over fire and which also refer to such processes as boiling and mixing, the latter sometimes including reference to tools such as a spoon or ladle. Examples can be found in *Bald's Leechbook*, a prose medical text that compiles Latin and Greek works and is derived from Galen. The *crocca* is used for mixing "the best honey" with vinegar and setting the liquid "over the fire in a cooking pot" (*þæt seleste hunig . . . meng togædere & do to fyre on croccan ofer*).[93] A similar recipe concerns the medical uses of the badger from the *Medicina de quadrupedibus*, also based on a Latin original.[94] The preparer is to "simmer its brain in three measures of oil in a new crock until a third part is boiled away, put it into a vessel and keep it" (*His brægen geseoð on þrim sestrum eles on niwon croccan oðþæt þrydda dæl sy beweallen, fætelsa & heald hyt*).[95] The recipe calls for the use of a new vessel, presumably as a precaution against contamination. The *crocca*, the vessel in which the remedy was prepared, is distinguished from the vessel in which it was stored. The only texts calling for unused or new containers are medical, and most of them indicate that the pot is to be set over a fire. The recipe including the badger's brain also includes the *fætels* (found some 325 times), a vessel for storage. To judge from its frequent appearance in the corpus, *fætels* designated an open vessel used mainly for fluids (found about thirty times). A *fætel* is mentioned by the leatherworker in *The Colloquy*, so this object could also have been made of leather or other material. The same is true of the *buteruc* (*buterícas*) or bottle that the leatherworker mentions.[96] The "Metrical Epilogue" of the Old English translation of the *Pastoral Care* urges the reader to drink of the Lord's wisdom and

[91] For *Ordal* 1b, see Liebermann, *GDA*, pp. 386–87.
[92] A related term not included here is *cytel*, meaning kettle, and usually of metal. See *DOE, cytel*.
[93] London, British Library, MS Royal 12 D.xvii (Winchester, mid-tenth century); N. R. Ker, *Catalogue of Manuscripts Containing Anglo-Saxon*, p. 322. See *Bald's Leechbook*, Book II, ch. xxviii, ed. Cockayne, *Leechdoms*, 2: 224–25.
[94] London, British Library, MS Cotton Vitellius C.iii, early eleventh century, with text based on a fifth-century Latin source "directly descended from an Anglian original." See Ker, *Catalogue of Manuscripts Containing Anglo-Saxon*, p. 285. See Hubert Jan de Vriend, ed., *The Old English Herbarium*, p. lxi, on the Anglian original.
[95] Vriend, *The Old English Herbarium*, p. 236, para. 6. For commentary, see M. L. Cameron, *Anglo-Saxon Medicine*, p. 60.
[96] G. N. Garmonsway, ed., *Ælfric's Colloquy*, p. 35, ll. 172–74.

fill a vessel, *fætels* or *kylle* (*cyll*, leather bottle, or vessel), at the Lord's well (*drihtnes welle*).[97]

Narrative texts based on Latin sources associate pots with food-related processes but shed little light on Anglo-Saxon customs. Homilies that describe cooking processes used in the Bible might have reinforced notions of Anglo-Saxon Christians' identity as children of God and as a Chosen People. Ælfric's "De Populo Israhel" contrasts food sent as a sign of God's favor with ordinary food and ordinary cooking. The Israelites in the desert are given "heavenly food" that had "the taste of all the sweetness that any food has, and was also more to be valued than the herbs that they boiled with meat in their cooking pots at home" (*se heofonlica mete hæfde ælcne swæc ælcere werodnysse þe ænig mete hæfð, and wæs eac wurðlicor þonne ða wyrta wæron þe hi æt ham sudon on heora croccum mid flæsce*).[98] A description from Numbers 11:8, which recounts the Israelites gathering and preparing manna, mentions both grinding and baking: "the heavenly food [i.e., manna] that they gathered and ground in a hand-mill or crushed and boiled in cooking pots and made into loaves: they were such as they were baked in oil" (*þone heofonlican mete þæt hi gaderodon & grundon on cwyrne oððe brytton & sudon on croccan & worhton hlafas ðærof: þa wæron swylce hi wæron elebacene*).[99] Leviticus 6:19–21 also refers to cakes "baked in oil and warm" (*þa sceolon beon elebacene & wearme*).[100] *Elebacan*, baked in oil, is a word found nowhere else in the Old English corpus, suggesting that this method was not used in early England.[101] In these references it seems taken for granted that the Hebrews and the Anglo-Saxons would have boiled grain in the same way. Lack of comment on significant differences (such as cakes baked in oil or in ashes), on the other hand, might suggest that sacred texts were not expected to correspond to modern methods of food preparation. Genre matters. Homilies exploit implicitly shared identities, a strategy essential to narratives about the saved or damned and the audiences hearing these accounts.

Here and there we glimpse a detail that is more revealing. Baking in ashes is mentioned in the late ninth-century translation of the *Dialogues of Gregory the Great*. Monks are baking a hearth cake in ashes (hence *axebakenne*) and have neglected to put the sign of the cross on it. The holy man Martirius blesses it, putting his hands over the ashes: "And immediately as he was making the sign, the loaf gave out a crackling sound, as though a great cooking pot had burst in the fire" (*And him þa swa segniendum sona se hlaf dyde unmæte bærstlunge, efne swylce þær toburste sum mycel crocca in þam*

---

[97] For the "Metrical Epilogue" to the *Pastoral Care*, ll. 24–26, see Elliott van Kirk Dobbie, ed., *The Anglo-Saxon Minor Poems*, p. 112.

[98] Ælfric, "De Populo Israhel," ed. John C. Pope, *Homilies of Ælfric*, 2: 646, ll. 124–27.

[99] For Numbers 11:8, see S. J. Crawford, ed., *The Old English Version of the Heptateuch*, p. 310. See also Chapter 4, p. 95, above.

[100] For Leviticus 6:19–21, see Crawford, ed., *The Old English Version of the Heptateuch*, p. 291.

[101] *DOE, elefæt* (found ten times) refers to a bottle or vessel for oil, but the oil seems to be consecrated (or chrismatory) oil, not oil for cooking.

fyre).[102] The Latin source refers to the baking pan, but the translator instead evoked a sound with which he expected his readers to be familiar, a crock breaking over the fire (because it was poorly made, perhaps, and could not withstand the heat).

No Old English texts about cooking pots address the potter's craft. There are only three references to the *crocwyrhta*, including the famous quotation about vessels in Psalm 2:9: God shall smite his enemies "and dash them in pieces like a potter's vessel" (NRSV). Following a continental tradition, the translation of the Paris Psalter (late ninth century), says that this will be done easily (*eaðe*): *and hi miht swa eaðe abrecan swa se croccwyrhta mæg ænne croccan* ("and you may shatter them as easily as the potter may shatter a pot").[103] The mid-eleventh-century Cambridge Psalter refers to a clay vessel (*fæt lamys*), and the Lambeth Psalter (second half of the eleventh century) adds to the potter (*crocwirhtan*) the brickmaker (*tygelwirhtan*).[104] *Crocc-sceard*, meaning sherd or broken piece of pottery, is also rare, occurring four times, once in a homily by Ælfric about Job (who uses a sherd to scrape away worms that have infested his sores) and elsewhere as a gloss for *testa*.[105]

Medical recipes point to food-based identity in more specific ways, underscoring the rarified equipment required for some tasks (where copper or brass is specified, for example), the patient skills required of practitioners, their knowledge of herbs and other foods, and, by implication, their well-connected lines of supply. Recipes as texts do so only indirectly, however, since presumably they were available, in either oral or written form, only to those equipped to do what the formulae required. But they describe a world of objects and procedures to be performed with them, activity known to many people, even if most of them saw only the product and not the process. Comparable texts for cooks and their helpers are unknown. The cook in *The Colloquy* does not mention pots, for example, although he refers to boiling.[106] We do not think of cooking or storage pots as components of identity because we do not see them as specialized objects, either in their manufacture or in their use, whereas high-status objects and learned texts are usually seen as tools for articulating social distinction. Storage pots and other vessels were partners with the human agents who prepared and served food, as much the tools of their trade as the quern, knife, awl, or any other instrument deployed by skilled hands. Elegant wares needed for the feast serve as barometers of international contact and political standing, while ordinary pots document the less glamorous world

---

[102] Hans Hecht, ed., *Bischof Wærferths von Worcester Übersetzung der Dialoge Gregors des Grossen*, book 1, ch. 11, p. 87, ll. 16–20.

[103] Patrick P. O'Neill, ed., *King Alfred's Old English Prose Translation of the First Fifty Psalms*, p. 101; see notes to verse 9, p. 169, on the translation of *facilis* (easily).

[104] For the Cambridge Psalter text of Psalm 2:9, see Karl Wildhagen, ed., *Der Cambridger Psalter*, p. 3, and for the Lambeth Psalter version of Psalm 2:9, see U. Lindelöf, ed., *Der Lambeth-Psalter*, p. 2.

[105] Job 2:8. For citations, see *DOE*, *crocc-sceard*.

[106] Garmonsway, *Ælfric's Colloquy*, p. 37, ll. 197–99.

of interregional trade and the slow processes of technological change in the world of seasonal potters. Objects from these levels are mixed in the archaeological record and attest to the connection of social identities rather than to discrete worlds of elite and common consumption. More revealing than the mix of imported and domestic wares used for the same purposes, it seems to me, is the mix of older wares with new shapes and fabrics. That mixture may point to a preference for an older way of doing things and for older things themselves. In the modern world many old things retain the power to evoke history. Was it different at Hamwic or Mucking? Blinkhorn believes that some residents of Mucking clung to older ways of making pots because the tradition behind those techniques mattered more than "other, and arguably more efficient, possibilities."[107] Even later sites such as Goltho show that older forms survived the introduction of new ones, at least for some purposes. No ware was closer to food than the pots in which it was cooked. Judging from a handful of sites ranging from early to late, we can see that there were more changes in storage vessels than in cooking vessels. Storage and shipping vessels were responses to new goods and new lines of supply. When it came to preparing some of that merchandise, cooks used old wares, new food in old pots. That their preferences were directed by tradition and ancestry is very likely in the early period, less so in the tenth or eleventh centuries, when Anglo-Saxon cooks, like many modern chefs, used what they had on hand simply because, whatever its imperfections, they knew how it worked.

---

[107] Blinkhorn, "Habitus," pp. 119–20.

6

Food Objects in Iron

Simply by virtue of its abundance, pottery contributes to our understanding of Anglo-Saxon identity at many social levels. We can tell that certain forms and fabrics were valued for certain tasks and can see that ordinary wares were sometimes retained when they might have been replaced by newer pots, perhaps because what was ordinary was also familiar and traditional. Ironwork was also ubiquitous in Anglo-Saxon settlements, but not all of it yields insights into social identity. Food objects in iron did not last. When they broke they were not discarded or put to new uses, as were fragments of quernstones or pots, but instead were melted down and refashioned. The old disappeared into the new. Iron had advantages over both pots and querns, however, in that its manufacture was associated with fire and hence with spectacle. As a result, iron and ironworkers were sometimes noticed in narratives that describe how ironwork and ironworkers were understood.

The character of iron

The most famous story about ironworking concerns Bede's contemporary, Ecgwine, bishop of Worcester, a figure about whom our sources date from the eleventh century and later. A zealous reformer, Ecgwine made many enemies and eventually had to seek support in Rome. Before setting out, he bound himself in fetters and tossed the key into the River Avon. In Rome, he asked his followers to catch a small fish from the Tiber, which they did. When the cook prepared it, he found Ecgwine's key in the fish's belly. Freed from his bonds, Ecgwine was absolved of the charges that had burdened him in Worcester. His spiritual integrity now beyond question, he returned there and founded Evesham Abbey; he died in 717.[1]

Accounts of miracles do not usually focus on the ordinary objects – the lock and key – around which the wonders occur. An exception of double value occurs in Adomnan's *Life of St. Columba*, in an episode in which Molua, one of the monastic brethren, brings an "implement" for Columba

---

[1] See Michael Lapidge, "Byrhtferth and the *Vita S. Ecgwini*," pp. 307–8, for the versions of the story.

to bless while the saint is copying a manuscript. Without putting down his pen, the saint blesses the object and later asks his servant what implement had been blessed. It was a knife for "the slaughtering of bulls or cattle," the servant says. Columba responds that the implement "will not harm man or beast," and indeed when Molua tries to kill a bull he is unable to do so. "Having discovered this fact, the monks who knew the blacksmith's craft melted down the iron of that knife and then coated the liquid metal on to all the other iron tools in the monastery," ensuring that they too would be "unable to harm any flesh."[2] It is important that these monks are skilled smiths who can refashion iron for new uses.

Ecgwine's key and shackles are not the saint's only connection to iron-work. The early thirteenth-century *Chronicle of Evesham* recounts Ecgwine's confrontation with pagan smiths at Alcester.[3] He preached to "the miners, charcoal burners, and smiths" there, "smudged and sturdy worshippers of Wodin and Freya every one of them," according to G. W. Wood. Enraged at the bishop's sermon, they "dashed hammer on anvil, drowning the holy man's exhortations, and finally driving him with aching ear drums into the peace of the forest." The bishop cursed them, whereupon "the earth opened and swallowed the smiths."[4] Ecgwine's anathema "long prevented any one from carrying on the trade in that town for fear of the caudal appendage threatened by the irate bishop."[5] The fiery destruction of Alcester, meant to invoke the Last Judgment, underscores the association of forges with the fire, smoke, and noise of Hell; the "caudal appendage" surely recalls the devil's own.

A less impassioned but no more appealing account of smithing emerges in the Old English dialogue known as *The Colloquy*. After monastic students take up the roles of various craftsmen, the schoolmaster asserts that the plowman's is the foremost *woruldcræft*, or secular occupation. When the smith replies that there would be no plowing or fishing without his skills, the master reasserts the primacy of agriculture and gives a glimpse of the smith at work. The plowman supplies bread, "but you [ironsmith], what do you give us with your forging, except iron fire sparks and blows of beating of a sledgehammer and fanned bellows?" (*þu, hwæt sylst us on smiþþan þinre buton isenne fyrspearcan & swegincga beatendra slecgea & blawendra byliga?*).[6] The smith is an environmental nuisance rather than the indispensable worker he claims to be.

Given this reputation, it is easy to see why Weland, the legendary Germanic smith, is seen in terms of his craft's products, including Beowulf's coat of mail and Mimming, Waldere's sword, rather than its

---

[2] Adomnan, *Life of St. Columba*, trans. Richard Sharpe, book 2, ch. 29, pp. 177–78. See Sharpe's notes on the translation, p. 332, concerning the high heat needed to melt iron as opposed to softening it for reworking.

[3] For the episode, see Jane Geddes, "Iron," p. 175. For the text, see W. D. Macray, ed., *Chronicon Abbatiae de Evesham*, pp. 25–26.

[4] See G. W. Wood, "The Vision of Eoves and What Came of It," p. 816.

[5] Anonymous, "Three Abbots of Evesham."

[6] G. N. Garmonsway, ed., *Ælfric's Colloquy*, p. 40, ll. 226–28.

processes.[7] It is often assumed that smithies were located in areas remote from domestic spaces. But some Anglo-Saxon excavations suggest otherwise. The eleventh-century clay-built furnace at Stamford (Lincolnshire) was found in the middle of the town.[8] At Hamwic the smithies were located at major junctions on the major north–south streets.[9] Ecgwine confronts smiths in the city of Alcester, which he leaves before he invokes his curse. It would seem that smiths practiced their trade near the living and working spaces of their customers. Woodworking was also noisy, and so was milling. But the smith's triumvirate of racket, stink, and smoke was unique, and no other workers were surrounded by flying sparks that threatened conflagration.

Ironwork has been found at nearly all Anglo-Saxon sites. I describe evidence from a selection of sites and then look at common iron cooking implements, ranging from knives to fish hooks. Iron was available in "almost every county" of England, either collected as bog ore or mined from shallow pits.[10] The ore had to be extracted and smelted, a process that required a large facility equipped with fuel and room for waste and disposal. Smelters worked near the sources of ore. Smiths managed iron's next step on the way to the kitchen and table. They made iron into knives, forks, keys, hooks, skewers, cauldrons, chains, and tools as small and seemingly simple as the fish hook. If smithies were centrally located, as some evidence suggests, that was because smiths were in steady demand. They made new instruments and refashioned remnants into new forms, the fate of many broken or worn out forks, spoons, pans, kettles, skewers, and trivets. Knives, like keys, survive in large numbers in part because they had symbolic value that earned them a place in burials. Most food objects made of iron are less numerous. Some categories of larger implements are poorly represented. No iron cauldrons survive, for example, although ladles of iron are found in pagan graves. According to Patrick Ottaway, "of all the groups of tools known from Anglo-Saxon England, it is those used in agriculture which are the least commonly found, perhaps because ironwork was more assiduously recycled in rural communities than elsewhere."[11] The same conclusion seems to apply to objects used in preparing and serving food.

Standard assumptions about the development of ironwork parallel those about the development of pottery. It has been thought that early, small settlements were served by local, occasional, potters who were conservative in their methods, whether for technical reasons, cultural reasons, or some mixture of the two. About ironwork, Ottaway writes, "At a time

---

[7] See R. D. Fulk, Robert E. Bjork, and John D. Niles, eds., *Klaeber's* Beowulf, p. 17, ll. 454–55. For "Waldere," see Elliott van Kirk Dobbie, ed., *The Anglo-Saxon Minor Poems*, pp. 4–5, ll. 1–4.

[8] David M. Wilson, "Craft and Industry," p. 262.

[9] P. Andrews, ed., *Excavations at Hamwic*, p. 222.

[10] Geddes, "Iron," p. 167.

[11] Patrick Ottaway, "The Products of the Blacksmith" (online resource, cited by part and page number); Ottaway's selection of sites is discussed at 1: 2; see also 1:15.

when England was primarily a country of dispersed rural settlements, smithing was probably undertaken, for the most part, either by itinerant smiths or on a part-time basis by people also active in other crafts." As a result, "assimilation of new techniques was probably slow" and there was probably little experimentation with new forms. Aristocratic estates employed specialists who turned out such high-status objects as those seen from Sutton Hoo, including the cauldron and chain from Mound 17 and various weapons.[12]

Changes in pottery production came about as a result of specialization and the development of markets. Ottaway likewise associates changes in ironworking with markets and external contacts. He suggests that innovations could be expected in monasteries, towns, and rural sites of some standing, such as Flixborough.[13] Few such signs have surfaced, however. Compared to cooking pots, culinary objects in metal do not seem to have changed greatly over time. One does not read about ironwork in a particular style or fabric comparable to Ipswich or Thetford ware, for example. As we have seen, Paul Blinkhorn believes that some forms of pottery persisted because they communicated ancestral identity, not because they functioned in a superior way.[14] It is possible that certain forms of ironwork, like certain pots, encoded identity in ways not obvious to us. Ironwork is not easily marked, but some specimens are grooved and sometimes inlaid with, for example, brass. Such evidence (discussed below) indicates status and hence addresses identity. Many iron food objects required handles of wood, bone, antler, or other materials that could be given identifying details through color or finish. They are not well preserved in most soil types, however, meaning that in the world of iron signs of the *habitus* are difficult to detect.

My selection of ironworking sites has been guided by Ottaway's introduction to Anglo-Saxon smithing, which describes well-stratified objects from recent excavations or those described in site reports with extensive findings of ironwork. Mid-Saxon sites in his survey include Flixborough, Hamwic, Thwing, and York (Fishergate); later sites include Goltho, Repton, Thetford, Winchester, and York (Coppergate).[15] I add some earlier sites, including Mucking, and also the large smithy findings from Wharram Percy. More sites supported ironwork than supported smelting. Ottaway notes that iron was usually smelted near the source of the ore and transported to smiths in bars, although the ore could also be transported for processing, as it was transported to York (16–22 Coppergate).[16] Other sites at which smithing has been documented include Hamwic (Six Dials), Ramsbury, Flaxengate, and Lincoln. "While smithing slag and pieces of bar iron and scrap are frequently found on excavations," Ottaway writes,

[12] Ottaway, "The Products of the Blacksmith," 3:7.
[13] Ottaway, "The Products of the Blacksmith," 3:8.
[14] Paul Blinkhorn, "Habitus, Social Identity and Anglo-Saxon Pottery," p. 121.
[15] Ottaway, "The Products of the Blacksmith," 1:2.
[16] Ottaway, "The Products of the Blacksmith," 1:4.

"a smithing site cannot be securely identified unless the material is found in direct association with a suitable hearth." Even where hearths have been identified, basic equipment, including an anvil and bellows, has seldom been found. Smaller pieces, such as punches, clippers, and others do survive.[17] Like pottery production, smithing took place on two scales, one attuned to the needs of a settlement and serving many purposes, the other more highly specialized. Smiths at prominent trading sites, such as Hamwic, London, Ipswich, and York, resemble those at rural sites with extensive economic activity, such as Flixborough. Evidence of metalworking on an industrial scale and of highly specialized ironwork is rare.

Ironworking and food objects at early sites

Shakenoak was occupied through the middle years of the eighth century. When published in 1972, finds from Site F there constituted "a greater variety of objects than [had] yet been published from any Anglo-Saxon settlement site."[18] Structural ironwork (nails, staples), horse furniture, and other fittings were prominent. Included are two bucket handles and buckets made from sheet iron and over twenty knives, including types found in cemeteries.[19] The bucket handles found at Shakenoak have been compared to those found at Portchester Castle, another early site; at Portchester the handles were retrieved from a ninth-century context.[20] These items apart, however, no other food objects in iron were found at Shakenoak.[21] It is significant that Shakenoak produced both tap slag and cinder, and a furnace lining, since they are evidence of smelting, not just of smithing. The ore probably came from the region if not the immediate area of the settlement.[22]

Several huts at Mucking were associated with or near ironworking sites but were considered peripheral to "the main focus of the settlement" (i.e., agriculture). One might say that smithing was central to the mechanics of agriculture, however, and in that sense also central to Mucking and other rural sites. Iron bars and fragments from Mucking have been compared to those found at Site F at Shakenoak and at York (see below).[23] At Mucking local sources were likely used for bog ore, as it is called, or ironstone from gravel deposits. "The evidence emerging from Essex indicates that ironworking during the Anglo-Saxon period took place on a small

---

[17] Ottaway, "The Products of the Blacksmith," 1:4–6.
[18] P. D. C. Brown, "The Ironwork," p. 86. On the date of the settlement's probable abandonment, see A. C. C. Brodribb, A. R. Hands, and D. R. Walker, *Excavations at Shakenoak Farm*, p. 29.
[19] Brown, "The Ironwork," p. 92 (bucket handles), p. 114 (iron buckets), and pp. 112–13 (knives, illustrated pp. 86–89 and 111).
[20] Barry Cunliffe, *Excavations at Portchester Castle*, p. 200 and p. 201, fig. 132, nos. 16–17, and pp. 88–89 on the context of Phase 3c.
[21] Brown, "The Ironwork," p. 90 and p. 91, fig. 39.
[22] H. Cleere, "Anglo-Saxon Iron-Working Debris," and H. P. Powell, "Geology of the Area around Shakenoak Farm," p. 143.
[23] Helena Hamerow, *Excavations at Mucking*, pp. 17 and 69–70.

scale to satisfy local needs" rather than some kind of industrial production. Nonetheless, smithies such as those found at Mucking could produce high-quality wares, especially knives.[24]

Compared to Mucking and Shakenoak, Hamwic is considered an "urban" context. Industry of various kinds is well represented at this major mid-Saxon trading center. Some 3,600 iron objects survive, many of them unidentified fragments of bar and rod.[25] Little of the ironwork relates to food objects. Mark Brisbane describes metalwork of various kinds at the site: "ironworking (mostly smithing, but perhaps also smelting), copper-alloy working, leadworking, goldworking (including mercuric gilding)," and, in addition, crafts requiring iron tools, including work in bone, wool, textile, leather, and glass.[26] Smithing would be small-scale, smelting more likely to be associated with industrial production. Both smithies at Hamwic, as I have noted, were located on the major north–south street. They might have been linked to domestic structures, suggesting permanent rather than seasonal work with iron.[27]

Household ironwork discovered at Hamwic includes "hooks, strike-a-lights, chain links, and rings; some of the plate fragments may be the remains of cauldrons." Bucket handles were also found, and some knives had copper-alloy inlay, suggesting that they conveyed status for those who carried them.[28] Even when non-ferrous objects are included in the cooking-implement category, however, the results for so large a settlement seem meager. P. Andrews lists "spoons and 'forks,'" but no "high-quality decorative objects" that might be regarded as "characteristic of 'non-urban' (probably monastic) sites such as Flixborough."[29] As Hamwic shows, trade and industrial ironwork did not invariably go together. Lundenwic is another example. Brian Hobley describes ironwork at Lundenwic as "operating on a non-specialist, non-zonal, domestic scale." He continues, "This is especially true of iron and alloy-working, for crucible and mould fragments are very common in domestic assemblages." But he argues that in the Saxon periods there was no industry as such in Lundenwic. It was not a manufacturing center and is "the only major late Saxon town not to have its own pottery industry."[30]

Ironwork at later sites

With the exception of Lundenwic, the sites discussed so far seem to have been abandoned by the ninth century or shortly after; Hamwic did not retain its importance much later than the ninth century.[31] Flixborough, by

---

[24] Gerry McDonnell, "Slags and Ironworking Residues," p. 83.
[25] Andrews, *Excavations at Hamwic*, p. 225.
[26] Mark Brisbane, "Hamwic (Saxon Southampton), p. 104.
[27] Andrews, *Excavations at Hamwic*, pp. 222 and 225.
[28] Andrews, *Excavations at Hamwic*, p. 226.
[29] Andrews, *Excavations at Hamwic*, p. 221.
[30] Brian Hobley, "Lundenwic and Lundenburg," p. 80.
[31] Andrews, *Excavations at Hamwic*, p. 13.

contrast, is known to have passed through several different occupational sequences from the seventh to the twelfth centuries. It had, for example, a phase as a monastic or religious settlement but was also a secular location with variable status. Metalworking at Flixborough is more revealing of food culture than is ironwork elsewhere. The site is rich in small finds of a domestic nature, although kitchen utensils such as pottery, cutlery, sharpening stones, and other portable objects account for less than 10 percent of the recorded finds. Food objects, in whatever material, would probably have accounted for a higher percentage of things used by the occupants. Among domestic items related to food, "a very wide range of iron fittings" was turned up, including "hooks, suspension chains, pot hooks, wall hooks," along with 250 knives, flesh hooks, and one skewer.[32] These ample finds hold the promise of an integrated understanding of the role of iron in cooking and in related agricultural processes. Some twenty-two vessel handles were recovered, all originally semicircular with looped terminals. Some handles had spans of 20 cm or more, and it is assumed that they were used for buckets or possibly cauldrons. A curved plate, with a rim that might have come from a metal cauldron, was found. Various other vessel suspension fittings were presumably intended for use with wooden containers such as buckets. Several more such fittings, thought to have been used with cooking vessels, are listed as "pot hooks." They are generally U-shaped rather than semicircular, meaning that the pots to which they were attached were not widemouthed. Some of these hooks are 16 mm in length, slightly over six inches (two are illustrated).[33]

Iron handles from one site can be connected to pottery shapes from others. Hooks of the shape and size just described would match the dimensions of cooking pots such as those found at Ipswich, for example (discussed in the previous chapter). There, according to J. G. Hurst, the "basic form" of the "small squat cooking pot" had an approximate diameter of four to six inches and was five to seven inches high (see also Figure 6, a whole pot from York).[34] Similar pots were found at Flixborough, where jars with lugs might have been suited to handles like those at Flixborough.[35] Although, so far as I know, there has been no speculation about the ethnic origins associated with one kind or shape of handle, we should remember Blinkhorn's claims about the shape and finish of cooking pots, and also the location of pierced lugs used to hang pots over fires (see Chapter 5, pp. 109–10, and Figure 5, the pottery sequence from Flixborough showing forms with lugs). Lugs might have been intended for iron handles as well as leather straps or cords, and it is therefore possible that the ironwork, like the pottery it was attached to, communicated information about identity in ways modern observers are not yet in a position to decipher.

---

[32] Patrick Ottaway *et al.*, "Domestic Fittings and Implements," p. 165.
[33] Ottaway *et al.*, "Domestic Fittings and Implements," pp. 171–73; the pot hooks are seen in p. 172, fig. 5.4, nos. 1769 and 1771.
[34] J. G. Hurst, "The Pottery," p. 300, citing Stanley West, "Excavations at Cox Lane."
[35] Jane Young and Alan Vince, "The Anglo-Saxon Pottery," pp. 340–41.

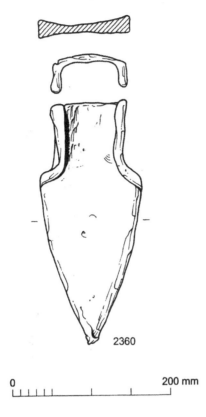

2360

0   200 mm

Figure 7. Plowshare, Flixborough; no. 2360. Scale 1:4.

Among the remarkable ironwork finds at Flixborough are a cauldron
chain and a plowshare, two objects "probably deliberately buried together
as a hoard." The plowshare, seen from the top in the drawing, would have
been fitted as a shoe to a wooden ard (a light plow without a moldboard to
turn over furrows) for cutting into the soil (see Figure 7).[36] Ottaway compares the chain (see Figure 2) to the Sutton Hoo chain and suggests that
it would have been hung approximately three meters above the ground;
the Sutton Hoo chain would have been suspended from a height of five
meters. The Flixborough chain is less elaborately worked than the one at
Sutton Hoo and that found at Burrow Hill, Butley (another Suffolk site). It
is significant that the Flixborough chain does not come from a burial but
rather from a hoard. Such a context might suggest that, at the time it was
buried, the chain was functioning in a feasting setting and highly valued.
However, it was buried with a plowshare, not an object associated with

---

[36] For detailed descriptions, see Ottaway *et al.*, "Domestic Fittings and Implements," pp. 173–74
(chain) and p. 245 (plowshare).

social status. [37] The plowshare, which shows no sign of use or damage, is not the only object of this kind to have been recovered from the sort of hoard that is not likely to make the evening news. It would seem that both the chain and the plowshare were valued less for what they did than for the material and work that had gone into their fashioning. They were hidden not because they had symbolic meaning or conveyed status, but rather because, as objects, they were difficult to replace.

Other ironwork related to food culture at Flixborough includes hooks that were attached to wall posts or ceiling beams and served "a number of functions, including hanging of lamps, meat and other objects." The hooks (there are twenty-three of them) ranged in length from 32 mm to 90 mm. [38] The skewer, thought to be as early as the mid-eighth century, is the only example of its kind from an Anglo-Saxon context; 312 mm in length, it was presumably used "for holding meat or other food-stuffs over a fire while cooking, or for skewering them afterwards." [39] Middle Saxon ironwork from Flixborough has parallels to that found at North Elmham (Norfolk), including a bucket or cauldron handle and a chain hook possibly for use with a cauldron or cooking vessel. No hooks were found at North Elmham, where, as elsewhere, knives were the most common iron objects. Knives from the Early and Middle Saxon periods at North Elmham have whittle tangs for use with wooden handles. [40]

At Wharram Percy (Yorkshire) there is some uncertainty about which objects came from the smithy, which has been described as a setup typical of a "village" blacksmith (use of quotations advisable), and which came from "specialised sources." [41] Wharram is one of the most extensively investigated ironworking areas in the Anglo-Saxon period. The site included "a permanent smithy, housed in a timber building, with a waist-high smithing hearth." A "possible metalworking hollow" was nearby. There were miscellaneous pottery finds in the smithing area, which were somewhat useful in dating the site, but nothing from the smithy area suggests objects for cooking or food use. [42] Many iron objects survive from the mid- and late Saxon periods. Except for knives, few of them relate to food culture. Over forty knives were found, along with other household ironwork, but forks, metal pots, skillets, and similar objects are not mentioned. Wharram Percy seems to have had access to two grades of ironwork, the local or "household" kind and the work of specialized smiths. The two sources of production could, potentially, illustrate the contrast between work of a traditional kind manifesting the operation of the *habitus* and newer work manifesting outside influences. Specialized work might also

---

[37] On the plowshare, see Lisa M. Wastling and Patrick Ottaway, "Cultivation, Crop Processing and Food Procurement," p. 245.

[38] Ottaway *et al.*, "Domestic Fittings and Implements," p. 175.

[39] Ottaway *et al.*, "Domestic Fittings and Implements," p. 218 and p. 220, fig. 5.31, no. 2309).

[40] Ian H. Goodall, "The Iron Objects," 2: 514–15, fig. 267, no. 89 (chain hook) and no. 90 (handle).

[41] Ian H. Goodall and E. A. Clark, with L. Webster and J. G. Watt, "Iron Objects," p. 132.

[42] P. A. Stamper and R. A. Croft, eds., *Wharram: A Study*, pp. 32–35. See p. 35 for a description of the smithy.

have communicated traditional significance, but inhabitants of small sites would not have recognized it. Such objects as ornate chains from which cauldrons were suspended, for example, would have required special- ized skills and would have been at the center of a settlement's gathering space. A fragmentary chain at Goltho is included among Beresford's list of "household ironwork."[43] One thinks also of richly wrought chains dis- played in the small halls at West Stow and the prominence of such wares in similar small-scale structures . A chain, cauldron, and associated objects would have been "extremely visible" even in much larger halls, to quote Blinkhorn in reference to pots in similar locations.[44] The chain might incor- porate details that communicated identity to those who saw both it and the cauldron with which it was associated. The style, history, and origin of these two objects would have been matters of interest and pride to all. But this is not to say that humbler objects from the local smith, such as forks with tines set at familiar spaces and angles, would not also have conveyed information that was equally significant to the residents.

Cooking and eating utensils in iron

Food utensils in iron include knives, forks, spoons and ladles, and pots; also included in this category are fish hooks, the size of which are important in differentiating marine and freshwater fishing.

Knives

Knives survive in great numbers from almost every settlement. They have long been analyzed for evidence of social identity, in part because the knife was both a weapon (the *seax*) and a tool. It has been studied more for the former association than the latter. Hundreds of blades survive, in many kinds and sizes. Knives were used for more than eating and food prepa- ration, although these are their chief applications within food networks, including hunting and butchery. They were also used in leatherwork and woodwork, both media from which food containers were fashioned. H. E. M. Cool notes that a ready supply of iron in Roman Britain allowed the manufacture of cleavers and "very intensive butchery" on cattle carcasses.[45]

Smaller knives presumably were reserved for personal use, including preparing and consuming food. It is assumed that nearly everybody wore a knife, perhaps attached to a girdle hanger, a common iron grave object. The *Rule* of St. Benedict requires each brother to have a knife and a needle but warns them that they are not to sleep with their knives attached to their belts lest they injure themselves.[46] We might be able to generalize

---

[43] Guy Beresford *et al.*, *Goltho*, pp. 183–84; for illustrations of the chain and associated fittings, see p. 182, fig.159, nos. 122–25.

[44] Blinkhorn, "Habitus," p. 123

[45] H. E. M. Cool, *Eating and Drinking in Roman Britain*, p. 89.

[46] For the Old English *Rule* of St. Benedict (Winteney Version), see Arnold Schröer, ed., *Die*

from this requirement to standards of dress for those outside the monastery. A copper-alloy ring found in a grave in Bury St. Edmunds holds three similar personal implements, including a circular spoon and a pick.[47] Such tools might have been tokens of status. A small knife from Flixborough might have been used for personal care. It is one of a number from the site that were inlaid, as were those above, from Hamwic, which marks them in terms of status and hence identity.[48]

Small knives are common in graves from the Early Saxon period, as, for example, at Lakenheath.[49] Knives found at Shakenoak resemble those found in later cemeteries at Yelford, Chadlington, and Sutton Courtenay, but differ in style from knives found in other local cemeteries of the sixth century.[50] Evidence from Flixborough shows knives homogeneous within the settlement but, in the later period, differing from knives found elsewhere. Ottaway describes the composite group of Flixborough knives as homogeneous, with little variation in dimensions between those from the earlier settlement periods (seventh to late ninth century) and later periods (late ninth century onward). However, in the later period knives from Flixborough were somewhat different from aggregate samples from various other late Anglo-Saxon and Anglo-Scandinavian sites. Knives from the latter tended to have longer tangs (the part of the blade inserted into the handle) and handles than knives from the mid-Saxon period.[51] Traditions of ironwork and knife-making were both spread across regions but, as Flixborough shows, sometimes maintained consistent in form over long periods, even though, as we have seen, Flixborough as a settlement shifted its focus several times.

Given their personal ties, it is not surprising that knives are often found in graves. Links between grave finds and settlement life can be but are not always strong links to the lives of those who used them.[52] In reference to the settlement and cemetery at seventh-century West Stow, J. D. Richards comments that "iron tools are found in domestic contexts but almost never in Anglo-Saxon graves."[53] Richards notes that rich Viking burials often include smithing and farming tools, while Anglo-Saxon burials do not. Citing a study by Heinrich Härke, Richards notes that "many of those buried with weapons" elsewhere "were not warriors."[54] Knives might be found in graves because they were personal objects used for eating every day and other personal tasks that were worthy of commemoration. But it is

Winteney-Version der Regula S. Benedicti, ch. 22, p. 63, on how to sleep, and ch. 55, p. 113, on the knife and needle.
[47] Stanley West, *A Corpus of Anglo-Saxon Material from Suffolk*, p. 14, item 13.1, and p. 129, fig. 13, no. 2.
[48] Ottaway *et al.*, "Domestic Fittings and Implements," p. 215.
[49] West, *A Corpus of Anglo-Saxon Material from Suffolk*, p. 77, nos. 110.14–110.16, and p. 228, fig. 110, nos. 14–16.
[50] Brown, "The Ironwork," p. 112. Sixth-century knives had slightly humped backs; those at Shakenoak and elsewhere have a straight blade edge and back.
[51] On the knives, see Ottaway *et al.*, "Domestic Fittings and Implements," pp. 203–12.
[52] See, for example, Lloyd Laing and Jennifer Laing, *Anglo-Saxon England*, pp. 77 and 84.
[53] J. D. Richards, "Anglo-Saxon Symbolism," p. 136.
[54] Richards, "Anglo-Saxon Symbolism," p. 136, citing Heinrich Härke, "'Warrior Graves'?".

also possible that the object represented something other than a connection to lived experience.

Forks

Flesh forks and meat hooks (or flesh hooks) are difficult to distinguish in texts, since there is only one Old English word for the two devices, *awel*. In finds the two are differentiated. The fork is Y-shaped with two prongs; the meat hook consists of a shaft or tang (to be inserted into a wooden handle) with two or three curved prongs projecting at right angles from the tang. Seven flesh forks or parts thereof were found at Flixborough. The longest measures 106 mm (approximately 4.05 inches) and the shortest 45 mm (a stub). The width given for a fork 77 mm long was 30 mm wide.[55] The tines of these forks are not set at right angles to the tang but curve outward instead, a design detail that might carry traditional or cultural significance.

Finds from Flixborough have parallels at Thetford and North Elmham. A series of meat forks was found at Thetford.[56] The term "meat fork" might suggest a massive implement meant to hold a thick joint over the fire, but all four examples from Thetford measure only 80 mm to 90 mm. Each would have been affixed to a wooden handle, as is a fork found in Birka, Sweden, which had a long handle attached.[57] Prongs on one of the Thetford forks are approximately 6 mm wide and, like the "pot hooks" or handles described above, suit the dimensions of such cooking pots as those from Ipswich, which have a mouth diameter of four to six inches.[58] The hooks from Thetford, with wooden handles, could have been used to pull meat out of broth or lift it off a roasting surface. Somewhat similar to the flesh forks from Flixborough, these have tines that curve outward rather than project at a right angle to the stem.[59] Such forks would not have been useful for holding any but small cuts of meat directly over a fire, however, since the handles could easily have burned.

Although knives dominate the iron finds from the 16–22 Coppergate site at York, with dates ranging from the ninth to the eleventh centuries, forks and other implements are also abundant. For example, a socketed fork was "probably a flesh fork used for holding meat over a fire during cooking or extracting it from cooking vessels." It is approximately 12 cm long, with two prongs about 5 cm long and about 2.5 cm apart at the widest spread. Ottaway notes that several objects of comparable size and shape were recorded as "boat hooks" at Dorestad, while "substantially larger forks of similar form" were found at Birka (Sweden) and Hedeby (Denmark). The

---

[55] Measurements from Ottaway *et al.*, "Domestic Fittings and Implements," p. 228.
[56] Ian H. Goodall, with Blanch Ellis and Brian Gilmour, "Iron Objects," p. 94 (figs. 133, 193–96) and p. 95.
[57] Patrick Ottaway, *Anglo-Scandinavian Ironwork from 16–22 Coppergate*, p. 599.
[58] Hurst, "The Pottery," p. 300.
[59] Ottaway, *Anglo-Scandinavian Ironwork*, p. 600, notes the curvature of the Thetford tines and compares them to forks at York, for which see below.

forks from York and Dorestad seem very small for use as boat hooks, an application for which the larger, long-handled Birka and Hedeby objects were no doubt better suited.[60] Also found at York was a curved prong or tip, probably broken off from a stem that would have held another prong like it to form a flesh hook. The curvature of this flesh hook is comparable to those from Flixborough and Thetford discussed above.[61] Elsewhere examples of such hooks are also socketed, but sometimes they also have whittle tangs so they could be inserted into wooden handles as were knives.[62] A second site at York, 46–54 Fishergate, also yielded a meat hook with curved tips forming prongs and with a tang to be fitted into a wooden handle. In this case there is evidence of development and perhaps innovation. Nicola Rogers writes that "this type of flesh hook, with two or three prongs split from the same tang, originates in the late Anglo-Saxon period and continues in use until the thirteenth century." The context of the York hook she illustrates is twelfth century. She cites other examples from York (6–8 Pavement), Thetford, and Goltho, the latter with two arms and a short, angled tang.[63]

At Flixborough no forks were found with the tines set at right angles to the tang, a configuration that is common elsewhere. Instead, at Flixborough the tines are curved, as they are on forks from Thetford. There could be several explanations. One might be that the form encoded tradition or other elements of the *habitus* at both Thetford and Flixborough. It is possible that other forms were unknown or that the surviving form was not, in fact, exclusive and that forks which differed in form were not preserved (only a small part of the evidence survives). The handles, the most eloquent part of a fork, are missing. The importance of fork handles can be adduced from some knife blades at Flixborough, which were decorated with inlay, suggesting that they "were considered suitable for making statements about their owner's social status."[64] Rogers believes that the form in which tines are split from the same tang was developed in the late Anglo-Saxon period and that it persisted for some three centuries. Cultural connections reaching from tenth-century York so far forward would be extraordinary by any standard. It is more probable that the form, once it had evolved to a certain point, became generic. It must have been highly satisfactory, since, over centuries, no improvements were needed. The treatment of the handle might have varied, but handles have disappeared.

Spoons and ladles

Items sometimes made of iron include spoon and ladles, but these forms, like iron cauldrons or cooking vessels, are rare. It is not clear, moreover,

---

[60] Ottaway, *Anglo-Scandinavian Ironwork*, p. 599, illustrated p. 600, fig. 247, no. 2989.
[61] Ottaway, *Anglo-Scandinavian Ironwork*, p. 600, notes the comparison to Thetford.
[62] Ottaway, *Anglo-Scandinavian Ironwork*, p. 600, no. 2990.
[63] Nicola S. H. Rogers, *Anglian and Other Finds from 46–64 Fishergate*, p. 1331, fig. 643. Beresford et al., *Goltho*, pp. 183–84; for an illustration, see p. 182, fig.159, no. 119.
[64] Ottaway et al., "Domestic Fittings and Implements," p. 215.

that ladles and iron pots were exclusively used for cooking. Six tinned spoons were found at York with a flat bowl at either end of the stem, one larger than the other; they compare to bone and non-ferrous metal spoons and "may have been used for measuring or dispensing such materials as cosmetics and spices."[65] An iron spoon found at 16–22 Coppergate is tin-plated and whole. Thought to have been made on the site, it has two bowls, one larger than the other, with a triangular handle and chamfered (i.e., beveled) shoulders (the context is c. 930–c.975).[66] A second spoon, missing one bowl, was found in a post and wattle building nearby. Made of iron and tin-plated, it has a grooved stem and it too is thought to have been made on the site.[67] A copper-alloy spoon was found at Whitby, and, like the plated and decorated spoons from York, cannot be grouped with ordinary, unornamented kitchen wares.[68] They were intended for special uses requiring a finer finish than iron, or perhaps were intended for kitchens or tables of the prosperous.

Pans and cauldrons

Other iron cooking implements are even rarer than forks and spoons. Among them is the pan, in Old English the *panne* or *cocerpanne*. The pan was a shallow metal vessel with a handle, sometimes made of iron but also of non-ferrous metals. Two bronze skillets, both with bronze handles, were found at the monastery of Whitby and classified as "objects of domestic use." According to Charles Peers and C. A. Ralegh Radford, these skillets are "descendants of the well-known Roman *patella*" that was developed "in the Gaulish workshops, and exported to every province during the early Empire."[69] Cool describes a variety of cookware forms in metal from Roman Britain, but few of them were made of iron.[70] The Whitby vessels are seen as poor examples of the type since they lacked "effective strengthening of the handle, rim, and base." Both showed repairs.[71] At Flixborough five copper-alloy vessel fragments were recovered from late seventh- to early eighth-century contexts. Rogers suggests that they might represent bowls, a cauldron, or skillets similar to those found at Whitby.[72] An iron pan with a long handle (again, of metal) was found at Winchester and another at York. Ottaway writes that "vessels made of iron, rather than pottery, were, on occasion, used for cooking and large pans which have, or had, a long handle come from Winchester and York. These objects illustrate skill in a very important part of the smithing process, namely the working

[65] Ottaway, "The Products of the Blacksmith," 2:5–6.
[66] This is Period 4b. See Ottaway, *Anglo-Scandinavian Ironwork*, pp. 601–2, no. 3002.
[67] Ottaway, *Anglo-Scandinavian Ironwork*, pp. 601–2.
[68] Charles Peers and C. A. Ralegh Radford, "The Saxon Monastery of Whitby," p. 62, fig. 12, 7.
[69] *Patella* is glossed with *panne* in L. Kindschi, "The Latin-Old English Glossaries in Plantin-Moretus MS. 32," line 681.
[70] Cool, *Eating and Drinking in Roman Britain*, pp. 50 and 53.
[71] Peers and Radford, "The Saxon Monastery of Whitby," p. 66, illustration p. 67 (fig. 16).
[72] Nicola Rogers, "Copper-alloy Vessels and Container Mounts," p. 115.

of large pieces of sheet iron without allowing them to split."[73] It is not impossible that early forms of such pans were, for a time, associated with the Roman and Gaulish *patella*.

The metal pan is a continental form; its successor, the ceramic pan with wooden handles, is Scandinavian. Metal handles would transmit heat, so the pan would have required some form of insulation when placed directly over fire. One such iron pan was found in Norway at Jevnaker (Oppland), a Viking era artifact (eighth to tenth century), found in a grave mound, whole, circular, slightly concave, with a handle attached by rivet to the center (85 cm long, 25 cm wide).[74] Pans or skillets were also fashioned from shallow pottery vessels with sockets made to hold wooden handles. An example of a flat dish with two socketed handles was found at Vorbasse (Denmark).[75] These skillets are not characteristic Anglo-Saxon wares and, on this account, seem more likely than others discussed so far to have been seen by the Anglo-Saxons as encoding cultural and ancestral information.

Forms with handles are well documented outside England and seem to have been imports or wares used by traders. Two Viking-era skillets or frying pans, both ceramic, were found in York. One found at Hungate, possibly from the ninth century, consists of the upper part of a skillet with a socket and is, in Dudley M. Waterman's view, "almost certainly" an import from Holland in the Viking age.[76] The socket, made separately, was pressed into position. According to Waterman, late Saxon skillets have short sockets usually level with a flanged rim. A second pan found at Goodramgate is also Anglo-Scandinavian. Consisting of the upper part of the bowl with a socket for a wooden handle, it too is "almost certainly" an import from Holland in the Viking age.[77] Waterman considered this skillet to be typical of those found at sites in the Rhineland, Holland, Northern Germany, and also Hedeby.[78] Two skillets of St. Neot's ware from Bedford also feature socketed handles, although nothing is said about their origins. They are presumably the "plain" skillets to which Waterman refers, along with a decorated example from Downing Street, Cambridge. Waterman notes two distinct methods of attaching the handle. The East Anglian examples (Bedford, Cambridge) have a short socket that is level with the rim. The skillets from York have sockets that angle above the rim, like those imported from Holland, the Rhineland, and Germany.[79] This difference seems to relate both to function, since a skillet with an angled handle is easier to place over fire and manipulate, and also to fashion, since

[73] Ottaway, "The Products of the Blacksmith," 2:6 (fig. 11).
[74] Else Roesdahl, Jean-Pierre Mohen, and François-Xavier Dillman, eds., *Les Vikings*, p. 142 (image), p. 244 (description).
[75] C. J. Becker, "Viking Age Settlements in Western and Central Jutland," pp. 171–72 and fig. 34.
[76] Dudley M. Waterman, "Late Saxon, Viking and Early Medieval Finds from York," pp. 100–1.
[77] Waterman, "Late Saxon," p. 100 and p. 101, fig. 3.
[78] Waterman, "Late Saxon," pp. 100–1, and n. 5.
[79] Waterman, "Late Saxon," p. 101. See G. C. Dunning, J. G. Hurst, J. N. L. Myres, and F. Tischler, *Anglo-Saxon Pottery*, pp. 35 and 39, fig. 15, nos. 4 and 5.

the skillets with angled handles were either imports or locally made wares modeled on imports.

Since iron vessels are rare in Anglo-Saxon contexts, agricultural processes involving iron that parallel cooking processes are of interest. One example involves wool. Ottaway notes that vats were used for wool processing, which required ladles for handling hot fat or oil. He writes that "combing wool involved passing it from one comb to the other, but in order to do this effectively the teeth had to be heated and the wool greased." Middle Anglo-Saxon combs from Wicken Bonhunt were found with an unusual, elongated ladle, which, Ottaway suggests, was "used for greasing wool during combing."[80] This object survived in the context of animal husbandry rather than cooking, but the application of such a tool to food preparation is plausible.

Fish hooks

One implement involved in a particularly important area of the diet is the fish hook. Hooks were used in line fishing, both freshwater and marine. It is well known that many Anglo-Saxon sites had access to riverine or freshwater fish. The onset of marine fishing and the role of marine fish in the diet, however, are controversial, as we will see later (Chapter 10), making the fish hook a piece of ironwork of special interest. Fish hooks are not common, but they have been found in several mid-ninth- to eleventh-century sites, including 16–22 Coppergate, York. They are usually iron, sometimes barbed, and are variable in size. The longest of seven hooks from York measures 78 mm; another 55–56 mm in length, has a width of 20–22 mm. Some have loop-eyed terminals, others have terminals formed by flattening the head of the shank; tips are either barbed or pointed. Larger hooks from Anglo-Saxon contexts are rare. Another hook from elsewhere in York is larger than those from Coppergate. Ottaway considers a hook from Shetland measuring 105 mm in length exceptional in size; other large hooks he describes are from Denmark and Sweden.[81] In comments on Saxo-Norman London, Alan Vince links large fish hooks found at Billingsgate to the onset of deep-sea fishing in the middle decades of the eleventh century.[82]

Four fish hooks were found at Fishergate (three intact, one possibly a hook fragment). One, intact, is 49.2 mm long, its (possibly looped) terminal missing; another is only half that size. Rogers considers the former large enough for pike or cod and suggests it could have been used for marine or freshwater fishing, although it seems too small for the former compared to hooks from Coppergate.[83] The hooks were found in pits that

[80] Ottaway, "The Products of the Blacksmith," 1:12 and 1:14, fig. 5b (the Wicken Bonhunt ladle).
[81] Ottaway, *Anglo-Scandinavian Ironwork*, p. 601, fig. 248, nos. 2991–95.
[82] Alan Vince, "Saxon Urban Economies," p. 114.
[83] The larger hook is no. 5038 and the smaller hook is no. 5039 in Rogers, *Anglian and Other Finds*, p. 1319; illustrated p. 1318, fig. 637.

contained earlier fill, perhaps from the later eighth century. Rogers notes the similarity in size between the larger hook mentioned here and hooks found at Coppergate; she also notes that large fish hooks were found at 6–8 Pavement in York. The presence of smaller hooks, she believes, might have been overlooked in soil samples that were not sieved.[84] Given their size, it is perhaps remarkable that either large or small hooks survive.

It is useful to compare the aggregated evidence of ironwork from Anglo-Saxon sites to that from roughly contemporary sites in Jutland. No cooking utensils were found at Sædding, a village abandoned around 1100, for example, although knives, nails, and various agricultural tools, including a scythe, were recovered.[85] Finds from Trabjerg numbered nearly 4,000, but, astonishingly, only twenty-three of them were metal. However, several soapstone sherds revealed traces of iron handles (or rivets probably made for handles), and eight sherds retained traces of burned food.[86] At Vorbasse, a larger and better-known settlement, some longhouses within farming complexes were used for casting bronze and forging iron.[87] These buildings, part of the western (later) section of the settlement, were multi-purpose structures that housed animals. The report describes no surviving iron-work, but pottery finds included a flat dish with two sockets intended for inserts of wood.[88] Omgård was a multi-phased Viking site, having served as a trading location at one point and as a large farm at another. There was extensive evidence of smithing in various longhouses that were exca-vated, and some horse furniture was turned up. Pottery finds documented a strong presence of Slavic imported ware, but no ironwork connected to food preparation or consumption was found.[89] There were changes of pottery and of site function during the rebuilding (and relocation) of the site, but there is no evidence of the impact of such changes on ironwork.[90] At these sites, as in the Anglo-Saxon and Anglo-Scandinavian sites dis-cussed earlier, kitchenware in iron is either scarce or not at all in evidence. Even so, we have many reasons to assume that it was once abundant.

Iron and texts

Food objects in iron are hardly more prominent in texts than they are in archaeological data. Texts refer to smiths and smithies in both practical and mythical contexts, with examples as different as the *Chronicle of Evesham*, with its account of recalcitrant smiths, and *The Colloquy*.[91] Texts that refer

---

[84] Rogers, *Anglian and Other Finds*, p. 1319.
[85] Becker, "Viking Age Settlements," p. 115.
[86] Becker, "Viking Age Settlements," pp. 131–32.
[87] Becker, "Viking Age Settlements," p. 160.
[88] Becker, "Viking Age Settlements," pp. 171–72 and fig. 34.
[89] Becker, "Viking Age Settlements," pp. 173–206.
[90] Note the meat fork from the trading site of Hedeby, Jutland, in Herbert Jankuhn, *Die Ausgrabungen in Haithabu*, p. 128, illustration no. 62.
[91] The episode is mentioned in Geddes, "Iron," p. 175. For the text, see Macray, *Chronicon Abbatiae de Evesham*, pp. 25–26.

to cooking objects made of iron are very rare. The most important is *Be gesceadwisan gerefan* (*Concerning the Discriminating Reeve*), discussed in relation to glosses (see Chapter 3). This text draws on glosses that name iron implements related to food production and consumption, and embeds them in lists. The tools include:

> wagon-cover, plowing tackle, harrowing tackle, and many things. . . and also a measure, a fork (or hook), and, for the threshing floor, a flail, and many implements: a pot (bowl), a leaden cauldron, a kettle, a ladle, pans, a crock, a gridiron [a trivet supporting a kettle over fire], dishes, a handled vessel, a large jar for liquids, a tub, a churn, a cheese-vat, a pouch or basket, . . .

> wængewædu, sulhgesidu, egeðgetigu & fela ðinga, . . . ge eac mete, awel & to odene fligel & andlamena fela: hwer, lead, cytel, hlædel, pannan, crocca, brandiren, dixas, stelmelas, cyfa, cyflas, cyrne, cysfæt, ceodan, . . .

One hint of the list's literary heritage is the alliteration of the last words. A second list, which also has an academic origin, includes many implements of iron, including the auger, awl, adze, curry-comb, and others:

> axe, adze, bill, awl, plane, saw, spoke-shave, tie hook, auger, mattock, crowbar, share, coulter, and also goad-iron, scythe, sickle, hoe, spade, shovel, woad-trowel, barrow, broom, mallet, rake, fork, ladder, curry-comb and shears, fire-tongs, steelyard.

> æcse, adsan, bil, byrse, scafan, sage, cimbiren, tigehoc, næfebor, mattuc, ippingiren, scear, culter & eac gadiren, siðe, sicol, weodhoc, spade, scofle, wadspitel, bærwan, besman, bytel, race, geafle, hlædre, horscamb & sceara, fyrtange, wæipundern.[92]

Many of the tools in this list would have had agricultural uses, among them the coulter, hoe, spade, and shovel.

These are the only lists of food-related ironwork in Old English. Mark Gardiner associates only a few of these objects with the kitchen. Those likely to have been made of iron include *hwer* (small cauldron); *lead* (leaden vessel); *cytel* (large cauldron); *hlædel* (ladle); *pannan* (pans); and *brandiren* (gridiron). Two were probably made of wood: *dixas* (dishes) and *stelmelas* (scoop). The *crocca* was earthenware. Most of the containers are associated with the dairy, including *cyfa, cyflas, cyrne, cysfæt,* and *ceodan,* all of these likely to have been made of wood. Two of these items, *cyfa* and *cyflas,* might also have been found in the kitchen. Gardiner assigns other objects found in these two lists (not included in my excerpts above) to the pantry, known in Old English as the *cellarium* or *meteclyf,* or the *lardarium* or *spichus,* both words found only in glosses. It is not possible to tell if the pantry formed a recognized workspace in the Anglo-Saxon home or on estates (it would have been likely only in manor houses, in any case). Objects Gardiner assigns to the pantry might also have been kitchenware: *sealtfæt* (salt cellar);

---

[92] *Gerefa,* ed. F. Liebermann, *GDA,* pp. 453–55. For a discussion of the second list, see Chapter 3, pp. 74–75, and n. 63, above.

sticfodder (spoon-case); *piperhorn* (pepper-horn); *bearmteage* (yeast-boxes); *læflas* (bowls); and *cyllan* (leather bottle).[93] None of these is likely to have been made of iron but rather of wood. Most other food-related words in *Concerning the Discriminating Reeve* are found elsewhere only in glosses.[94]

Two important iron objects are not included in *Concerning the Discriminating Reeve*. One is the ordinary knife, the *seax*. The Old English *World History* of Orosius, translated in the ninth century, is the only place we find a reference to a knife used to cut meat, the *meteseax*, where it is mentioned as the murder weapon in the death of Caesar: "they stabbed him with their meat knives within their court chambers" (*hiene mid heora metseacsum ofsticedon inne on heora gemotærne*).[95] The phrase *mid heora metseacsum* indicates use of the men's personal knives for this deed. Ælfric's homily on the Holy Innocents notes that before he died Herod commanded his followers to hand him his *seax* to peel an apple (*þa het he him his seax aræcan to screadigenne ænne æppel*).[96] Numerous references to the *seax* are associated with plants, as in a charm that involves digging and chopping a herb and putting it, with the knife, beneath an altar so that Masses can be said over it.[97] *Bald's Leechbook* contains similar references. One describes how the knife, a surgical instrument, can be used to reform the edges of a hair-lip.[98] Another describes how a *seax* with an ox horn handle and brass nails can be used to cure a horse of elf-shot (a disease produced by evil spirits).[99]

Also missing from the reeve's list is the *angel*, fish hook, an object which might have been found on estates with rivers or ponds. *Angel* occurs fifteen times in the corpus, but predictably most occurrences have little to do with the work of catching fish. The most commonly cited example is from *The Colloquy*, in which the student impersonating the shipman explains how he goes about fishing: "I go on board my ship and throw my net into the river, and a hook, and bait, and a wicker basket (creel), and whatever they catch I take" (*Ic astigie min scyp & wyrpe max mine on ea, & ancgil vel æs ic*

---

[93] Mark Gardiner, "Implements and Utensils in *Gerefa*," pp. 264–65. Gardiner cites Christine Fell, "Some Domestic Problems."

[94] See Chapter 3 for a discussion of *Concerning the Discriminating Reeve*.

[95] Janet Bately, ed., *The Old English Orosius*, book 5, ch. 12, p. 129, l, 1.

[96] Ælfric, "Holy Innocents," in P. A. M. Clemoes, ed., *Ælfric's Catholic Homilies*, p. 222, l. 163.

[97] Charm 19, ed. Godfried Storms, *Anglo-Saxon Magic*, pp. 243–44: "Dig up the herb, stick it through with the knife. Immediately go as quickly as you can to church and put it [the herb] under the altar with the knife" (*Adelf þa wyrt, læt stician þæt seax þær on. Gang eft swa þu raþost mæge to ciricean, and lege under weofod mid þam seaxe*).

[98] *Bald's Leechbook*, Book I, ch. xiii, ed. Oswald Cockayne, *Leechdoms, Wortcunning and Starcraft*, 2: 56–57: "For a hair-lip . . . cut the false edges of the lip with a knife, sew up with silk, then smear with salve inside and out" (*Wið hærscearde . . . onsnið mid seaxse seowa mid seolce fæste smire mid þonne mid þære sealfe utan & innan*).

[99] *Bald's Leechbook*, Book II, ch. lxv, ed. Cockayne, *Leechdoms*, 2: 290–91: "If a horse is elf-shot, take a knife with a handle made of the horn of a fallow ox and on which there are three brass nails, then make Christ's mark on the horse's forehead" (*Gif hors ofscoten sie nim þonne þæt seax þe þæt hæfte sie fealo hryþeres horn & sien III ærene næglas on, writ þonne þam horse on þam heafde foran cristes mæl*). "Elf-shot" might mean wounded by an arrow shot by an elf, hence indicating an ill-defined malady.

wyrpe & spyrtan, & swa hwæt swa hig gehæftað ic genime). Later the iron-worker asserts the indispensability of his craft: "Whence the fisherman's hook, or the shoemaker's awl, or the sewer's needle, are they not of my making?" (*Hwanon fiscere ancgel, oþþe sceowyrhton æl, oþþe seamere nædl? Nis hit of minon geweorce?*).[100]

Other references to the fish hook are imbued with moral connotations. The word occurs in the translation of the *Consolation of Philosophy* undertaken during King Alfred's reign: "Adversity then very often draws all those who are subjected to it by force to the true felicities, as a fish is caught by a hook" (*Sio wiðerwerdnes þonne ful oft ealle þa ðe hiere underþeodde bioð neadinga getyhð to ðam soðum gesælðum, swa swa mid angle fisc gefangen bið*).[101] The word is common in the Gospels, as in Matthew 17:27, elaborated by Ælfric: "Lest we offend them, go to the sea and throw out your hook and (taking) the fish that swallows it most quickly, open its mouth and therein you will find a piece of money. Take it out and give it to them as the tax for yourself and for me" (*Ðe læs þe we hi æswician: ga to þære sæ & wurp ut þinne angel. & þone fisc þe hine hraðost forswylhð geopena his muð. þonne findst þu ðæron ænne gyldenne wecg nim þone & syle to tolle for me & for þe*).[102] This example invokes the miraculous topos seen in the life of Bishop Ecgwine. Another example is from Ælfric's homily for Palm Sunday, which draws on Gregory the Great's famous analogy of the humanity of Christ as fish bait: "It happens to the fierce devil just as (it happens) to the hungry fish that sees the bait but does not see the hook on which the bait is stuck (and) is then hungry for the bait and hence swallows up the hook with the bait" (*Þa getimode þam reðan deofle. swa swa deð þam grædian fisce. þe gesihð þæt æs. & ne gesihð þone angel. þe on ðæm æse sticað: bið þonne grædig þæs æses. & forswylcð þone angel forð mid þam æse*).[103] These references have more to do with psychology than with the mechanics of fishing or the properties of hooks or their making.

The reeve's list names two objects with multiple names and forms, the awl and the iron kettle. A single Old English word, *awel*, describes forks in metal, which are of two kinds, the meat hook and the fork. *Awel* is found nineteen times, almost always in glosses. Forks of unspecified function are mentioned in a few texts. *Awel* designates an agricultural implement (by context) only in this text, where it could be translated either as fork or hook. In glosses *awel* translates *fuscinula* or small fork and *tridens*, in the latter case paired with *meottoc* (translated as fork or trident). *Awel* also glosses *harpago*, talon or hook, and *uncus* and *ungule*, barb, both Latin

---

[100] Garmonsway, *Ælfric's Colloquy*, p. 26, ll. 91–93, and pp. 39–40, ll. 221–23.

[101] Malcolm Godden and Susan Irvine, eds., *The Old English Boethius*, 1: 284, ll. 25–27 (OE); 2: 31, ch. 20 (translation).

[102] Ælfric, "Dedicatio Ecclesiae Sancti Michaelis," ed. Clemoes, *Ælfric's Catholic Homilies*, pp. 465–75 at p. 470, ll. 163–66.

[103] Gregory described the devil as Leviathan, the sea monster. The humanity of Christ is the bait that disguises the hook with which God catches the monster. For Ælfric's homily on Palm Sunday, see *Ælfric's Catholic Homilies*, ed. Clemoes, p. 296, ll. 171–74, and see further commentary by Malcolm Godden, ed., *Ælfric's Catholic Homilies*, p. 117.

words referring to an instrument of torture (*DOE, awel*). Textual support for *cytel*, a cooking vessel made of iron, is also ample, some forty occurrences. References range from medicinal recipes requiring a copper kettle to a list of plate from a monastic community in which all the items seem to be made of metal. *Cytel* seems to have been used interchangeably with other words for containers. In one gloss, *cytel* and *crocc* seem to be interchangeable translations. The Latin *caccabos* is translated as *crocc, citiles, hweres* (i.e., crock, kettle, cauldron).[104]

Other words from the reeve's list that occur often elsewhere include *cyf*, a vessel used especially for wine or water, or possibly a tub. The word is used thirteen times and is found both in glosses and in narratives based on scripture or the early Christian era (*DOE, cyf*). *Panne* is found over thirty times and *cocorpanne* is found ten times; both words designate a skillet, but *cocorpanne* (or *cocerpanne*) is found only in translations of the psalms or in glosses (*DOE, cocorpanne*). The first element of this compound, *coc-*, informs several food-related words: *coc*, found seventeen times in a range of texts, meaning cook; *cocor-mete*, cooked food, in one gloss; *cocnung*, also meaning cooked food or perhaps a cake, found five times, including *Bald's Leechbook*; *gecocnod*, in two glosses, meaning "seasoned, made savoury"; and *gecocsod*, cooked or fried, also in two glosses.[105] Terms for iron cooking implements include *brædpanne*, found only in four glosses, and two variants, *brædingpanne* (in one gloss) and *bradpanne* in two glosses.

As this survey shows, textual evidence of food-related objects in iron is limited. Not surprisingly, texts are replete with mentions of finished forms of iron such as sword blades and armor. For example, there are over twenty references to iron weapons and armor in *Beowulf* and four *iren*-compounds. *Iren* means "sword" when Hrothgar talks with Beowulf about what might happen if "sickness or sword [should take] your lord, keeper of the people" (*adl oþðe iren ealdor ðinne / folces hyrda*).[106] *Iren* (iron) functions metonymically for "sword" in "The Battle of Maldon," when the thegn Leofsunu predicts that "weapons shall take me, spear and sword" (*ac me sceal wæpen niman, ord and iren*).[107] The rest of the poetic corpus contains only six references to iron, perhaps an indication of how closely connected the word *iren* was to the grimmest aspects of heroic topoi. Iron is mentioned once in *Andreas*, when the devil urges that Andrew be attacked with the "hard-edged sword."[108] In *Genesis B* Satan

[104] Aldhelm's glosses to "De Virginitate" contain several such pairings; for glosses to the prose version, see Louis Goossens, ed., *The Old English Glosses of MS. Brussels, Royal Library 1650*; see other sources listed in the *DOE* entry for *cytel*.
[105] All data from *DOE* entries for *coc* and its forms: *cocor-mete, cocnung, gecocnod*, and *gecocsod*.
[106] See Fulk, Bjork, and Niles, eds., *Klaeber's* Beowulf, p. 62, ll. 1848–49. My translation.
[107] For "The Battle of Maldon," l. 253, see Dobbie, ed., *The Anglo-Saxon Minor Poems*, p. 14.
[108] For *Andreas*, l. 1180–81, "the track of the weapon, the hard-edged sword" (*wæpnes spor iren ecgheard*), see George Philip Krapp, ed., *The Vercelli Book*, pp. 35–36.

complains of his iron bonds (twice).[109] Iron is mentioned three times in "Solomon and Saturn" (the devil pelts a wretched man with iron balls; age is said to consume iron with rust; apocalyptic beasts are said to have horns of iron).[110]

The Anglo-Saxons seldom registered the tension between ironwork for war and ironwork for peaceful purposes. We have seen that when Bishop Ecgwine was confronted by the smoky, noisy, obstreperous smiths, he retreated to a forest to invoke punishment on their satanic force, although the forest itself was probably imbued with pagan significance for the residents of Alcester. In the *Old English Martyrology*, the biographer of the obscure St. Eastorwine did much better by ironworkers and ironwork. Eosterwine was co-abbot of Wearmouth with Benedict Biscop and the cousin of Ceolfrith, who was the abbot of Jarrow. Once a thegn of King Ecgferth, Eosterwine "abandoned his weapons and worldly habits" (*he forlet þa wæpna ond ða woruldlican wisan*) and became a priest and then an abbot. He was so humble that he guided the plow, smithed iron, cultivated and shelled (or threshed) corn, milked ewes, led new-born calves to their mothers, baked bread, and planted leeks (or herbs) (*he sulh heold, ond on iren sloh, ond corn ðærsc and þæt windwode, ond ewa mealc, ond ða cealfas to cuum lædde, ond hlafas brædde, and leac sette*).[111] As if beating swords into plowshares (Isaiah 2:4), the holy man exchanged his weapons for the plow and other iron tools.

Eastorwine's agricultural and culinary talents were more varied than those of Ceolfrith, about whom it was written that, "while he held the office of baker, he was careful in the midst of sieving the flour, lighting and cleansing the oven and baking in it the loaves, not to omit to learn and also to practice the ceremonies of the priesthood."[112] Ceolfrith's association with the arts of baking seems to elevate them to a sacramental level. The list of Eastorwine's activities avoids ceremonial associations and confirms his humility. The list appears in somewhat different form in Bede's *History of the Abbots of Wearmouth and Jarrow*, its source. Bede writes that Eastorwine ceased to be a thegn "by laying down his arms and girding himself for spiritual warfare." He "took his share of the winnowing and threshing, the milking of the ewes and the cows; he laboured in the bakehouse, garden and kitchen." Although an abbot, Eastorwine put his hand "to the plough along the furrow, hammering iron into shape or wielding the winnowing-fan."[113] In this regard it is important that smithing – the abbot *on iren sloh*

---

[109] For *Genesis*, l. 371, "iron bands" (*irenbenda*), l. 383, "of hard iron" (*heardes irenes*), see George Philip Krapp, ed., *The Junius Manuscript*, p. 14.

[110] For "Solomon and Saturn," see ll. 28 (iron balls, *irenum aplum*), 301 (iron bitten by rust, *iren mid ome*), 471 (with iron horns, *irenun hornum*), in Dobbie, ed., *The Anglo-Saxon Minor Poems*, pp. 32, 41 and 47.

[111] Günther Kotzor, ed., *Das altenglische Martyrologium*, 2: 30. See Sarah Foot, *Monastic Life in Anglo-Saxon England*, pp. 186–87.

[112] "The Anonymous Life of St. Ceolfrith," ed. Dorothy Whitelock, *EHD*, pp. 758–70, at p. 759.

[113] Bede, *History of the Abbots*, pp. 194–95. See Kotzor, *Das altenglische Martyrologium*, 2: 291.

(struck on iron), to quote the *Old English Martyrology* – ranks with plowing and humble field work. The monastic master of *The Colloquy* treats the cook and some others with disdain, but Ceolfrith, Eastorwine, and others show that manual labor was seen in serious monastic literature as a dignified and worthy occupation.

Blinkhorn notes that "monk-smiths sometimes feature in Anglo-Saxon prose." In the *Ecclesiastical History* Bede describes a loose-living monk whom he knew himself. He was "much addicted to drunkenness and the other pleasures of a loose life" and would remain in his workshop rather than go to church. His monastic brothers, Bede writes, "bore with him patiently for the sake of his outward service, for he was an exceptionally skilled craftsman" (*ob necessitatum operum ipsius exteriorum, erat enim fabrili arte sigularis*).[114] Blinkhorn describes the monk as "skilled in metal-working" and "a skilled worker in metal," and *fabrili*, the only word for the monk's craft, can mean smith or forger (but other construction crafts as well). Blinkhorn also cites the "Carmen de Abbatibus," a ninth-century poem by Æthelwulf that refers to Cwicwine, whose hammer "crashed on to the iron placed under it in different positions on the anvil, while the forge roared." As the hammer "flew and smote the empty air, it decked the table of the brothers by beating out vessels."[115] Cwicwine presumably created plates, trays, and perhaps cups for the monks' table. He was not making iron tools only. Blinkhorn suggests that "the monastic manufactories" also played a role in trade associated with the monasteries, suggesting that some wares made by the monks "were destined for a wider market."[116] In the last chapter we noted that evidence from the Middle Saxon period (650–850) at North Elmham produced "a remarkably small number" of pottery sherds, suggesting "an almost aceramic phase" at this time. Perhaps there too food objects in iron were more common than elsewhere.[117]

We have seen throughout that ordinary objects associated with cooking seldom figure prominently in texts. Pots are overshadowed by decorated ceramics and special forms such as pitchers and cups, the feasting wares archaeologists describe. Querns are rarely thought of in close proximity to the glass and other luxuries riding above them in ships coming to England. Likewise, ironwork for field and kitchen is overshadowed by ironwork that took form in gleaming weapons, helmets, and shields, or in elaborate chains from which cauldrons were suspended and which have been found in ship burials, as at Sutton Hoo. Those objects communicate identity because they address elite consumption. Even observers who lack detailed knowledge of, for example, sword patterns or chain design that

[114] *Bede's Ecclesiastical History*, book 5, ch. 14, ed. Colgrave and Mynors, pp. 502–5.
[115] Æthelwulf, *De Abbatibus*, ch. 10, pp. 24–27, ll. 278–83, ll. 302–5, cited in Blinkhorn, "Of Cabbages and Kings," p. 10, and in Elizabeth Coatsworth, "The Material Culture of the Anglo-Saxon Church," pp. 784–85.
[116] Blinkhorn, "Of Cabbages and Kings," p. 10.
[117] Peter Wade-Martins, *Excavations in North Elmham Park 1967–1972*, 1: 120; see also 2: 423, and see Paul Blinkhorn, "Anglo-Saxon Pottery," p. 10.

might be characteristic of a given workshop, would be immediately aware of the prestige of weapons and feasting gear. Like decorated pots, this equipment points to exclusive circles traditionally seen as the center of the food network and comprising its densest, richest node.

If we think of production rather than consumption, however, we will see that ordinary ironwork, like ordinary cooking pots, occupied the center of the food network, and that feasting wares were at its margins. Without these useful forms and devices there could have been no cooking and hence no feasting. Simple iron forms also occupied the center of humbler food networks. Iron forks with wooden handles held meat over fires. Cooking pots hung from iron handles or simple chains or straps. Cakes were baked in iron pans. People who ate them and other things cooked in iron were surrounded by ordinary iron objects that, even without long histories of development specific to ethnic origins, spoke to them of what they did and how they did it, and hence helped to shape their identity.

Ironwork itself did not mark identity as clearly as pottery did, since opportunities for characteristic markings were limited. Yet ordinary iron objects created continuity with the past whether those who used it were aware of this continuity or not. Iron was reused and reshaped. Rogers observes that a type of Anglian meat hook originating in the late Anglo-Saxon period continued to be used until the thirteenth century.[118] As they were transported from place to place, melted down, and reshaped, iron objects carried iron forward in time, if not by centuries then by decades. Iron was a medium bearing no message – at least none that we can see and, perhaps, apart from signs of age, none that was visible to those who used iron objects. A molten stream flowing from object into object, iron filled new forms with old ones. New to the people who made and used them, whether nails or knives or forks, these objects were also as old as the fiery substance out of which they were fashioned.

---

[118] Rogers, *Anglian and Other Finds*, p. 1331.

7

Food Objects in Wood

The Anglo-Saxons lived in wood, sat on it, and ate and drank from it. Food was eaten from bowls and platters with wooden spoons, stored in jars and cooked in pots, some with wooden lids. Even feasters, as we know from the feast of Isaac's weaning in the *Old English Heptateuch* (Genesis 21:8), drank from wooden cups.[1] Households used wooden troughs for kneading bread and employed butter churns, trays, baskets, and other tools and containers made of wood. From hall to hut, tub to trough, bowl to barrel, wood was the most pervasive medium of their age. It is probable that most Anglo-Saxons used food objects in wood more often than they used pottery.

It is a paradox, then, that wooden artifacts are extremely rare among Anglo-Saxon finds. Almost all the wood that survives from early medieval England comes from York, where waterlogged, anaerobic soil conditions at three excavations – Coppergate, Bedern, and 22 Piccadilly – were well suited to the preservation of wooden objects.[2] The finds have been used to establish continuous occupation for well-defined, extended periods of Anglo-Scandinavian York, ranging from about 900 to 930, 930 to 975, and 975 to the early eleventh century.[3] Although spoons and spatulas, buckets and barrels, and wooden handles for iron implements have been found in various settlements, the evidence from York, some 1,500 wooden objects, is unique. According to Carole A. Morris, herself a woodworker, "No site in the rest of the world has yielded such rich and varied evidence of this important craft."[4] Only Dublin, another Viking settlement, produced comparable finds in wood; according to Morris, most of them remain unpublished.[5] She describes the objects from York as "the tip of an enormous wooden iceberg," the rest of which has vanished.[6]

---

[1] London, British Library, MS Cotton Claudius B.iv. "Abraham fashioned, as their custom was, a great feast as an entertainment for his people on that day on which the child was withdrawn from nursing" (*Abraham worhte, swa swa heora gewuna wæs, micelne gebeorscipe to blisse his mannum on þone dæg, þe man þæt cild fram gesoce ateah*). S. J. Crawford, ed., *The Old English Version of the Heptateuch*, p. 138 (my translation).

[2] Carole A. Morris, *Wood and Woodworking in Anglo-Scandinavian and Medieval York*, pp. 2073–94.

[3] Morris, *Wood and Woodworking*, p. 2076.

[4] Morris, *Wood and Woodworking*, p. 2093.

[5] Morris, *Wood and Woodworking*, p. 2090.

[6] Morris, *Wood and Woodworking*, p. 2094.

The nature of wood

Wood carving, along with ironwork and pottery making, was a common activity in Anglo-Saxon settlements. Like most domestic and agricultural tasks, woodworking began far from craft centers and depended on iron tools. Industrial woodworking required that trees be felled and processed into planks and blocks for further sizing and shaping. The Domesday Book records woods as the resources of manors and their lords, but Julian Munby points out that trees were also found on common lands to which peasants would have had some access for making hedges and houses.[7] Managing woodland resources (coppicing) was a specialized skill that ensured the availability of different kinds and sizes of tree for different tasks, ranging from the construction of large buildings to making table implements. Work in wood depended on a close relationship between craft workers and estate owners whose coppices produced the wood. Large objects in wood such as bowls, trays, and troughs could come only from trees of a certain diameter. The conversion of a tree trunk into wood was a precise and elaborate process, as Morris shows. She points to a large and largely invisible industry of cultivating and felling trees, transporting them, grading them, and converting them into units that could be made into useful objects. These stages of woodworking took place before the lathe-turners began.

Woodwork survives so poorly that many Anglo-Saxon site reports have nothing to say about it. Scandinavian sites, however, are known for woodwork.[8] A number of wooden culinary objects, including a trough, a bucket, and a bowl, along with a wooden shovel and fork, number among the objects catalogued for an exhibition of Viking artifacts that toured Paris, Berlin, and Copenhagen in 1992 and 1993. Some of the objects were retrieved from a well at Vorbasse, a Danish settlement.[9] It is believed that the search for new timber sources was one of the factors that prompted Viking voyages to Greenland and ultimately L'Anse aux Meadows.[10] Iron woodworking tools have been found at numerous Anglo-Saxon settlements where no worked wood turned up. At Flixborough, with its thousands of objects in other materials, items in wood are extremely scarce. Woodworking there is discussed largely in terms of iron tools.[11] A few woodworking tools were found at Goltho. At Wharram a single piece of burned wood was recovered along with structural planks. The excavation

---

[7] Julian Munby, "Wood," p. 380.

[8] Morris, *Wood and Woodworking*, p. 2116.

[9] Else Roesdahl, Jean-Pierre Mohen, and François-Xavier Dillman, eds., *Les Vikings*, p. 243, nos. 59–60, and p. 248, nos. 81–83.

[10] See, generally, Kirsten Wolf, *Daily Life of the Vikings*. At Greenland the Vikings had to import timber, but at L'Anse aux Meadows it was plentiful. See Else Roesdahl, *The Vikings*, pp. 274–75.

[11] P. A. Stamper and R. A. Croft, eds., *Wharram: A Study*, index, p. 223. See D. H. Evans and Christopher Loveluck, *Life and Economy at Early Medieval Flixborough*, p. 485.

at Six Dials, Hamwic, is devoid of objects in wood.[12] At Portchester Castle wooden fragments were found near iron bucket handles in a well, a ninth-century context.[13] At Thetford "the processes of construction of timber buildings and portable wooden objects, obviously a major occupation in the town, have left no trace apart from two adzes, a saw, and spoon bits."[14] Objects in wood were not included in the site report at North Elmham, which, as we saw in Chapter 5, was also remarkably poor in ceramic finds.[15] Despite the lack of evidence from other places, the survivals at York have been said to pertain more generally to Anglo-Saxon settlement cultures. Munby writes that "if more woodwork had survived, its domestic usage might be more prominent than pottery, in utensils, furniture, fittings, and gadgets."[16]

Wood at York was shaped both in shops equipped with lathes and in homes. The finds from Coppergate and the other York sites attest to different modes of production that, in some instances, interacted. Morris notes that some wooden lids were fashioned by unskilled carvers from pieces that had been discarded by lathe-turners.[17] Many other objects were carved in homes or small shops, spoons and knife handles included. Change in either the form or the finish of objects is a central concern of archaeology, as we have seen in all other media involved in food networks. Pottery fabrics and shapes yield specific geographical points of reference. Wood, dated through dendrochronology, constitutes even more precise evidence. The leap from objects to context is assisted by the dense finds at Coppergate, where distinct building phases have been charted. Continuous occupation of the site meant that buildings sealed and preserved deposit layers beneath them. Extensive ironwork, along with pottery finds, woodwork, livestock remains, and other data, will eventually enable a composite analysis likely to be much richer than comparable views of other locations.[18]

We have seen that archaeologists offer both functionalist and cultural explanations for changes in pottery form and fabric over time, with practices and preferences that embody tradition sometimes resisting the introduction of new and more efficient ways and products. The *habitus*, the mechanism proposed by Pierre Bourdieu and interpreted in Anglo-Saxon contexts by Paul Blinkhorn and others, was not a permanent feature of settlement life. The *habitus* evolved and adapted to new forms and new

[12] P. Andrews, ed., *Excavations at Hamwic*, see index, p. 268.
[13] Guy Beresford et al., *Goltho*, p. 178 for a list of woodworking tools, illustrated p. 177, fig. 156, nos. 2–6. Barry Cunliffe, *Excavations at Portchester Castle*, p. 224 and p. 225, fig. 143, nos. 90–91, and pp. 88–89 on the context of Phase 3c.
[14] Andrew Rogerson and Carolyn Dallas, *Excavations in Thetford*, p. 199; for the bone spoons, see p. 180, nos. 88–90.
[15] Peter Wade-Martins, *Excavations in North Elmham Park 1967–1972*, see contents.
[16] Munby, "Wood," p. 379. See pp. 379–84 for general comments on managing timber resources.
[17] Morris, *Wood and Woodworking*, p. 2262.
[18] See the overview of tenements and adjacent areas by Morris, *Wood and Woodworking*, pp. 2073–83.

purposes. The rules of the *habitus* might be unseen and unwritten, but that does not mean that they were also unchanging.[19] In discussing the finds from York, Morris, who makes no reference to Bourdieu's work, takes two views of regularity in the production of wooden objects. When commenting on the regular sizing of many objects in wood, such as cups and bowls, she writes, "There seems to have been a 'social pattern book' of different types of vessels for particular tasks, each material used to make those for which it was best suited."[20] Morris puts her key phrase in quotation marks to show that she knows there was no public, much less written, agreement guiding the use of certain woods for certain vessels. The last two words, "best suited," are ambiguous. Was the material "best suited" because it functioned well (e.g., a hard wood works better for certain tasks than a soft wood), or was it "best suited" because it was thought to encode cultural data that craft workers and their customers valued? It seems probable that Morris intends the former and regards it as a matter of function. It might have been the case that only one form was available, however, because its functional advantages had become traditional. Once a chosen form became standard – that is, part of the "pattern book" – it might have been difficult to distinguish its functional merits from the tradition that had selected it. Did a choice persist because it resulted in high performance, or did it persist because it had long since replaced other options and hence had no competition from them?

Morris takes a different view in a discussion of objects from "everyday life." She notes the "enormous number and range of wooden items" found at York. "The wide range reflects both the versatility of wood as a raw material, different species having properties suitable for different tasks, and also the lack of standarised production of some types of everyday objects."[21] The first point, which concerns "different species having properties suitable for different tasks," supports the suggestion of an unwritten "pattern book" for materials "used to make those for which [they were] best suited." But the second point, which concerns "the lack of standardized production of some types of everyday objects," suggests something different and seems to point to production outside the guiding force of the *habitus*. Significantly, Morris restricts the latter statement about lack of standardized production to "some types of everyday objects" for which makers did not have a "social pattern book." These humble objects include pot lids and spoons, which took many apparently *ad hoc* (i.e., irregular) shapes and seem to have been made by less skilled carvers. The "social pattern book" would seem to have guided lathe-turners and others who produced large quantities of wooden objects. Morris gives impressive testimony to the regularity of such production, using scattergrams to show that dimensions for spindle- and face-turned bowls fell

---

[19] For discussion, see Paul Blinkhorn, "Habitus, Social Identity and Anglo-Saxon Pottery."
[20] Morris, *Wood and Woodworking*, p. 2094.
[21] Morris, *Wood and Woodworking*, p. 2262.

into two sizes.[22] However, Morris also notes that bowls from many other sites elsewhere in Britain were of comparable size, perhaps "indicating the size of the roundwood most often used for turning bowls."[23] In that case, it might seem that the resource itself determined the scale of the object to be made from it, a matter of function. The *habitus* seems to be more involved with large-scale and self-consciously selected or preferred forms of production rather than with occasional or seasonal work. At the same time, ordinary people who did not have the time or resources of specialized craft workers might have developed traditions of their own, a *habitus* on the household level rather than the settlement or regional level. Fathers who learned to carve spoons or other objects from their own fathers passed that skill on to their sons in a process with its own regularities, however humble. Bourdieu uses the image of the "conductorless" orchestra to represent the directing force of the *habitus*, but it would seem that some musicians, to extend his analogy, especially those lacking polished skills, did not see themselves as members of an orchestra at all – that is, as part of a concerted productive force. These workers produced wares that did not replicate standard forms found at the site but that might have replicated the instructions of a very small "pattern book" known only to a family or a few families. Such woodworkers did what they could do with wood; woodworking was not their chief occupation.

An additional consideration guiding form is the relationship of woodwork to other crafts, including ironwork and pottery, that were integrated into the *habitus*. Morris comments that objects in wood were often made to suit food-related wares in other media, including "pottery jars, lugs and cooking pots, and metal cooking vessels." Thus woodwork was, in part, responsive to sizes and shapes controlled by other craft workers. Additional examples would include knives, forks, hooks, and other implements that required handles made of wood (some handles were carved from bone and antler). The handle, which had to be adjusted to the size and purpose of the implement to which it was joined, was also more likely to bear marks of identity, such as bands of color or carving, than the iron implement itself.

The wooden objects described below characterize food culture at York from roughly 850 to 1100, probably the best documented and most diversified settlement in all of Anglo-Saxon archaeology. Cultural history from the Viking period is popular, as anyone who has seen crowds of tourists outside the Jorvik Viking Centre in Coppergate will know.[24] The Jorvik Viking Centre offers an illuminating introduction that conveys, in life-size exhibits, the density of the tenements in a detailed and utterly unromantic

---

[22] Morris, *Wood and Woodworking*, pp. 2122–45. In spindle-turning, the grain is parallel to the direction of the lathe's rotation; in face-turning the wood is perpendicular to the direction of rotation. Face-turning is more common for bowls, and spindle-turning for cups and tool handles.

[23] Morris, *Wood and Woodworking*, pp. 2277–78.

[24] See the Jorvik Viking Centre site at http://www.jorvik-viking-centre.co.uk/.

way. The adjacent museum holds an extravagant display of small finds, especially well supplied with objects from everyday life. Inevitably, the military side of the Viking achievement dominates – blood-axes, coats of mail, helmets, and the rest – but visitors also get to see the much-injured skeleton of one of the warriors, so that the martial aspect of York's history acquires meaning in terms of personal, everyday experience, exposing the bare bones of heroism. West Stow is another celebrated stop on the Anglo-Saxon tourist circuit, much humbler and (when I visited) without high-tech innovations, which are hardly needed to bring the beautifully reconstructed wooden buildings to life. It too is a quick education in settlement life, and its superb museum also displays small finds, although far fewer than the number surviving from York.

Wooden cups and bowls

The most common wooden objects at York are bowls and cups. While much else perished, these forms survived in impressive numbers and shapes. They were the most common form of dining ware in the period, easily created and easily replaced, more durable than pottery, and suitable for a variety of uses. Bowls came in many sizes, small enough to drink from, large and wide enough to serve as trays and carving surfaces. Morris reports ninety-four lathe-turned bowls from Anglo-Scandinavian York and twenty-five cups, along with five lids. She was at pains to distinguish cups from bowls, since previous studies seem to confuse or merge these forms. She used the ratio of height to width to do so (cups in a 1:1 ratio, spindle-turned; bowls in a 1:5 and even 1:10 ratio, face-turned).[25] Wooden bowls were distinguished by the thinness of the rim, by details such as flanges to accommodate lids, and by turned bases. Morris was further able to establish that cups ranged from 70 mm to 130 mm in diameter, with most between 100 mm and 120 mm, while bowls ranged from 160 mm to 220 mm in diameter, with most falling between 180 mm and 200 mm.[26] The value of these measurements is clarified in Morris's demonstration of their reliability as guides to cup and bowl sizes elsewhere in Britain between 400 AD and 1500 AD. A sample of 338 vessels from this period shows that few measured more than 200 mm in diameter; only 5 percent were greater than 300 mm in diameter. The wider bowls were used for mixing in the kitchen, in the dairy, and for serving stews, Morris believes, all traditional uses for heavy, thick-walled vessels of this type.[27] Cups also varied in size and shape. Morris suggests that smaller examples were used for serving stronger, rare kinds of drink.[28] Some bowls from Coppergate show the effects of the food served in them, with grease stains or heat marks. Morris

[25] Morris, *Wood and Woodworking*, p. 2176. See p. 2437 for a list of sites and excavations from which these artifacts came.
[26] Morris, *Wood and Woodworking*, pp. 2175–78.
[27] Morris, *Wood and Woodworking*, pp. 2170–71.
[28] Morris, *Wood and Woodworking*, p. 2182.

discusses a bowl that has been repaired with a metal clip along the rim; the interior of the bowl shows grease stains and some food residue.[29] Another bowl, from Tamworth, was discarded in a millpool in a "very worn and abraded" condition.[30]

Objects in wood, like those in iron, could be repaired. For example, cracks in trays and in large bowls like the one just discussed were mended with metal clips.[31] Large vessels – some were 360 mm in diameter (over fourteen inches) – would not have been easy to replace. Wood was resistant. When dropped, wooden bowls and cups were less likely to break or crack than those made of clay. Once repaired, a bowl used for one purpose might be put to another. Morris supplies various reasons for these repairs. Making bowls might have been seasonal labor, and in the countryside perhaps wooden bowls were available only from itinerant sellers or woodworkers. The repair on the York bowl, it should be noted, is none too elegant, nor are the other repairs that are pictured. Morris points out that repaired wooden bowls were placed in graves, showing that the bowl itself was a marker of status and that the repairs were not seen as lessening its importance (indeed, the story of the repair might have enhanced the bowl's value in this context).[32] At the other extreme, some wares in wood were decorated with metal bands or carved, as are burrwood vessels from Sutton Hoo.[33]

Spoons and spatulas

After the knife, the spoon was the most common eating utensil in the Old English period. Surviving spoons are usually carved from wood. The length of the handle and the shape and depth of the bowl vary widely. Spoons are also made of iron, bone (see Figure 1), and, in the later period, from pewter and bronze.[34] Most textual examples refer to spoons used for consuming remedies, although some references to the spoon (*sticca*) pertain to mixing rather than eating. Wooden spoons were unknown to Anglo-Saxon archaeologists half a century ago and are still relatively rare; only seven examples were found at York, in contexts ranging from Anglo-Scandinavian through to early medieval (i.e., c. 1200). While metal spoons can be classified according to bowl shapes, the same is not true for wooden spoons, since their bowl shapes vary greatly. Morris describes an oval spoon with straight sides and a plain handle as possibly homemade; she

---

[29] Morris, *Wood and Woodworking*, p. 2190, fig. 1041.

[30] Morris, *Wood and Woodworking*, p. 2188.

[31] Morris, *Wood and Woodworking*, pp. 2176–77 and 2190–91.

[32] Staples found in a grave at Lyminge, Kent, "almost certainly repaired a long linear crack in a large bowl," Morris writes; see *Wood and Woodworking*, pp. 2190–91. See other repairs in illustrations p. 2189, fig. 1040.

[33] Both are decorated with silver mountings; see Stephen Pollington, *The Mead-Hall*, p. 131.

[34] The bone spoon is described by Evans and Loveluck, *Life and Economy at Early Medieval Flixborough*, pp. 231–33 (no. 2316, fig. 5.35 and plate 5.9).

traces it to ninth-century York (16–22 Coppergate).[35] A spoon from ninth-century Gloucester (Westgate Street) also has straight sides but the sides of other spoons are rounded.[36] Morris suggests that simpler, straight-sided shapes were homemade and that spoons with refined, rounded bowls were created by specialist carvers. She describes one spoon, for example, as "a finely smoothed, delicate utensil with very thin walls," a specimen of "high-quality workmanship."[37] The York spoons were small enough to have been used for eating rather than cooking; culinary spoons were larger. Some York spoon bowls show signs of scorching, which suggests that they were also used to prepare food. Another spoon from York, made of hazelwood, has an elongated oval bowl with straight sides; it is almost flat and hence spatulate. Possibly homemade, it is broken; its rounded handle survives. Also from York is a yew spoon with a broken handle and a carved, rectangular terminal below the bowl; the bowl is thin-walled and oval, with rounded sides.[38]

In addition to spoons, the York finds include a number of double-ended objects that are referred to as spoon-spatulas, with a bowl at one end and a wide blade at the other. Examples have also been found at Sevington, Kent. At Winchester a similar implement had a fork at one end and a spoon at the other; the fork was made of bone. Morris suggests that the size of such objects is more important to their function than the materials from which they were made.[39] The spatula, an implement for mixing or stirring foods and medicines, is not readily distinguishable from the spoon except by the depth of the bowl, which cannot always be ascertained. Spoons have a deeper bowl; spatulas might terminate in a shallow bowl or in a blade. Pre-Norman spatulas can have a flat blade at one end tapering to a handle, or can have a bowl at one end. Cast-iron spatulas from York have high-quality finishes (e.g., grooved stems) that suggest specialized use. Some spatulas have bowls that are not deep; these utensils were not used for consuming liquids but for mixing spices or ointments. Most references to them come from recipes and medical texts.

Two spatulas were found at 16–22 Coppergate, York. The first, from a Period 4b context (c. 930–c. 975), was found whole. It is made of yew with a long, flat blade and tapered handle (129 mm long, 14 mm wide). The second, also in wood, was found in six fragments but is complete and much larger (c. 329 mm long, 35 mm wide). This large implement, made of ash, tapers from a flat blade to a round handle.[40] Morris emphasizes throughout her discussion of both spoons and spatulas that the forms found in Anglo-Scandinavian York and elsewhere in the Anglo-Saxon period seem

---

[35] Morris, *Wood and Woodworking*, p. 2267 (fig. 1101, no. 8895). See also p. 2268.
[36] Morris, "Wood Objects," p. 199, fig. 17, no. 13; cited by Morris, *Wood and Woodworking*, p. 2268. For York spoon shapes, see Morris, *Wood and Woodworking*, p. 2267, fig. 1101.
[37] Morris, *Wood and Woodworking*, quotation from p. 2268; see p. 2267, fig. 1101, no. 8899 for a drawing of this object.
[38] Morris, *Wood and Woodworking*, p. 2267, no. 8899; see pp. 2267–68 for contexts.
[39] Morris, *Wood and Woodworking*, p. 2269.
[40] Morris *Wood and Woodworking*, p. 2270, nos. 8903 and 8905.

to have continued with very little change into the medieval period; she compares yew spatulas of the fifteenth century to the York examples in her survey.[41] This sign of continuity across so much time cannot be read as evidence of the *habitus* but rather shows, once again, that a simple form persisted because it worked well, a phenomenon we will see several times in the following account.

Churns and Troughs

Among the wood objects assumed to have been common in settlements with dairies was the butter churn. Lids and dashers for churns have been found in a few contexts. The churn was a wooden vessel with stave sides, a lid, and a dasher, which is a pole, fixed to either a rectangular block or circular disk, that was plunged into the churn to agitate the cream. No whole churns survive, but dashers of both types and lids have been found. A churn with a lid and dasher with a perforated disk (reconstructed), of an Anglo-Scandinavian type, was found at 16–22 Coppergate. It is from the early thirteenth century, but Morris believes that such items would have changed their form very little during the medieval period.[42] A churn dash from 16–22 Coppergate, dated from the ninth to the eleventh centuries, is rectangular and made of oak. It is whole and was found in backfilling in a mid- to late Anglian well shaft (i.e., eighth to ninth century).[43] A rectangular dasher from Gloucester is comparable to the one at York; Morris gives other, later examples, and again likens them to objects found at York.[44]

The trough (*trog* or *troh*) was a hollow vessel, a tray or rectangular container used for making bread. It had thick end walls, thinner side walls, and a U-shaped interior. The interiors of some surviving examples are stained with grease accumulated through culinary use.[45] An example from Coppergate is about one meter long and 400 mm wide (probable reconstructed measurements) and made of poplar. A second example, also dated tenth to eleventh century, is a fragment (traces of bottom and one end remain), made of alder.[46] An example from New Fresh Wharf, London, is also a fragment of internal end wall surface, showing adze and chisel marks that are traces of the hewing and shaping processes. Four troughs made of beech and fir were found in the Oseberg ship burial in Norway, one very large, over two meters long.[47] Traces of rye flour were found in the largest of the troughs from the burial.

Morris emphasizes that kneading bread was probably just one function for the trough, which was also used for sieving, sorting seeds, and

---

[41] Morris, *Wood and Woodworking*, p. 2271.
[42] Morris, *Wood and Woodworking*, p. 2278 (reconstructed churn).
[43] Morris, *Wood and Woodworking*, p. 2277.
[44] Morris, "Wood Objects," pp. 199–200; the objects are from the ninth century.
[45] Morris, *Wood and Woodworking*, p. 2275, fig. 1106.
[46] Morris, *Wood and Woodworking*, pp. 2275 and 2413.
[47] For these objects, see Morris, *Wood and Woodworking*, p. 2274

similar work associated with grain. She writes that "the shape of this sort of vessel changed little over time and illustrates the conservatism commonly found where wooden utensils evolve into a useful form and are then manufactured over a wide area with little alteration for a long period of time."[48] The functionalist assumptions behind this assessment seem well founded. There was "little alteration for a long period of time" because adaptations were not required. The possibility that such objects would transmit evidence of group identity seems very small but cannot be ruled out. Ancestral identity is not likely to have been communicated, admittedly, but family or group identity could well have been embodied in such objects. Other objects lending themselves to more than one application were barrel lids. Figure 3 shows a merchant's mark incised on the stave of a cask head.[49] Such marks might have had symbolic functions as "devices thought to protect the contents of the vessels." Morris reproduces the lid to a coopered vessel, showing that the lid sometimes served as a cutting board. It is difficult for a modern observer to look at this object and not wonder whose hands and knives were responsible for scoring its surface.[50]

Texts and food objects in wood

Bowls and cups

Like food objects in iron, those in wood took numerous forms and so could be mentioned in texts in many ways. When asking what the Anglo-Saxons called their wooden eating vessels, Morris, like so many others, turns to *Concerning the Discriminating Reeve*. In discussing bowls and cups, she notes that this text includes "at least six Old English words which may refer to this type of vessel – *dixas, beodas, bleda* and *melas*[,] which are probably different sorts of bowls, *stelmelas*[,] which are probably bowls with handles, and *cuppan* or cups."[51] Three of these words would seem to be especially useful since they are attested often and in a variety of sources: *disc* (eighty times); *bledu* (twenty-seven times); and *cupp* (thirty-five times; *DOE* figures). The value of the other terms is less clear. *Beod* usually means table, not drinking vessel or dish, and occurs in numerous compounds such as table-covering (*DOE*). *Beod* refers to "dish" just twice, including in *Concerning the Discriminating Reeve*; *stelmelas* occurs only in this text, and *melas* only in this text and once as a gloss on *ciatos* ("wine ladle") and *karchesia*, an unspecified drinking vessel. Unfortunately, none of the three common words from *Concerning the Discriminating Reeve* clearly refers to

---

[48] Morris, *Wood and Woodworking*, p. 2275.
[49] For Figure 3, see Chapter 2, p. 57, and Chapter 3, pp. 68–69.
[50] Morris, *Wood and Woodworking*, pp. 2259–61, figs. 1094 and 1097, for the cask head; see p. 2256, fig. 1092, for the scored lid. The quotation is from p. 2261.
[51] Morris, *Wood and Woodworking*, p. 2165.

wooden dishes.[52] *Disc*, for example, is used twice in *Beowulf*, both times as part of a hoard of precious metal and mentioned with the *bune* (drinking cup).[53] Many other references also suggest metal dishes, such as the list of plate from St. Cuthbert's and the tray on which the head of John the Baptist was delivered to Salomé.[54] *Bledu* is a wide-ranging word, meaning cup, bowl, goblet, or dish. *Cuppan* describes both simple and ornate vessels, with or without lids. It is possible that the medicinal references are to objects in wood as well as pottery, but there is no way to tell from context.[55] Such an object, left in a will, might be a fine object of wood or (more probably) metal, as were those listed among the plate of St. Cuthbert's.

Spoons and spatulas

Textual evidence of spoons appears mainly in medical recipes as an implement for sipping, tasting, or otherwise ingesting, as in "spoonful," "full spoon," or "half spoon." All textual references to the spoon come from medical texts such as *Bald's Leechbook*, which advises the reader to serve juice "in a spoon" (*on cuclere*).[56] Very similar is this reference from the *Lacnunga*: "put one morsel into the mouth with a spoon" (*do in muð mid cucylere ane snade*).[57] Also from *Bald's Leechbook* is a recipe that indicates the spoon as a unit of measure, "mix in a cup a full spoon of mustard and a half-spoon of honey" (*senepes dustes cucler fulne & huniges healfne cucler gedo on calic menge*).[58] The *Herbarium* apportions spoons of wine by age: "To a young man give to drink five spoons full of wine, and to a younger (man) and a sick (man) and to a woman, three (spoons full), and to a little child one (spoon full) (*Syle þycgean on wine geongum men fif cuceleras fulle & gingrum & untrumrum & wifum þry cuculeras, litlum cildum ane*).[59] Such directions are common in texts of this kind, which do not differentiate between what must have been varied sizes of bowls that formed spoons.

The Old English *cucler* (also *cucelere, cuculere, cucere*) also designates a spatula or instrument for mixing. *Cucler* occurs about twenty-seven times,

---

[52] I report the results of *DOEWC* searches on these words. *Concerning the Discriminating Reeve (Gerefa)* is edited by F. Liebermann, *GDA*, pp. 453–55, and translated by Michael Swanton, *Anglo-Saxon Prose*, pp. 30–35. See *Gerefa* 17, p. 455, for *beodas, dixas, stelmelas*.

[53] R. D. Fulk, Robert E. Bjork, and John D. Niles, eds., *Klaeber's Beowulf*, p. 94, l. 2775, and p. 103, l. 3048 .

[54] A. J. Robertson, *Anglo-Saxon Charters*, App. II, no. 4, pp. 250–51. For Matthew 14:8 (John the Baptist) as found in the Rushworth Gospels, see Walter W. Skeat, ed., *The Holy Gospels in Anglo-Saxon*, pp. 120–21.

[55] *Bald's Leechbook*, Book III, ch. ii, 6, ed. Oswald Cockayne, *Leechdoms, Wortcunning and Starcraft*, 2: 308–9: "Take butter, boil in a pan, skim the foam off, and purify the butter in a dish" (*Nim buteran, wyl on pannan, afleot þæt fam of & ahlyttre þa buteran on blede*). The *Leechbook* (Book III, ch. x, 2: 314–15) includes a remedy for spewing blood that uses the dish: "Take good barley meal and white salt, put it into cream or good skimmings stir in a dish" (*Genim god beren mela & hwit sealt, do on ream oþþe gode flete, hrer on blede*).

[56] *Bald's Leechbook*, Book I, ch. xlviii, 1, ed. Cockayne, *Leechdoms*, 2: 120–21.

[57] J. H. G. Grattan and C. Singer, *Anglo-Saxon Magic and Medicine*, pp. 150–51.

[58] *Bald's Leechbook*, Book I, ch. i, 17, ed. Cockayne, *Leechdoms*, 2: 24–25.

[59] For the *Herbarium*, ch. xxvi, 3, see Hubert Jan de Vriend, ed., *The Old English Herbarium*, p. 73.

mainly in medical recipes; however, as an instrument for mixing rather than delivering food to the mouth, the word seems to occur unambiguously just once. This is in *Bald's Leechbook*, where a recipe for a liquid emetic instructs the reader to take "three slices of houseleek and peeled elderbark in equal portions, twenty-five medicinal seeds ground together, add a like portion of honey, stir with a spatula [*mid cuclere*], [and take it with a sip] of hot or cold water" (*Spiwedrenc, hamwyrte III snæda & ellenrinde berende gelice micel, XXV lybcorna gegnid, do huniges swilce an snæd sie, onete þonne mid cuclere, onsup hates wæteres oððe cealdes*).[60]

Churns and troughs

There are just three occurrences of *cyrn* (churn) in Old English, one from *Concerning the Discriminating Reeve* and two from glosses. The most revealing textual evidence of the churn in Old English is Riddle 54, which does not name the object itself, the identity of which must remain ambiguous for the sake of humor; the solution is usually given as "churn." This is a pseudo-sexual description of a hard object thrust into a chamber to induce the growth of a treasured object. The riddle gives us an idea of what churning butter looked and possibly felt like.

A youth came along to where he knew she stood in a corner. He stepped forth, a hardy young man, with his own hands lifted her up, thrust under her girdle as she was standing there something stiff. He worked his will; both of them shook. A thegn hastened, useful at times, a capable servant. Although he was strong at first, nevertheless he grew weary eventually, tired of the work. In her began to grow, beneath the girdle, that which good men often love heartily and buy with money.

Hyse cwom gangan, þær he hie wisse
stondan in wincsele, stop feorran to,
hror hægstealdmon, hof his agen
hrægl hondum up, hrand under gyrdels
hyre stondendre stiþes nathwæt,
worhte his willan; wagedan buta.
Þegn onnette, wæs þragum nyt
tillic esne, teorode hwæþre
æt stunda gehwam strong ær þon hio,
werig þæs weorces. Hyre weaxan ongon
under gyrdelse þæt oft gode men
ferðþum freogað ond mid feo bicgað.[61]

The object stands *in winsele* or *in wincsele*. If *win-sele*, a wine hall, the location is very unexpected. The Old English for "corner" is *wincel*, and that is the reading of several editors, which makes much more sense. The dress that is lifted up is the churn's lid; the object described as "something stiff" would

---

[60] *Bald's Leechbook*, Book II, ch. i, 3, ed. Cockayne, *Leechdoms*, 2: 272–73.
[61] George Philip Krapp and Elliot van Kirk Dobbie, eds., *The Exeter Book*, pp. 207–8; my translation.

be the dasher, the dowel with projections or a disk at one end to agitate the milk when worked up and down or wiggled. The prize that begins to grow is the solidifying butter, a commodity that could be purchased or made at home. That churning butter was exhausting is not in doubt. There has been some discussion about the sex of the worker, obviously male for the sake of the sexual humor of the riddle.[62] We should infer that men as well as women performed the work of churning, in keeping with Christine Fell's suggestion that such tasks were undertaken by those with the time to do them and were not assigned by sex according to modern conventions.[63]

The word for trough, *troga*, is found in *Concerning the Discriminating Reeve*, among agricultural rather than culinary tools: *hriddel, hersyfe, tæmespilan, fanna, trogas, æscena, hyfa, hunigbinna* ("a sieve, a hair-sieve, a sieve-frame, a winnowing fan, a trough, a bucket made of ash, a hive, a vessel for honey").[64] It appears in the record of gifts of Bishop Æthelwold among items in the property inventory at Yaxley (Geaceslea): "six baskets [or perhaps casks] and two tubs and three troughs, and a lead plumb and a trivet."[65] The other container mentioned here, the *cyfel*, is also found in *Concerning the Discriminating Reeve* and in a charter (*DOE, cyfel*). In *Bald's Leechbook* we see an example that explains how some troughs (and perhaps large wooden bowls) obtained burn marks. To make a medicinal steam bath, or *stufbæð*, for an open sore or ulcer, a mixture of plants was placed over a hot stone set into a trough, and hot water was poured over the stone (*lege on hatne stan on troge, geot hwon wæteres*; "lay on a hot stone in a trough, pour some water over it").[66] Another recipe uses the same procedure with a slightly longer list of herbs.[67] *Bald's Leechbook* also provides a treatment for hemorrhoids or piles using a hot bath or *beþinge*. Red ryden, a herb (*reade ryden*), is placed in the trough and hot stones placed over it. The patient, who has taken a drink for the condition, sits on a stool over the trough: "Put [red ryden] in a trough, heat the stones very hot, lay them in the trough, and let the man sit on a stool over the hot bath" (*do on trig, hæt þonne stanas swiþe hate, lege on þæt trig innan & he sitte on stole ofer þære beþinge*).[68]

In addition to troughs and churns, implements mentioned in *Concerning the Discriminating Reeve* that archaeologists have documented include spades and shovels. Among those not mentioned in this text but also documented are rakes and manure forks made of wood, both common agricultural implements. These objects were at some distance from food preparation, and occupied nodes in the food network far from the table. This was also true of most iron implements used on farms and in fields.

---

[62] Nina Rulon-Miller, "Sexual Humor and Fettered Desire in Exeter Book Riddle 12."

[63] Christine Fell, *Women in Anglo-Saxon England*, pp. 48–49, on the distribution of labor.

[64] For the list in *Gerefa* 17, see Liebermann, *GDA*, p. 455.

[65] P. H. Sawyer, *Anglo-Saxon Charters*, charter no. 1448. See Ann Hagen, *A Second Handbook of Anglo-Saxon Food and Drink*, p. 114.

[66] *Bald's Leechbook*, Book III, ch. xxx, 1, ed. Cockayne, *Leechdoms*, 2: 326–27.

[67] Grattan and Singer, *Anglo-Saxon Magic and Medicine*, para. 76.1, pp. 148–49.

[68] *Bald's Leechbook*, Book III, ch. xlviii, ed. Cockayne, *Leechdoms*, 2: 340–41.

These large objects might have supplied shapes for smaller versions that were used in conjunction with foodstuffs, scooping or shoveling grain, for example. Other examples include flails used to thresh grain, objects that would have consisted of both wood and leather.

The network of food objects in wood involved workers of two distinct skill levels. Some food objects made of wood were created by skilled craft workers using sophisticated machines; others were fashioned by workers with basic skills and their hands. As we know, nearly every Anglo-Saxon carried a personal knife. One purpose was to make simple tools, including spoons and spatulas. Another, possibly, might have been to incise wooden food objects with markers of personal identity and status, a gesture not possible with objects in other media. There is evidence that wooden objects were used as records in this way. A recent discovery on Baffin Island, northwest of Newfoundland, included "suspected Norse artifacts such as Scandinavian-style spun yarn" and "distinctively notched and decorated wood objects," whetstones, and other things.[69] These have been used to support arguments for sustained Viking occupation west of L'Anse aux Meadows after that colony collapsed in the eleventh century. Wooden objects, some of them notched and decorated, are possibly "fragments of what seemed to be tally sticks, used by Vikings for recording trade transactions," which would have been an obvious use of this easily incised medium. Uses of writing were not only academic. In the ancient world, weights and measures were recorded on jars in which oil was shipped, for example (as noted in Chapter 3).[70] Weights and measures also mattered in domestic settings in which food rents had to be calculated, as numerous charters indicate. But those transactions also required documentation at levels at which the apparatus of literacy took a different form. Wood and wax were the among the few affordable media available for such record-keeping. Wood was also the medium of containers that could have been easily marked by anyone with a knife and a need to record data or a message, as, for example, on the cask head (Figure 3) discussed above.

Unlike any other food medium, wood dominated the visual world of the Anglo-Saxons, as numerous references to woods and wooded areas in texts ranging from poems to charters attest. The tree was the material of the cross, the gallows from which criminals were hanged in Anglo-Saxon England, and the tree and gallows are invoked three times each in "The Dream of the Rood" (*syllicre treow*, l. 4; *wuldres treow*, l. 14; *hælendes treow*, l. 25; *fracodes gealga*, l. 10; *gealgan heanne*, l. 40; *gealgtreowe*, l. 146).[71] The gallows also emerges in *Beowulf* and in a boundary clause.[72] The double

---

[69] Heather Pringle, "Vikings and Native Americans" (online resource).
[70] On commercial amphorae, see James Graham-Campbell and Magdalena Valor, eds., *The Archaeology of Medieval Europe*, pp. 290–92. See also Simon Keay, "The Amphora Project" (online resource).
[71] See "The Dream of the Rood," ed. George Philip Krapp, *The Vercelli Book*, pp. 61–65.
[72] For *Beowulf*, l. 2940 (*on galgtreowum*), see Fulk, Bjork, and Niles, *Klaeber's* Beowulf, p. 100. The boundary clause occurs in charter no. 592 (*fram Hunan bricge to þam galhtreowe on deopandene*); see Sawyer, *Anglo-Saxon Charters*, p. 209.

identity of wood as glorified and shamed is preserved in "The Dream of the Rood" and also seen in many early medieval crosses in which a gold and bejeweled surface is laid over wood. Such a cross is suggested in "the timber cross" riddle (Riddle 30a) from the *Exeter Book*:

> I am fire-busy, at play with the wind, wound about with glory, made one with the surrounding air, eager for the journey, [but] consumed by fire, flourishing in the grove, a burning coal. Very often comrades present me with their hands so that proud men and women may kiss me. When I rise up they bow to me, many with reverence, where I shall add to the coming blessedness of humanity.

> Ic eom legbysig,   lace mid winde,
> bewunden mid wuldre,   wedre gesomnad,
> fus forðweges,   fyre gebysgad,
> bearu blowende,   byrnende gled.
> Ful oft mec gesiþas   sendað æfter hondum,
> þæt mec weras ond wif   wlonce cyssað.
> Þonne ic mec onhæbbe,   ond hi onhnigaþ to me
> monige mid miltse,   þær ic monnum sceal
> ycan upcyme   eadignes.[73]

The phrase "wound about with glory" might also describe the cross of "The Dream of the Rood," which is covered with gold. The speaker of the riddle connects the home of wood in the forest, "flourishing in the grove" (*bearu blowende*), to its cultural identity as an object of veneration, held out with hands so others can honor it with a kiss. The solution to the riddle is a "timber" or wooden cross.

Timber in Old English means both "timber" and "material out of which something is made." In one herbal remedy the liver is described as *blodes timber & hus*, "the material and home of the blood."[74] The association of the object with the material it is created from is clear in a canon from the *Penitential* of Theodore translated as part of the Old English *Canons of Theodore*: "Timber from a church must not be put to any other use except for another church, or one may burn it up entirely for some benefit which is necessary for the servants of God who are in the monastery, and it should never be used by lay people" (*Ne sceal cyrcean timber to ænigum oðrum weorce buton to oðre cyrcean oððe hit man forbærne to sumere freme þe ðam godes þeowum þearf sy ðe in þam mynstre syn & hit næfre sy gedon þam leawedum to bryce*). Theodore's version allowed that the wood could be used to bake bread (*vel coquere cum eis panes licet*), a use omitted by the translator.[75] Morris notes that wood that had outlived its purpose was either burned or discarded; this regulation shows that consecrated wood could be burned or used for another church but not used in any other way.[76]

---

[73] Riddle 30a, Krapp and Dobbie, eds., *The Exeter Book*, pp. 195–96. See Ilse Schweitzer, "The *Crux Gemmata* and Shifting Significances of the Cross" (online resource).

[74] *Bald's Leechbook*, Book II, ch. xvii, ed. Cockayne, *Leechdoms*, 2: 160–61.

[75] *Penitential* of Theodore, book 2, ch. 1, c. 3, ed. A. W. Haddan and W. Stubbs, *CED*, p. 190. For the Old English, see Frantzen, *ASP*, *OEC*, B63.04.01

[76] Morris, *Wood and Woodworking*, p. 2194.

Conclusion: Food things and words

The culinary culture in wood that survives from Anglo-Scandinavian York has been the focus of most of this chapter. This evidence cannot be taken as typical of Anglo-Saxon sites. Artifacts in other media, including querns, pots, and ironwork, have been found at multiple sites. How much can be assumed about other Anglo-Saxon sites on the basis of what has emerged at York? Why was so much wood in use there? Morris points out that many of the artifacts catalogued were not made at home and that, with some exceptions, few were made by carving. Instead they were the creations of skilled lathe-turners and stave-builders, and a concentration of specialists in such crafts suggests commerce and trade, and hence production on a large scale. Morris points out that woodworkers shared their tenements with those who specialized in many other crafts. These tenements were points at which many lines of supply and production intersected. The domestic objects they produced were not only sold but also furnished the workers' own shops and dwellings. The non-domestic objects in wood were widely distributed among shipbuilders, textile workers, farmers, leatherworkers, and others, but these people also used domestic objects in wood. The findings at York point to a unique pairing of concentrated craft working spaces and domestic settlements. Yet artifacts from York sites can tell us some things we need to know about food culture more generally. The Anglo-Saxons made some objects in wood for themselves and bought or traded for others. The more specialized the object – the larger the bowl, for example – the more likely it was to come from an outside source; the simpler – a basic spatula – the more likely it was to be made at the settlement. Morris believes that the range of objects made at home was very small; she writes that "very few domestic vessels seem to have been made by carving." Morris points out that wood was not used as an inexpensive substitute for pottery or wares made of metal. Wooden vessels complement those in pottery: the "social pattern book" directed which material better suited which task.[77] It seems likely that even a simple Anglo-Saxon kitchen contained wares of iron, wood, and clay.

No other medium used in food culture encompassed so much of the Anglo-Saxon world as did wood. It was a medium for the largest objects in that world, the halls of great lords, and some of the smallest, such as spoons and tiny cups for precious drink. Wooden objects have special value because wood had aesthetic advantages over other materials. Every object has its own beauty, one could argue, but such woods as yew, alder, and maple added aesthetic value to cups, bowls, and other objects. Morris writes that the woods were "decorative in themselves," with "distinctive grain patterns and colors."[78] The same might be said of leather, another important source of food objects that is almost impossible to study because

---

[77] Morris, *Wood and Woodworking*, p. 2094.
[78] Morris, *Wood and Woodworking*, pp. 2185–86.

so little of it survives from culinary contexts.[79] A spare and utilitarian leather bottle or wooden bowl might have been an object of great beauty prized for that reason if no other.

Wood is synonymous with building in Old English, and its fundamental importance to the networks comprising settlement and civilization is nowhere clearer than in Alfred's preface to the translation of Augustine's *Soliloquies*. The author begins in the forest, gathering staves and branches for his purposes. "In every tree I saw something for which I had a need at home. Accordingly, I would advise everyone who is strong and has many wagons to direct his steps to that same forest where I cut these props." The emphasis is on building "many splendid houses" and "a fine homestead" in which to live "pleasantly and in tranquility both winter and summer" in preparation for a longer stay in a better, heavenly home. This activity, according to *Concerning the Discriminating Reeve*, was best undertaken in May and June.[80] But the preface also notes that once a man has constructed "a hamlet on land leased to him by his lord and with his lord's help," he will want to dwell there and hunt, fish, and go fowling.[81] Such occupations and countless others required the use of objects made of wood – bows and spears for hunting, cages for birds, and others.

We take it for granted that such objects as gold-covered crosses were used for contemplation and meditation; that was one reason why they were written about. Contemplation of a metal object might be described as a reverie in which flashing gold resembles fire fanned by the wind or a glowing, burning coal. Humbler objects were also closely regarded, if not meditated on with the discipline of those steeped in learned, Latinate traditions. Alfred's preface might be said to split the difference when he muses on branches and wagons, his reverie reaching to buildings and then fishing and fowling before the king's mind turns to the weightier matter of the afterlife. Alfred is beholding building materials, not art objects. Every tree he looks at suggests something he needs, the raw stuff from which a tool can be created. Such reverie, I believe, might have been extended by other thoughtful Anglo-Saxons to food objects. I imagine someone looking at a wooden cup, or a cooking pot, or a knife, and thinking, "This was my mother's" or "My father made this." Others looking at the object thought of the identity of the present owner and might not have known the previous owner. In their unobtrusive way, ordinary things helped the Anglo-Saxons to shape ideas of where they came from, who they were, and where they might go.

---

[79] Shoes, sheathes, and other objects in leather survive, but a detailed study of leatherwork in York includes no evidence of cooking objects made of leather; references to bottle-makers are to medieval rather than Anglo-Saxon contexts. See Quita Mould, Ian Carlisle, and Esther Cameron, *Leather and Leatherworking in Anglo-Scandinavian and Medieval York*.

[80] These were months for constructing in timber (*timbrian*) and cutting wood (*wudian*). See the translation by Swanton, *Anglo-Saxon Prose*, p. 31; text in Liebermann, *GDA, Gerefa* 9, p. 454.

[81] Thomas A. Carnicelli, ed., *King Alfred's Version of St. Augustine's "Soliloquies,"* pp. 47–48, translated by Simon Keynes and Michael Lapidge, *Alfred the Great*, pp. 138–39.

I began this survey of food objects with quernstones, which many archaeologists think would have been found in nearly every household in the early Middle Ages, and turned next to pottery, the most common archaeological find related to food culture. Food objects in iron and wood proved less informative than those in either of the other media, chiefly because they are relatively rare. But there is another side to be considered. Although using the quern was a task that anyone might have performed, the quern served a single function. Grinding and milling were noisy tasks, and quernstones must have been in near-constant use. Querns would have been hard to miss and so too the muscles on those who operated them. Those devices required tremendous energy and might be said to have used their operators, just as the flour the mills produced ate those who consumed it. Flour was filled with tiny fragments of granite that wore through the enamel of those who ate bread or porridge made from the flour.

Pottery, in comparison, served many ends, ranging from cooking to shipping and all the phases in between. Pots bore distinguishing traces, whether they were intended as decoration or not, because they were hand-produced and easily marked. Objects in wood and iron would also have been distinctive. Of the two, wood communicated much more about its substance. As a result of small differences in grain and color, it is unlikely that any two pieces of wood were identical, even if they were made from the same source. We associate identity with individuality, a modern notion that cannot safely be mapped onto the elements of daily life a thousand years ago. In the Anglo-Saxon era, many objects were, like the quernstone, communal, even though only a few people used them; the iron cauldron and its chain are other examples. We should expect that such objects spoke to communal identity, as if they said to those who used or beheld them, "We are a people who use this object, which has come to us from our ancestors," and so on. The closer to the table objects came, the more they had to do with personal identity. Food, after all, is personal, something from outside one's body that is put into the body and made part of it. The point of consumption, the act of eating, is the most identity-producing point in a food network. Did an Anglo-Saxon worker drink from his or her own cup or instead from a cup that others used at different times? The more exclusive the use of the object, the more likely it was to convey the user's station, and the less situational it would have been: the cup that touches his lips or hers, the spoon that carries her soup or his to the mouth.

Objects seem not to lend themselves to situational identity, unless we think of identity as an attribute so unstable that it shifted with the hours in the day, which is hardly productive. Objects point to the people who used them and who possessed them. If they could be marked, or if constant use itself marked them, they were easily identified as belonging to somebody. Mobile objects were likely to signify the station and habits of those who used them. Large objects like the quernstone, iron hook, or iron fork, signaled identities also – the identity of the maker, if he or she were local to the community, as well as the user. Offices such as that of grinder, ironworker, wood carver, or potter were one form of identity. Those workers operated within the confines of the *habitus* to pass on through their techniques, and through the objects they shaped, social identities that were linked to form and color. For the people who used those objects, the identities to which the objects contributed were stable, not situational. Food objects spoke to the claim that "We are a people who use this object," which is not a claim we would make today, when we would say instead that "I am a man or woman who uses this object." For the Anglo-Saxons, I propose, it was different. "We are a people whose cooking pots look like this," they might have said. "We are a people whose wooden cups are made by our brothers and sisters from our trees." Day in, day out expressions of identity were broadcast by objects rather than proclaimed in words, evidence easily overlooked for the simple reason that, like the objects to which it referred, it was ordinary.

Part III

Food Offices

8

Food Officers in Handbooks of Penance

Objects communicate the presence and identity of those who use them. Knives, hooks, bowls, and cups served as badges of identity among the Anglo-Saxons, just as objects today are one way we show others how we see ourselves. Many people who worked with food are identified in Old English sources, including the beekeeper, the cheesemaker, and others. Some food workers also acquired identities as food officers, the term I use for those who monitored supplies to last through the winter; managed the diet during fasting periods; and, when necessary, assessed the quality and acceptability of the food and drink. When food workers exercised this authority, which they did only on occasion, they changed the way other people saw them. They acquired a temporary identity – what I have described earlier as a "situational" identity – in addition to what William O. Frazer calls the "social identity" that was ordinarily theirs.[1]

The role of food officer is one of the less conspicuous ways in which food culture generated identities that formed the "storied lives" of the Anglo-Saxons. A settlement's beekeeper became a food officer when someone was stung by bees and died as a result. Two Old English penitentials refer to this case. On such an occasion, the bees were to be killed, although the honey they had produced could be consumed.[2] The beekeeper was presumably responsible for killing the bees and preserving the honey. This was not a routine event, and the case is not mentioned among the beekeeper's duties in the *Rectitudines Personarum Singularum*, the *Rights (or Duties) of Individuals*.[3] The beekeeper's actions certified the purity of the honey, a valuable sweetener, and ensured access to it. In this case his authority and expertise also gave him, temporarily (and unusually), even more: the authority to execute symbolic justice, since life had to be given to pay for life taken.

---

[1] William O. Frazer, "Introduction," pp. 3–4. See also Chapter 1, pp. 18–19, above.
[2] Frantzen, *ASP*, *OES*, X26.01.01; *OEP*, Y44.31.01 (the *OES* is the source of the canon in the *OEP*). "If bees kill someone let them be killed quickly, and one is allowed to eat the honey they produced" (*Beon gyf hi mannan acwellað cwelle hy man hraðe & ete man þæt hunig þæt hy wrohton*).
[3] The rights and duties of the *beo-ceorl* are discussed in *Rectitudines Personarum Singularum*, ed. F. Liebermann, *GDA*, p. 448, para. 6.

The most prominent food officers mentioned in Old English ecclesiastical texts were bishops and priests; in the laws, the most important food officers were reeves. In the next chapter I examine food purity and food officers in the law codes and related texts. Here I describe food purity and food offices, show how handbooks of penance treated these food-related identities, and then consider what various categories of food purity would have meant for food officers, cooks in particular. Some officers, including the reeve (*gerefa*), who served the king or the bishop, and the dish-thegn (*discþegn* or *discberend*), who was the seneschal or steward of the hall, had formal titles.[4] Most food officers did not. They acted as food officers only on occasions that inserted them, by virtue of their food-related expertise, into the chain of agents linking the clergy to the laity. Priests and bishops controlled the ideology of food culture, but, like the reeve, they could not have known how well food purity was maintained in every settlement or household. At that level someone else would have been charged, informally but necessarily, with enforcing both requirements for fasting and ecclesiastical prohibitions of foods considered to be impure.

Food purity

Food purity refers both to food itself and how food (including liquid) is consumed. All food had to be protected from contamination, and, during seasons of fasting, some foods had to be avoided. Food itself could be pure or impure, fit for consumption or not, and pure food could be used in acceptable or unacceptable ways. To eat meat during a fasting period was, for an adult Christian in good health, an offense against food purity, not because of the food itself but because of the dietary demands of the season. Food purity has traditionally drawn more interest from anthropologists than from archaeologists. This is understandable, since anthropology emphasizes the power of ideology to shape material culture, while archaeology has traditionally been more concerned with things than with what they represent.

Mary Douglas's *Purity and Danger*, first published in 1966 and issued with a new preface in 2002, remains the most influential anthropological study of pollution and taboo. Douglas argued that food prohibitions in the Book of Leviticus, along with other dietary laws in the Gospels and letters of St. Paul, warned people away from abominations. She constructed systems of animal classification that identified anomalous species such as crawling animals and those with "deviant feet" – rabbits, for example. The Book of Leviticus prohibits eating rabbit, "for though it chews cud, it does not divide the hoof, [so] it is unclean to you."[5] Paul Sorrell made effective use of Douglas's schema when discussing Aldhelm's riddles, the Old

---

[4] According to *DOE* searches on *discþegn* and *discberend*, the former is found ten times: seven times in charters, twice in glosses, and once, as *discten*, in a homily about St. Clement by Ælfric. The latter word is found three times in glosses.

[5] Mary Douglas, *Purity and Danger*, p. xiv. See Leviticus 11:6.

English *Maxims,* and other texts that describe the suitability of animals to habitats and classify animals in terms of their means of locomotion. Sorrell also noted some difficulties with Douglas's views, particularly regarding her use of anomalous characteristics to define classificatory systems.[6] Douglas revised her arguments in a new preface to the work some forty years after the book appeared. She decided that the prohibitions existed not to warn believers away from abominations but instead to imitate the rules that formed God's covenant with the Chosen People. Food consumed by the body should be seen as parallel to food sacrificed on the altar, she wrote: "The dietary laws intricately model the body and the altar upon one another."[7]

Douglas's views pertain to the study of Anglo-Saxon food purity with reference to both the details of food culture and the link between food purity and social organization. Douglas identified E. E. Evans-Pritchard, her teacher, as the greatest influence on her work. Evans-Pritchard demonstrated that social organization might operate undetected beneath externally visible frameworks. He believed that structures of authority were not simply concentrated in "central organs of government" but could also be found at other levels of authority.[8] This assertion is relevant to my discussion of food officers, figures who can be found at several levels of the social body but are difficult to detect "beneath externally visible frameworks." Other than Evans-Pritchard, Douglas wrote, she was heavily influenced by her husband, who forced her to "take a stand on the relativity of dirt." The "relativity of dirt" seems trivial when juxtaposed to frameworks and "central organs of government." However, to decide what constitutes dirt, and how much dirt can be tolerated and when, is to exercise authority and to execute what I call a food office. Dirt upsets public order, the social agreement about the way things are supposed to be, and forces someone in a community – the food officer – to decide what to do about it.

Handbooks of penance monitor food purity not by explaining an animal's place in a system of classification but by warning that something about an animal's condition prior to being consumed – the manner of death in particular – made it unfit for consumption. In a discussion of early continental evidence, Rob Meens notes that that "penitentials are the oldest texts in Latin Christianity in which dietary prescriptions are found." He summarizes Douglas's work in four points: "medical materialism" or rules of hygiene; contemporary reaction to pagan rituals; a "cherishing of Old Testament traditions" in order to create Christian identity; and "a contribution to the identity of man in his relationship with the animal world."[9]

---

[6] Paul Sorrell, "Like a Duck to Water."

[7] See Douglas, *Purity and Danger,* pp. xv–xvi. See also Douglas's essay, "Land Animals: Pure and Impure," in *Leviticus as Literature,* pp. 134–51.

[8] Douglas, *Purity and Danger,* p. viii. For recent discussion, see R. M. J. Meens, "A Relic of Superstition."

[9] Rob Meens, "Pollution in the Early Middle Ages," p. 5 (which appeared before the revision of Douglas's book).

All four considerations pertain to the Anglo-Saxon penitentials as well as to the continental (i.e., Frankish) handbooks Meens discusses. Each point is relevant to the formation of new identities for new Christians.

Some Anglo-Saxon dietary rules demonstrating "medical materialism" include those that prohibit the consumption of carrion, of food contaminated by animals, or of animals that had eaten human flesh or drunk blood. The Anglo-Saxons, early and late, also proscribed pagan practices and the identities associated with them. For example, one penitential assigns a penance of five years to whomever, in order to ensure the well-being of others, "burns grain in a place where a man died" (*corn bærne in ðære stowe þær man dead wære*). Sacrifices "offered to demons" (*demonis immolantur*) incurred penances of seven and ten years.[10] The Church did not permit such rituals, whether or not they involved foodstuffs that represented the natural world. In Aron Gurevich's words, the Church disapproved of pagan "identification of man and nature" and attempted "to tear people away from it, for the only clerically approved contact with a higher power was in and through the church of God."[11] Identity is also at the heart of the third point Meens offers, which is respect for Old Testament traditions. The Anglo-Saxons assumed continuity between ancient food cultures and their own. They associated querns in their own settlements with querns in biblical texts and assumed that their pots and pans were similar to those used by the Israelites.[12] Meens's fourth point concerns identities that relate humans to "the animal world." This tradition also has roots in the Hebrew Testament. We have seen how Psalm 8, for example, relates humans to animals, offering a vision of cultural dominion: "All creation you put under his feet and under his power: sheep and all oxen and all the beasts of the field and the birds of the air and fish of the sea that move through the sea paths."[13] For the Anglo-Saxons, cherishing Old Testament traditions was a way to confirm their identity as a Chosen People, an analogy pursued in various forms in Old English poetry and prose.[14] When bees turned deadly, they upset this dominion. As a food officer, the beekeeper restored Christian order to the natural world.

Much evidence of food purity in this chapter comes from vernacular handbooks of penance. Since, as Meens has noted, some historians discount the importance of the penitentials as historical sources, their value is worth reasserting.[15] Over three decades ago John Boswell argued that the penitentials were not an "index" to medieval morality. Indeed they are not, and no such cultural indices are to be found to confirm the empiricist

---

[10] Frantzen, *ASP, OES*, X16.01.01–X16.03.01.
[11] Aron Gurevich, *Medieval Popular Culture*, p. 97. See Allen J. Frantzen, "All Created Things," pp. 116–18.
[12] For querns, see Chapter 4; for plants, e.g., the *hellebore*, see Chapter 3.
[13] Translated from James L. Rosier, ed., *The Vitellius Psalter*, p. 12; see Chapter 1.
[14] See Stephen J. Harris, *Race and Ethnicity in Anglo-Saxon Literature*, pp. 169–74; Nicholas Howe, *Migration and Mythmaking in Anglo-Saxon England*, pp. 72–107.
[15] Meens, "Pollution in the Early Middle Ages," pp. 4–5. See also R. D. Fulk and Stefan Jurasinski, eds., *The Old English Canons of Theodore*, pp. xlii–lx.

assumptions supporting Boswell's critique. No matter what we choose to conclude about the frequency of confession in the early medieval period, we will never know how closely devout Christians followed the terms of the penitentials, and even if we did know how often people confessed, we could not be sure they carried out the penances that had been assigned to them. Without doubt, the penitentials reveal society and culture in indirect ways that inform our understanding of Anglo-Saxon food culture, the history of sex, and other matters. Their historical value can be established in several ways not noticed by Boswell, who, in order to argue for normalized same-sex relations in medieval sources, incorrectly maintained that homosexual acts were punished less severely than hunting.[16] The early ninth-century penitential of Halitgar, bishop of Cambrai (d. 829), assessed penances ranging from one to seven years for clerics who hunted; the same text assessed a penance of fifteen years for male same-sex intercourse.[17] It is clear that the early Irish and Anglo-Saxon penitentials also contradict Boswell's claims.

The mere existence of regulations does not prove that the regulations, whether about food or sex, were enforced. As Sarah Foot has shown in her discussion of monastic life in England before 900, it is ill-advised to attempt to write religious or cultural history on the basis of regulatory texts, or what Foot calls "advisory or prescriptive literature." She argues that such sources offer "an idealized picture of a perfect and harmonious" monastic institution, thus obscuring the mixed rules and regulations that governed English monastic life.[18] Foot stresses the need to consult hagiographies and narrative texts for details of monastic life, and these sources, as we have seen, also illuminate details of food culture. The penitentials might encourage an equal and opposite bias, since they have suggested depravity to some, as they did to Charles Plummer at the end of the nineteenth century.[19] At the least, the regulations themselves indicate what bishops taught priests to expect of lay people and of each other, and what the clergy communicated to the laity. I believe that the penitentials show us more. If they were ossified forms that mechanically transmitted ancient standards, we would have little reason to parse their testimony. R. D. Fulk and Stefan Jurasinski have advanced debate about one of the vernacular handbooks by arguing that its translator sought to tighten the standards of its Latin source.[20] Whatever the merits of that argument, we will see that Anglo-Saxon penitentials, although often textually conservative in matters of food purity, were vital and notably innovative in matters of form.

---

[16] John Boswell, *Christianity, Social Tolerance, and Homosexuality*, pp. 179–84.

[17] See Pierre J. Payer, *Sex and the Penitentials*, pp. 135–39, and Allen J. Frantzen, *The Literature of Penance*, pp. 15–16. Halitgar's Latin is given in the notes to Josef Raith, ed., *Die altenglische Version des Halitgar'schen Bussbuches*, p. 59 (no. 27), hunting; pp. 18–19 (no. 6), male same-sex acts.

[18] Sarah Foot, *Monastic Life in Anglo-Saxon England*, pp. 6–7.

[19] As noted in Frantzen, *The Literature of Penance*, pp. 1–2.

[20] Fulk and Jurasinski, *The Old English Canons of Theodore*, pp. liii–lv.

The food officer in early Latin penitentials

The penitentials contain many references to food purity but seldom give an idea of how food regulations were to be enforced. Although the Church relied on its own officers to suppress pagan customs and to establish its new patterns of social organization, priests and bishops could not be everywhere at once. A degree of responsibility for the new discipline rested with the laity. Enforcement was not a comparable problem in penitential practice centered on monastic, communal life closely supervised by an abbot and a confessor. The early Latin penitentials were among the first written rules about food purity. They were brought to England by Irish missionaries and were in use before Theodore (d. 690) arrived from Rome in 669 to become archbishop of Canterbury. We associate the beginnings of a distinctively English disciplinary tradition with him. His penitential, dated to the early eighth century and attested in early manuscripts of both insular and continental provenance, is attributed to a follower known as the "Discipulus Umbrensium" and is divided into two books.[21] The preface to the *Penitential* explains how the regulations came to be collected. "Not only many men but also women" came "in crowds" to visit Theodore, who was "a man undoubtedly of extraordinary knowledge for our age." These consultations resulted in "conflicting and confused" rules gathered in the second book of the *Penitential*, which was compiled from cases Theodore judged.[22]

Food purity was one of many topics of concern to these apparently anxious converts to Christianity. Theodore's treatment of food culture differs from that of Irish penitentials, which quote some of the scriptural and canonical authorities he would have known about, especially the Book of Leviticus. Theodore knew Irish handbooks and derived a number of canons from Cummean's work, as P. W. Finsterwalder has shown. The *Penitential* of Cummean appears in several of the same manuscript collections as Theodore's.[23] In turn, later Irish authorities were quick to borrow from canons attributed to Theodore, some of which were quoted in Irish documents within a generation of the archbishop's death. Theodore was cited in a version of the Irish text called the *Collectio Canonum Hibernensis*, which is known to have been compiled before 725. The *Hibernensis* drew from a version of Theodore's penitential known as the *Judicia Theodori*; the *Bigotian Penitential*, a ninth-century Latin text, cites Theodore by name in reference to food purity.[24]

---

[21] On the manuscript traditions of Theodore's decisions and their continental distribution, see Meens, "Pollution in the Early Middle Ages," pp. 7–8. For a description of Theodore's work, see Thomas Charles-Edwards, "The Penitential of Theodore and the *Iudicia Theodori*." See also Frantzen, *The Literature of Penance*, pp. 63–66.

[22] Translation from John T. McNeill and Helena M. Gamer, *Medieval Handbooks of Penance*, p. 183.

[23] Paul Willem Finsterwalder, *Die Canones Theodori*, pp. 229–31. See further Charles-Edwards, "The Penitential of Theodore and the *Iudicia Theodori*," p. 171.

[24] See Fulk and Jurasinski, *The Old English Canons of Theodore*, pp. xlii–xlvii, and Charles-Edwards, "The Penitential of Theodore and the *Iudicia Theodori*." For the *Bigotian Penitential*

Theodore was an innovator in legislating food culture. He must have encountered numerous difficulties in shaping monastic discipline into a tool for lay life. We can compare the treatment of food purity in penitentials attributed to Finnian, Columbanus, and Cummean to Theodore's extended treatment of the topic. In its Irish form the penitential addressed monks and those who lived near them and centered on an exchange between a monastic counselor or confessor and someone who understood the monastery's social organization, a group that would include laity who lived in monastic *paruchia* or monastic federations.[25] Finnian's and Columbanus's penitentials were compiled for their own monks.[26] Neither discusses food purity in detail, chiefly because matters of diet were regulated by the monastic rule, and opportunities for sins related to food were scarce. When Columbanus mentions drunkenness that leads to vomiting, or eating and drinking beside temples, the sanctions pertain to the laity.[27] These penitentials predate Theodore's own collection, which borrows canons from Cummean's work; Theodore's *Penitential* and the penitentials of Finnian and Columbanus do not overlap. There are extensive parallels between penitentials attributed to Columbanus and Finnian and between Cummean's *Penitential* and the *Bigotian Penitential*; the latter two cast a wider net concerning food purity. Both of the latter works categorize food regulations under the sin of gluttony or as part of offenses related to the Eucharist, with the *Bigotian Penitential* adding canons from Theodore's text and others not of Irish origin.[28] There are many provisions protecting the handling of the Eucharist in a chapter that includes food offenses unrelated to the sacrament (e.g., the contamination of food or drink by animals or insects).[29]

Irish handbooks are replete with learned paragraphs quoting authorities by name, an important indication of their monastic audience. The *Penitential* of Cummean begins with a homily attributed to Caesarius of Arles (but derived from Origen and John Cassian) that follows the structure of the eight deadly sins.[30] The *Bigotian Penitential* gathers provisions from Jerome, Isidore, Ambrose, Theodore, Benedict of Nursia, and others. Food offices in these works seem to be modeled on monastic rules, which, in the early Anglo-Saxon period, varied in their requirements for fasting.

see Ludwig Bieler, ed., *The Irish Penitentials*, pp. 200–1, para. 19–23, and pp. 202–3, para. 32. It is traditional to call these texts "Irish" and to see them as "penitentials," but the corpus includes work in Old Irish and Latin of Breton and Welsh as well as Irish origin.

[25] John Reubin Davies, "Ecclesiastical Organization," pp. 242–45.

[26] On these penitentials' monastic focus, see Bieler, *The Irish Penitentials*, p. 4 and pp. 92–95 (Finnian), pp.106–7 (Columbanus), and pp. 122–25 (Cummean).

[27] The *Penitential* of Columbanus, c. 22, c. 24, in Bieler, *The Irish Penitentials*, pp. 104–5.

[28] See the *Penitential* of Cummean, ch. 1 (concerning gluttony), Bieler, *The Irish Penitentials*, pp. 110–13. See also "Of petty cases" in Cummean, pp. 124–27, ch. 10, c. 1 and c. 10 (the Eucharist) and c. 16 (carrion). For the *Bigotian Penitential*'s food regulations, see Bieler, *The Irish Penitentials*, pp. 215–19.

[29] See the *Penitential* of Cummean, ch. 11, cc. 12–18 (concerning the Eucharist), Bieler, *The Irish Penitentials*, pp. 130–33.

[30] For Cummean's text, see Bieler, *The Irish Penitentials*, pp. 110–23.

As Foot has noted, monastic culture was not monolithic.[31] The two rules of Columbanus were very strict. The *Communal Rule* required fasting every day until *none*, or 3 p.m., a rule later relaxed and observed only on Wednesday, Friday, and other designated days; violators fasted on bread and water for two days.[32] Columbanus described a daily diet of vegetables, beans, "flour mixed with water," and "the small bread of a loaf," the fare of the evening meal, the only one permitted by the *Monks' Rule*.[33]

Such detailed provisions required careful supervision. Monastic rules and saints' lives describe the duties of the officer who was responsible for ensuring that regulations were followed. The *Communal Rule* of Columbanus refers to the *economus*, a high-level administrator described by G. S. M. Walker as "a sort of bursar, cellarer, and master of works in one."[34] The *economus* adjudicated disputes and oversaw hospitality to strangers; he gave instructions to a subordinate overseer and also to monks, and handled disputes not brought to the abbot.[35] Other food officers presumably reported to him, including the *pincerna* or butler, the cellarer, the baker, and the cook. The *Communal Rule* singles out the brothers "to whom the care of cooking or serving has been entrusted" (*cui sollicitudo coquinandi vel ministrandi commissa est*). If these persons spilled anything, all the brothers prayed for him at the end of the office. If a quantity of food or drink was lost, he prostrated himself while they sang psalms.[36] Drink might have been involved in such accidents. The *Life of Columba* by Adomnan recounts Columba's prediction that a visitor to Iona named Colgu would know, when he saw his "butler enjoying himself at dinner with friends and swinging the serving jug round in a circle by its neck," that he would soon die.[37] Another form of Columba's name, Columcill, is also evidence; according to Bede it refers to his duties as a cellarer.[38] As the happy butler's behavior suggests, those bound by Irish monastic rules enjoyed few private moments. In such a culture it would have been difficult to skirt regulations about food purity.

The rules of Columbanus are stricter about food purity than rules associated with St. Benedict, who outlined the duties of the cellarer: "Let him

[31] Foot, *Monastic Life in Anglo-Saxon England*, pp. 233–39.
[32] Columbanus, *Communal Rule*, ch. 13, in G. S. M. Walker, ed., *Sancti Columbani Opera*, pp. 160–63.
[33] Columbanus, *Monks' Rule*, ch. 3, "Of food and drink," in Walker, *Sancti Columbani Opera*, pp. 124–27.
[34] Columbanus, *Communal Rule*, in Walker, *Sancti Columbani Opera*, p. 161, n. 1.
[35] Columbanus, *Communal Rule*, ch. 8, in Walker, *Sancti Columbani Opera*, pp. 152–53.
[36] Columbanus, *Communal Rule*, chs. 2 and 3, in Walker, *Sancti Columbani Opera*, p. 146–47.
[37] Adomnan, *Life of Saint Columba*, book 1, ch. 17. The *pincernus* is one in charge of drinks, a butler. The word sometimes refers to the cellarer. The object the butler swings, the *hauritorium*, might be a "bucket, ladle, jug – in short, anything in which water or the like may be drawn or drunk." Richard Sharpe lists various possibilities in the *Life of Saint Columba*, p. 179, n. 104.
[38] According to Bede, "Columba is now called Columcill by some, which is a compound of the world *cella* and the name Columba" (*Qui videlicet Columba nunc a nonnullis composito a Cella et Columba nomine Columcelli vocatur*) (*Bede's Ecclesiastical History of the English People*, book 5, ch. 9, pp. 478–79).

regard all the vessels of the monastery and all its substance, as if they were sacred vessels of the altar. Let him neglect nothing and let him not give way to avarice, nor let him be wasteful and a squanderer of the goods of the monastery; but let him do all things in due measure and according to the bidding of his Abbot."[39] In large communities Benedict excused the cellarer from kitchen duties assigned other monks on a weekly basis; they were to clean their utensils and return them to the cellarer when their work period was complete.[40] The *Rule* of St. Benedict, like the rules of Columbanus, depends on a strong administrative structure that ensured the monks' accountability.

An exception in Irish writing about food purity is the *Canons of Adomnan*, a Latin work based on Mosaic law and only nominally associated with the Irish abbot (d. 704). Nineteen of the text's twenty canons concern food purity; none assign penances for offenses.[41] Bieler hypothesizes that this and other canonical texts, including the *Judicia Theodori*, were collected between 725 and the date of the earliest exemplar, roughly 800.[42] The text adapts its sources to local and even geographical conditions. For example, it treats the case of marine animals that were cast ashore and cattle that fell from a rock. The text includes unusual categories such as the chicks of hens that had tasted human blood. John T. McNeill and Helena M. Gamer suggest that these conditions are those of seventh-century Ireland, a possible but not certain link.[43] The text acknowledges material circumstances in a way no other collection of food regulations does, Irish or Anglo-Saxon. Had more regulatory texts pertaining to food culture included comparable detail, the history of medieval regulations concerning food purity would be more informative. The *Canons of Adomnan* presents a contrast to the treatment of food in Irish penitentials and in Theodore's work as well.[44]

Although Theodore refers to an Irish handbook (*libellus scottorum*) in his preface, his two-part *Penitential* marks a new phase in the integration of food offices and penitential discipline. The concluding paragraphs indicate that Theodore's collection was to be used along with a "booklet on penance," perhaps Cummean's *Penitential*, especially since, as noted above, this text appears in some manuscript collections with Theodore's work.[45] Theodore's achievement was to center penitential discipline, including

---

[39] Benedict, *The Rule of St. Benedict*, ch. 31, pp. 48–50.
[40] Benedict, *The Rule of St. Benedict*, ch. 35, pp. 52–54.
[41] For the *Canons of Adomnan*, see Bieler, *The Irish Penitentials*, p. 9 (introduction), pp. 176–81 (text, with the scriptural parallels indicated), and pp. 253–54 (notes). The *Canons* belongs to the core of a group of six manuscripts of canonical works, three of them written by Breton scribes and two others of "Breton origin" or based on "a Breton exemplar" (and bearing Breton glosses; see Bieler, pp. 21–24 at p. 21).
[42] The earliest manuscript dates from the end of the eighth century; others are from the ninth century. See Bieler, *The Irish Penitentials*, pp. 21–24.
[43] McNeill and Gamer, *MHP*, p. 131.
[44] Bieler, *The Irish Penitentials*, "Concordantiae canonum," pp. 285–87, shows no shared content between the *Canons of Adomnan* and other Irish penitentials; there are none with Theodore's *Penitential*.
[45] Frantzen, *The Literature of Penance*, pp. 68–69.

the regulation of food, on the bishop and the priest. Theodore modified what Meens describes as the Irish "inclination" to strict discipline.[46] It was not an inclination, I would say, but rather a deliberate attempt to create demanding standards of discipline in sexual conduct, diet, and social interactions of many kinds outside the monastery. The kinds of settlements in which Theodore's handbook was likely to have had the most influence, I think, were monastic estates, which involved large numbers of lay people in various capacities. A minster commanded the administrative resources to spread the discipline of Theodore's text to its lay population, a kind of influence that would have been more difficult to exert in secular estates with less well-formed administrative structures. Building on work by Margaret Gelling, Foot writes that "some minsters were established specifically to meet the wider pastoral needs of the local population, particularly during the conversion period." She cites Theodore's concern with staffing minster churches.[47] Early in the conversion period, the administrative structure of a minster church would have been essential to the enforcement of new dietary rules, including fasting periods and matters of food purity. Estates around minsters would have felt the impact of the new rules most keenly, I suggest, because food officers within the minster might have exercised similar judicial power outside it among the laity.

Both books of Theodore's *Penitential* define standards of conduct for the laity and clerics. Most of the first book follows the protocol of a tariff penitential or handbook of penance, assigning a specific penance for each sin. The canons concerning food purity, like some others, do not follow this formula but merely state what the accepted practice is (e.g., one may eat horsemeat, but not everybody does). The whole of the second book comprises customs Theodore recommended and encouraged, and none of the behavior outlined there is accompanied by penances to be assigned if the standards are violated. The chapter dealing with food in the first book concerns "many and diverse evils" and comprises twelve canons, eight of which address food purity.[48] Penances are attached only to three canons: for drinking blood or semen, a penance of three years; for eating flesh torn by beasts, a penance of forty days (except in case of "the necessity of hunger"); and for knowingly eating "any unclean thing," penance "according to the degree of the pollution." The sinner's account would suffice for the first two matters, but a food officer might be required to determine the "degree of pollution."[49] The other five canons describe "harmless" cases. Three canons provide for violations committed out of

---

[46] Meens, "Pollution in the Early Middle Ages," p. 17. The conflicts between Irish and Roman standards, both within Ireland and in England, are much discussed. See "Ireland," in Allen J. Frantzen, *Anglo-Saxon Keywords*, pp. 151–55.

[47] Foot, *Monastic Life in Anglo-Saxon England*, pp. 85–86; see also pp. 317–18.

[48] Theodore, *Penitential*, book 1, ch. 7, ed. A. W. Haddan and W. Stubbs, *CED*, pp.182–83, translated in McNeill and Gamer, *MHP*, pp. 190–91.

[49] Theodore, *Penitential*, book 1, ch. 7, cc. 3, 6, and 12, ed. Haddan and Stubbs, *CED*, pp.182–83, translated in McNeill and Gamer, *MHP*, pp. 190–91.

necessity (eating or drinking contaminated supplies).[50] Two canons treat the violations as harmless if they were committed without the sinner's knowledge (both concerning pollution by blood).[51] If one touched food with unwashed hands, "there is no offense." Nor was it an offense to eat an unclean animal "from necessity," drink polluted water after it had been blessed, or ingest blood with saliva.[52] According to Cummean's *Penitential*, in contrast, one who touched "liquid food" (*limphaticum alimentum*) with soiled hands received one hundred blows; one who consumed food tainted by "a household beast" (*a familiari bestia*) performed special fasts. Fasts were assigned for giving another person food contaminated by a mouse or weasel, but the food itself was spared. Only the portions around the bodies of "those little beasts" (*bestiole*) were to be discarded and the rest was to be "taken in good faith" (*omne reliquum sana sumatur fide*).[53]

A chapter on the use of animals in Theodore's second book comprises nine canons. They concern eating carrion, eating food contaminated by small animals, consuming animals that had eaten carrion, and eating horsemeat, among others. None of the canons entails a penance, implying that the primary goal of the text was to inform the faithful and their priests about new matters, a function secondary to penitential practice.[54] Theodore's authority was sufficient to establish the new norms. Many cases that required penance under the Irish rules were seen as harmless under Theodore's. One canon in the *Bigotian Penitential* requires a penance of seven years for drinking blood or human urine, but notes that Theodore said three years instead. Another canon assigns a five-day penance for drinking liquid a cat has contaminated, but observes that Theodore said "it does not matter."[55]

The food-related chapter in Theodore's first book addresses "necessary things that are harmless" and outlines cases in which, to quote Meens, "necessity broke law." Meens adds that "Theodore's lenient approach to dietary rules probably was a reaction against other, more austere texts."[56] But what kind of a reaction? To the extent that we can gauge his intentions as an author (obscured as they are by the collaboration of unnamed assistants and a complex textual tradition), we can say that he was a pragmatist who understood that there were limits to the clergy's reach into the lives

---

[50] Theodore, *Penitential*, book 1, ch. 7, cc. 6, 7, and 9, ed. Haddan and Stubbs, *CED*, pp. 182–83, translated in McNeill and Gamer, *MHP*, p. 191.

[51] Theodore, *Penitential*, book 1, ch. 7, cc. 10–11, ed. Haddan and Stubbs, *CED*, p. 183, translated in McNeill and Gamer, *MHP*, p. 191.

[52] Theodore, *Penitential*, book 1, ch. 7, cc. 7, 9, 11, ed. Haddan and Stubbs, *CED*, p, 183, translated in McNeill and Gamer, *MHP*, p. 191.

[53] For these canons in the *Penitential* of Cummean, see Bieler, *The Irish Penitentials*, pp. 130–31, "Of questions concerning the Host," ch. 12, c. 15 (touching food), c. 18 (the household pet), c. 14 (preserving contaminated food).

[54] Theodore, *Penitential*, book 2, ch. 11, ed. Haddan and Stubbs, *CED*, p. 198, translated in McNeill and Gamer, *MHP*, pp. 207–8. These matters are described by Meens, "Pollution in the Early Middle Ages," pp. 8–14.

[55] The *Bigotian Penitential*, ch. 5, c. 2 and c. 8, ed. Bieler, *The Irish Penitentials*, pp. 216–17.

[56] Meens, "Pollution in the Early Middle Ages," p. 9.

of the laity. Yet his rules could be strict, as we see in decisions on sexual behavior, marriage, ordination of the clergy, and other problems. Through Theodore's penitential the early Church exerted influence both directly by assigning penances for specific sins and less directly by specifying standards not enforced by penances. Compared to Irish sources, his penitential reduced the number of food-related offenses requiring penitential discipline and hence reduced the need for food officers to supervise them. Theodore seems to have recognized that food was never so plentiful that it could be discarded without good cause. Although he did not dispense with the implied need for someone to determine if the standards had been violated, neither did he explain how, outside the strict vertical organization of a monastery, this oversight was to be achieved. This gap carried over into the vernacular texts based on Theodore's work.

Food purity and food offices in vernacular handbooks

Theodore's *Penitential* was influential in both its two-book form and as the *Judicia Theodori*, a work that revised that structure and incorporated other canons into it. These texts dominated the first handbooks to appear in the English language. A long penitential claiming his authority but traditionally assigned to "pseudo-Theodore," recently dated to between 820 and 850, has been assigned a part in the reform of handbooks of penance undertaken in the Frankish church. "The context of high-level discussions about the authority of, and inconsistencies in, older handbooks of penance," Carine Van Rhijn and Marjolin Saan write, "may ... have given pseudo-Theodore reason enough for his collecting, organizing and amending" older handbooks ("amending" is a word that should be used advisedly).[57] This author kept Theodore's influence current in the eleventh century; pseudo-Theodore's work survives in two English manuscripts that contain vernacular handbooks of penance.[58] Theodoran texts form just one element in the stream of regulatory literature informing the vernacular handbooks of penance. Other texts used by the compilers of penitentials in Old English include reform-oriented works by Theodulf of Orléans (d. 821) and Halitgar of Cambrai, authors who were translated into Old English in the tenth century if not before.

Three of the four vernacular English handbooks created between the second half of the ninth century (if not earlier) and the closing decades of the tenth include canons drawn from Theodore's work. The tradition of vernacular handbooks was a vigorous and developing one. Their manuscript traditions, along with evidence of language change and the emergence of new textual forms, provide rich testimony to the vitality of this

[57] Carine van Rhijn and Marjolin Saan, "Correcting Sinners, Correcting Texts," p. 40.
[58] In Appendix 1 to this chapter, Table 1, see Cambridge, Corpus Christi College, MS 190, and Brussels, Bibliothèque royale, 8558–63. See also Rhijn and Saan, "Correcting Sinners, Correcting Texts," p. 24.

textual tradition.[59] Although their dates remain undetermined, the Anglo-Saxon vernacular penitentials can be seen as emerging in a sequence. Using structural complexity as a guide, we can place the *Canons of Theodore* first. Translating provisions from Theodore's *Penitential* but without apparent system or plan, the *Canons of Theodore* shows few signs of Carolingian sources.[60] The *Scriftboc*, in contrast, includes a variety of ninth-century continental sources, among them texts falsely attributed to Bede (d. 735) and Egbert of York (d. 766), and reformed monastic rules, among them one by Chrodegang of Metz (d. 766) and another by Theodulf of Orléans. The compiler of the *Scriftboc* gathered food-related canons from various chapters of pseudo-Egbert's and Theodore's collections into a series of five chapters on food purity.[61] This text contains a fuller assembly of regulations concerning food and diet than that found in any of its sources and is the most extensive document on food regulation in the Old English period. There is no comparable attempt at planning in the *Canons of Theodore*, which does not use chapter headings, although several canons from one book of Theodore are grouped together near the beginning of the text.[62] The third text, the *OE Penitential*, also has a clear structure that adapts source materials, in this case the six-book Latin penitential of Halitgar. The *OE Penitential* includes excerpts from the *Scriftboc* but also draws independently on Theodore's *Penitential*. The fourth vernacular text, the *OE Handbook*, draws many of its canons from the second and fourth parts of the *OE Penitential* and takes innovation in this genre to its zenith.

The vernacular penitentials show many signs of innovation. The elaborate synthesis and reorganization of source materials in the *Scriftboc* is one example. Another is the development of a quasi-liturgical introduction to confession, supplemented by advice for the confessor, a text known as the *OE Introduction*. This material appears in manuscripts with both the *Scriftboc* and the *OE Penitential*. (see manuscripts SXY, Table 2, in the appendix to this chapter). Instructional material for the priest was greatly expanded in the *OE Handbook*, the last of the vernacular texts with some links to Wulfstan, archbishop of York and bishop of Worcester and London (d. 1023). The *OE Handbook* breaks with tradition, drastically shortening the list of sins the priest was to use in hearing the penitent's confession and greatly increasing instructional materials for the priest as a confessor.

---

[59] For details on Anglian forms and structural changes to these texts, see Allen J. Frantzen, "Food Words in the Anglo-Saxon Penitentials" and "Making Sense: Translating the Anglo-Saxon Penitentials." See also Franz Wenisch, *Spezifisch anglisches Wortgut*, pp. 63 and 327.

[60] On the relationship of the *OEC* to materials related to Theodore's *Penitential*, see Fulk and Jurasinski, *The Old English Canons of Theodore*, pp. xlii–lii.

[61] They concern the Eucharist; carrion and other prohibited food; pork, chickens, and other animals; fish and fowl; and miscellaneous matters, including bees, as well as the theft of animals. All of these were drawn from the Latin handbooks of pseudo-Egbert and Theodore's two-book collection. See Frantzen, *ASP*, *OES*, X23.01.01 through X26.13.01. Most provisions in these chapters concern food purity.

[62] See Frantzen, *ASP*, *OEC*, B63.05.01 through B64.03.01. Most provisions are drawn from Theodore's *Penitential*, book 2, ch. 11. See further Fulk and Jurasinski, *The Old English Canons of Theodore*, pp. xlii–xlvii.

Although innovative in matters of form, the compilers of Old English handbooks were conservative in matters of content. Theodore's regulations were incorporated into the vernacular texts with few changes. Two chapters of his *Penitential*, as we have seen, are devoted chiefly to food. Eight of the twelve canons in the chapter concerning "many and diverse evils" address food purity.[63] All twelve canons were translated into Old English. The chapter in Book 2 concerned with food regulations comprises nine canons, eight of which were translated into Old English.[64] These two chapters contain a total of twenty-one food-related regulations, twenty of which appear in a tenth-century vernacular penitential, including sixteen of the seventeen canons that concern food.[65] These canons comprise the bulk of the food-related content of the vernacular handbooks. In order to analyze food-related canons, I examine how these texts treat fasting periods and the fasting diet and then trace the distribution of key food-related vocabulary in them.[66]

The most common food word in the penitentials is *fæsten*, to fast. The liturgical year revolved around three fasts connected to three feasts: forty days before Christmas, forty days before Easter, and forty days after Pentecost. Fasts assigned in private confession would have been additional and would have required the penitent to fast at times and in ways in which others did not. Such fasts shaped a situational identity for the one fasting, setting him or her apart from others who were not bound to fast at the same time. Periodic or seasonal fasting requirements in the early Middle Ages were extensive. Discussing twelfth-century evidence, J. Patrick Greene estimates that those in monasteries would have fasted 175 days, or nearly half the year.[67] In a study of early monastic rules, Maria Dembinska suggests up to 200 fasting days.[68] For lay people we must count the three forty-day periods (Advent, Lent, Pentecost) and include other fasts, such as Ember days. We can assume a minimum of 150 fasting days for them, as well as any additional fasts assigned by confessors to individuals. Because seasonal fasts were communal, they would have been the easiest to enforce, exceptions being made for the sick, the young, and the elderly.

Penitential fasts, as opposed to seasonal fasts, would have been more difficult to monitor. They varied in length and intensity from a week of

---

[63] Theodore, *Penitential*, book 1, ch. 7, ed. Haddan and Stubbs, *CED*, pp.182–83, translated in McNeill and Gamer, *MHP*, pp. 190–91.

[64] Theodore, *Penitential*, book 2, ch. 11, ed. Haddan and Stubbs, *CED*, p. 198, translated in McNeill and Gamer, *MHP*, pp. 207–8.

[65] The exception is a canon concerning consumption of an animal with which a human had had sexual intercourse. See Theodore, *Penitential*, book 2, ch. 11, c. 9, ed. Haddan and Stubbs, *CED*, p. 198, translated in McNeill and Gamer, *MHP*, p. 208. Some of this material appears in Frantzen, "Food Words in the Anglo-Saxon Penitentials."

[66] Fulk and Jurasinski suggest that the translator of the *OEC* sometimes revised Theodore's canons, if inadvertently, by misunderstanding the source; see *The Old English Canons of Theodore*, pp. liii–lv.

[67] J. Patrick Greene, *Medieval Monsteries*, pp. 124–25.

[68] Maria Dembinska, "Fasting and Working Monks," p. 155.

fasting to several years during which fasting was required two or three days each week. Those who fasted had to change their diet and behavior, and hence, during the fasting interval, alter their social identity by assuming a temporary identity. In considering what foods the penitential fast permitted the faithful to consume, we might assume a diet of bread and water. But to judge by the *Penitential* of Theodore and vernacular texts based on it, such was not the custom in the early Anglo-Saxon period. Theodore assigned penances without specifying a diet. The two earliest vernacular handbooks followed suit. The phrase *on hlafe & on wætere* ("on bread and water," translating *pane et aqua*) is found only once in the *Canons of Theodore*, in a penance for suffocating a child, translating an as yet unknown source.[69] The expression does not occur at all in *Scriftboc*. In contrast, penances in the *OE Penitential* are routinely described as fasts of bread and water, sometimes divided into one year of such a fast and two years "as his confessor prescribes for him." The provision for two years "as his confessor prescribes for him" might mean a lightening of the penance for the second period (assuming that the more intense of the two periods would take place first). All the penances in Book 4 of the *OE Penitential* that were taken from Halitgar's sixth book follow the formula requiring bread and water.[70] There are signs that this diet was becoming the norm. The compiler of the *OE Penitential* revised canons taken from the *Scriftboc* to follow this form and often assigns fasts of bread and water, and prescribes penances of one or two years, with a longer portion sometimes added at the confessor's discretion. Some of these canons also appear in the *OE Handbook*.[71]

It is difficult to see how anyone could have monitored fasts of varying lengths for several adults. In the end, penitents were accountable to their confessors and must have been responsible for monitoring their food intake in accordance with the confessor's instructions, avoiding meat even if others ate it and adhering to a diet of bread and water on the appointed days if they had been told to do so. Such modifications would have been much easier to accomplish within the monastery, where, as we have seen in the case of the monastic cooks and servers who spilled food or drink, knowledge of offenses was communal. Many sins committed by those living in settlements would also have been common knowledge. Some, such as theft, were punished by law as well as the Church, making

---

[69] Frantzen, *ASP, OEC*, B66.06.01. The *OE Handbook* includes a canon on suffocating a child (Frantzen, *ASP, OEH*, D54.39.01). This seems to parallel *Canons of Theodore* B66.06.01, a canon not in the *OE Penitential* or *Scriftboc*. See also Fulk and Jurasinski, *The Old English Canons of Theodore*, p. 35, note to A32.

[70] Raith, *Die altenglische Version des Halitgar'schen Bussbuches*, pp. 46–69, gives Latin sources for the Old English canons.

[71] Compare Frantzen, *ASP, OEP*, S44.25.01, to *OES*, S25.03.01. Both canons concern animals caught in nets. The *OEP* adds a fasting diet for one who eats an animal that was killed this way: *gif his hwa bruce fæste iiii wucan a operne dæg on hlafe & on wætere*. Compare also *OEP*, Y44.39.01, to *OES*, X22.01.01. The *OEP* adds a fasting diet of bread and water: *fæste iii lengtenu ælce frigedæg on hlafe & on wætere & þa opre dagas bruce his metes buton flæsce*. *OEH*, D54.31.01, D54.33.01, and D54.34.01 require fasting on bread and water.

anonymity impossible and increasing the likelihood that the penitent would adhere to the special fasts that had been assigned in confession. We will see that the *OE Handbook* sought to make a virtue of this kind of publicity by enlisting the penitent's associates in his or her fast.

Food words other than those related to fasting are unevenly distributed in the vernacular handbooks. As a way of linking these words to possible occasions for food officers to exercise their expertise, I analyzed the distribution of eighty-one food words; they are listed in the appendix (Tables 3–8; Table 10 summarizes the use of food words in each text).[72] The analysis is limited to nouns, which are divided into six categories, in descending order of frequency: animals as food and in relation to food purity; foodstuffs in general; food-related processes; the body; drink; and food objects. My count shows that the *Scriftboc* includes 54 percent of these words, the *OE Penitential* 48 percent, and the *Canons of Theodore* 38 percent. The *OE Handbook* includes just seventeen of these words, or 21 percent. Only the *OE Introduction*, which does not assign tariffs or penance for specific sins, includes a lower figure, just 10 percent of them.

These percentages show a marked drop in food-related content in the *OE Handbook*. Twenty-eight words in this list name animals (Table 3). The *Scriftboc*, the *Canons*, and *OE Penitential* each contain at least twelve of them; there are none in the *OE Handbook*. Seven words relate to punishments for ingesting the body or its wastes (Table 6), all represented in the three early works while, again, none appear in the *OE Handbook*. The *OE Handbook* also omits canons dealing with the Eucharist, a matter treated fully both in the *Scriftboc* and the *OE Penitential*.[73] The *OE Handbook* names only one food object; all the others name two or more (Table 8). In other areas, the *OE Handbook* shares the interests of the earlier handbooks, including foodstuffs (Table 5, a category including generic terms such as *æt*, meaning food, and medical terms, such as abortifacients). Words for drink, defined as any liquid not coming from the body, occur in all four vernacular handbooks (Table 7). The data from the use of food-related verbs are similar to the data on nouns. The *OE Handbook* includes just two of nine verbs related to food, while each of the earlier handbooks uses four or more and the *OEI* uses three (Table 9).

The penitentials say more about practices and processes than about objects or actors associated with food (see Table 4 and Table 9). The largest category, the use of animals and contamination by animals, would have presented many opportunities for decisions based on expert assessment (see Table 3). Other categories involving specialized knowledge include clerical conduct, especially consumption of alcohol, and the purity of

---

[72] To see the relevant canons, use the canon finder or the glossary (available when any Old English text is on the screen). The category of "food words" is not an objective one, and numerical data based on words included, although reliable as more than general indicators, are not, obviously, scientific.

[73] For examples, see Frantzen, *ASP*, Cultural index, Eucharist. The *OEC* contains just one reference to the Eucharist.

medicinal mixtures, another area that would have been overseen by those equipped to prepare such remedies themselves. The cook was presumably charged with ensuring the quality of animals used as food. Tradition would have determined some matters. The Anglo-Saxons were permitted to eat rabbits, cited by Douglas as having "deviant feet" and forbidden by Leviticus (11:6). Horses were forbidden in some places because pagans ate them (both wild and tame), according to the eighth-century pope, Gregory III, who told the Anglo-Saxon missionary Boniface that he was "in no wise" to permit this "filthy and abominable practice."[74] However, following Theodore, both the *Canons of Theodore* and the *Scriftboc* permit horses to be eaten, noting that not everybody does eat them.[75]

The cook's interests sometimes might have conflicted with those of purveyors, including hunters, trappers, or fishers. The cook would have asked the hunter or other food-gatherer about the condition of carcasses in dubious condition. The cook would need to know the circumstances of the animals' death. Birds and other animals found in nets could not be eaten if they had suffocated, a prohibition taken from the Acts of the Apostles, which prohibited eating animals that had been strangled.[76] The hunter in *The Colloquy* reports that he uses nets, but the three early handbooks prohibit the eating of animals trapped this way if they had suffocated (but not, presumably, if they had been killed by the one who found them).[77] Animals that had been found dead could not, in most cases, be eaten. Hens and pigs that had consumed human blood could only be eaten after a certain period.[78] In cases of necessity, animals that had died of "natural causes" could be eaten (i.e., those not killed by a hunter or butcher).[79] The *Scriftboc* and the *OE Penitential* both include penances for consuming blood in half-cooked meat and for accidentally swallowing blood, canons drawn from Theodore's penitential by the compiler of the *Scriftboc* and taken into the *OE Penitential* from that source.[80]

In these cases, there would have been possibilities for concealment on the cook's part as well as on the hunter's. If food were in short supply, it is easy to suppose that expediency, or, to use Theodore's word, "necessity," ruled. An important clue, perhaps, is a passage from Theodore's *Penitential* translated in the *Canons of Theodore*. This canon assesses a penance for

---

[74] For the letter of Gregory III to Boniface, written around 732, see Ephria Emerton, trans., *The Letters of St. Boniface*, pp. 57–58.

[75] Frantzen, *ASP, OES*, X25.02.01; *OEC*, B64.03.04.

[76] For these canons, see Frantzen, *ASP, OES*, X25.03.01; *OEP*, Y44.25.01; and *OEC*, B64.03.02, B64.03.03.

[77] G. N. Garmonsway, ed., *Ælfric's Colloquy*, p. 23, ll. 57–61. Frantzen, *ASP, OES*, X25.03.01 and *OEC*, B64.03.02 (both concerning birds and other animals caught in nets or torn by hawks); *OEP*, Y44.25.01 (deer caught in nets).

[78] In the *OEC*, see B64.03.01; in the *OEP*, Y44.54.01. For all references to animals, consult Frantzen, *ASP*, Cultural index, Animals, which contains all references to animals in the OE penitentials, and see also Appendix 2, Table 5.

[79] For these canons, see Frantzen, *ASP, OES*, X25.02.01; *OEC*, B64.03.04 and B68.04.01 ("natural causes").

[80] For these canons, see Frantzen, *ASP, OES*, X23.07.01, X23.08.01; *OEP*, Y44.37.01, Y44.38.01.

consuming contaminated food. "Therefore, that which is polluted with blood or with any unclean thing, if someone eats it and does not know (that it is unclean), that does not harm him. If he knows it, he must repent for it according to the measure of pollution" (*bete be ðæs widles gemete*, translating Theodore's *juxta modum pullutionis*).[81] Either a supervisor or a cook might have been able to judge the "measure of pollution." Such a rule might originally have been intended for the administrative structures of religious houses, in which various offices could have been used to enforce food standards. In a settlement, I believe, the cook alone could assess the "measure of pollution" of the food supply.

The rules were sometimes corrupted. For example, the *Scriftboc* requires that if a small pig (*lytle fearh*) fell into liquid, the liquid was to be blessed and consumed. *Fearh* is an error, obviously, since a farrow or young pig is not likely to have had access to a vat of water; the Latin is *surrex* (mouse). However, if the animal died, the liquid had to be discarded, apparently because decay would have begun.[82] The same regulation occurs in the *OE Penitential*, which correctly refers to a mouse, evidently based on a better version of Theodore's work than that known to the compiler of the *Scriftboc*. According to the *OE Penitential*, again following Theodore directly, or using a version of the *Scriftboc* no longer available, the liquid was to be discarded if the animal died and the vessel (*fæt*) was to be cleaned (the Old English *þwean* might mean either washed and cleansed or blessed ritually).[83] The *Scriftboc* makes no reference to cleaning the vessel.

According to another canon in the *Scriftboc*, if a "large amount of liquid" (*on mycelre wætan*) were contaminated by a mouse or weasel, the liquid could be consumed once it had been blessed.[84] The *OE Penitential* also stands closer to Theodore on this matter, making it clear that the compromise is necessary because the contaminated liquid contains much food (*metes mycle*); there is no reference to *mete* in the *Scriftboc* version. Here we get a representation of what must have been a common way of preparing meat, simmering it with other ingredients in liquid: "It is also said that if [there is] a great deal of food altogether there [in the liquid], one is to sprinkle it with holy water and consume it if he needs it, but [only] out of necessity" (*Eft hit cwyð on oþre stowe gif þæs metes mycel sig ætgædere strede man*

---

[81] Frantzen, *ASP, OEC*, B76.06.09; the source is Theodore, *Penitential*, book 1, ch. 2, c. 12, ed. Haddan and Stubbs, *CED*, p. 183, translated in McNeill and Gamer, *MHP*, p. 191.

[82] The confusion, McNeill and Gamer note, stems from *sorex*, shrewmouse or shrew. See *MHP*, p. 191, n. 75. For the text, see Frantzen, *ASP, OES*, X26.02.01. All three manuscripts of the *Scriftboc* read *fearh*.

[83] Frantzen, *ASP, OEP*, Y44.32.01: "If a little mouse falls into water, one is to do away with it and sprinkle that water with holy water. If the animal is alive, one is to use that water and if it is dead, one is to throw it out and clean the vessel." (*Gif mus on wætan befealle do hy man aweg. & astrede mid halig wætere. & gif heo cucu sy. þicge man þæne wætan. gif heo þonne dead sy. Geote hit man ut. & þwea þæt fæt.*)

[84] Frantzen, *ASP, OES*, X26.04.01: "If a mouse or a weasel falls into a large amount of liquid and is dead there, one is to sprinkle it with holy water and drink it." (*Gyf on mycelre wætan hwylc mus oððe wesle fealle· & ðær dead sy sprencge man mid halig wætere & ðicge.*)

hit mid haligwætere & þicge gif his þearf sig & þæt þonne for neadþearfe).[85] The *Canons of Theodore* include a provision from Theodore not found elsewhere. If bird dung fell into liquid to be drunk or used for cooking, the dung was to be removed and the remaining food and broth (*se mete*) blessed with holy water and then regarded as clean.[86] The handbooks supplied conflicting advice on other matters, such as the case of pigs or chickens that ate carrion or ingested human blood. The *Scriftboc* allowed these animals to be eaten after they were purified; the hen could be eaten about three months after this happened.[87] Theodore's penitential did not specify the three-month period or the process of purifying the animal but said only that the animals were not to be discarded.[88] The *OE Penitential*, by contrast, required that contaminated animals be killed and fed to dogs.[89]

It is not likely that lay people would have been aware of these discrepancies, which would have been more readily detected in monastic communities. Lay decisions would have been governed by tradition. The cook was probably not the only person who was held accountable for food purity. Everyone in a settlement might know if a pig or chickens had eaten flesh or drunk blood and all might have been aware of the time that had to lapse before the animals could be consumed.[90] Both the *Canons of Theodore* and the *Scriftboc* specify that if diners were aware that food was unclean and ate it anyway, they (not the cook) were assessed penance for their wrongdoing.[91] Other violations would have been public and difficult to conceal, especially drunkenness and its consequences, the subject of the first chapter of Theodore's first book and so especially prominent.[92] Social decorum was affected by food and drink, including vomiting because of inebriation, causing another to vomit, or such practices as mixing blood with other fluids. Drunkenness might cause pollution (e.g., vomiting the

---

[85] Frantzen, *ASP, OEP*, S44.32.02.

[86] Frantzen, *ASP, OEC*, B76.06.08.

[87] Frantzen, *ASP, OES*, X24.01.01–X.24.02.01: "If swine eat carrion and taste man's blood, we believe that they nevertheless are not to be disposed of; however, one may not eat them until they are made clean again. If a hen drink man's blood, one is allowed to eat it afterward up to about 3 months later; but for this we do not have ancient authority" (*If swyn eteð myrten flæsc & mannes blod byrigeð we gelyfað þæt hi swa þeah ne syn to worpenne· þeah hi mon þonne gyt etan ne mote oððe hi eft clæne syn. Gyf henfugel mannes blod drince eft his man mot brucan ymbe þreo monað. be þysum swa þeah we nabbað ealde gewitnesse*).

[88] Theodore, *Penitential*, book 2, ch. 11, c. 7: *Si casu porci comedent carnem morticinorum aut sanguinem hominis, non abiciendos credimus, nec gallinas; ergo porci, quo sanguinem hominis gustant, manducentur*. In Haddan and Stubbs, *CED*, p. 198. Translation by McNeill and Gamer: "If by chance swine eat carrion flesh or the blood of a man, we hold that they are not to be thrown away; nor are hens; hence swine that [only] taste the blood of a man are to be eaten" (*MHP*, p. 208).

[89] Frantzen, *ASP, OEP*, Y44.54.01: "If a pig or a chicken or any sort of creature eat someone's body or drink his blood, one is to slay that creature and give it to the dogs" (*Gif swin oððe henna oððe æniges cynnes yrfe ete of mannes lichaman oððe his blode slea man þæt yrfe & sylle hit hundum*).

[90] Frantzen, *ASP, OEC*, B64.03.01; *OES*, X24.01.01.

[91] Frantzen, *ASP, OES*, X26.03.01; *OEC*, B76.06.03.

[92] In Haddan and Stubbs, *CED*, p. 198. See McNeill and Gamer, *MHP*, p. 184. There is a wide-ranging discussion of drunkenness and gluttony in Hugh Magennis, *Anglo-Saxon Appetites*, pp. 92–120.

Eucharist) as well as violence and death. Few canons address drunken behavior and what followed from it. The *Canons of Theodore* and *Scriftboc* include only one canon each about drunkenness or gluttony; the *Scriftboc* provides a penance for vomiting the Eucharist while drunk, and the *Canons of Theodore* for manslaughter caused by drunkenness.[93] Both are drawn from Theodore's chapter. The *OE Penitential* includes six canons related to alcohol, some drawn from the chapter on drunkenness in Theodore's handbook. The canons concern nocturnal emission caused by inebriation; intoxicated bishops, monks, priests, and laity who vomit because they are drunk; and deceit used to cause another to become intoxicated.[94] The *OE Handbook* refers to intoxication four times, although only once in a penance, which concerns an adult, who, while asleep, rolled over on and suffocated a child. If this happened because the adult was drunk, the penance was intensified. This is not an abuse related to food purity; nor are other references to drunkenness in the *OE Handbook*.[95]

All the vernacular penitentials incorporate canons that relate food to medicinal uses, an important context for food purity. In these cases the food officer would have been the one who prepared the estate's remedies and recipes. Many recipes refer to food objects (including spoons and pots of metal or ceramic) and food (such as honey, eggs, and herbs). An example, quoted earlier from *Bald's Leechbook*, uses the spoon as a unit of measure, instructing that one should "mix in a cup a full spoon of mustard and a half-spoon of honey" (*senepes dustes cucler fulne & huniges healfne cucler gedo on calic menge*).[96] The penitentials prohibited some mixtures. One regulation, derived from Theodore's collection, prohibits combining semen with food as a love potion.[97] The *OE Penitential* and *OE Handbook* contain similar prohibitions but refer only to "food and drink" used this way and also prohibit incantations that involve gathering herbs.[98] The *OE Penitential* and the *OE Handbook* include the same canon concerning abortions induced by food or drink. The *Scriftboc* also prohibits abortion but does not mention the means of inducing it.[99] The continuity across these three handbooks suggests that these customs, however despised, were difficult to repress.

In assessing the continuity of regulations for food purity over the centuries from Theodore to Wulfstan, we should consider two points. First, when the Latin texts were compiled in the early stages of the Christian conversion, food discipline was less important than other matters. The longest chapters in the second book of Theodore's penitential concern marriage,

[93] Frantzen, *ASP, OES*, X22.05.01; *OEC*, B76.03.04.
[94] Frantzen, *ASP, OEP*, Y43.14.02–Y43.14.04; for intoxicated bishops, see Y44.28.01–Y30.01.01.
[95] Frantzen, *ASP, OEH*, D54.39.01. See the list of sins to be avoided, D55.10.01.
[96] *Bald's Leechbook*, book I, ch. i, 17, ed. Oswald Cockayne, *Leechdoms, Wortcunning and Starcraft*, 2: 24–25. See also Chapter 7, p. 166, above.
[97] Frantzen, *ASP, OES*, X14.08.01; see Meens, "Pollution in the Early Middle Ages," p. 12.
[98] Frantzen, *ASP, OEP*, Y44.14.01; compare *OEH*, D54.37.01, a longer form. For prohibitions on incantations that involve gathering herbs, see *OEP*, Y42.24.01.
[99] See Frantzen, *ASP, OEP*, Y42.02.01, and *OEH*, D54.10.01; for the *Scriftboc*, see X14.09.01.

the organization of the church, and the ordination of priests. Food purity must have been simpler to adjudicate than questions of divorce, clerical discipline, and others that reached beyond the domestic and dietary. Second, in setting standards of food purity, Theodore (who had lived in a monastic community before coming to Canterbury) and his followers seem to have used monastic models of social organization similar to those implied in the Irish penitentials. The monastery's central administration, clearly defined lines of authority, and simple reporting structure ensured the enforcement of the required diet. Such conditions could not have obtained in most settlements where Christians were to be found.

As they outlined dietary standards for all Christians, the scholarly archbishop and his workers did make an important concession when they decided not to assess penances for food violations, revealing an accommodating and pragmatic spirit. Theodore and his assistants knew that Christian food standards had to be introduced and rationalized, whether in humble settings in which the cook worked alone with few or no helpers, or in large communities with more organized and hence more readily regulated food cultures. Whatever the form in which they were communicated, ecclesiastical standards in either setting would have been limited by common sense. The cook and his or her assistants were in constant contact with food, drink, and food objects. Trapped or hunted game would have been brought to them. They would have been the most aware of the vulnerability of storage vessels to small animals and other sources of contamination. They were also aware of how much food had been stored and how long it would last. When rules had to be bent "of necessity," they were the ones who made the decision. How their judgments were reported to the priest or to the bishop's reeve, and how widely their authority was accepted, are matters we cannot know. The cook was a figure around whom both power and resentment accrued, as we see in *The Colloquy*. In this classroom dialogue the monastic master (i.e., the teacher leading schoolboys in the dialogue) dismisses the cook, who claims that "without my craft every table would seem empty" and that no food would taste good without bread (meaning that this cook is also doubling as the baker). He also boasts that he makes hearts strong and that he is "the stamina of men" (*Ic heortan mannes gestrangie, ic mægen wera*).[100] Anybody can cook, the master replies, whether boiling vegetables or roasting meat. The master skips the hard work of preparing things to be cooked, taking a consumer's view and ignoring the need for decisions about the quality of the foodstuffs. The cook insists that without his services all will be servants "and none of you will be lord." The cook's language reinforces the image of a pyramid in which the top rests on the base (i.e., the position the cook himself occupies). The monastic master and the cook himself fail to see the significance of the cook's words, which demonstrate the interdependence of labor within a network. Lords (i.e., other workers) might

---

[100] Garmonsway, *Ælfric's Colloquy*, pp. 36–37, ll. 190–91.

drive out the cook, but they would not thereby master his craft, without which, the cook says, "You won't be able to eat." He, in turn, could not cook without the hunter and the plowman and a host of other, unnamed agricultural workers. Cooks were powerful; they were among the few food workers who were – by definition – always acting in the lordly capacity of food officers, an identity that other food workers acquired only when circumstances demanded.

Conclusion

The compilers of the *OE Handbook*, working in the early eleventh century, took little interest in food, incorporating about only one in five of eighty-one keywords related to food culture. Since Wulfstan and his followers were tightening the Church's regulation of society, how can we explain this development? Douglas offers the roots of an explanation in the "rela-tivity of dirt." "There is no such thing as absolute dirt: it exists in the eye of the beholder," she writes. We shun dirt because "dirt offends against order."[101] In the eighth century, the penitentials redefined dirt and the order that dirt offends against by intervening into existing foodways. Contamination of food supplies by animals or by other means was the same in the eleventh century as in the seventh. But the relative importance of dirt had changed. It is possible that food regulations found in the earlier penitentials were still consulted, since manuscripts containing them exist with those of the *OE Handbook* (Tables 1 and 2 in the appendix to this chapter). Just as Theodore's followers expected his penitential to be sup-plemented by earlier Latin handbooks, the compiler of the *OE Handbook* might have expected clergy to use earlier handbooks in the vernacular. Wulfstan himself culled earlier documents and quoted them when he found it useful. For example, in *The Canons of Edgar* the provision forbid-ding the clergy to hunt is drawn verbatim from the *OE Penitential*.[102] The *OE Handbook* draws many of its canons from the same source.

Given Wulfstan's well-documented and vigorous refashioning of legal discourse to incorporate more ecclesiastical matters, however, it seems more likely that the earlier penitentials, which had been in use by the time of Alfred, or earlier, were found wanting. Dirt in Wulfstan's time included contaminated food supplies, but there was a greater pollution to be seen in the failing power of Christian ways and the rejection of the Church itself. As an advisor to two kings, Wulfstan could see that the landscape was changing and that new centers of power were taking shape. He could, when he chose, create a vivid image of the consumption habits of his carousing clergy and their lax congregations, as readers of the *Sermon of the Wolf to the English* have observed. With the enemy not only at but within

---

[101] Douglas, *Purity and Danger*, p. 2.
[102] See Roger Fowler, ed., *Wulfstan's Canons of Edgar*, p. 15, c. 65. Compare to Frantzen, *ASP, OEP*, Y44.27.01.

the gates, Wulfstan faced difficulties different from those Theodore knew. The pious who came to Theodore for guidance were working out new identities for themselves, looking for guidance in new practices that told others who was Christian and who was not. For Wulfstan and his contemporaries, it was not enough to differentiate pagan from Christian identity. Christian identity itself had become diluted, and pagans, Wulfstan said, were sometimes more honorable than those who belonged to the Church.[103] Solutions, then, had to be framed in conjunction with powers above the Church's own. For this purpose Wulfstan exploited his close alliance with the king and used laws, sermons, rules for clergy, and other texts in order to position the public observance of fasting and feasting as the most important and closely regulated aspect of food culture. It was certainly the most obvious way to articulate and monitor the social order that, Douglas insists, stands behind food purity. Wulfstan's ecclesiastical legislation abandoned the monastic model of Theodore, with its implied hierarchy of officials charged with enforcing discipline. Wulfstan lived in a world of intoxicated priests who shirked their duties and thieving reeves. If priests were not sober, how could they judge the sobriety of their charges? If reeves were not honest, how could their lords trust those whom the reeves managed? These were not new problems; Bede, Alfred, and others complained about the clergy. Theodore's *Penitential* and Irish penitentials contained the same criticisms. But authors of those texts did not have the long arm of the law to use; Wulfstan did. That is why, I believe, Wulfstan chose to emphasize the fast. Fasting, like feasting, took place at authorized times that had now become as prominent in law codes as they had been in ecclesiastical documents. These cycles determined what could be eaten and when. They ordered the year and also ordered social space. As it emerges in ecclesiastical texts from Wulfstan's time, food culture was imagined as a shared interest of the royal and the regional. Under Wulfstan there was a convergence of penitential and legal practice that had not been seen since seventh-century Kentish laws drew from the penitential of Theodore. The textual tradition had carried the penitentials forward in time but left behind information necessary to understanding how the words had worked in the world. A gap had opened between the penitentials and the social contexts in which the Church functioned. That gap was closed by the *OE Handbook*. The Church now approached food culture and penitential discipline on a level comparable to that of law codes. Confession was still a conversation between a priest and a penitent, but in Book 5 and Book 6 the *OE Handbook* embraced practices of secular law to assert the Church's authority in public discourse.

In the *OE Handbook* lesser questions about food purity, whether about mice in flour or distribution of grain, were left to those best able to answer them, beginning with the reeve and reaching down to cooks. What now mattered was when and how the faithful fasted and feasted. Wulfstan's

---

[103] Wulfstan, *Sermo Lupi ad Anglos*, in Dorothy Whitelock, ed., *EHD*, pp. 929–34 at p. 930.

work was not concerned with the field or the kitchen but with the manor house and the field system. In the following chapter we will see that the *OE Handbook* took explicit measures to integrate penitential discipline into the size and complexity of estates. The *OE Handbook* was far from a retreat from the battlefront of food purity. Instead, it created a more powerful position for the Church by integrating some aspects of penitential discipline into the social networks of the wealthy on whose patronage the Church depended. In this new expression of ecclesiastical power, food and food objects mattered more rather than less than they had heretofore.

Chapter 8: Appendix

Table 1: Manuscripts of Anglo-Saxon penitentials

B: Brussels, Bibliothèque royale, 8558–63, s. xi[1]; southeastern (Ker, no. 10; Gneuss, no. 808)*

C: Cambridge, Corpus Christi College, 265, s. xi[med.]; Worcester (Ker, no. 53; Gneuss, no. 73)

D: Cambridge, Corpus Christi College, 201, s. xi[med.]; Winchester (Ker, no. 49; Gneuss, no. 66)

N: London, British Library, Cotton Tiberius A.iii, f. 96v, s. xi[med.]; Canterbury (Ker, no. 186, art. G; Gneuss, no. 363)

S: Cambridge, Corpus Christi College, 190, s. xi[med], XI[2]; Exeter (Ker, no. 45B; Gneuss, no. 59)

X: Oxford, Bodleian Library, Junius 121, s. xi¾; Worcester (Ker, no. 338; Gneuss, no. 644)

Y: Oxford, Bodleian Library, Laud Misc. 482, s. xi[med]; Worcester (Ker, no. 343; Gneuss, no. 656)

---

* Numbers in parentheses refer to descriptions in N. R. Ker, *Catalogue of Manuscripts Containing Anglo-Saxon*; Helmut Gneuss, *Handlist of Anglo-Saxon Manuscripts*.

Table 2: Distribution of texts in manuscripts

Manuscripts	B	C	D	N	S	X	Y
Texts							
OEC	complete				excerpts		complete
OES					complete	complete	complete
OEP	Book 4				complete	truncated*	complete
*OEH***	4-part	4-part	6-part**	4-part		excerpts	excerpts
OEI	excerpts			excerpts	complete	excerpts	excerpts

The manuscripts form two groups. MSS SXY are the main witnesses for *OEC*, *OES*, and *OEP*, the earlier penitentials; MSS CDN are the main witnesses for the *OEH*, the last of the vernacular handbooks. MS B, bridges these groups.

* In MS X Book 4 of the *OEP* is truncated and the entire *OES* is appended to it. This is a unique arrangement; other MSS BSY present Book 4 in its entirety (MS B contains only Book 4).

** The *OEH* appears as both a 4-part and 6-part text. The latter form is found only once and then imperfectly (D). Roger Fowler presents the text in six parts in "A Late OE Handbook for the Use of a Confessor." See Frantzen, *ASP, OEH*, Description & Index, for details.

Table 3: Animals*

---

beo (bee), *OES* (X26.01.01), *OEP* (Y44.31.01)
bera (bear), *OEP* (Y44.23.01)
deor (animal, beast), *OEP* (Y44.23.01)
deorcyn (wild animal), *OEP* (Y44.23.01)
eowu (ewe), *OEP* (Y43.16.01)
fearh (young pig), *OES* (X26.02.01)
feoðerfotneat (four-footed animal), *OES* (X26.06.01)
fisc (fish), *OES* (X25.01.01), *OEP* (Y44.26.01)
fugel (bird), *OEC* (B64.03.02), *OES* (X25.03.01)
hara (hare), *OEC* (B64.03.02), *OES* (X25.04.01)
heafoc (hawk), *OEC* (B64.03.02)
heafocfugel (hawk), *OES* (X25.03.01)
henfugel (hen), *OES* (X24.02.01)
henn (chicken), *OEC* (B64.03.01), *OEP* (Y44.54.01)
heort (hart), *OEC* (B64.01.01), *OEP* (Y41.02.01)
herd (herd), *OEP* (Y43.16.02)
hors (horse), *OEC* (B64.03.04), *OES* (X25.02.01)
hryðer (ox), *OES* (X26.06.01)
neat (animal, cattle), *OEC* (B64.01.01), *OES* (X02.03.01)
mus (mouse), *OEC* (B76.06.03), *OES* (X22.08.01)
orf (cattle), *OEP* (Y44.24.01)
ra (roe), *OEC* (B64.01.01)
storf (flesh of animals dead of natural causes), *OEC* (B68.04.01)
swyn (swine), *OEC* (B64.01.01), *OES* (X24.01.01), *OEP* (Y44.54.01)
wesle (weasel), *OES* (X23.05.01), *OEP* (Y44.35.01)
wildeor (wild beast), *OEC* (B76.06.04), *OEP* (Y43.16.02)
wyrm (worm, serpent), *OES* (X23.04.01)
yrfe (also *ierfe*, creature), *OEP* (Y44.54.01)

---

* In this and the following tables each word is counted only once, no matter how many times it is used in a text.

Table 4: Food processes

afæsten (fasting period), *OEC* (B62.02.01), *OES* (X01.02.01)
freolstid (festival time), *OEH* (D53.06.01)
freolstow (festival place), *OEH* (D53.06.01)
gereord (feast), *OEI* (S33.10.02)
gifernes ætes (greediness in eating), *OEH* (D52.02.02)
hærfest (autumn, harvest time), *OES* (X26.09.01), *OEP* (Y44.07.01), *OEH* (D54.30.01)
healfsoden mete (half-cooked meat), *OES* (X23.07.01)
hungor (hunger), *OEC* (B68.04.02), *OEP* (Y44.20.01)
huntað (hunting), *OEP* (Y44.27.01)
huselgang (reception of the Eucharist), *OES* (X15.01.09)
lenctenadl (dysentery), *OES* (X25.04.01)
Lengten (Lent), *OES* (X26.09.01), *OEP* (Y42.23.02), *OEH* (D54.30.01), *OEI* (S31.06.02)
Lengtenfæst (Lenten fast), *OES* (X26.11.03)
mæl (meal), *OEC* (B62.02.01)
oferdruncennes (drunkenness), *OEP* (Y44.29.02)
oferflownes (excess), *OEP* (Y43.14.02)
oferfyll (gluttony, drunkenness), *OEC* (B72.01.01), *OES* (X22.05.01), *OEP* (Y44.42.01)
samsoden mete (half-cooked meat), *OEP* (Y44.37.01)

Table 5: Foodstuffs

æt (food), *OEP* (Y43.14.02), *OEH* (D52.02.02)
attor (poison), *OEH* (D55.05.01)
biglifa (sustenance), *OEI* (S33.07.01)
corn (corn), *OEC* (B78.01.03), *OES* (X16.03.01)
dægswæsende (food or provisions for a day), *OES* (X26.09.01)
flæsc (meat), *OEC* (B63.03.01), *OES* (X09.04.01), *OEP* (Y44.05.02), *OEH* (D52.02.07), *OEI* (S33.05.02)
fodder (sustenance, fodder), *OEH* (D55.15.01)
gealla (bile), *OEC* (B64.03.05), *OES* (X25.04.01)
hlaf (bread, incl. Eucharist), *OEC* (B63.01.01), *OEP* (Y42.01.01), *OEH* (D54.05.01), *OEI* (S33.02.01)
hunig (honey), *OES* (X26.01.01), *OEP* (Y44.31.01)
husel (Eucharistic bread, Eucharist), *OEC* (B77.04.06), *OES* (X09.05.01), *OEP* (Y41.10.00), *OEH* (D56.06.01)
hwit (white foods such as cheese and eggs allowed when meat was forbidden), *OEI* (S31.06.02)
mete (food, meat), *OEC* (B76.06.03), *OES* (X11.06.01), *OEP* (Y43.16.02), *OEH* (D54.25.01), *OEI* (S33.05.03)
morten (myrten) (carrion), *OES* (X04.02.02)
peoper (pepper), *OEC* (B64.03.05), *OES* (X25.04.01), *OEH* (D55.16.01)
sealt (salt), *OES* (X23.01.01)

Table 6: The body

blod (blood), *OEC* (B64.03.01), *OES* (X05.01.01), *OEP* (Y44.22.01)
hreofel (scab), *OES* (X23.04.01)
meox (dung), *OEC* (B76.06.08)
micga (urine), *OES* (X23.04.01)
sæd (seed [semen]), *OEC* (B66.05.02), *OES* (X02.04.01)
scearn (feces, dung), *OES* (X23.04.01)
spatl (saliva), *OES* (X23.08.01), *OEP* (Y44.38.01)

Table 7: Drink

drinc (*drenc, drænc*) (drink), *OEP* (Y42.02.01), *OEH* (D54.10.01), *OEI* (S33.05.02),
druncen (drunkenness), *OEC* (B76.03.04), *OEP* (Y41.08.02), *OEH* (D54.39.01)
ealu (ale), *OEC* (B63.03.01)
liþ (mead), *OEC* (B77.04.02)
meolc (milk), *OEP* (Y43.16.02)
wæta (moisture,drink), *OES* (X23.06.01), *OEP* (Y44.32.01), *OEH* (D52.02.010)

Table 8: Food objects

calic (chalice), *OES* (X22.11.01), *OEP* (Y44.50.01)
fæt (vessel), *OEP* (Y44.32.01)
fiscpol (fishpond), *OEP* (Y44.26.01)
fyr (fire), *OES* (X22.06.01), *OEP* (Y44.44.01), *OEH* (D55.15.01)
nett (net), *OEC* (B64.03.02), *OES* (X25.03.01), *OEP* (Y44.25.01)
ofen (oven), *OEC* (B78.01.02), *OES* (X16.02.01)

Table 9: Food verbs

(ge)drincan (to drink), *OEC* (B76.06.01), *OES* (X05.01.01), *OEP* (Y42.22.01), *OEH*
(D55.07.01)
etan (to eat), *OEC* (B64.01.01), *OES* (X04.02.01), *OEP* (Y42.22.01)
fordrencan (to make intoxicated), *OEI* (S33.05.02)
fretan (to eat, used of animals), *OES* (X22.06.01), *OEP* (Y41.08.01), *OEI* (S33.11.01)
oferdrincan (to drink to excess), *OEP* (Y44.28.01)
onbitan (to taste, to eat), *OEH* (D55.10.01)
onbyrgan (to taste), *OEC* (B75.06.01), *OEP* (Y44.56.01)
(ge)reordian (to feast), *OEI* (S33.10.02)
þicgan (to eat, to consume), *OEC* (B76.06.03), *OES* (X11.06.01), *OEP* (Y44.32.01)

Table 10: Summary of distribution of food words in texts

Category	No. of words	OES	OEC	OEP	OEH	OEI	% of total
Animals	28	15	12	14	0	0	35%
Processes	18	8	4	8	5	2	22%
Foodstuffs	16	10	7	6	8	5	20%
Body	7	6	3	2	0	0	9%
Drink	6	1	3	4	3	1	7%
Objects	6	4	2	5	1	0	7%
Totals:	81	44	31	39	17	8	
% of total		54%	38%	48%	21%	10%	

9

Laws, Food, and Settlement Change

Early law codes, like early handbooks of penance, offer detailed accounts of obligations involving food and food purity. They are rich in kinds of information missing from later codes. Certain aspects of the treatment of food in later law codes can be illuminated by texts about status, works that are sometimes (misleadingly) called legal tracts. In this chapter I describe food culture in the laws and analyze the most important of the tracts that help to bridge gaps between ecclesiastical and secular views of food culture. I then describe a form of fasting in the *OE Handbook* that introduces some remarkable applications of foodways into the performance of penance.

Law codes and foodways

All the Anglo-Saxon law codes engage food culture, often through the agency of the reeve. He was, by definition, the culture's chief food officer and was sometimes answerable both to the lord and to the bishop, although the lord and the bishop might each have had a reeve of his own. In the laws, the reeve's office is first mentioned in the late seventh century. The reeve mediated between the lord or the bishop and those who answered to him. His position was a corruptible one, which is no doubt why the *OE Penitential*, passing on a regulation derived from its early ninth-century source, did not permit a priest or deacon to serve as reeve.[1] Numerous activities required his oversight. Most of the codes issued before the eleventh century refer to food culture by addressing hospitality (feeding visitors), fosterage (providing food for dependent people), food rents (paid to a lord or an abbey), and pannage (the right to pasture pigs in a forest, or income from the right). Four seventh-century codes trace the emerging shape of English law codes, simultaneously revealing what Patrick Wormald describes as "the Church's tightening grip on Anglo-Saxon society."[2]

---

[1] "It is not permitted to any masspriest or deacon that they be a reeve or steward" (*Nis nanum mæssepreoste alyfed ne diacone þæt hy gerefan beon ne wicneras*). Allen J. Frantzen, *ASP, OEP*, Y43.08.01. See also Chapter 3, pp. 72–73.
[2] Patrick Wormald, *MEL*, p. 96.

The earliest of these are the laws of Æthelberht (d. 616), which list *domas* or judgments that formed precedent; the exception is a set of clauses concerning the Church, which needed protection for new rights and privileges.[3] The Church's views on food and food purity are not mentioned; Æthelberht's laws concern food culture rather than food. Anyone who committed an offense while the king was feasting *æt mannes ham* (at someone's home) paid double compensation; the word for "feasting" is drinking (*drincæþ*).[4] Intercourse with a grinding slave (*grindende þeowa*) is punished with a fine of twenty-five shillings, or twelve shillings if she is "of the third class" (*þridde*). These two clauses have been used to document the presence and legal status of slaves and to link the work of grinding grain to female slaves – a link, as we saw in discussing querns, that is not necessarily reliable.[5]

Æthelberht's successors include Hlothhere and Eadric (c. 685), an uncle and nephew who seem to have ruled together and whose code describes judgments issued to extend what the code calls *æ*, the law of their predecessors. This code, the first to mention the reeve, enlarges the king's grasp, using syntax more nuanced than Æthelberht's. Hlothhere and Eadric punished violence at feasts anywhere, not only where the king might be. If one seized another's drinking cup without cause, a fine had to be paid to the householder, to the one whose cup was seized, and to the king. Drawing a weapon at a feast (*þær mæn drincen*) meant that fines were paid even if no harm had been done; much greater fines were required if blood had been shed. A visiting trader could be brought to justice if one had "fed him from his own food" (*hine þonne his mete fede*) for three days and the guest harmed someone in the host's care.[6] Like Æthelberht's, these clauses concern hospitality and the legal bonds it creates.

Wihtred's laws, issued in 695 and also Kentish, show the influence of Theodore's *Penitential*. Priests were punished if they were too drunk to perform their duties; work on Sunday was forbidden; hospitality had to be shown to tonsured men.[7] The last two clauses of the code address the fasting diet. One clause punishes the owner who gave his household (including slaves) meat during a fasting period, thus implicitly identifying the owner as a food officer who determined the household's diet. The other fines a slave who of his or her own free will consumed meat during a fasting period.[8] We do not associate slaves with eating meat, which even the

---

[3] References to the Anglo-Saxon laws are to F. Liebermann, ed., *GDA*, and are given by name and chapter. Translations are based on F. L. Attenborough, ed., *LEEK*, and A. J. Robertson, ed., *LKE*. For Æthelberht 1, see Liebermann, *GDA*, p. 3, and Attenborough, *LEEK*, pp. 4–5.

[4] For Æthelberht 3, see Liebermann, *GDA*, p. 3, and Attenborough, *LEEK*, pp. 4–5.

[5] See my comments on quern operators in Chapter 4, p. 94.

[6] For Hlothhere and Eadric 11–15, see Liebermann, *GDA*, pp. 10–11, and Attenborough, *LEEK*, pp. 20–21.

[7] For Wihtred, 6 (drunk priest), 11 (freeman), see Liebermann, *GDA*, pp. 12–13, and Attenborough, LEEK, pp. 26–27. See also Lisi Oliver, *The Beginnings of English Law*, for comments on *The Laws of Wihtred* and their relationship to ecclesiastical discipline (with parallels in the *Penitential* of Theodore), pp. 170–74.

[8] For Wihtred 14 and 15, see Liebermann, *GDA*, p. 13, and Attenborough, *LEEK*, pp. 26–27. On

free are thought to have consumed infrequently. But modern understandings of slavery do not correspond to the realities of status in the Anglo-Saxon period, when being a slave might have been an acquired identity (one could sell one's children, or oneself, into slavery, for example). Slaves, like servants, could own property and had to pay fines or, if unable to pay, atone by being whipped, as they did when they violated Wihtred's rule about eating meat during the fasting period.[9] Wihtred's code is distinctive in vocabulary and "massively ecclesiastical," Wormald writes; it might have been "a synodical decree in Latin" that was later translated. There are apparent borrowings from the contemporary code of Ine, king of Wessex. Wormald sees the distinctive vocabulary, and the Church's influence, as signs that legal culture was becoming increasingly textual.[10]

Ine's code (688–726) survives only as appended to the laws of Alfred. Ine's laws concern Wessex in the early eighth century, nearly two centuries before Alfred's reign (872–99). Ine offers the most detailed account of food culture in all the Anglo-Saxon codes. Like Wihtred's code, Ine's begins with a preface acknowledging the role of two bishops in the compilation of the clauses. It is a disorderly code if read by topic, but Wormald argues that its clauses were added as the judgments were rendered, and the core of older pronouncements steadily expanded as the king's power grew.[11] In Wormald's words, "law-making in writing had gone 'live.'"[12] There is a gap between Ine's predominantly secular concerns and the strong ecclesiastical presence in the Kentish laws, Wihtred's especially. Ine's code contains fewer interactions with ecclesiastical regulations than we might expect. For example, meat is mentioned in reference to stray animals and theft, not in the context of fasting, as it is in Wihtred's laws.[13] The king's interests extend deep into daily matters involving livestock and crops. Ine's laws refer not only to such matters as fosterage and the value of livestock, but also to the staples of food rent, including barley, bread, cheese, and honey. Outbreaks of violence in the king's house could be punished with death, a clause followed by several regulating the outbreak of fighting elsewhere.[14] Ine's code requires land to be kept under cultivation and protects the homestead, which had to be fenced.[15] Requirements for pasturing pigs and the value of sheep are also specified. The food rent of ten hides is spelled out: bread, ale, cows, geese, hens, cheeses, and butter, as well as salmon – a luxury item – and eels.[16] The Church's status is clear,

the distinction between violating a fast at the lord's orders or because of one's own free will, see Oliver, *The Beginnings of English Law*, pp. 170–74.

[9] See David A. E. Pelteret, *Slavery in Early Mediaeval England*, pp. 92, 138, 144, and 244 on slaves and their status in Wihtred's code.

[10] Wormald, *MEL*, p. 102, n. 355.

[11] Wormald, *MEL*, p. 105.

[12] Wormald, *MEL*, p. 105.

[13] For Ine 17 and 42.1, see Liebermann, *GDA*, pp. 96 and 106–8; Attenborough, *LEEK*, pp. 40–41 and 50–51.

[14] For Ine 6, see Liebermann, *GDA*, pp. 90–91, and Attenborough, *LEEK*, pp. 38–39.

[15] For Ine 64–66, see Liebermann, *GDA*, p. 118, and Attenborough, *LEEK*, pp. 56–59.

[16] For Ine 70.1, see Liebermann, *GDA*, pp. 118–19, and Attenborough, *LEEK*, pp. 58–59.

and not only in the protection of its property. Ine reduced a freeman who worked on Sunday to the status of a slave.[17] For breaking into fortifications or enclosures the code requires restitution to the bishop as well as to the king's officers.[18] Ine's code, in Wormald's view, inserts the king into as many transactions as possible, making "fiscal gains from disturbers of the stability" that the laws sought to maintain. This code reveals close integration of social order and food culture and demonstrates more fully than any earlier laws the role of food in establishing one's social – that is, here, legal – identity.

Alfred's code, issued in the 890s, makes many references to Christian observance and mandates observation of times for fasting and feasting.[19] His code is the first to name the reeve in connection with obligations involving food. Food figures into the punishment of one who made a lawful pledge and failed to keep it. This man was required to surrender his arms and possessions (*his wæpn 7 his æhta*) to friends and spend forty days imprisoned on one of the king's manors (*cyninges tune*), performing the penance the bishop assigned him. His family was to feed him; lacking relatives, he was to be fed by the king's reeve (*feda cyninges gerefa hine*).[20] The responsibility for feeding those seeking sanctuary is also specified. One who sought asylum could not be fed and could claim protection for seven days provided "he is able to live despite hunger" (*gif he for hungre libban mæge*).[21] Alfred's code singled out offenses committed during Lent, including theft, breaking into a fortification, enclosure, or a dwelling, and other disregard for Church laws. This code provides special punishment for theft during Rogation Days, an innovation.[22] Food culture is still regulated in detailed ways. For example, theft of bees, horses, cows, and calves is punished, evidence of Alfred's concern with food supply as wealth.[23] Alfred edged his innovations with caution. He claims to have annulled some laws and revised or approved others and to have introduced few of his own because, he explains, "I did not know which of them would be pleasing to those who would (come) after us" (*forðam me was uncuð, hwæt þæs ðam lician wolde, ðe æfter us wæren*).[24] Among the provisions strongly affirmed by his successors are the protection of times for feasting and

---

[17] For Ine 3–3.2, see Liebermann, *GDA*, p. 90, and Attenborough, *LEEK*, pp. 36–37.

[18] For Ine 45, see Liebermann, *GDA*, p. 108, and Attenborough, *LEEK*, pp. 50–51.

[19] For Alfred's preface, see Liebermann, *GDA*, pp. 27–47. On the question of Alfred's authorship of the introduction, see Malcolm Godden, "Did King Alfred Write Anything?" pp. 4–10 and 17–18.

[20] For Alfred 1.1–4 see Liebermann, *GDA*, pp. 46–47, and Attenborough, *LEEK*, pp. 62–63.

[21] For Alfred 1.2, 1.3 and 5.2, see Liebermann, *GDA*, pp. 48–52, and Attenborough, *LEEK*, pp. 62–63 and 66–67.

[22] For theft in Lent and on Rogation days, see Alfred 5.5, in Liebermann, *GDA*, p. 52, and Attenborough, *LEEK*, pp. 66–67.

[23] For Alfred 9.2 (theft of horses and bees) and 16 (cows or calves), see Liebermann, *GDA*, pp. 54 and 58; and Attenborough, *LEEK*, pp. 68–71 and 72–73.

[24] For this quotation from Alfred 49.9, see Liebermann, *GDA*, p. 46, and Attenborough, *LEEK*, pp. 62–63.

fasting and the expansion of regulations related to Lent, matters which, in later law codes, become major factors in the calendar year.

Subsequent to Alfred's laws are three tenth-century codes, including those of his son, Edward the Elder (d. 924); Edward's son and Alfred's grandson, Æthelstan (d. 939); and Edgar (d. 963). The codes of Æthelstan are notable for their broad demonstration of ecclesiastical influence. His laws make scattered references to Lenten fasts and require a fast before an ordeal. Clauses refer to specific foodstuffs, including bread, as part of Church taxation. The code resembles Ine's in its attention to the details of food culture, including pannage, and includes several terms not seen in previous codes. For example, the *gesufel* or "soul loaf" was assessed to members of a guild upon the death of one of the guild's members. Food rent is included in the code, which also specifies the Rogation period as the time for maintenance of fortifications.[25] By the time of Æthelstan's reign, Rogation Days, Lent, and other ecclesiastical periods had become standard matters of legal discourse.

Æthelstan issued an "ordinance relating to charities," one of the most important legal tracts (as opposed to a law code) issued in the tenth century.[26] This work was composed at the behest of (or perhaps by) Wulfhelm, bishop of Wells and later archbishop of Canterbury, who, Wormald hypothesized, might have written and preserved Æthelstan's laws.[27] The ordinance describes what a "destitute Englishman" (*an earm Engliscmon*) was to receive from the king's reeve. Every month the reeve was to take from the king's rents (*feorm*) an *amber* of meal (perhaps a unit of measure indicating the amount required for sustenance; *DOE, amber*), a shank of bacon or a ram worth four pence, and clothing. If the reeve failed to perform this duty he was fined and the fine was divided, with the bishop's supervision, among the poor on the negligent reeve's estate, the fine becoming sustenance for those whose welfare the reeve had failed to protect.[28] The reference to the "destitute Englishman" offers unique insight into the role of food in shaping social identity as well as situational identity for both the poor and for the reeve who oversaw their welfare. Two models of identity are contained in the phrase. One, *Engliscmon*, is racial or (to speak anachronistically) national: the identify of the person known to be English. The other, *earm*, might be an example of William O. Frazer's social identity, in this case one who is "destitute, poverty-stricken, poor, indigent."[29] But it might also be situational identity, since that person might not have always been impoverished (although that might have been the case). A legal provision for feeding such a person might have an occasion behind it,

[25] For II Æthelstan 13 (repair of fortresses), see Liebermann, *GDA*, p. 156, and Attenborough, *LEEK*, pp. 134–35.
[26] For the "Ordinance Relating to Charities," see Liebermann, *GDA*, pp. 148–49, and Attenborough, *LEEK*, pp. 126–27.
[27] Wormald, *MEL*, p. 300.
[28] "Ordinance Relating to Charities," c. 1 (food rents) and c. 2 (penalties), see Liebermann, *GDA*, pp. 148–49, and Attenborough, *LEEK*, pp. 126–27.
[29] William O. Frazer, "Introduction," pp. 3–4.

i.e., someone who fell into poverty and so came to the reeve's notice. The law speaks to the estate's administration, that being the territory under the reeve's jurisdiction, but should the reeve fail in his duty, it was the bishop who oversaw the distribution of the fine. Æthelstan authorized the bishop to fine the reeve if he was insubordinate.[30] The reeve's role as a food officer is also evident in the second of Edgar's codes, which required observance of Sunday as a festival time and commanded that all appointed fasts be rigorously observed.[31] Edgar's laws also required the tithing of young animals at Pentecost, of crops at the equinox, and of church dues by Martinmas. If the tithe was not rendered, the king's reeve, the bishop's reeve, and the priest, working together, were authorized to go to the offender and confiscate his holdings, taking the tithe, setting aside one tenth for the offender (a biting irony), and dividing the remaining part equally between the bishop and the lord of the manor.[32]

The cooperation of law and ecclesiastical discipline became Wulfstan's aim for the laws he wrote for Æthelred (d. 1016) and Cnut (d. 1035), but Æthelstan's code shows how far this connection had developed by the mid-tenth century. Wulfstan found precedents in Æthelstan's codes. Examples include Æthelstan's clauses charging the king's reeves to ensure that *ciricsceattas* and *sawlsceattas*, church dues and burial fees, were collected at the right places.[33] One of several methods of increasing church revenue, these fees found favor with Wulfstan in 1016, when he revised laws first issued in 1008.[34] Among the later codes, the so-called "treaty of Edward and Guthrum," issued during the time of Wulfstan rather than in the reign of Edward (d. 924), specifies a penalty for a priest who misdirected the faithful concerning periods *æt freolse oððe æt fæstene*, the "time of a feast or a fast." This language is often found in later codes. Fines are assessed in both English and Danish currencies. A fine of thirty shillings was assessed to the priest who misinformed lay people about feast and fast days, showing the king's concern with uniform observance of the Church's periods.[35] Ordeals and legal proceedings involving oaths could not be held on fast or feast days.[36] Payment of both plow-alms and "Peter's Pence" was required. A freeman who worked during a festival was reduced to the status of a slave, a provision we can compare to Ine's legislation concerning the freeman who worked on Sunday.[37] This was one way in which the

---

[30] For II Æthelstan 25.1, see Liebermann, *GDA*, p. 165, Attenborough, *LEEK*, pp. 141–42.

[31] For II Edgar 5 and 5.1, see Liebermann, *GDA*, pp. 198–201, and Robertson, *LKE*, pp. 22–23.

[32] For II Edgar 3, see Liebermann, *GDA*, pp. 196–99, and Robertson, *LKE*, pp. 20–23.

[33] For 1 Æthelstan 4, see Liebermann, *GDA*, pp. 146–48, and Attenborough, *LEEK*, pp. 124–25.

[34] Wormald, *MEL*, pp. 314–15.

[35] The fine in a Danish district was three "half-marks" (*gylde XXX scillinga mid Englum & mid Denum ðreo healfmare*). For Edward and Guthrum 3.1, see Liebermann, *GDA*, p. 130, and Attenborough, *LEEK*, pp. 102–5.

[36] *Ordel & aðas syndan tocwedene freolsdagum & rihtfæstendagum.* For Edward and Guthrum 9–9.1, see Liebermann, *GDA*, p. 132, and Attenborough, *LEEK*, pp. 106–7.

[37] For Edward and Guthrum 6 (concerning Peter's Pence and plow-alms) and 7 (concerning Sunday), see Liebermann, *GDA*, pp. 131–32, and Attenborough, *LEEK*, pp. 104–7. For Ine 3–3.2 (concerning Sunday), see Liebermann, *GDA*, p. 90, and Attenborough, *LEEK*, pp. 36–37.

"Englishman" of Æthelstan's charity ordinance might have come to be poor (*an earm Engliscmon*).

The later codes say less about specific aspects of food culture – that is, rams and bacon – and more about times of feasting and fasting. This shift corresponds with what the *OE Handbook* seeks to achieve, as we will see below. Ann Hagen observes that Anglo-Saxon life involved "an annual pattern of fasting and feasting" seen as "a Christian duty." She suggests that fasting enabled feasting by saving food, especially during early spring, when food supplies might be low.[38] Hagen implies that the connection between fasting and feasting was long-standing, but there are few references to fasting in the laws until the eleventh century. As we saw, Wihtred's laws punished one who gave members of his or her household meat during a fasting period, a provision paralleled in Theodore's *Penitential*.[39] These are unusual clauses. Among tenth-century codes, II Edgar commands fasting and Æthelstan cites the need to fast before an ordeal. Both parties in a dispute to be settled by an ordeal had to fast; the accused had to fast on bread, water, salt, and herbs.[40]

References to fasting are plentiful after 1000, some eighteen clauses in codes by Æthelred and eleven in codes by Cnut (many of these clauses are repeated from code to code). The lexical evidence often takes the form of the pairing of *freols* and *fæst* (e.g., *mid fæstene & syþþan mid freolse*).[41] This expression is not usually associated with a fine but rather occurs in an exhortation to observe the proper season. There is no penalty attached to failure to observe fast or feast times, although presumably prohibitions against such procedures as ordeals at such times was enforceable. For example, VI Æthelred forbade ordeals during festivals, on Ember days, and at other holy times.[42] No one could hunt, go to market, or hold meetings on Sunday. Christians were bound to observe some fasts "fittingly" or conscientiously (*freolsa 7 fæstena healde man rihtlice*), including all those honoring Mary.[43] This code describes the observance of feasts and fasts as a revival: they are to be observed now "as they were observed by those who observed them best" (*swa swa þa heoldan þa þe betst heoldan*).[44] To underscore the point, the following clause refers to fasts prescribed for the English by

---

[38] See Ann Hagen, *A Handbook of Anglo-Saxon Food and Drink*, p. 76.

[39] Oliver, *The Beginnings of English Law*, *Laws of Wihtred*, cc. 11–11.1, pp. 158–59. On the relationship of these and other regulations to ecclesiastical discipline (with parallels in the Latin *Penitential* of Theodore), see pp. 170–74.

[40] For II Æthelstan 23.2, see Liebermann, *GDA*, p. 162, and Attenborough, *LEEK*, pp. 140–41, also translated by Dorothy Whitelock, ed., *EHD*, p. 421; for II Edgar 5.1 see Liebermann, *GDA*, p. 198, and Robertson, *LKE*, pp. 22–23.

[41] For V Æthelred 12.3, 14, 14.1, 15, 17, 18, see Liebermann, *GDA*, pp. 241–47, and Robertson, *LKE*, pp. 82–85; for VI Æthelred 22, 22.2, 22.3, 23, 24, 28.2, 43, see Liebermann, *GDA*, pp. 252–58, and Robertson, *LKE*, pp. 96–105. For I Cnut, II Cnut, see Liebermann, *GDA*, pp. 278–371, and Robertson, *LKE*, pp. 154–219.

[42] For VI Æthelred 25, see Liebermann, *GDA*, pp. 252–54, and Robertson, *LKE*, pp. 98–99.

[43] For VI Æthelred 22 and 22.2, see Liebermann, *GDA*, p. 252, and Robertson, *LKE*, pp. 96–97.

[44] For VI Æthelred 22.3, see Liebermann, *GDA*, p. 252, and Robertson, *LKE*, pp. 96–97 (where the provision is marked 22.4, part of 22.3 in Liebermann's edition).

Gregory the Great himself.[45] II Edgar contains a similar backward glance to "the highest standards of the past."[46] This note often sounds in estates literature, which laments the decline in social standards and implicitly reproaches those responsible for it.

Law, estates literature, and food offices

As the laws accommodated more Christian practices, they began to sound more ecclesiastical. By Wulfstan's time legal discourse was plainly pious. The code known as II Cnut quotes the Lord's Prayer and exhorts all "to submit in their inmost hearts to his Lord" (*þæt he inweardre heortan gebuga to his Drihtne*) and to seek "to please our Lord" (*urum Drihtene cweman*).[47] Piety in legal writing emerged much earlier, as we have seen, in Æthelstan's "ordinance relating to charities." I regard this and various quasi-legal tracts that became more numerous in Wulfstan's time as examples of estates literature. They offer glimpses of food culture not to be found in the laws and show how both secular and ecclesiastical leaders were responding to social change.[48] The status and some of the foodways of those she calls the "new rich" of late Anglo-Saxon England have been studied by Robin Fleming. She comments on the "optimism and anxiety" of prosperous thegns and earls and regards these emotions as "perfectly reflected in those two quintessential late Anglo-Saxon texts: the treatise on estate management and the tract on status." Fleming asserts that these tracts are "about improving one's ability to consume and keeping others in their place." This characterization might be deft but it is only partially accurate.[49] Associating these texts with "improving one's ability to consume" suggests that they had something in common with the "lifestyle" section of today's metropolitan newspapers; suggesting that they were written to keep "others in their place" is no less misleading, since these tracts actually address social mobility at several levels. Estates literature reveals aspects of food culture and food-related identities that other genres do not, that much is clear, but we cannot characterize its effects so neatly as Fleming does.

The first work I consider is known as IV Æthelred. It is not a law code but a Latin translation of "a statement of current London customs" concerning tolls and taxes accompanied by a statement about tolls in relation to the town peace.[50] The text details cargo, including planks, cloth, and fish, along with pepper, vinegar, hens, eggs, and cheese, that passed through the port of London from Rouen, Flanders, Normandy and elsewhere.[51] Anonymous documents such as this one show that writing was

---

[45] For VI Æthelred 23, see Liebermann, *GDA*, p. 252, and Robertson, *LKE*, pp. 98–99.
[46] II Edgar 5.3. See Liebermann, *GDA*, p. 200, and Robertson, *LKE*, pp. 22–23.
[47] II Cnut 84, in Liebermann, *GDA*, pp. 368–71, and Robertson, *LKE*, pp. 216–19.
[48] On estates literature, see Chapter 3, pp. 67–68.
[49] Robin Fleming, "The New Wealth, the New Rich, and New Political Style in Anglo-Saxon England" pp. 3–4.
[50] Wormald, *MEL*, p. 371; see also pp. 322 and 328.
[51] IV Æthelred, in Liebermann, *GDA*, pp. 232–37, and Robertson, *LKE*, pp. 70–79.

used to record local customs that we might otherwise have assumed were preserved only in memory or by word of mouth. A large mechanism of social and economic regulation obviously stands behind the text, which concerns what people do, not who they are. The material elements of the food network, down to hens in their cages, come more clearly into view as bureaucratic discourse diminishes.

Most estates texts do not focus on the most particular levels of food culture. *The Colloquy* and *Concerning the Discriminating Reeve* (*Be gescead-wisan gerefan*) are usually cited as quasi-journalistic or documentary sources for Anglo-Saxon food culture. They are more plausibly seen as teaching tools for monastic schoolboys and are related to glosses, word lists compiled for teaching purposes (see Chapter 3). Both works should be regarded as literary fictions attesting to a social ideology in which power is wielded by ecclesiastical officers. These works inform us about food culture, although not in the ways others have assumed.

The Colloquy represents the food network through personal relations between consumers and producers. Some are positive: the hunter is paid with gifts for his services to the king. Others are negative: the master asks the merchant why he marks up his goods (i.e., does not sell them for what he paid for them) and mocks the fisher for being afraid of venturing on the ocean.[52] The master is deferential to the king's hunter, however, and to some of the other workers – not incidentally, for the social meaning of hunting, its capacity to establish aristocratic identity, far exceeded its value as a food source.[53] Part of the exercise is to decide "which trade among these seems to you to be superior."[54] A councillor decides that "the service of God" holds first place and that, among secular crafts, the honor belongs to agriculture "because the plowman feeds us all." The master positions learned men at the peak while disguising their dependence on workers' skills. "Each one should diligently practice his craft," he says, "for he who neglects his craft, by his craft he is forsaken." He adds that "it is great humiliation and shame if a man does not to wish to be that which he is and that which he is obliged to be."[55] There, clearly, is language designed to keep people in their place. These sententious passages are described by Garmonsway as "studied and bookish" in comparison to the "spontaneous" earlier sections.[56] "Spontaneous" isn't quite the word for this methodical, overbearing interrogation and play-acting, although Garmonsway is right to mark the difference between the clipped questioning of the workers and the moralized discussion of their duties, a hint that the text was compiled from different sources.

The learned figures, including the master, the monk, and the councillor, are situated in a network of labor related to food. But they do not recognize

[52] G. N. Garmonsway, ed., *Ælfric's Colloquy*, pp. 33–34, ll. 250–66.

[53] See N. J. Sykes, "The Impact of the Normans on Hunting," pp. 163–64.

[54] Garmonsway, *Ælfric's Colloquy*, p. 38, ll. 208–10.

[55] Garmonsway, *Ælfric's Colloquy*, pp. 41–42, ll. 233–43.

[56] Garmonsway, *Ælfric's Colloquy*, p. 8, n. 3.

food culture as a network – that is, as an exchange of skills and materials that requires recognition and respect. Rather, they interpret labor and
its material bases as a pyramid of power in which they stand above the
workers. Their assertion of ecclesiastical dominance, like the concept of
competition among crafts, seems to authenticate *The Colloquy* by reinforcing modern assumptions about ecclesiastical control. But that control is a
rhetorical gesture intended to impress ecclesiastical authority on students.
The text is not a source for the Anglo-Saxon diet, although a useful description of the schoolboy's daily fare is provided when the master asks a boy
what he did that day. The boy describes a generous and varied diet and is
called greedy (*waxgeorn*) because he eats so well.[57] The only personal relations that *The Colloquy* models with authority are those between teacher
and student.

Concerning the Discriminating Reeve has more value as a text about the
Anglo-Saxon material world, thanks to much-studied lists of tools (see
Chapter 3 and Chapter 6). But this tract is as naive as *The Colloquy* in its
representation of food culture. Countering those who read the text at its
face value, P. D. A. Harvey interprets *Concerning the Discriminating Reeve*
"as a literary work, not as a practical manual."[58] Others have commented
on the text's tell-tale use of alliteration. John Hines has bolstered Mark
Gardiner's view that the text is indebted to gloss-like lists. It is reasonable,
for example, that the churn is associated with a cheese-vat in the list, but
one can see here and elsewhere that parts of the list alliterate.[59] The first
two parts of *Concerning the Discriminating Reeve* idealize the relationship
between the reeve and his lord, and the reeve and his hired workers as one
of unquestioning obedience. The reeve governs within *folcrihte*, customary
law, and "if those whom he should govern govern him," he should lose his
job (*gyf hine magan wyldan ða ðe he scolde wealdan*). One is reminded of the
injunction in *The Colloquy* that "he who neglects his craft . . . is forsaken" by
his craft.[60] Every section of *Concerning the Discriminating Reeve* is invested
in imperatives: what must be done, and when, and with what. The text
expresses attitudes about work and social order similar to those in *The
Colloquy*, compelling the reeve to his duties: "he must," *he sceal*. Frequent
self-references underscore the author's didacticism. "Because what I say
is true" (*Forðam to soðe ic secge*), he says at one point, and at another, "But
I instruct that he do as I have said before" (*Ac ic lære, þæt he do, swa ic ær
cwæð*).[61] He comments that he "may not recount all that a good reeve must
attend to" (*Ic eal geteallan ne mæig, þæt god scirman bycgan sceal*), which
includes "many things that I cannot now name" (*fela ðinga, ðe ic nu genæmnian ne can*), although he has "related that about which I know; let the one

---

[57] Garmonsway, *Ælfric's Colloquy*, p. 46, l. 290.
[58] P. D. A. Harvey, "*Rectitudines Singularum Personarum* and *Gerefa*," p. 12.
[59] John Hines, "*Gerefa* §§15 and 17: A Grammatical Analysis of the Lists of Nouns."
[60] Garmonsway, *Ælfric's Colloquy*, p. 41, ll. 240–41.
[61] *Gerefa* 3.1 and 4 (my translation). For the text, see Liebermann, *GDA*, p. 453; also translated by
Michael Swanton, *Anglo-Saxon Prose*, pp. 30–33.

who knows better explain it more fully" (*Ic gecende be ðam ðe ic cuðe; se ðe bet cunne, gecyðe his mare*).[62] *Concerning the Discriminating Reeve* imparts rudimentary information but does so with frequent assertions of authority. No doubt such texts would have been useful in the schoolroom, but hardly elsewhere. Reeves acquired their working knowledge of farms and the operations of agriculture and animal husbandry first-hand, from each other, from their predecessors, and from laws about the reeve's duties.

The fictionality of food work and food offices represented in *Concerning the Discriminating Reeve* and *The Colloquy* emerges when they are compared to *Rectitudines Personarum Singularum*. Wormald emphasizes the discursive connection between the text *Be gesceadwisan gerefan* and *Rectitudines*, which appears just before the text on the reeve in Cambridge, Corpus Christi College, MS 383, an important late Old English law book. Wormald considers *Concerning the Discriminating Reeve* a "supplement" to *Rectitudines*.[63] Gardiner downplays a possible association with Wulfstan; Wormald sets that connection aside with definitive clarity.[64] Once associated with south-central Mercia, *Rectitudines* has been linked by P. D. A. Harvey to Bath Abbey and the manor of Tidenham, which belonged to Bath Abbey. Harvey sees the text as "two quite different documents in one," both an eleventh-century treatise "on the ordering of society in a rural community" and "a tenth-century record of estate administration."[65] We have this text only because the core of the administrative document was adapted to didactic purposes by a later writer. The administrative content survived through the hybridity of the form; other records of this kind have vanished. It is significant that the Old English *lagu* (law) is used in two compounds in *Rectitudines*: *Ðegenlagu* (thegns' law) and *landlagu* (estate law).[66] Neither term appears in *Concerning the Discriminating Reeve* (DOEWC). Merging the didactic function of Christian discourse with practical matters of social organization, *Rectitudines* is rich in detail about fields, grain, and animal husbandry, revealing the interconnected nature of agricultural work and the offices assigned to workers of various levels of responsibility.

Rectitudines is organized by categories of rank confirmed in other sources. Its provisions lack the universalized, moralized point of view found in *Concerning the Discriminating Reeve* and some sections of *The Colloquy*. One discursive mode shared by *Rectitudines* and *Concerning the Discriminating Reeve* is use of the first-person pronoun. Both texts use

---

[62] For *Gerefa* 12, 17, 19, see Liebermann, *GDA*, pp. 454–55, and Swanton, *Anglo-Saxon Prose*, pp. 30–31.

[63] Wormald, *MEL*, pp. 232 and 387. For *Rectitudines*, see *GDA*, pp. 444–53 and for *Gerefa*, pp. 453–55; both are translated by Swanton, *Anglo-Saxon Prose*, as "estate memoranda," pp. 26–33. See N. R. Ker, *Catalogue of Manuscripts Containing Anglo-Saxon*, no. 65, pp. 110–13, for the contents of the manuscript.

[64] Patrick Wormald, *Legal Culture in the Early Medieval West*, pp. 248–49.

[65] Harvey, "*Rectitudines Singularum Personarum* and *Gerefa*," pp. 19 and 22. See also Wormald, *MEL*, p. 233.

[66] The citation from *Rectitudines* is from Liebermann, *GDA*, pp. 453–55; see c. 4.4 and Harvey, "*Rectitudines Singularum Personarum* and *Gerefa*," p. 13. Harvey notes that *lagu* is the only Scandinavian term in the text.

the phrase *ic ær cwæð* ("as I said before"), the only texts in the legal corpus to do so. *Rectitudines* uses the expression twice and uses *ic sæd* ("I said") and *ic ymberehte* ("I spoke about") once each; the text on the reeve uses *ic ær cwæð* once and *ic secge* ("I say") once.[67] *Rectitudines* makes concessions to history and tradition, gestures lacking in *Concerning the Discriminating Reeve* and *The Colloquy*, with their universalizing points of view, although the text about the reeve does say to "let the one who knows better explain it more fully" (*se ðe bet cunne, gecyðe his mare*).[68] The author of *Rectitudines* allows that experience of the world might cause the regulator to adjust the rules:

> Estate laws [*landlaga*] are various, as I said before. Nor do we apply these regulations, which we have previously spoken about, in all districts. But we tell what the custom is where it is known to us. If we learn better, we will readily delight in and maintain it, according to the custom of the people among whom we then live. Wherefore one must learn the laws in the district lovingly, if one does not wish to lose good opinion on the estate.

> Landlaga syn mistlice, swa ic ær beforan sæde. Ne sette we na ðas gerihtu ofer ealle ðeoda, ðe we ær beforan ymbe spræcon; ac we cyðað, hwæt ðeaw is ðær ðær us cuð is. Gyf we selre geleorniað, þæt we willað georne lufian & healdon, be ðære ðede ðeawe, ðe we ðænne onwuniað. Forðam laga sceal on leode luflice leornian, lof se ðe on lande sylf nele leosan.[69]

Rectitudines begins its assessment of food offices at the center, with the thegn, who is "entitled to his estate," for which he renders the "three necessities," as they are known elsewhere: military service, repair of fortresses, and repair of bridges. "Further land-duties" include supplying "almsgiving and church dues." The rights and duties of the cottager, the *kotsetla*, follow and include working for the lord each Monday and, in harvest time, three days each week. His holdings are limited to five acres because "his labor must always be available." The *geneat*, or man of service, was assigned many duties, including reaping, mowing, and carrying messages. Things are important: tools for his work and equipment for his house were to be supplied for his use. One step lower than the cottager, the *gebur* was heavily burdened, working two days each week for the lord and three days in harvest time and from Candlemas to Easter. His food rent includes barley, hens, and sheep. He was to give six loaves to the swineherd. He is assigned seven sown acres, two oxen, and one cow; and he is to have "tools for his work and utensils for his house," all of this passing to his lord when the *gebur* dies. Lesser workers' duties are also listed, including those of the beekeeper, two categories of swineherd, the oxherd, cowherd, and shepherd. The text differentiates "men's provisions" and "women's

---

[67] Results of a Boolean search of legal texts (Cameron number B14+) in the *DOEWC* (*ic, ær, cwæð*).

[68] For *Gerefa* 12, 17, 19, see Liebermann, *GDA*, pp. 454–55, and Swanton, *Anglo-Saxon Prose*, pp. 30–31.

[69] For *Rectitudines* 21.1–21.3, see Liebermann, *GDA*, p. 452, and Swanton, *Anglo-Saxon Prose*, pp. 28–30.

provisions" (although the only woman worker mentioned among the specialists is the cheesemaker).[70]

Rectitudines refers to social levels seen in other Anglo-Saxon sources. In place of didacticism the text describes working relations among those who labor within food networks. Both food-related objects and the social identities they create are contextualized by rights and duties. In *Rectitudines* everyone has a share in the grain or livestock for which he or she cares. By no means does work move down a pyramid as its products move up, contrary to Fleming's implication. Every producer is also a consumer. This reciprocity is true even on the authorial level, since the author calls attention to his role as mediator. All those who do their duty, we can assume, will, like the hay-keeper, be "fully entitled to a good reward" (*godes leanes ful wel wyrðe*).[71]

Rectitudines Personarum Singularum pairs well with *Geþyncðu* (meaning "rank" or "status"), which is found in Cambridge, Corpus Christi College, MS 201, an important eleventh-century collection of laws and ecclesiastical works associated with Wulfstan, including the *OE Handbook*.[72] *Geþyncðu* limits its focus to the thegn, his rights and responsibilities, and those of his followers, and is one of the "Wulfstanian 'private' texts" (that is, of special interest to the archbishop and his circle) aimed at restoring the importance of social ranks and ensuring that the clergy's place was recognized and legally protected.[73] *Geþyncðu* begins with an appeal to the standards of prior generations, a note often found in satire (i.e., standards have declined and need to be revived). The author recalls a time when "people and rights went by dignities, and councillors of the people were entitled to honour, each according to his rank whether noble or *ceorl*, retainer or lord."[74] Wormald suggests that the text is tinged with "nostalgia for good times gone" and that it seeks to "restore past proprieties."[75]

But the tract is also, and arguably more importantly, about social mobility. Its most famous clauses concern the ceorl who can become a thegn, traders who can acquire the rights of thegns, and scholars who gain rank by remaining celibate.[76] One version shows how secular and ecclesiastical interests had converged around settlement planning in the late Anglo-Saxon period. As preserved in the twelfth-century *Textus Roffensis*, *Geþyncðu* reveals that a church was considered an essential element of a thegnly residence – although not that of just any thegn. A ceorl who had

---

[70] Swanton, *Anglo-Saxon Prose*, p. 29, and Debby Banham, *Food and Drink in Anglo-Saxon England*, p. 54 (see also p. 56).
[71] For *Rectitudines* 20.1, see Liebermann, *GDA*, p. 452; translated in Swanton, *Anglo-Saxon Prose*, p. 30.
[72] See Wormald, *MEL*, pp. 391–94. On Cambridge, Corpus Christi College, MS 201, see Ker, *Catalogue of Manuscripts Containing Anglo-Saxon*, pp. 82–90.
[73] Wormald, *MEL*, p. 391.
[74] Liebermann, *GDA*, p. 356: *þa wæron þeodwitan wurðscipes wurðe, ælc be his mæðe*; translation from Whitelock, *EHD*, p. 468.
[75] Wormald, *MEL*, pp. 393–94.
[76] Whitelock, *EHD*, paragraphs 6 and 7, p. 469.

five hides of his own land, "[church and kitchen], bell [house] and *burh-geat*, seat and special office in the king's hall," was "entitled to the rank of a thegn" (the words in brackets are found only in the *Textus Roffensis*).[77] Ann Williams (who, like Wormald, attributes the text to Wulfstan) analyzes the meaning of these markers of status for the developing aristocracy. The church near the manor house (itself indicated by the gate in the walls surrounding the manor), was, Williams thinks, an "estate-church" that was built to serve "the needs of the lord and his family," a custom that operated through the twelfth century and in her view "gave rise to the parochial structure of the later middle ages."[78] In *Geþyncðu* we see, on one hand, a pyramid held in place by an authorial gaze fixed on the social order of the past – the reality Fleming sees. On the other, we find ways to improve one's status. Wormald writes that *Geþyncðu* was meant "for the drilling of a Christian society," a comment that might be seen as reinforcing a mechanistic view of the culture. If "drilling" was the aim, we should understand that *Geþyncðu* communicates more than one point of view. There is, as we would expect, a fixed social order, but there are ways to ascend within it.[79]

Manorial sites, central planning, and fasting

Geþyncðu shows that ideas about status and rank were changing at a time when rural elites were finding impressive ways to express their authority and wealth. Large estates required centralized field systems and the clustering of workers around manor houses and churches. I hope to show that the Church responded to these changes with ambitious forms of penance that exploited social networks in new ways. Fasting and other forms of penance had always taken into account the social status of the sinner but rarely considered him or her in connection to peers. One inspiration was suretyship, or *borg*, a guarantee of security reaching back to the earlier law codes. For example, III Æthelred 13 required anyone who fed a man who had broken the peace to "clear himself with three times twelve compurgators who shall be nominated by the reeve."[80] The *OE Handbook* envisions groups of this and much greater size acting as – or on behalf of – penitents. Organizational changes taking place in settlements and estates would have made it feasible to engage social groups in penance on behalf of one person within the group. Among the obvious motives for such a change is revenue, a long-standing concern of secular and ecclesiastical law.

The rural elites who occupied large estates form a recognized social class in historical and archaeological analysis but remain unfamiliar to literary historians, although their lives are attested in the *Anglo-Saxon Chronicle*,

---

[77] For the text, see Liebermann, *GDA*, pp. 456–59, translated in Whitelock, *EHD*, pp. 468–69. The text is quoted by Ann Williams, "A Bell-house and a *Burh-geat*," p. 225.

[78] Williams, "A Bell-house and a *Burh-geat*," p. 233; Wormald, *MEL*, p. 394.

[79] Wormald, *MEL*, p. 208. See further pp. 391–99 and 457–62.

[80] For III Æthelred 13, see Liebermann, *GDA*, pp. 230–32, and Robertson, *LKE*, pp. 68–69. The number is expressed as *þrinna XII*, a Scandinavian form (see *LKE*, p. 321, note to 13).

in charters, and elsewhere. We know about rural elites chiefly because of the manorial settlements associated with them. Williams singles out Goltho, rebuilt several times, where a large hall, surrounded by a banked enclosure and a ditch, shows "what a pre-Conquest aristocratic *burh* was like."[81] At Flixborough Chris Loveluck finds a tenth-century rural elite occupying a manorial center that eventually included a stone church, a structure that seems to certify power and authority.[82] "What we see in the remains of Flixborough-Conesby," Loveluck writes, "is the emergence of the secular elite lifestyle of the 'countryside,' as opposed to that of the town."[83] Additional signs of the development of manorial settlements come from the village of Raunds (Northamptonshire), which was a center of county administration in the Anglo-Saxon period. Two large timber buildings dominated the settlement until it was re-planned in the tenth century. In the early eleventh century four buildings associated with the church shared a continuous walled trench.[84] Rectangular plots were laid out, fronting a central street. "On such estates the king's thegns built their residences," Williams writes, "sometimes encouraging or compelling their depending peasants to settle around the manor-house, and re-organiz-ing the layout of their tenements in the surrounding fields." This process reinforced the dependency of the tenants on the lord's will.[85]

A similar pattern, including a stone church, large hall, and uniform plots of land, emerges at West Cotton, where Tom Saunders points to a "qualitative change in the character of many landscapes and settle-ments" in this period. Both at Raunds and West Cotton a "bounded spatial pattern" indicated a "new settlement morphology" extending to an open field system. Saunders notes that the stone church and hall at Raunds were placed on higher ground and ditched and banked, suggesting both isolation and military fortification, and also underscoring the cooperation between the Church and landowners.[86] Saunders notes comparable devel-opments at Goltho (Lincolnshire) and at Sulgrave (Northamptonshire).[87] He see "local lords" who had gained "rights of jurisdiction over private estates" as the principal organizing force behind settlement planning.[88] Williams proposes that settlements comparable to Goltho might include Hillesley (Gloucester), Barton upon Humber (North Lincolnshire), and

[81] Williams, "A Bell-house and a *Burh-geat*," p. 230.
[82] Christopher Loveluck, *Rural Settlement*, pp. 8–30 and 154–57. The excavators also outlined two further, later phases.
[83] Christopher Loveluck, "The Dynamics of Elite Lifestyles in the Rural World," pp. 156–57.
[84] See Stephen Parry, ed., *Raunds Area Survey*, p. 223, and Graham Cadman and Glenn Foard, "Raunds: Manorial and Village Origins," pp. 82–83.
[85] Williams, "A Bell-house and a *Burh-geat*," p. 233.
[86] Tom Saunders, "Class, Space and 'Feudal' Identities in Early Medieval England," p. 218. See also Gill Campbell, "The Preliminary Archaeobotanical Results."
[87] Saunders, "Class, Space," p. 223.
[88] Saunders, "Class, Space," p. 221. See David Hall, "The Late Saxon Countryside," who notes that at Raunds the strips of the field system "overlie ninth- to tenth-century occupation" (p. 108).

Earl's Barton (Northamptonshire).[89] Richard Hodges includes Portchester (Hampshire) as a site of an emerging manor-centered culture similar to those at Raunds and Sulgrave.[90] Concerning Flixborough, Loveluck notes "very close similarities to this country-based elite lifestyle" in other "manorial" settlements, including, in addition to those already named, Thwing (East Yorkshire); Wharram Percy (North Yorkshire); Faccombe Netherton (Hampshire), Trowbridge (Wiltshire), and Bishopstone (Sussex).[91] These are among the people Fleming describes as "rural elites," thegns "who dominated the hinterlands" and who were connected by trading to centers where manufacturing took place.[92]

Centralization of estates and consolidation are not entirely distinctive features of the later Anglo-Saxon period. Della Hooke notes that by the end of eighth century "large multiple estates were well-established features across England," consisting of "a system of federated holdings" with peasants maintaining royal vills.[93] Hooke shows that settlement nucleation moved forward "most efficiently within arable regions," with a manor at the center of dependent settlements, "often with a patch of mainly arable land farmed under an open field system."[94] Dominic Powlesland identifies examples of planned settlements at West Heslerton (North Yorkshire), Sutton Courtenay (Berkshire), and West Stow (West Suffolk). These sites show "remarkable uniformity" in structural styles that, Powlesland thinks, points to "a similar and equally sophisticated overall structure within the settlements of which these structures form a part." He concludes that "early Anglo-Saxon settlements were well organized, well maintained and formed part of a sophisticated network of trade and exchange."[95] Sir Frank Stenton describes "innumerable villages where the lord's hall and outbuildings adjoin a church . . . and are surrounded by fields representing the hides which had yielded Danegeld to the kings before the Conquest."[96] Peter Fowler has also commented on widespread evidence of nucleation.[97] But in the later period, it is agreed, comparable changes were spurred by small numbers of aristocrats whose social and economic conditions were improving, Fleming's "new rich." These people are not always visible in the textual record, but with the increased flow of writing about and for them in the late Old English period, seen in Ælfric's homilies for his lay

[89] Williams, "A Bell-house and a *Burh-geat*," p. 231.
[90] Richard Hodges, *The Anglo-Saxon Achievement*, p. 170.
[91] Loveluck, *Rural Settlement*, pp. 48–50. Among others, see Guy Beresford *et al.*, *Goltho*; Barry Cunliffe, *Excavations at Portchester Castle*; Alan H. Graham and Susan M. Davies, *Excavations in the Town Centre of Trowbridge, Wiltshire*; P. A. Stamper and R. A. Croft, eds., *Wharram: A Study*; and J. R. Fairbrother, *Faccombe Netherton*.
[92] Robin Fleming, "Rural Elites and Urban Communities in Late-Saxon England," p. 19.
[93] Della Hooke, "The Anglo-Saxons," p. 73.
[94] Hooke, "The Anglo-Saxons," p. 80.
[95] Dominic Powlesland, "Early Anglo-Saxon Settlements, Structures, Form and Layout," pp. 110 and 115.
[96] Sir Frank Stenton, *Anglo-Saxon England*, p. 487.
[97] Peter Fowler, *Farming in the First Millennium AD*, pp. 32–33.

patrons and in Wulfstan's homilies and legal texts, their presence, as M. R. Godden has shown, becomes more marked.[98]

Wormald writes that these people were "drilled" in new modes of behavior, as if this meant that they had to be catechized.[99] It is not likely that they were more resistant to Christian teaching than were previous generations, although the rhetoric of reformers like Wulfstan (and King Alfred, for that matter) strives to create that impression. Reformers by nature fault the present and idealize the past. Rather than think of Wulfstan's faithful being "drilled" in Christian teaching, we can think of them being "drilled" in new expectations concerning Christian behavior. The new tracts on rank and status associated with Wulfstan help to close the gap between the Church's ambitions and the social conditions of the faithful. These texts seek to guide the formation of new modes of behavior and to model situational identities, new ways for the faithful to be seen as penitents. Cambridge, Corpus Christi College, MS 201, one of the manuscripts Wormald discusses, is the chief witness for the kinds of social change I am describing. It contains law codes, "private" Wulfstanian texts (to refer to Wormald's description of status tracts), and the *OE Handbook*, the last of the vernacular penitentials (see Chapter 8). Some elements of this penitential, I believe, are uniquely suited to the kind of social change the archbishop witnessed and was seeking to further. The Christians for and about whom Wulfstan wrote were not interchangeable figures in his mind. He was concerned with all classes, but he had the most to gain by influencing people of means, including the rural elites whose large settlements were drawing attention across the landscape. Wormald numbers among Wulfstan's distinctive traits his propensity for laws that enhanced the Church's revenue. The later law codes, Wormald shows, inserted the king into more and more judicial matters that might profit him. In Wulfstan's tracts on status we see a comparable interest in elevating the status of the clergy. Fully in this spirit, the *OE Handbook* inserts the Church into the lives of landed aristocrats who did penance, outlining ways for them to use their material status and their command over large numbers of workers, as well as their networks of others of their own class, to alleviate the burden of lengthy penances.

In writing about food culture at Flixborough, Loveluck has observed that the hall provided a "'theatre' for feasting and gift-giving" – that is, for consumption and social display.[100] Fleming has summarized documentary and archaeological evidence of conspicuous consumption of food, which she calls "a major site of aristocratic consumption on the eve of the Norman Conquest." In the eleventh century both wild birds and fish alike figured into the diets of the wealthy, and even into those of the "not-so-

---

[98] M. R. Godden, "Money, Power, and Morality," where the focus is the moral discourse surrounding wealth.

[99] Wormald, *MEL*, p. 208.

[100] Loveluck, *Rural Settlement*, pp. 31–74. Social display is a running feature of the built environment at Flixborough; on the hall as a theater, see p. 149.

great," as never before.[101] Another and seemingly paradoxical form of that display, I contend, was the fast and an attendant practice of shortening fasting periods known as the commutation. The late Anglo-Saxon Church used the *OE Handbook* to introduce a commutation related to food practice that was without precedent in its scope and complexity. Although commutations are found in the earlier handbooks and involve ways to shorten periods of fasting by giving alms or giving food to the hungry, those found in the *OE Handbook* surpass anything previously seen in the English penitential system. [102]

The relevant provisions are found in the last two of the six books of the *OE Handbook*.[103] Only in Cambridge, Corpus Christi College, MS 201 do the six books form a reasonably coherent whole, and only there do books five and six have headings: Book 5 is *Be dædbetan* ("Concerning penance") and Book 6 is *Be mihtigum mannum* ("Concerning people of means"). These two books of the *OE Handbook* are relevant to changes in settlement plan and food use. Both show how the lives of the great were tied to the lives of their inferiors. The fifth book of the *OE Handbook* appears in all six manuscripts, the sixth only in two, both of them important.[104] Book 6 appears both in Cambridge, Corpus Christi College, 201, and in Bodleian Library, Laud Misc. 482, a small, hand-sized book of the kind a pastor might have carried with him.[105] We could hardly find two collections less likely to share a text; one is a grand codex containing laws as well as homilies and a penitential, the other a slim handbook containing two earlier handbooks, texts for the sick and dying, and three parts of the *OE Handbook*, including both liturgical works and handbooks of penance, thus suggesting it was for the use of priests.[106]

Book 4 of the *OE Handbook* is a tariff penitential matching penances to sins. As I showed in the previous chapter, it radically revises the list of sins about which the priest was to ask the penitent, omitting many food-related offenses. Book 5 and Book 6 are also revolutionary. Book 5 outlines an extraordinarily material approach to penitential acts, far beyond the fasting required in Book 4. Book 5 seems to be a composite text that mixes the familiar – advice to the priest on grading penances according to the

[101] Fleming, "The New Wealth, the New Rich," pp. 3–7.
[102] Frantzen, *ASP*, *OES*, X26.09.01, and *OEP*, S44.57.01; note that MSS BY contain a shorter form of this canon and omit those that follow it. For details, see Frantzen, "Food Words in the Anglo-Saxon Penitentials." See also Thomas P. Oakley, *English Penitential Discipline and Anglo-Saxon Law*, pp. 88–103, and Frantzen, *The Literature of Penance*, pp. 73–74.
[103] Frantzen, *ASP*. Go to Texts, *OE Handbook*, Description & Index, and see Table 1 for the structure of this text.
[104] At Frantzen, *ASP*, go to Texts, *OE Handbook*, Description & Index, Table 2, to see the distribution of Books 5 and 6 in each manuscript. In Oxford, Bodleian Library, MS Laud Misc. 482, the contents of Book 5 are divided into three parts (as can be seen in both Table 1 and Table 2 in the database), casting doubt on the integrity of Book 5.
[105] On this manuscript, see Ker, *Catalogue of Manuscripts Containing Anglo-Saxon*, pp. 419–22.
[106] Victoria Thompson has argued that because it was glossed by the "Tremulous Hand" the book belongs to the Worcester Cathedral Library and was used by the cathedral clergy. See Thompson, "The Pastoral Contract in Late Anglo-Saxon England," and Catherine Cubitt, "Bishops, Priests and Penance in Late Saxon England," pp. 57–58.

strength of the penitent – with innovative commutations that are found nowhere else. The first half of Book 5 compares the confessor to a physician, part of the ancient tradition of the medical metaphor. The author stresses that penance must be assigned "according to the person's works" and "by his power, and his means, and how one understands the sorrow of his heart and his own earnestness" (*be mannes gewyrhtum hit man mot secan æfter canon dome & eac medemian be mihtum & be mæðe & be þam þe man ongit his heortan reowsunge & his silfes geornfulnesse*).[107] Terms relevant to status, including *had* (rank), *miht* (power), and *mæðe* (abilities) occur several times in the first half of Book 5. The second half of Book 5 admonishes the confessor that:

> It is a serious penance that a layman lay aside his weapons and wander widely barefoot and not be one night where he was the one before, and fast greatly, and watch, and pray earnestly day and night, and put on wool, and be so unshorn that iron not come on hair nor on nail, nor that he come into a warm bath, nor onto a soft bed, nor taste meat, nor anything from which drunkenness come, nor that he come into church.

> Deoplic dædbot bið þæt læwede man his wæpna lecge & weallige bærfot wide & ne beo niht þar oðre & fæste swiðe & wacige & gebidde georne dæges & nihtes & willen werige & swa æscære beo þæt iren ne cume on hære ne on nægle ne þæt he cume on wearmon baðe ne on softum bedde ne flæsces ne onbite ne he æniges þinges þe druncen of cume. ne he innan cirican ne cume.[108]

These clauses describe comforts to which the well-to-do were accustomed and which, as penitents, they would have to forgo. No grooming was permitted; wool was to be worn (presumably coarser fibres than those to which one was accustomed); bed, a warm bath, and meat and alcohol were forbidden, and the penitent was not to enter a church. He or she might "seek holy places and make his offenses known" but may "kiss no one," a sign of exclusion from the body of the faithful about to receive the Eucharist.

The following sections of Book 5 are more ambitious. The penitent "may redeem much with alms," even to the extent that he or she "should raise a church" and donate the land for it and find young who might "serve for him and minister to God daily." Other contributions included those that benefited the whole community. The penitent could "improve people's journeys with bridges over deep water and over foul ways, and distribute earnestly what he has for God's worship, so far as it is possible for him. And let him help poor men earnestly, and widows and stepchildren and all foreigners." These demands correspond to one of the *trimoda necessitas* of the laws, the "three necessities" of repairing roads and bridges, maintaining fortifications, and serving in the *fyrd* or army.[109] Other provisions

---

[107] Frantzen, *ASP, OEH*, D55.09.01.
[108] Frantzen, *ASP, OEH*, D55.11.01.
[109] Frantzen, *ASP, OEH*, D55.13.01. For the charter mentioning the *trimoda necessitas*, see P. H. Sawyer, *Anglo-Saxon Charters*, no. 230; the authenticity of the text is in dispute. See Dorothy

require that he free "his own slaves and redeem to freedom their slaves from other men, and also poor captured men, and feed the needy, and clothe, house, warm, bathe, and make beds for them according to their own needs." To free slaves was a traditional practice, while caring for the needy involved the penitent in work normally associated with the Church.[110] In addition, the sinner should also seek the "Lord's mercy, reprove himself very greatly with severe abstinence from food and drink and every bodily desire."[111] A person of "fewer means" who was assigned penance "according to his degree (rank)" could tithe, give alms, and "give house-shelter and food and protection to those who have need of it, and fire and food and bed, and bathe and clothe and help the needy if he may do anything." This same category of penitent could visit "those who are sad in mind and sick, and bury the dead," and keep vigils.[112] These provisions require less expenditure, instead making use of the penitent's existing resources for hospitality and care of those in need. Some of these tasks, such as visiting the sick and burying the dead, are pastoral in nature, aiming to draw the well-to-do into pastoral care.

Book 5 also includes forms of penance for one "who has yet fewer means." These acts include fasting, vigils, and other forms of deprivations, penances to tax the body rather than draw on the penitent's material resources. The penitent is again seen in a pastoral role. If he or she has led anyone into sin, an effort should be made to bring that person back to holiness. Speaking in the first person, which is very rare, the author adds that the penitent is to help reform anyone he corrupted: "What I mean is, that if he has enticed anybody into sin, he is to do what is necessary and bring him from that (sin) and lead him to his right way" (*ðæt is þæt ic mæne gif he ænigne man on sinne bespeone. do swa him þearf is. gebringe hine of ðam. & læde hine on his riht wege*).[113] The anomaly of the first-person pronoun, which is found in all manuscripts of Book 5, points to a phase of a composition process; one would have expected its traces to have disappeared. The phrase *ic mæne* occurs only six times in Old English and nowhere else outside a narrative context.[114] The author seems to feel that the point might be misunderstood and needed clarification. Book 5 suggests that the penitent "distribute all that he possesses and forsake home and homeland together and all the love of the world, and serve his Lord day and night,

---

Whitelock, *The Beginnings of English Society*, pp. 64–65, 76–77, and 85. The repair of bridges is among the public charges of a nobleman in *Rectitudines* 1; see Liebermann, *GDA*, p. 453. In II Cnut 65 (1020–23) maintenance of bridges is one of the "three necessities" (*Trimoda Necessitas*), and failure to repair a bridge is fined 120 shillings; see Liebermann, *GDA*, p. 352, translated in Robertson, *LKE*, pp. 206–7. See also David Harrison, *The Bridges of Medieval England*, and Alan Cooper, *Bridges, Law and Power in Medieval England, 700–1400*.

[110] See Pelteret, *Slavery in Early Mediaeval England*, pp. 101–5.

[111] Frantzen, *ASP, OEH*, D55.14.01.

[112] Frantzen, *ASP, OEH*, D55.16.01.

[113] Frantzen, *ASP, OEH*, D55.16.01.

[114] Other texts include Riddle 61 (*Ræd hwæt ic mæne*), in George Philip Krapp and Elliott van Kirk Dobbie, eds., *The Exeter Book*, p. 229, l. 9; and "Solomon and Saturn" (*Saga hwæt ic mæne*), in Dobbie, ed., *The Anglo-Saxon Minor Poems*, p. 39, l. 237.

mortify himself as greatly as he can against his own desire all the days of his life." It would be difficult to imagine a more thorough transformation of identity than this one, which turns an opportunity for situational change created by confession into a new and presumably permanent social identity. This evokes the Gospel adjuration to leave all one has and follow Christ (Matthew 19:21), a tradition observed by Anglo-Saxon kings such as Oswald, whose charity Bede describes.[115]

Book 6 supplies a further and more ambitious set of commutations for the wealthy and their friends: "Thus may a man of means and many friends lighten his penance with his friends' help" (*Þus mæg mihtig man & freondspedig his dædbota mid freonda fylstan mycclum gelihtan*).[116] The word for "commute" is *gelihtan*, to lighten, the same verb used in the commutations outlined in the *OE Introduction* ("one is allowed to lighten his penance," *man mot lihtan his dædbote*).[117] The sinner is told to confess, lay aside weapons and "idle ornaments," take "staff in hand," don a hair shirt, and sleep on the floor away from home. Then, during three days, the sinner is to do penance that equals the number of days in seven years:

> Let him receive assistance and first take with him twelve men and fast three days on bread and on green herbs and on water, and obtain in addition, howsoever he may, seven times one hundred and twenty men who shall also fast for him three days. Then will be fasted as many fasts as there are days in seven years.

> Fo on mid fultume. nime him to ærest xii men & fæstan iii dagas be hlafe & be grenum wyrtum & be wætere & begite þar to eacan swa hu swa he mæge septies cxx manna þæt fæstan eac for hine iii dagas. þonne wyrð gefæst swa fela fæstena swa bið daga on vii gearum.[118]

The penitent is to ask twelve others to undertake a three-day fast, so that thirteen people would fast a total of thirty-nine days. Then he or she is to request another 840 people (that is, seven times one hundred twenty) to undertake a three-day fast, for a total of 2,520 days. If we add the latter figure to the previous number of days of fasting (thirty-nine), we reach a total of 2,559 days of fasting. Divided by the number of days in the year (365), that does indeed give a total of a seven-year fast of consecutive fasting days (not a fast consisting of two or three fasting days each week that would extend for seven years). Among the grave sins for which the *OE Handbook* assigns lay people a fast of seven years are homicide, adultery,

---

[115] Frantzen, *ASP, OEH*, D55.17.01. The closest examples are the holy kings and queens in Bede's *Ecclesiastical History*, the chief example being Oswald, who had an officer whose duty it was "to relieve the needy" and distribute food and silver in the king's name. See Bertram Colgrave and R. A. B. Mynors, eds., *Bede's Ecclesiastical History of the English People*, book 3, ch. 6, pp. 230–31.

[116] Frantzen, *ASP, OEH*, Y56.01.00. Cambridge, Corpus Christi College, MS 201, substitutes *fultume* for *fylstan*; see D56.01.00.

[117] Frantzen, *ASP, OEI*, S33.08.01.

[118] Frantzen, *ASP, OEH*, D56.01.01–03.01; for parallels in Book 5, see D55.10.01.

and selling Christians to heathens.[119] Such calculations also appear in the "Dialogue of Solomon and Saturn," which indicates that a contribution of 720 loaves per year is adequate for a serving man, or an allotment of two loaves per day (although 720 seems to be an error for 730, which is twice 365).[120]

The penitent was to "distribute to all God's needy the dishes that he would have used," i.e., his or her uneaten food.[121] He is to remain in a church "with a taper bought for charity," and "earnestly watch there and call to God and ask forgiveness with a lamenting mind, and kneel often in the sign of the cross," weeping and lying prostrate. During this three-day period, the penitent was required to feed "as many people in need as he can and on the fourth day bathe them all and shelter them and distribute possessions, and let the penitent be (busy) about washing their feet, and let one offer as many Masses that day for him as can possibly ever be obtained." Then he is to go to Mass, be absolved, and return to the Eucharistic community (unless other conditions pertain, perhaps restitution).[122]

It will be useful to summarize the functions that Books 5 and 6 assign to food and eating in order to see how the texts address and manage the penitent's material resources. The most traditional role of food is in fasting, which is mentioned in several forms, including to "fast greatly" and abstain from meat and "anything from which drunkenness comes" (*ne flæsces ne onbite ne he æniges þinges þe druncen of cume*). The directions to feed the needy (*fede þearfan*) imply access to resources; even those of lesser means addressed by Book 5 were to feed the needy, as well as house and cloth them (*mete & munde þam ðe þæs beþurfe*). Penitents of lesser means had to fast but were not compelled to charity.[123]

Food in Book 6 is more complex. A diet of bread, water, and green herbs was required for the penitent, his twelve companions, and the large number of others observing the three-day fast. The penitent himself or herself had to distribute the uneaten food (from the non-fasting diet) to the poor and feed "as many of the needy as possible," a requirement that assumes great means (*fede man þa ðri dagas þearfena swa fela swa man mæst mæge*).[124] The obligation to the hungry required supplies beyond the food one penitent would have eaten during the same period. There is an implication of restitution in this requirement, as if what the penitent normally

---

[119] On Christians selling other Christians, see Wulfstan, "Sermo Lupi ad Anglos," in Dorothy Bethurum, ed., *The Homilies of Wulfstan*, pp. 270–71. This is not a penance calibrated on the basis of fasting three days each week but rather "seven years fully." See Frantzen, *ASP, OEH*, D54.41.01. Other penances in the *OE Penitential* and *OE Handbook* are less severe.

[120] Stephen Pollington, *The Mead-Hall*, pp. 122–23. See James E. Cross and Thomas D. Hill, eds., *The Prose Solomon and Saturn* and *Adrian and Ritheus*, p. 34, c. 59, and notes, pp. 123–34.

[121] Frantzen, *ASP, OEH*, D56.04.01.

[122] Frantzen, *ASP, OEH*, D56.05.01.

[123] See, in order, Frantzen, *ASP, OEH*, D55.10.01 (concerning alcohol), and D55.14.01, D55.16.01, and D55.17.01, concerning penances for those of lesser means.

[124] For bread, water, and herbs, see Frantzen, *ASP, OEH*, D56.03.01, and for the open-ended commutation, D56.05.01.

consumed was food that might have been given to the needy. The expense of a feast, if invested in humble fare, would have purchased supplies for far more than the number of those at the feast. Book 6 juxtaposes conspicuous consumption with human need in a way unflattering to the wealthy, especially if the wealthy penitent himself or herself, rather than the usual intermediaries, was to be involved in distributing food to the needy in the surrounding district. These commutations did not affect the wealthy only. Ways of shortening or alleviating penances are provided for penitents at several ranks, and for the sick as well as the hale. However, it seems clear that certain penances in Book 5 (donating the land for a church) and most of those in Book 6 address Christians whose wealth could benefit the Church and the community as a whole. Building a church, donating land for it, and staffing it with young men are acts that could be connected to locating churches on newly centralized and, sometimes, enclosed settlements.

There are parallels between some features of these commutations and the laws, chiefly in the tradition of surety that had a long history in both continental and English law. Alfred's treaty with Guthrum (886–90) allows the accused to clear his name with the assistance of his equals; II Æthelstan requires those who witness an ordeal to fast along with the one who is to undergo it.[125] In commenting on laws issued by Æthelred before his work with Wulfstan, Wormald contrasts Æthelred to Edgar, who "stressed the role of community sureties," whereas Æthelred "sought to integrate the activity of lord and neighbourhood" and emphasize "district and household sureties."[126] We see the role of the lord and the neighborhood in III Æthelred 13, which requires one who supplied food to a man who had broken the peace to "clear himself with three times twelve compurgators who shall be nominated by the reeve."[127] The commutation in the *OE Handbook* likewise links the lord to his neighborhood. The provision calls for many more than a dozen witnesses, which was the usual number in surety; it calls 852 people besides the penitent, to be exact (twelve and 840 in addition). Such figures seem improbable but hardly impossible if we think of manorial estates with extensive holdings – i.e., a manorial center from which large resources of labor could be commanded – and a network of "rural elites" that populated and linked such centers in a landscape dominated by powerful figures.

A specific parallel between these provisions and the law codes involves food. The code known as VII Æthelred (1009), drawn up when the "great army" had invaded (*ða se micele here com to lande*) requires a nation-wide fast on green herbs and bread and water (*be hlafe 7 wirtum 7 wætere*), a provision found in no other penitential of the period except the *OE Handbook*. The law mandates this fast for everybody (*eal folc to gemænelicre dædbote*)

[125] For Alfred's treaty with Guthrum 3, see Liebermann, *GDA*, p. 126, and Attenborough, *LEEK*, pp. 98–99. For II Æthelstan (Grately), see Liebermann, *GDA*, p. 162, and Attenborough, *LEEK*, pp. 138–39.
[126] Wormald, *MEL*, p. 328.
[127] For III Æthelred 13 see Liebermann, *GDA*, pp. 230–32, and Robertson, *LKE*, pp. 68–69.

and requires that everyone go to church in bare feet without "gold or orna-ments" in order to confess. A special assessment of one penny per hide was to be collected, divided, and distributed to the poor. During the fast the food not eaten was to be distributed among the poor.[128] The public nature of fasting and almsgiving was obvious, and compliance was monitored. The priest, the reeve of every village, and the tithing supervisor (*presbiter et tungravis et decimales hominess*) were required to attest that the fast was performed and the alms paid. One recension of VII Æthelred is preserved in Cambridge, Corpus Christi College, 201, which, as we have noted, also contains all six books of the *OE Handbook*.[129]

The commutations in Books 5 and 6 of the *OE Handbook* were, I suggest, created for the advantage of lords, whether "middling" thegns or "king's thegns," by someone with an interest in connecting ecclesiastical struc-tures to the organization of the land.[130] Wormald has shown Wulfstan and his followers to be adept at reworking existing materials and traditions for new purposes, creating new texts out of parts of old ones.[131] An advisor to Æthelred (1008–12) and Cnut (1012–23), Wulfstan shaped both ecclesiasti-cal regulations and Cnut's laws, which require the use of "instruction or teaching contained in books (of penance or ecclesiastical law)."[132] The *OE Handbook* offers the occasion to connect this oversight to the political and social organization of the landscape.[133] That bishops would have overseen penitential discipline in their diocese is obvious. The late Saxon church began using the term *scir*, meaning district, as a unit for the Church's juris-diction. The so-called *Canons of Edgar* make it clear that the *scriftscir* is the unit of the priest's authority and its extent. He is responsible for what takes place at the bishop's synods. One of the priest's duties is to report anyone who commits a mortal sin (*heafodleahtra*) or who is "disobedient to God."[134] How the terms *scir* and *scriftscir* correlate with estate boundaries or other units of land is unclear, but we can expect some association of these terms with the "parish" in the Late Saxon period.[135]

---

[128] For VII Æthelred, 2.1–3, see Liebermann, *GDA*, p. 262 , and Robertson, *LKE*, pp. 114–15. For a detailed discussion of the political context, see Simon Keynes, "An Abbot, an Archbishop, and the Viking Raids," especially pp. 179–81.

[129] Wormald, *MEL*, pp. 330–33.

[130] See Stenton, *Anglo-Saxon England*, pp. 487–88, on classes of thegn. The term "middling" thegn dates from Sharon Turner, *The History of the Anglo-Saxons*, 3: 190.

[131] Wormald, *MEL*, pp. 389–97.

[132] I quote the *DOE* definition of *boctæcinge*. See Liebermann, *GDA*, p. 338, and Robertson, *LKE*, pp. 194–95, where the word is translated as "canon law." Whitelock, *EHD*, p. 460.

[133] Roger Fowler, "A Late OE Handbook," discusses Wulfstan's authorship of parts of the *OEH*, pp. 6–12. See Carole Hough, "Penitential Literature and Secular Law," p. 141, n. 56. Hough repeats Wormald's view that Wulfstan might simply have quoted or adapted the *OEH*.

[134] Roger Fowler, *Wulfstan's Canons of Edgar*, c. 6, p. 3. In "Bishops, Priests and Penance," Cubitt argues that the *Handbook* is even more strongly connected with Wulfstan than Fowler pro-posed (pp. 53–54). Such claims need to be seen in the context of Wormald's view that the archbishop's reach might easily be confused with that of his followers or assistants. See Wormald, *MEL*, p. 352.

[135] See, most recently, John Blair, *The Church in Anglo-Saxon Society*, where *scriftscir* as "parish" is mentioned several times (pp. 429–30, 495, and 497).

Scriftscir and *rihtscriftscir* are seldom found outside texts associated with Wulfstan, such as the *Institutes of Polity*, the *Canons of Edgar*, and late law codes, including V Æthelred, and I Cnut.[136] The bishop relied both on the priest to report affairs in his *scriftscir* and on the bishop's own reeve, who had a legal brief similar to the priest's. The priest heard confessions in his district, and, according to the *Canons of Edgar*, reported serious offenses and defiance of the Church's authority at the bishop's synod. Failure to observes rules of fasting and feasting so prominent in the laws would have been among these offenses. No longer concerned with bees, mice, and bird droppings, the priest became a more important food officer. One can imagine the expensive penances of Book 5 or the commutations of Book 6 coming into play as the bishop and the *freondspedig* (literally, friend-rich) penitent met and the latter, facing seven years of penance, considered ways the bishop offered him to shorten the period. Those who submitted to these commutations would have attracted attention to their penitential status by the conspicuous nature of their deeds.

If the commutations and penances of Book 5 and Book 6 of the *OE Handbook* worked as I have suggested, they were a shrewd calculation on the part of the Church to use the sinner's material status to benefit the Church and the poor. Food was central to this strategy. The acts required by the *OE Handbook* went beyond the conventions of *noblesse oblige* and, however briefly, closed the gaps that otherwise kept rich and poor apart. The commutations and penances reverse the dynamic of workers and lord or lady, requiring the well-to-do penitent to feed the workers rather than be fed by them. The commutation directs the penitent to return that food, uneaten because of the fast, to those who produced it. The massive commutation that involved hundreds dispenses just enough for sustenance – bread, water, and perhaps green herbs, the penitential diet Æthelred demanded of the whole people at Michelmas in 1009, a precedent sure to have been familiar to many and an event that would have built awareness of the kind of fast to which the *OE Handbook* refers.

The Church used the commutations of the *OE Handbook* to spread the expense of caring for the poor to persons of rank. The commutations reveal the extent to which the social network was also a food network, a web in which the Church caught the powerful. The powerless were already caught by the powerful, it is safe to say. All members of the Church who lived in large settlements would have been affected if the lord or lady sought to commute a long penance. Swept up by the commutation into a fast by proxy, the faithful who were not among the *mihtigum mannum* would have borne the consequences of this accommodation of the wealthiest Christians. "But one not powerful may not go ahead with such steps," we read in Book 6. That one instead "must seek it [i.e., the remedy of sin] in himself more earnestly. And that is also most just, that everyone avenge

[136] *Scriftscir* also occurs in II Æthelstan 26 (a code known as "Grately"); see Liebermann, *GDA*, p. 164, and Robertson, *LKE*, pp. 142–43. See Wormald, *MEL*, pp. 294–300.

his own misdeeds on himself with earnest repentance. For it is written, each one will carry his own burden."[137] The commutation, however, suggests that the *unmaga* might have carried others' burdens as well, not only undertaking the fast by proxy but producing the bread required for large numbers of people and managing the distribution of food to the poor to whose needs the *OE Handbook* refers.

In one way, the commutations and redemptions merely reinforced what people already knew about wealth and social position. In another way, however, displays of piety – and power – such as those I have described created new, if temporary, identities that were actualized through days of discipline. The new pairing of fast and feast in the law codes was not a spiritual matter only. It also expressed a concern with public order and with a kind of purity that food culture required. The commutations outlined in the *OE Handbook* made extraordinary demands on the food supply. They humbled the mighty and showed the power of the Church over them, while also reinforcing the very social distinctions that piety might have minimized. Fasting had become a way to demonstrate social superiority.[138]

---

[137] *Scriptum est enim quia unusquisque onus suum portabit.* Frantzen, *ASP*, *OEH*, D56.07.01.

[138] Some material from this and the following chapter appears in earlier form in Allen J. Frantzen, "*Be mihtigum mannum*: Power, Penance, and Food in Late Anglo-Saxon England."

10

Fasting and the Anglo-Saxon "Fish Event Horizon"

Many of the foods known to the Anglo-Saxons remained the same through-out the Anglo-Saxon period. Studies of fauna note changes from settlement to settlement and period to period, but they generally report more or less beef, pork, or mutton.[1] Animal bones are among the factors that reflect settlement wealth. Older animals were killed for consumption when they became less efficient at traction, the chief task they performed. Butchery of young animals is evidence that their value as food exceeded their work capacity – obviously a sign of wealth.[2] Anomalies in patterns of animal bone distribution that show a preponderance of one species are taken as indications of high status. At the East Anglian site of Wicken Bonhunt, there was a high proportion of pig bones; Wicken Bonhunt might have been a market or perhaps a royal farm.[3] Another sign of a site's status is the presence of fish bones. Delicate and difficult to transport and store, fish are no ordinary food. Whether from marine or freshwater sources, fish were not a constant factor in the Anglo-Saxon diet. The fish is an ancient Christian symbol, and much that has been written about fish has been connected to fasting. In the *City of God* Augustine commented on an acrostic that linked the first letters of five Greek words to form the Greek *ichthus*, which means fish. Augustine saw the fish as an allegory for Christ, who "was able to remain alive – that is, without sin – in the abyss of our mortal condition, in the depths, as it were, of the sea."[4] Fish have long been regarded as a fasting food, but were formerly seen as a luxury, as they were in Anglo-Saxon England and in the later Middle Ages. How can we reconcile this discrepancy? Arguments about the place of fish in relation to fasting present an opportunity to compare evidence from fish bone assemblies to texts that determined how and when the Anglo-Saxons fasted.

Anglo-Saxon Christians fasted several times a year. The fasting diet of lay people seems to have consisted chiefly of bread, water, and some greens. Textual details for lay fasting diets are sparse. We know more

---

[1] For an overview, see Peter Fowler, *Farming in the First Millennium AD*, pp. 245–90.
[2] See Jennifer Bourdillon, "The Animal Provisioning of Saxon Southampton," pp. 121–22.
[3] Pam Crabtree, "Animal Exploitation in East Anglian Villages," p. 50. Also useful is Terence O'Connor, "8th–11th Century Economy and Environment in York."
[4] Augustine, *City of God*, book 18, ch. 23, p. 790.

about fasting in monasteries. Some scholars have argued that fish were an established fasting food in monasteries and that, following the tenth-century revitalization of monastic life, fish became a fasting food for lay people as well. Knowledge of fish consumption is uneven. I have noted H. E. M. Cool's description of a lecture by "a highly enthusiastic fish bone specialist" and its impact on a dig Cool supervised. Fish bones "had rarely appeared in the preceding weeks," Cool writes, but suddenly more and more were found.[5] Sieving and other recovery techniques have evolved, and it would seem plausible that evidence of fish consumption has often been minimized. James H. Barrett, Alison M. Locker, and Callum M. Roberts have charted an increase in consumption of fish in general and of marine species in particular in the late Anglo-Saxon period. They suggest that the increase was partly driven by the Church's fasting requirements because, they hypothesize, fish played a key role in the fasting diet. To be sure, more extravagant claims have been made. In *Fish on Friday*, for example, Brian Fagan suggested that the need for fish during Lent drove oceanic exploration and was among the factors leading to the settlement of the Americas.[6] I will review the archaeologists' assessment and examine evidence in laws and penitentials that pertains to the fasting diet. Texts have been said to play too great a role in shaping our understanding of material culture. In this case, I believe, texts might have been emphasized more rather than less.[7]

The "fish event horizon"

According to Barrett, Locker, and Roberts, between 975 and the late eleventh century there was an increase in consumption of both marine and freshwater fish, and an increase in sea fishing and trade related to it.[8] "The marked increase in marine fishing was probably revolutionary in archaeological terms," they write, and they hypothesize that a "'fish event horizon' must have occurred within a few decades either side of the end of the first millennium AD." People were eating more fish, especially more fish from the sea. "As the marine species became more important, the proportion of freshwater taxa in the bone assemblages declined."[9] In their study, which ranges from 600 to 1600, Barrett, Locker, and Roberts use fish consumption to divide a "dark age" of undefined markets and gift exchange from "later medieval trade." The transition from exchange to trade is disputed by some, and although I have reservations about the claims scholars make for the late Anglo-Saxon period, I see the merits of the long view they take.

---

[5] H. E. M. Cool, *Eating and Drinking in Roman Britain*, p. 104. See also Chapter 1, pp. 14–15, above.
[6] Brian Fagan, *Fish on Friday*, p. 90.
[7] See Chapter 1, above, and Barbara J. Little, "Texts, Images, Material Culture."
[8] See James H. Barrett, Alison M. Locker, and Callum M. Roberts, "'Dark Age Economics' Revisited," p. 623.
[9] Barrett, Locker, and Roberts, "'Dark Age Economics' Revisited," p. 630.

They make their case within the larger context of Richard Hodges's "Dark Age economics."[10] We have seen Hodges's arguments in several areas of food culture, especially the distribution of pottery, a bulk commodity that was cheaply produced and transported, and hence important to the growth of markets. The authors define fish as a bulk commodity to "contextualise the significance of 'Dark Age' commerce," their aim being to test Hodges's thesis using this highly perishable commodity.[11]

Barrett, Locker, and Roberts tally fish specimens for "the eight most common fish taxa," which they divide into three categories.[12] Marine taxa included herring and cod-like fish, or gadids. Migratory specimens included European eel, salmon, trout, smelt, and various others, flounder among them. Freshwater fish included carp (cyprinids) and pike. Assemblages of specimens from the seventh to the tenth centuries comprised primarily freshwater and migratory fish. Later assemblages (i.e., eleventh century and on) were richer in herring and cod-like fish. Herring were found in seventh- to tenth-century sites, but this species "increased fourfold in the eleventh to twelfth centuries." Cod were "virtually unexploited prior to the end of the first millennium AD" and "first appeared as a significant component of the medieval 'catch' in the eleventh to twelfth centuries." While "virtually all 'catches' from the seventh to the tenth centuries were dominated by freshwater and migratory species," most eleventh-century and later catches included more marine fish, especially herring.[13]

Barrett, Locker, and Roberts surveyed evidence from about sixty-five sites, sampling some of them in multiple phases, for a total of 127 settlement phases, rural and urban, coastal and inland, from the Early to Late Saxon periods and beyond (roughly from the seventh to the sixteenth century).[14] Evidence of increased consumption is based on the number of identifiable specimens and the species represented. The authors used isotope evidence drawn from fish bones to distinguish freshwater from marine species. The sites studied were nearly evenly distributed between inland (sixty-two) and estuarine (fifty-nine), with only six coastal sites included. Barrett, Locker, and Roberts concentrated on nineteen assemblages that could be dated to within about one hundred years.[15] They regard inland sites as "under-represented prior to the eleventh century,

[10] See Richard Hodges, *The Anglo-Saxon Achievement*; *Dark Age Economics*; and "Dark Age Economics Revisited," ch. 4 of *Goodbye to the Vikings?*, pp. 61–71. For a spirited commentary on Hodges's work, see Ross Samson, "Illusory Emporia and Mad Economic Theories."
[11] See Chris Wickham, *Framing the Early Middle Ages*, pp. 699–700, for an analysis of exchange of bulk goods.
[12] Barrett, Locker, and Roberts, "'Dark Age Economics' Revisited," notes to Acknowledgements and notes to figure 2.
[13] Barrett, Locker, and Roberts, "'Dark Age Economics' Revisited," pp. 618–20. On forms in which cod and herring were traded, see pp. 624–25.
[14] Barrett, Locker, and Roberts, "'Dark Age Economics' Revisited," p. 624.
[15] These sites included York between c. 975 and the mid-eleventh century; London, c.1050 to 1070; Southampton before c. 1300; Norwich, the late tenth to late eleventh century; Eynsham Abbey, the late eleventh to early twelfth century; and Northampton, by the eleventh century.

not vice versa," strengthening the view that "non-marine species were preferred prior to the end of the first millennium AD." In their view, "changes in fishing in the eleventh to twelfth centuries were more dramatic than better known later developments."[16]

It is not clear that more fish were being consumed at all these sites. Sometimes the number of specimens declined around the "horizon." At York, 16–22 Coppergate, from about 930 to 975 (Period 4b at the site), 6,918 specimens were found. In the next two periods the numbers declined: at about 975 (Period 5a), there were 1,873 specimens, and from about 975 to the mid-eleventh century (Period 5b), there were 2,895 specimens; numbers fell sharply in later periods. At York's Fishergate site, there were 4,484 specimens in eighth- to ninth-century contexts (Period 3z) and 1,874 specimens in Period 4, eleventh to twelfth century. In support of the authors' thesis, it is important that the representation of marine species in these samples increased, although the overall number of identified specimens fell at both York sites. These data are not conclusive; older sieving methods would probably have missed important evidence.

It is worth noting that sites in York have been studied from several perspectives, including an analysis of economic and environmental change by Terence O'Connor. He describes Fishergate in the eighth century as a community "possibly not free to trade for food resources," with a fish diet consisting of "mostly eels and cyprinids, some herring." Coppergate in the late ninth century, a "poorly developed market with little 'gravity,'" gave evidence of "mostly eels and cyprinids, some salmon and pike." In the tenth century Coppergate was an "urban community diversifying diet by using locally available resources," these comprising "mostly eels, cyprinids, herring, salmon, smelt, perch and pike," while in the late tenth and early eleventh century it was a "market big enough to draw in commodities from wide area by consumer demand" – that is to say, with considerable "gravity," it would seem – and with a diet of "mostly herring, eel, and cyprinids, some cod and pike."[17] Herring occur already in the eighth-century catches at Fishergate as well as in Coppergate evidence from the tenth and eleventh centuries. "Mostly herring" and "some cod" in the late tenth and early eleventh century offer the only evidence of increased consumption of marine fish. These data amount to modest evidence of a "fish event horizon" at best. Equally clearly, they suggest continuity rather than a marked change in the fish diet. The significant element supporting an "event horizon" is that the scope of Coppergate's market changed and that consumer demand seems to account for some of this development. About tenth-century Coppergate and Fishergate, O'Connor writes, "The fish bones from this period of occupation show an intensive exploitation of the river. There are herrings and other marine species in the assemblages, but eels and cyprinid species predominate." The "marked increase" at this

---

[16] Barrett, Locker, and Roberts, "'Dark Age Economics' Revisited," p. 621.
[17] O'Connor, "8th –11th Century Economy and Environment in York," p. 145.

time, however, was in use of geese, pigs, and fowls, not fish. In the late tenth century at Coppergate there was "little change in the exploitation of the main domestic animals," but at that time "the fish bone assemblages show an increased exploitation of inshore marine fish, especially cod *Gadus morhua*, at the expense of freshwater cyprinid taxa."[18]

Evidence from other sites suggests that the "fish event horizon" did not emerge uniformly. Tenth-century Flixborough yielded the lowest number of identified specimens, barely 3 percent of the total of fish remains recovered at the site. The mid-eighth century produced a quarter of the total specimens from the site, and the early ninth- to early tenth-century period over a third.[19] Fish consumption has been difficult to document at other sites. At West Heslerton, twelve miles or so inland in North Yorkshire, only a single fish bone was discovered among 80,000 identified specimens. At Sedgeford, five kilometers east of the estuary known as The Wash, Gareth Davies found only a few flatfish bones amid masses of mammal bone and a substantial find of oyster shells.[20] The background against which the "event horizon" was constructed is, therefore, uneven. It seems most strongly attested in urban settings, although, as we have seen, even in York the specimen patterns do not consistently support arguments for increased consumption of fish marine species.

According to Barrett, Locker, and Roberts, three factors precipitated the "event horizon": the Church's requirements for fasting, the environment, and technology. The urban connection is important. They consider it likely that "the concentration of population in England's (and continental Europe's) early towns produced a demand for fish, particularly during periods of fasting, which outstripped the potential of freshwater resources (due to both social and environmental limitations on this resource) – leading to an increase in sea fishing and the development of long-range trade in this product."[21] On the link between evidence of fish consumption and urban settlements, the work of Barrett, Locker, and Roberts overlaps with conclusions offered by others. Fish assemblages "of any size are rare outside urban contexts such as York," Christopher Loveluck writes.[22] "Urban contexts" might mean "town" or "early town," although usage is not settled. The majority of people did not live in towns, where the shift that Barrett, Locker, and Roberts propose would have appeared first. That shift is marked by an increased demand for fish, "particularly during periods of

---

[18] O'Connor, "8th –11th Century Economy and Environment in York," p. 144. These data are put into wider contexts of food remains recovered in York by Keith Dobney, Allan Hall, and Harry Kenward, "The Bioarchaeology of Anglo-Saxon Yorkshire."

[19] My figures show 226 finds from the latest period (3 percent), 1,486 from the second I mention here, or 25 percent, and 1,987 or 33 percent from the third period. Based on data from Barrett, Locker, and Roberts, "'Dark Age Economics' Revisited," appendix, at http://antiquity.ac.uk/ProjGall/barrett301/ (accessed September 1, 2013).

[20] Gareth Davies, *An Archaeological Evaluation of the Middle-Late Saxon Settlement at Chalkpit Field*, p. 182.

[21] Barrett, Locker, and Roberts, "'Dark Age Economics' Revisited," p. 630.

[22] Christopher Loveluck, "Wealth, Waste," p. 92.

fasting." Because the supply of freshwater fish was inadequate, this new demand is thought to have stimulated both sea fishing and long-range trade.[23] Their reference to increased consumption during fasting periods should prompt us to look for evidence in ecclesiastical and administrative sources for decrees driving this change.

The other proposed causes – the effects of technology and the environment – are more difficult to analyze. Environmental change would be impossible to narrow to the millennium, although it would be a factor influencing fishing over the longer term. Technology is more likely to be relevant, since it figured into the expansion of both marine and freshwater fishing and also into conflicts between fishing and other uses of waterways. Technology that negatively affected freshwater fishing could have stimulated efforts to harvest marine species. Della Hooke has described how the proliferation of mills and dams created obstacles to freshwater fishing. Fishing weirs also impeded transport. Methods of fishing for both freshwater and marine species inevitably responded to these changing conditions.[24] Barrett, Locker, and Roberts suggest that after 1000 fishing became more regulated and that the growth in marine fishing was "concurrent with attempts (successful or unsuccessful) to expand and secure access to supplies of freshwater fish."[25]

The role of the Church in the increased demand for fish seems to matter more than technology or environmental change in explaining the change. That is how I read the authors' assertions that "temporal changes in Christian fasting practices may have influenced the level of marine fish consumption." They observe that "the role of fish in early medieval Christian diet remains poorly understood" and emphasize "that the practice of fasting formalised by St. Benedict's Rule and subsequent monastic regulations was also applied to the English *secular* community by seventh century and later Anglo-Saxon law."[26] Most of these laws were passed in the reigns of Æthelred and Cnut under Wulfstan's guidance (i.e., 1010–23). The authors note that fasting had "a major impact on the demand for fish in the later Middle Ages." That was also, they suggest, the case in the Anglo-Saxon period, although they allow that "some authorities dispute that [fish] were widely accepted as components of monastic fasts prior to the twelfth century."[27]

The analogy between the eleventh century and later periods should be challenged. The authors cite an analysis by C. M. Woolgar that begins around 1275 and argues for a connection between fasting and increased fish consumption. He points to the role of Norman monasticism in imposing

---

[23] Barrett, Locker, and Roberts, "'Dark Age Economics' Revisited," p. 630.
[24] Della Hooke, "Use of Waterways in Anglo-Saxon England," and Ann Cole, "The Place-Name Evidence for Water Transport in Medieval England."
[25] Barrett, Locker, and Roberts, "'Dark Age Economics' Revisited," p. 628.
[26] Barrett, Locker, and Roberts, "'Dark Age Economics' Revisited," p. 629. They cite Maria Dembinska, "Fasting and Working Monks," on the first point, and Ann Hagen, *A Handbook of Anglo-Saxon Food and Drink*, p. 131, on the second.
[27] Barrett, Locker, and Roberts, "'Dark Age Economics' Revisited," p. 629.

stricter (i.e., meatless if not vegetarian) diets at Winchester and St. Alban's.[28] Late medieval evidence also dominates a separate study by Woolgar and Dale Serjeantson which concludes that, in periods up to around 1000, "the place of fish in the monastic diet might be opaque."[29] This plausible statement underscores the fact that Woolgar and Serjeantson did not establish a link between fasting and fish consumption in the Anglo-Saxon period.

According to Barrett, Locker, and Roberts, it "seems likely that fish were part of [the] monastic diet (and by implication presumably secular fasts) long before the 'fish event horizon.'"[30] Fasting is mentioned in seventh-century law codes, and, as the authors note, became pronounced in later laws. However, the fasting requirement does not also imply a place for fish in the diet. The authors emphasize "temporal change" in ecclesiastical regulations. If so, one would expect to find regulations requiring fish as part of the fasting diet and other evidence to demonstrate the change, especially given the role of Wulfstan and his followers in producing regulatory texts. "Christian fasting practice" is outlined in laws, monastic rules, and handbooks of penance. Textual evidence from the early ninth century as well as from the tenth century shows that fish, when they were to be had, were sometimes included in the monastic diet but almost always as a delicacy. Beyond that, the authors' view that fish "by implication presumably [figured into] secular fasts" proves difficult to support. Texts do not clearly support the assumption that fish formed a significant part of the fasting diet in monasteries, in Lent or at other times, and offer some evidence to the contrary.

Fish and fasting in texts

Charters and monastic rules suggest continuity rather than change in fasting practices and contain little evidence to support the assumed link between fish and a fasting diet. Most textual references concern the consumption of both freshwater fish, eel especially, and herring. Gifts of fish to monasteries in charters are sometimes large, eels especially in the thousands. This often-cited evidence, drawn from documents of the ninth and tenth as well as the eleventh century, establishes only that monasteries took in large quantities of fish.[31] Two documents refer to fish as a substitute for meat. First is a grant to Christ Church, Canterbury, 805 x 815 AD, for a commemoration. Oswulf, alderman, and his wife, specify different foods for fast days and *fugeldæg* (fowl days), when meat could be eaten: "A good cow, four sheep, two flitches, five geese, ten hens, and ten pounds of cheese, if it be a meat (fowl) day. If it [i.e., the commemoration] be a fast

---

[28] C. M. Woolgar, "Take this Penance Now." Another relevant study is Christopher C. Dyer, "The Consumption of Freshwater Fish in Medieval England."

[29] Dale Serjeantson and Christopher M. Woolgar, "Fish Consumption in Medieval England," p. 104.

[30] Barrett, Locker, and Roberts, "'Dark Age Economics' Revisited," p. 630.

[31] Ann Hagen, *A Second Handbook of Anglo-Saxon Food and Drink*, pp. 165–66.

day, then one is to give a measure of cheese, fish, butter, and eggs" (*an hriðer dugunde & IIII scęp & tua flicca & V goes & X hennfuglas & X pund caeses, gif hit fuguldaeg sie, gif hit ðonne festendæg sie, selle mon uuęge cæsa, & fisces & butran & aegera*).[32] I take this to mean that if the donation is made during Lent one is to give *in addition* to all that goes before cheese, fish, butter, and eggs. In themselves, these latter four elements do not constitute an offering comparable to the animals and foodstuffs (including ten pounds of cheese) already mentioned. Second is an annual donation to Denewulf, bishop of Winchester, dated to 909. It concerns his commemoration after death, which is designated as *edmeltide* or "festival time" (*DOE*). The food donation was to be used at the celebration: "If it occurs in Lent, then the value of the meat shall be taken in fish, unless this is impracticable" (*Gyf hit on lencten gebyrige þæt þæ þonne þære flæscun geweorð on fisce gestriene buton þæt þis forgenge sie*).[33] While this text supports the substitution of fish for meat, it accommodates a feast, not a fast, and an option as well, not a necessity.

Two charters from the turn of the millennium link fish to fasting periods. In the will of Æthelgifu, dated 990–1001, fish occurs in a list of foods to be donated every Lent: "That he give every Lent [or spring?] to Braughing six measures of malt and with it meal [or flour], and fish, and the same [amount] to Welwyn and to both churches four pigs at Martinmas [Nov. 11]" (*þe he selle ælce lengtene to Brahingum vi mittan mealtes, & þær meolo to, & fisc, & swa micel into Welingum & to ægðeran mynstre iiii swin to mærtines mæssan*).[34] The link of fish to fasting is not clear. *Lengtene* can mean either Lent or spring; was this a donation made because it was Lent, or because it was spring? Given the pairing of the earlier time of year with Martinmas, the choice of spring seems better paired with late autumn. There is no reference to fasting in the text. A Worcester food rent from 996 directs: "Fifteen salmon, good ones, to the bishop who then is seated at Worcester, and that to be done on the principal fast day and brought to the bishop" (*XV leaxas, and þa gode, þam biscope þe þonne beo into Wiogornaceastre, and þis beo gelæst on forme fæstenes dæg, and to þam biscope gebroht*).[35] This suggests luxury consumption, not ordinary fare, even for a bishop. The reference is to the principal fast day, a special occasion for which the salmon are to be especially good – as if, it would seem, for a feast. Fish are mentioned in a mid-eleventh-century charter concerning the bounds of Tidenham, another text that does not refer to fasting. This text declares that every other fish belongs to the lord of the manor and "all rare fish that are

[32] Florence E. Harmer, ed., *Select English Historical Documents*, pp. 1–2; see P. H. Sawyer, *Anglo-Saxon Charters*, no. 1188, pp. 349–50. See Joseph Bosworth and T. Northcote Toller, *An Anglo-Saxon Dictionary, Supplement*, p. 583.
[33] A. J. Robertson, ed., *Anglo-Saxon Charters*, pp. 39–43; Sawyer, *Anglo-Saxon Charters*, no. 385, p. 165. The *DOE* notes that the word has been less plausibly interpreted as "abundant" (*DOE, forgenge*).
[34] Sawyer, *Anglo-Saxon Charters*, no. 1497, p. 419. Dorothy Whitelock, ed., *The Will of Æthelgifu*, pp. 7–17.
[35] Sawyer, *Anglo-Saxon Charters*, no. 1381, p. 391, edited by T. Hearne, *Hemingi Cartularium Ecclesiae Wigorniensis*, pp. 190–91.

valuable, sturgeon and porpoise, herring and other sea fish" (*ælc seldsynde fisc þe weorðlic byð, styria & mereswyn, healic other sæfisc*). No fish was to be sold without the lord's permission. Note that *sæfisc* are *seldsynde* and *weorðlic*, "rare" and "valuable.[36] The texts that most explicitly link fish to fasting are the grant of Oswulf and his wife to Christ Church, and the donation to Denewulf. Both date from the ninth and early tenth century, long before the supposed stimuli for widespread use of fish in the fasting diet have been hypothesized. The latest of them, the Tidenham document, with its reference to "rare fish that are valuable," implies that the "event horizon" had not reached what is now west Gloucestershire.

What do these donations suggest about the monastic diet during seasons of fasting? Debby Banham observes that the reform forbade monks to consume meat. This seems to be a reference to the *Rule* of St. Benedict, translated into Old English in the tenth century, which restricted the consumption of four-footed animals to all but the very sick (*fiðerfete flæsc si forhæmed butan wanhalum & þa metruman*, "four-footed flesh is forbidden except for the infirm and the sick").[37] Banham emphasizes the role of fasting in increasing the demand for fish and claims that fish was "a substitute for meat" whenever meat was forbidden; she also notes that few ordinary people could have afforded fish, undercutting the likelihood that fish could have been a common food for fasting periods.[38] Cool shares Banham's view.[39] Although the *Rule* did not permit flesh to be consumed, this stipulation does not mean that fish were automatically a substitute. Hagen's claim that "the monks would have to eat fish on fast days" is also is open to question.[40] Monastic documents treat fish as a delicacy, not a staple of the diet. So far as I know, there is no text that specifies that "monks would have to eat fish on fast days," or even that they ought to do so.

Maria Dembinska's study of early monastic rules undercuts arguments linking fish consumption to fasting. According to Dembinska, "fish were originally not considered suitable for fasting, but were regarded as delicacies, *deliciae*, to be eaten only with the abbot's permission on holidays."[41] Barrett, Locker, and Roberts cite Dembinska's work without acknowledging its implications for their claims. Dembinska's study of pre-Anglo-Saxon evidence is more relevant to Anglo-Saxon conditions than the discussions by Woolgar and Serjeantson summarized above. Monastic rules in Old English, translated from Latin texts, treat fish as a delicacy. Among the important monastic texts of the tenth century carrying forward

[36] Sawyer, *Anglo-Saxon Charters*, no. 1555, p. 434, translated by Robertson, *Anglo-Saxon Charters*, no. 109, pp. 204–7.
[37] H. Logeman, ed., *The Rule of St. Benet* , ch. 39, p. 71 (*carnium vero quadrupedum omnino ab omnibus abstineatur commestio, preter omnino debiles et aegrotos*).
[38] Debby Banham, *Food and Drink in Anglo-Saxon England*, p. 64.
[39] Cool, *Eating and Drinking in Roman Britain*, p. 105, citing a popular source, Mark Kurlansky's *Cod*, p. 24.
[40] Hagen, *A Second Handbook*, p. 170.
[41] Dembinska, "Fasting and Working Monks," p. 155.

this tradition are translations of the *Rule* of Chrodegang (bishop of Metz, d. 766) and the *Capitula* of Theodulf (bishop of Orléans, d. 821). Hagen has proposed both works as models for lay regulatory texts that might have promoted fish as a fasting food.[42] The *Rule of Chrodegang* includes a chapter on moderation in the monastic diet. All monks are to have a portion of meat every evening except during fasting periods:

> In the time when they must forgo meat, including Lent, then one is to give them at the mid-day meal a good piece of cheese (in a portion to be divided into two) and some delicacy with it. If one has fish or vegetables, give it to them as a third course. And in the evening, cheese (in a portion to be divided into two) and some delicacy.

> On þam tidum þe hi sceolon flæsc forgan, ealswa on Lengtenne, þonne sylle man to middægþenunge twam and twam an tyl cyssticce and sumne smeam-ete; and gif man fisc hæbbe oððe wyrta, sylle ma him to þriddan sande; and on æfen twam and twam an cyssticce and sume smeamettas.[43]

Another chapter, although not about the Lenten fast, is relevant to fish: "But if it is a light evening meal, bread with herbs and with fruit (or legume) and meanwhile, if they also have fish, they are to consider that a great delicacy" (*Ac sy eaðelic æfenmete, hlaf mid wyrtum and mid ofæte, and amang þam gif ma fisc hæbbe, healde þæt for healicne est*).[44] Fish makes the meal notable and in both cases constitutes supplementary fare. "If they also have fish" is an important qualifier in the first case, and the second is also qualified; there being fish, they constitute "a great delicacy." These are not rules that require monks to eat fish as a fasting food.

The most informative source about the status of fish in the fasting diet is the *Capitula* of Theodulf, translated from the Latin in the tenth century. This text is found in two versions, known as A and B, and they differ somewhat in their accounts of fasting food. Both versions include fish with cheese, eggs, and wine as foods that can be given up by those wishing to undertake an "intense fast." The A version says:

> At this time there ought to be *moderation of all luxuries....* Those who in the holy season are able to forgo cheese and eggs and fish and wine, <u>that is a very great fast</u>. Those who then because of sickness or for some other cause are not able to give up these things, it is necessary for them to use them in moderation and (use them) at the time at which it is permitted, that is, after evensong.

> On þas tid sceal beon *forhæfednes gehwylcra smeametta,* .... Þa þe on þas halgan tide magon cyse & ægru & fisc & win forgan: *swiðe healic fæsten þæt bið.* Þa þonne þe for untrumnesse oððe for hwylcum oðrum þingum hit forgan ne magon, him is þearf þæt hig his gemetlice brucan & þæm tidum þe hit alyfed is, þæt is æfter þæm æfensange. (my emphasis)

---

[42] Hagen, *A Second Handbook*, p. 165.

[43] Arthur S. Napier, ed., *The Old English Version of the Enlarged Rule of Chrodegang*, p. 15. *Twam and twam* refers to a portion for two monks served in one bowl. See Dembinska, "Fasting and Working Monks," p. 154. The passage is translated in Hagen, *A Handbook*, p. 121.

[44] Napier, *The Old English Version of the Enlarged Rule of Chrodegang*, p. 69, taking *ma* as "further" or "in addition to."

The B version differs:

> Moderation on these days shall indeed pertain *to almost all delicacies (luxuries)*, ... He who truly abstains from eggs and cheese and butter and fish and wine, *he is of great virtue.*

> Forhæfdnes soðlice on ðysum dagum sceal beon *forneah ealra esta*, ... Se þe soðlic fram ægrum and cyse and buteran and fixum and wine forhæbban mæg, *he is myceles mægenes.* (my emphasis)[45]

Whereas the A version comments on the quality of the fast (*healic fæsten*) the B version comments on the merits of the faster (*he is myceles mægenes*, "he is of great virtue"). The phrases in both versions translate the Latin *magne uirtutis est*. Abstaining from eggs, cheese, fish, and wine seems to be something only the very virtuous would do. In both versions the next sentence exempts the sick and those who "for some other reason" (*for hwylcum oðrum þingum*) are unable to fast, suggesting that most monks were expected to forgo eggs, cheese, butter, and fish in fasting time. Moreover, both versions include fish among delicacies (*smeametta* in A, *esta* in B). The translator of the A text adds that "drunkenness from wine and sinful desires are to be avoided, not milk and cheese" (*Wines druncennes ond synlustas synt forbodene, næs meoloc ne cyse*); the B version refers to milk and eggs rather than milk and cheese (*Soþlice wines and ælces wætan druncennes and galnes synt forbodene, næs meoluc and ægru*).[46] Neither version mentions fish except as a food to be abstained from by those wishes to observe a strict fast.

Healic could be translated as "principal" rather than "great" or "noble." Version A's *swiðe healic* presents a difficulty perhaps resolved with "a most principal feast." According to the *Rule* of St. Benedict the superior could not be excused from a *healic* fast: "The superior may break his fast for the sake of a guest, unless it happens to be a principal fast day which may not be violated; the brothers, however, keep the customary fast" (*Abrece se ealdor his fæsten for cumena þingum, butan hit hwylc healic fæsten sy, þe man abrecan ne dyrre; þa gebroðra healdan þeahhweþere hyra fæsten æfter gewunan*).[47] This pairing of the elevated and the ordinary, the *healic fæsten* and the *fæsten æfter gewunan*, or fast according to custom or use, is not made in the *Capitula* of Theodulf but is perhaps the distinction implied. It seems clear that in the *Rule* of Chrodegang and the *Capitula* of Theodulf fish was regarded as a delicacy and that it was to be given up in the chief fasting seasons, certainly during Lent. It seems reasonable to suggest that fish was more likely to be eaten during feasts than during fasts. Alternately, however, in a reading that supports arguments for the growing importance of fish in the fasting diet, this stipulation could mean that eggs, cheese, and fish were fasting foods and that those keeping a strict fast should avoid them. Given the commonly accepted view that to exclude

---

[45] Hans Sauer, ed., *Theodulfi Capitula in England*, ch. 40, p. 391 (both versions).
[46] Sauer, *Theodulfi Capitula in England*, ch. 40, p. 391 (both versions).
[47] Arnold Schröer, ed., *The Rule of St. Benedict*, ch. 53, p. 83.

meat is to include fish, the absence of clear and unambiguous references pertaining to fish as a fasting food is important. My conclusion is that fish was a delicacy, not a regular part of the diet in or out of fasting periods.

If Lent is a time when one does not eat meat, what, then, does one eat? One possibility lies in the word *hwit* (literally "white"), said to mean that "white foods (cheese, eggs, fish) [were] allowed when meat was forbidden."[48] The word occurs in the *OE Introduction*, which serves as a preface to two of the vernacular penitentials: *Fæst ælce dæge on ðis lenctene to nones and forgang hwit* ("Fast every day this Lenten period to *nones* [i.e., 3 p.m.] and abstain from *hwit*").[49] *Hwit* is also found in a text for the confessor in London, British Library, MS Cotton Tiberius C.i: "And forgo *hwit* on Holy Thursday unless sickness prevent [it], so that you may not forgo it or fast as I have now said" (*And forga hwit æt þunresdæg nyhst eastran butan þe untrumnys forwyrne þæt þu hit forgan ne mæge ne swa fæstan swa ic þe nu gesæd habbe*).[50] A homily in this same manuscript also refers to *hwit*: "We then ask of those who have sinned that they fast every day until *nones*, have one meal except on Sunday, and forgo *hwit*" (*Þonne beode we þam mannum þe forwyrhta habbað, þæt hi fæstan ælce dæg oð non, and to anes mæles butan þam halgan sunnandæge, and forgan hwit*). A pseudo-Wulfstan homily contains a similar direction: "Fast every day to *nones* and [have] only one meal except on Sunday, and forgo *hwit*" (*Fæst nu ælc dæge to nones and to anes meles buton sunnandæg, and forga hwit*).[51] In each of these five instances, the verb used with *hwit* is *forgangan*, that is, "to forgo or abstain from." In these sources, *hwit* indicates what the penitent is *not* to eat. In no case does a text prescribe a diet of *hwit* for the one who fasts.

An Anglo-Saxon Dictionary, Supplement, by Joseph Bosworth and T. Northcote Toller, seems to be responsible for getting fish onto the list of *hwit* foods as well as for defining *hwit* incorrectly as what is eaten rather than what is abstained from. The *Supplement* quotes the grant to Christ Church, Canterbury, 805 x 815, by Oswulf and his wife (discussed above). The text permits the substitution of cheese, fish, butter, and eggs for gifts of meat on a fast day as opposed to a fowl day: "one is to give them a measure of cheese, fish, butter, and eggs" (*selle mon uuẹge cæsa, & fisces & butran & aegera*).[52] Cheese, fish, butter, and eggs are grouped, but not in a phrase that defines any of them as *hwit*, a word not found in this grant. The instructions to forgo *hwit* do not name food groups, and the text that names food groups does not call them *hwit*. It seems reasonable to conclude that the term *hwit* has no probable, much less necessary, relationship to fish.

---

[48] Bosworth and Toller, *An Anglo-Saxon Dictionary, Supplement*, p. 583.

[49] Frantzen, *ASP, OEI*, S31.06.02. In London, British Library, MS Cotton Tiberius A.iii, the expression occurs in an extract from the *Introduction* on fol. 54v (*OEI*, N31.06.92). See also Hans Sauer, "Zwei Spätaltenglishe Beichtermahnungen."

[50] Neil R. Ker, "Three Old English Texts in a Salisbury Pontifical, Cotton Tiberius C.I," pp. 262–79.

[51] Arthur S. Napier, ed., *Wulfstan: Sammlung der ihm zugeschriebenen Homilien*, pp. 289–91.

[52] Bosworth and Toller, *An Anglo-Saxon Dictionary, Supplement*, p. 583. The charter is Sawyer no. 1188, early ninth century; see Sawyer, *Anglo-Saxon Charters*, pp. 349–50.

However, it is very important that *hwit* includes eggs, cheese, and butter, all foods which, along with fish and wine, the *Capitula* of Theodulf classifies as delicacies not to consumed during a principal fast. In the matter of the fasting diet, then, it seems untenable to argue that the use of fish as a fasting food passed from monastic to lay regulatory literature. It is clear that in the monastic literature fish is not a fasting food but a delicacy. It is highly unlikely that fish, which was, thanks to food renders, easier to get in a monastery than outside of it, was a fasting food among lay people if monks were not permitted to have it during seasons of fasting.

Fasting is the chief form of penance in the penitentials, fairly constant as a percentage of the canons across the corpus. About one-half of the penances in a given handbook require fasting and about one-half require some other form of sacrifice (prayer, almsgiving) or do not require a penance but rather state a decision about, for example, contaminated food.[53] The standard fast in the penitentials consists of bread and water; meat is always forbidden. A typical reference, taken from the *OE Handbook*, reads: "If someone pollute himself willingly, he is to fast for three years on each of the three forty-day periods on bread and water and forgo meat every day except Sunday" (*Gyf hwa hine silfne besmite his agenes willes fæste iii gear on ælcon iii xl daga on hlafe & on wætere & forga flæsc ælce dæg buton sunnandæge*).[54] The penitentials, as we have seen, supply penances for both laity and clergy, including monks. Fish is never named as a fasting food in the penitentials, and the texts do not substitute fish for meat. Sources that concern lay people's fasting do not address foodstuffs in detail comparable to that found in the monastic rules. Texts regulating the fasting diet for the laity refer to bread and water, with some variation, as we saw in the last chapter. Indeed, fish is mentioned only one time in only one vernacular handbook, the *OE Penitential*, and then in reference to eating dead fish (permitted if the fish was found in a stream, but not in a pond).[55]

It is clear that the government and the Church greatly increased attention to fasting and feasting in the period Barrett, Locker, and Roberts examine. But the link between fasting and fish consumption cannot be documented in the textual sources from the period. Fish are not regarded as a substitute for meat in any of the texts written in the late (eleventh-century) period, nor do texts that discuss the fast in detail – including provisions in the *OE Handbook* related to commutations – refer to fish.

---

[53] In the *Scriftboc* there are 92 references to fasting out of 202 canons, or 45 percent; in the *Canons of Theodore* there are 65 references to fasting out of 141 canons or 46 percent. In the *OE Penitential*, probably written in the second half of the tenth century, there are 84 references to fasting out of 162 canons, or 52 percent, roughly the same as in the *OE Handbook*, which has 45 references to fasting out of 88 canons, or 51 percent.

[54] Frantzen, *ASP, OEH*, D54.34.01.

[55] Frantzen, *ASP, OEP*, Y44.26.01: "If anyone find a dead fish in a fishpond and he eats it, he is to fast 4 weeks on Wednesdays and Fridays on bread and water and the other days forgo meat. And if one finds a dead fish in a stream, he may partake of it lawfully" (*Gif hwa finde deadne fisc on fiscpole & he his bruce· fæste ·iiii· wican wodnesdagum && frige dagum on hlafe & on wætere. & þa oðre dagas for ga flæsc. & gif hwa finde deadne fisc on ea bruce his man be leafe*).

There is, then, scant textual evidence to connect fish consumption to Lent, even on a modest scale, in the Anglo-Saxon period. Indeed, there is significant archaeological evidence to the contrary. Fish consumption in the mid-eleventh century was conspicuous at the site of Westminster Abbey. The Abbey, which James Rackham describes as "one of the richest in the London area," yielded nineteen species of marine fish, over three-quarters of the fish bones. At other Strand sites marine species accounted for less than 10 percent of the bones; over eleven species of wild bird were consumed at the Abbey, another sign of its wealth. The rising tide of marine fish, so to speak, did not lift all boats. The Abbey's concentration of wealth is apparent in its sea fish-rich diet, a vivid contrast to the sea fish-poor sites nearby.[56]

If fish became more plentiful in the late Anglo-Saxon period, it was not, I conclude, because the Church's fasting requirements had increased demand. Given the modern association of fish with the Friday fast, it is easy to understand that scholars might assume that more laws requiring fasting would produce an increase in the consumption of fish – provided that there were also evidence that fish was a regular, much less a mandatory, part of the fasting diet. To require fish as part of the fasting diet would have been a significant and expensive change. More fasting does not necessarily mean increased consumption of fish. Likewise, increased consumption of fish does not necessarily mean that people were fasting more than they had fasted before. Robin Fleming concludes that freshwater fish "was primarily eaten by the aristocracy," and that sea fish was for "the very rich." Monks, "with their fish dinners," she observes, wanted "to eat like thegns." Her view is that "marine species begin to appear in great numbers in the archaeological record only in the decades before the Norman Conquest, and they are closely associated with high-status sites."[57] Fish was not in demand because the Church was insisting that lay people should fast; fish was in demand because the wealthy could afford it and sought the status it conferred. They probably did so before the Conquest, as the data compiled by the data Barrett, Locker, and Roberts suggest.

Fleming's comments on the social aspirations of fish-eating monks give us a fine opportunity to turn to a small group of fish-eating priests working in what I take to be an urban setting where fish might be more available than elsewhere. They enjoy wine, fish, and oysters during a season of fasting in which they should have abstained from all three. Most unusually, these clerics afford us a chance to see Anglo-Saxons not only eating but having a good time, although in a season when they should not be doing either.

[56] James Rackham, "Economy and Environment in Saxon London," in Rackham, ed., *Environment and Economy*, pp. 132–33.

[57] Robin Fleming, "The New Wealth, the New Rich, and New Political Style in Anglo-Saxon England" pp. 5–7, citing James Rackham's work with Westminster Abbey, p. 5, n. 24. See also Fleming, *Britain after Rome*, pp. 298–99. The work by Barrett, Locker, and Roberts is included in the book's bibliography but not factored into the conclusions.

11

Conclusion: Anglo-Saxons at the Table

"The Seasons for Fasting," fish, and clerical discipline

One of the subjects of this book is the importance of coordinating textual and material evidence of food culture. Few texts about food are poems, making "The Seasons for Fasting" a rarity. The poem is cited by James H. Barrett, Alison M. Locker, and Callum M. Roberts as evidence of the "fish event horizon" discussed in the last chapter.[1] I suggest that the poem should be read as an example of estates literature and grouped with other texts that lament the loss of old ways and criticize new ones. "The Seasons for Fasting" addresses a controversy about the fasting periods known as Ember days, three-day fasts that were assigned to each of the seasons of the year, the *quattor anni tempora*. The poem sets out two traditions for determining the Ember fasts. One places the fasts in the first week of Lent, the week following Whitsunday, the week before the autumn equinox, and the week before Christmas. The poem endorses another method that specifies the first week of March, the second week of June, the third week of September, and the week before Christmas (ll. 39–102). The latter plan was established by Gregory the Great (l. 94); the alternative tradition is dismissed as "Frankish," *bryttan Franca* (l. 87).[2]

Chadwick B. Hilton asserts that the dates of the Ember observance changed as part of the monastic reforms of the late tenth century and argues that the poem takes a "nationalistic stance" on the appropriate times for fasting.[3] Ælfric's *De ieiunio quattuor tempora* follows the pattern criticized by the poet, and so does a text in Oxford, Bodleian Library, MS Laud Misc. 482, an important eleventh-century manuscript containing

---

[1] "The Seasons for Fasting," in Elliott van Kirk Dobbie, ed., *The Anglo-Saxon Minor Poems*, pp. 98–104; all references are to this edition, with line number given. James H. Barrett, Alison M. Locker, and Callum M. Roberts, "'Dark Age Economics' Revisited," pp. 629–30; Debby Banham, *Food and Drink in Anglo-Saxon England*, pp. 64–65.

[2] Dobbie, ed., *The Anglo-Saxon Minor Poems*, p. xciii, n. 4. Kenneth Sisam, "The Seasons for Fasting," argues that *bryttan Franca* should read *Bryttan oððe Franca*, i.e., Breton or Frankish; see Sisam, *Studies*, p. 55.

[3] See Chadwick B. Hilton, "The Old English *Season for Fasting*," and Hugh Magennis, *Anglo-Saxon Appetites*, pp. 85–92 and 135–37.

penitentials and prayers.[4] References to the "Frankish" tradition are "in a minority," according to Kenneth Sisam, but Ælfric's support would suggest that the matter was unsettled.[5] The poem's reference to Gregory the Great might be a clue to its date. The law code known as VI Æthelred (issued in 1008) urges the observance of feasts and fasts in accordance "with the highest standards of the past," meaning as they were observed by those who observed them best, and cites Gregory as the origin of the custom.[6] The manuscript of the poem was destroyed in the Cotton library fire of 1731; the text is known through two transcriptions, one encompassing only the first seven lines (by Humphrey Wanley, published in 1705), the other by Laurence Nowell, made in the mid-sixteenth century.[7] The now-lost manuscript contained a copy of the Old English version of Bede's *Ecclesiastical History* as well as a copy of the Parker Chronicle, and laws. The poem was placed after a collection of texts about hides and before a collection of recipes, contents ranging from the mid-tenth century to the first half of the eleventh century.[8]

"The Seasons for Fasting" is unusual in its lay-centered point of view and its vigorous anticlerical satire. Most writing about the behavior of the clergy is addressed to the clergy by their superiors, not addressed to the laity, *folces mann*, about the clergy, as this poem is (l. 208). The focus shifts to the present only in the last quarter of its 230 lines. The poet urges that, like Christ himself, the faithful should fast "to the ninth hour" (*oþ þa nigoþan tid*, elsewhere *non*, the ninth hour, i.e., three o'clock) and abstain from meat and from sins (*he na bruce flæsces oþþe fyrna*, ll. 182-83). Fasting draws the priest closer to God so that he may be "a friend to people throughout the world" and hear their confessions (ll. 184–91). An intercessor who can plead on behalf of another (*þingan*), he must be able to approach the Lord without fear, which he cannot do if he has sinned and not repented (ll. 195–98). The speaker warns the lay person to behave honorably even if the priest does not, and to profit from the priest's instruction. "Let him drink muddy water from the wayside; let the pure water of divine teaching benefit [you]" (the Old English is confused: *drince he him þæt drofe duge hlutter þe wæter of weg þæt is wuldres lar*, ll. 206–7).[9] The reason for this disclaimer becomes clear in the description of drinking priests that follows. The author attacks priests as a class, *sacerdas* (i.e., priests, plural at ll. 184,

---

[4] For the contents of Oxford, Bodleian Library, MS Laud Misc. 482, fol. 27b, see Frantzen, *ASP*, Manuscripts, Description for this manuscript (in Table 1, search Y81.01.01) .
[5] Sisam, "Seasons for Fasting," p. 49.
[6] For VI Æthelred 23, see F. Liebermann, *GDA*, p. 252; A. J. Robertson, *LKE*, pp. 98–99. See Sisam, "Seasons for Fasting," p. 50, n. 3, on the use of this phrase in a homily associated with Wulfstan. Gregory is also mentioned in Alfred's code but not in reference to the Ember fasts. For Alfred 43, see Liebermann, *GDA*, p. 78, and Robertson, *LKE*, pp. 84–85.
[7] Scholarship on the poem is reviewed by Magennis, *Anglo-Saxon Appetites*, pp. 85–86. See also Sisam, "Seasons for Fasting," *passim*.
[8] N. R. Ker, *Catalogue of Manuscripts Containing Anglo-Saxon*, art. 180, pp. 230–34. The poem is listed as item 10 in London, British Library, MS Additional 43703.
[9] I accept Sisam's emendation of the transcription, "Seasons for Fasting," pp. 56–57; see further Magennis, *Anglo-Saxon Appetites*, pp. 136–37.

193, and 209), not one wayward priest (singular at l. 200). Immediately after Mass, the Eucharistic meal of Christ's body and blood, priests are said to be both consumed with thirst and compelled by it. They follow a tapster (*tæppere*) through the streets (along which, no doubt, dirty water ran), a detail that suggests an urban setting. *Stræt* has many meanings in Old English, from road to path to street, but *tæppere* does not: it means wine-seller:

> Lo! Falsely they begin to lie. They constantly exhort the wine-merchant, say that without sin he would be able to provide oysters for food and fine wine in the morning. It seems to me that the dog and wolf carry on the same way in this world and do not know when they will eat next. So they seize food without restraint. Then, sitting, they begin to satisfy themselves, bless the wine, pour [it] often, say "Good day" to passersby, explain that they have tired themselves [*meþig þicgan*, loosely rendered as "become tired"] by saying Mass, and can eat oysters and other fish from the waters.

> Hwæt! Hi leaslice   leogan ongynnað
> and þone tæppere   tyhtaþ gelome,
> secgaþ þæt he synleas   syllan mote
> ostran to æte   and æþele wyn
> emb morgentyd,   þæs þe me þingeð
> þæt hund and wulf   healdað þa ilcan
> wisan on worulde   and ne wigliað
> hwæne hie to mose fon,   mæða bedæled.
> Hi þonne sittende   sadian aginnað,
> winne semað,   syllað gelome,
> cweðað goddlife   gumena gehwilcum
> þæt wines dreng   welhwa mote,
> siþþan he mæssan hafað,   meþig þicgan,
> etan ostran eac   and oþerne
> fisc of flode.   (ll. 216–30)[10]

The satirist mocks the priests by suggesting that thirst compels them to tag after the wine seller, *æfter tæppere teoþ geond stræta* (l. 215). Using the same verb, *teon*, which means "to draw," the author shows that the priests not only follow the *tæppere* but try to educate him. The phrase *þonne tæppere tyhtaþ* might be translated as "then instruct the wine-merchant," but "seduce" is also an appropriate choice, since these priests teach falsely and misleadingly. Sisam notes that the priests mislead their followers, the *folces manna* (the laity), *mid æfeste* ("with neglect of religious law").[11] They assert that they can do what they wish *synleas* (without sin), *emb morgentyd* (in the morning), but their wishes seem to go against the merchant's better judgment. He should know when Christians may drink and dine on fast days, since these were matters of law. The *OE Introduction* instructs

[10] Dobbie emends the manuscript reading, *win semað*, to *sinne semað*, admitting that it "leaves much to be desired" (*The Anglo-Saxon Minor Poems*, p. 198). I follow Sisam in giving *winne semað*, i.e., bless the wine; see "Seasons of Fasting," p. 58; see also Magennis, *Anglo-Saxon Appetites*, p. 90.
[11] Sisam, "Seasons of Fasting," p. 57.

the penitent to "Fast every day this Lenten period to *none* [i.e., 3 p.m.] and abstain from *hwit*" (*Fæst ælce dæge on ðis lenctene to nones and forgang hwit*).[12] The laws of Edgar (959–63) specify that the Sunday feast begins at *nontid* on Saturday (3 p.m.) and lasts until dawn Monday (*healde man ælces Sunnandæges freols fram nontide þæs Sæternesdæges oð ðæs Monandæges lihtinge*).[13] The same requirement appears in Cnut's code of 1020 and in I Cnut.[14] The so-called "treaty of Edward and Guthrum," one of Wulfstan's tracts, assesses a fine "if the priest misinformed the people about the time of a feast or a fast" (*gif mæssepreost folc miswyssige æt freolse oððe æt fæstene*).[15] The priests cannot wait to eat and are compared to dogs and wolves when they seize their food (ll. 221–23). Food ought to be blessed before being eaten. Instead, the priests "bless the wine," *win semað*, a blasphemous gesture in a tavern, especially soon after Mass, and "pour [it] often" or "repeatedly," *syllað gelome*. As they greet passersby, the priests excuse their indulgence by saying that their Mass duties have worn them out. They claim that they deserve to eat "oysters and other fish from the waters" (l. 230).[16] Just when we might learn more about the fish themselves, whether freshwater or marine, the poem ends, *fisc of flode* comprising its unfinished last line.[17] These fish could be either freshwater or marine, since *flode* refers to both environments. If marine, then perhaps herring would be a likely choice; the possibilities of freshwater fish are much greater.

The breakfast described in "The Seasons for Fasting" is the opposite of the strict fast recommended in the *Capitula* of Theodulf, which required that both fish and wine be given up.[18] The priests' meal is gluttonous, not only untimely but public, set in what seems to be a wine – and perhaps also a fish – shop. The *Capitula* says that priests "should not eat and drink at ale-stalls or benches" (*ne sceolon mæssepreostas æt ceapealeðelum ne etan ne drincan*).[19] The Church was concerned not only with fasting but with the appearance of fasting, which is to say that the practice created identity for the fasters in their own minds and in the eyes of the communities around them. Texts for the instruction and regulation of the clergy such as Wulfstan's *Institutes of Polity* stress the importance of the clergy's appearance. Bishops "must set an example [*bysnian*] of the spiritual duty of a

---

[12] Frantzen, *ASP, OEI*, S31.06.02.

[13] For II Edgar 5, see Liebermann, *GDA*, p. 198; Robertson, *LKE*, pp. 22–23.

[14] For Cnut 1020, c. 18, see Liebermann, *GDA*, p. 275; Robertson, *LKE*, pp. 144–45. The text of I Cnut 14.2 is verbatim; Liebermann, *GDA*, p. 294; Robertson, *LKE*, pp. 166–67 (*man Sunnandæges freols mid eallum mægene healde & weorðige fram Sæternesdæges none oð Monandæges lyhtinge*).

[15] For Edward and Guthrum 3.1, see Liebermann, *GDA*, p. 130; F. L. Attenborough, *LEEK*, pp. 102–5.

[16] "Flod" could refer to fish from a channel, a pond, a river, or perhaps the sea. See Angus Cameron *et al.*, *Dictionary of Old English*.

[17] The poem was already incomplete when it was transcribed in the modern era; see Ker, *Catalogue of Manuscripts Containing Anglo-Saxon*, art. 10, p. 232.

[18] Hans Sauer, ed., *Theodulfi Capitula in England*, ch. 40, p. 391.

[19] Translating *neque per tabernas eatis bibendo aut comedendo*; Sauer, *Theodulfi Capitula in England*, ch. 13, p. 319.

Christian nation," Wulfstan wrote, and priests must "set a good example [*wel bysnian*] to others."[20] Clergy were not to linger in alehouses: "And indeed it does not become a bishop ever in an alehouse that he stick to the bench, nor remain too long at home, or on the road, but to moderate both" (*And huru ne geriseð biscopum æfre on ænigum ealasele, þæt hy to lange clyfian on bænce ne æt ham ne on siðe, ac ægðer gemedmigan*).[21] Wulfstan's *Canons of Edgar* does not deny the priest the occasional drink but rules out excessive joviality. The priest was warned to avoid getting drunk and also to discourage drunkenness in others.[22] He was to be wise and honorable at all times, and not to be an alehouse singer (*ealusceop*) nor "in any way to make merry with himself or other people (*ne on ænige wisan gliwigeb mid him sylfum oðrum mannum*).[23] Drinking wine and eating fish in a fasting period established a visible and strongly negative situational identity for the priests – if it were situational, that is, rather than occupational and routine.

Barrett, Locker, and Roberts believe that the poem's reference to oysters (mentioned twice) and fish supports their claim about fish and the fasting diet, but it seems unwise to put too much confidence in "The Seasons for Fasting" as support for arguments for or against the place of fish in the fasting diet. Whatever the fasting rules in effect at the time of the poem, they clearly forbad eating and drinking in the morning. The priests go wrong, Barrett, Locker, and Roberts believe, by eating before they were permitted to break their fast; the issue, in their view, is when the priests eat, not what they consume. It is important, as Hugh Magennis and others note, that the Old English term for this offense, *ær-æt*, "early eating," is found in a range of anonymous homilies and confessional prayers, always in a list that includes gluttony or drunkenness (*ealugalnesse, oferdruncennessa, galness; DOE, ær-æt*). The poem also emphasizes their fondness for wine, oysters, and fish. As we have seen, monastic documents treat fish as a feasting food, not as part of the fasting diet (see Chapter 10). Priests so callous as to drink wine in the presence of parishioners before the proper time would hardly eat fish merely because fish were appropriate to a fast. It seems probable that the clerics enjoy fish, as they enjoy wine, as one of the finer things to which their taxing labors entitle them, seasons of fasting be damned. In the context of estates satire, the poem's use of fish and wine makes better sense if the men of the Church are both eating at the wrong time and also consuming luxuries, a gesture of double defiance. Estates satire traditionally points to a decline from formerly high standards, as we saw in the tract on status known as *Geþyncðu*, which evokes an age in which "councillors of the people were entitled to honour, each according

---

[20] Karl Jost, ed. and trans., *Die "Institutes of Polity, Civil and Ecclesiastical,"* ch. 60, p. 68; ch. 102, p. 85.
[21] "Ermahnung an die Bischöfe," quoted from Jost, *Die "Institutes of Polity,"* pp. 262–67.
[22] Roger Fowler, *Wulfstan's Canons of Edgar*, c. 60, p. 15.
[23] Fowler, *Wulfstan's Canons of Edgar*, c. 59, p. 15.

to his rank."[24] "The Seasons for Fasting" is bitter rather than melancholy or nostalgic, but there is no doubt that its aim was, as Patrick Wormald describes that of *Geþyncðu*, to "restore past proprieties," in this case by observing a regulation dating from the arrival of Augustine, Gregory's messenger, in Canterbury in 597.[25] Like other estates texts, the poem makes a good case for social order. Wine-sellers ought to obey the law, priests even more so.The laws and status tracts give us the clergy's view of the ranking laity, those moving up in the social world. The poem gives us the laity's view of the clergy, a group of dissolute priests who are not "entitled to honour" but who seize pride of place for themselves and constitute a group, in the author's view, on its way down.

Food things and "The Seasons for Fasting"

"The Seasons for Fasting" represents food-loving Anglo-Saxons, not merely drinkers, making it a good place to end an inquiry into words and things having to do with food. As the priests enjoy their bit of heaven on earth, we can take a look around the alehouse. I imagine them on benches gathered at a table. We seldom find people at the table in Old English texts, and if they have food rather than drink before them the scene is rarer still. In Riddle 46, Lot sits *æt wine* with his two wives and his two daughters, those women and their (and his) two sons each in double relationships with Lot who, *æt wine* himself after the destruction of Sodom, had sex with his daughters. Riddle 42 also mixes sex and alcohol. Through "runic letters" (*runstafas*) the assembled warriors will learn the names of two creatures "playing openly at love" (*ute plegan hæmedlaces*), the cock and the hen, when their names are "revealed to the men as they drink (*nu is undyrne werum æt wine*).[26] Documenting examples of the preposition *æt* (at) that refer "especially to a table at which a meal is eaten," the *Dictionary of Old English* supplies eight quotations, only one of which concerns a diner – in this case, the king of the Vandals – instead of a drinker.[27] The *DOE* entries for *beod*, meaning table, sometimes even furnish food – or not. The cook in *The Colloquy* notes that without his labor "every table would seem empty" (*butan cræfte minon ælc beod æmtig byþ gesewen*.)[28] The cheesemaker in *Rectitudines Personarum Singularum* makes butter "for the lord's table" (*to hlafordes beode*).[29] In the poem, the priests are not said to be *æt wine*, but

---

[24] Liebermann, *GDA*, p. 356: *þa wæron þeodwitan wurðscipes wurðe, ælc be his mæðe*; translation from Dorothy Whitelock, ed., *EHD*, p. 468.

[25] Patrick Wormald, *MEL*, pp. 393–94.

[26] See Riddle 46, ll. 1–2 (Lot), and Riddle 42, ll. 15–17 (cock and hen), in *The Exeter Book*, ed. George Philip Krapp and Elliott van Kirk Dobbie, pp. 204–5.

[27] *DOE* æt, sense I.B.2. For the passage, see Hans Hecht, ed., *Bischof Waerferths von Worcester Übersetzung der Dialoge Gregors des Grossen*, book 3, ch. 1, pp. 181–82. Elsewhere, in monastic texts, *on beoderne*, "in the refectory," is translated *ad mensam*, "at table." See *DOE*, *beodern*, "refectory" (sense a).

[28] G. N. Garmonsway, ed., *Ælfric's Colloquy*, p. 36, ll. 188–89.

[29] Michael Swanton, *Anglo-Saxon Prose*, p. 29; Liebermann, *GDA*, p. 448, para. 6.

like other feasters they enjoy some fare that is out of the ordinary, including fish, oysters, and wine, and it is safe to say that they are at table as they do so.

What did an Anglo-Saxon tavern look like? We know something about church interiors (and even their measurements) and about halls, but, so far as I know, nothing about taverns and alehouses.[30] "The Seasons of Fasting" requires us to furnish the tavern with a table and alebenches to which, as Wulfstan would have it, the clerics' behinds are unbecomingly stuck. We can set the table with a wooden tray or bowl for oysters, another for their shells, and wooden cups for drinking the wine from the pitcher that they bless and pour from liberally.[31] Perhaps the priests, like the monks of the *Monasteriales Indicia*, cut open their own oysters, so we would add a special knife for this purpose.[32] The oysters might have been kept in a barrel and doled out by the shopkeeper who tracked purchases on a wax tablet, or by notching a stick with a knife worn on his belt. Other food might have been on hand, including bread from the bakehouse served with *gesufle* (cooked vegetables) and soup. Since they hail passersby, the priests' bench and table might have been located outside the shop, although on a chilly spring day they more likely watched the townspeople come and go from inside the shop, close to a fire over which a kettle hung suspended from a chain, with cooking pots below bubbling on a trivet. Oil and spices might have been nearby, kept in jars with wooden stoppers, part of a pantry overseen by a cook with whom the priests would keep up bawdy banter. Perhaps, as Wulfstan seems to have suspected, they even broke into song. This being the Middle Ages, we should also supply a pair of hungry dogs milling around and fighting for the occasional scrap. Eventually, coins would change hands and the priests would head off, although not before stepping out to the privy.

However humble, the tavern was a node in a regional food network. To find the tavern, the priests followed a tapster through the streets. Along with foot traffic, carts laden with goods would have traveled up and down the same streets. The tavern keeper's wine and fish might have come from distant sources. But wooden bowls, cups, and plates would have been locally made, and so too pots and ironwork. The wine jar or pitcher, a specialized form, might in an earlier time have come from Ipswich and have been used to ship the wine. When the fisherman of *The Colloquy* says that he sells his fish in town (*on caestra*) to town-dwellers (*caesterwara*), he reminds us that purveyors looked to commercial centers to market their products.[33] Adriaan Verhulst has remarked that "the location of a fish market denotes one of the oldest urban nuclei," suggesting, Barrett, Locker, and Roberts note, "the possible relationship between urbanism,

[30] Paul Meyvaert, "Bede and the Church-paintings at Wearmouth-Jarrow."
[31] See Magennis, *Anglo-Saxon Appetites*, p. 89, on the emended line *win seniað, syllað gelome*, "bless the wine, pour it freely."
[32] Debby Banham, *Monasteriales Indicia*, pp. 34–35, no. 72.
[33] Garmonsway, *Ælfric's Colloquy*, p. 27, ll. 97–99.

fishing and fish trade."[34] It makes sense to set "The Seasons for Fasting" in a market town, its transient feel an advantage for clerics who show little regard for their reputation. Some traders and foreign merchants would not have known that the carousers were supposedly holy men.

"The Seasons for Fasting" could also be set in or near any one of several kinds of Anglo-Saxon settlements. An urban atmosphere seems plausible, but these priests would stand out no matter where they lived. Settlements thought to be "rural" could be as small and agricultural as West Stow and Mucking, for example (fifth to seventh centuries), or as extensive and complex as Flixborough, a "rural" settlement inhabited from the sixth to the twelfth centuries. West Stow and Mucking were in the hinterland and so might have been the center of their own small food networks, contributing renders to the Church or the local lord. Mucking also had strategic importance and might have been a point at which trade and defensive considerations merged, an example of a small site with several contemporary identities.[35] "Rural" does not mean "small," only that "the site was a net producer of agricultural resources rather than a net consumer."[36] Localities balanced the other way – consuming more foodstuffs than they produced – would be more suitable for the priests. Places regarded as "urban" include not only London and York but smaller market centers as well. They shared features with settlements we think of as distinctively rural. In some periods York and other densely settled areas were somewhat independent of their hinterlands for food, as Terence O'Connor has shown; some residents raised their own goats and geese and obtained fish from York's rivers.[37]

The food network linked not only countryside to town but church to tavern. The poem sketches what Chris Loveluck might call a "theatre" for eating and drinking and hence for displaying identity, both social and occasional.[38] However unedifying, the poem's tavern feast counts as conspicuous consumption, a modest version of celebrations seen in *Beowulf* or events held at Goltho and other sites of elite culture. In the spirit of their times, the priests ape their betters, although they are compared to other animals, to dogs and wolves (ll. 221–23), predators that did not contribute to the food supply but rather contaminated it (neither dogs nor wolves were eaten; they killed livestock and game). "'The kingdom of God is not eating and drinking,' but righteousness and peace and joy in the Holy Spirit," warns the *Capitula of Theodulf*, quoting Romans 14:17. This ninth-century Carolingian reform text, known in a tenth-century English translation,

---

[34] See Barrett, Locker, and Roberts, "'Dark Age Economics' Revisited," p. 630. They quote Adriaan Verhulst, *The Rise of Cities in North-West Europe*, p. 84.

[35] On Mucking's connections, see Sue Hirst, "Mucking/East Tilbury: Lower Thames Meeting Place and Mart in Early and Middle Saxon Periods?"

[36] Terence O'Connor, "8th–11th Century Economy and Environment in York," p. 139.

[37] O'Connor, "8th–11th Century Economy and Environment in York," pp. 143–45.

[38] Christopher Loveluck, *Rural Settlement*, pp. 31–74, where social display is a running feature in the analysis of the built environment at Flixborough. For the reference to the hall as a theater, see p. 149.

continues : "Some people believe that true love (*caritatem*) is to be found in food and drink, but it is not so." Rather, "there where people give food and drink for the true love of God, that is truly God's work and it is counted among other holy works" (*Ðonne wenað sume men þæt on mete ond on drence sy soð lufu, þonne nis hit na swa. Be þon cwæð se apostol: "Godes rice nis hyt naðer ne mete ne drync." Ac þeah þær þær mon mete ond drync for soðre Godes lufan seleð, hyt bið swiðe god weorc, ond hit bið gemong oðrum halgum weorcum geteald*).[39] The priests are not concerned with acts of charity or with feeding others, as were the penitents discussed in relation to commutations in the *OE Handbook* (see Chapter 9, pp. 227–28). Dispensing food as charity was a function of the food network the clerics disdain, and in this regard they are like Chaucer's lively, likeable, and yet contemptible Friar Hubert, who "knew well the taverns in every town, and every innkeeper and barmaid, better than the lepers or a women beggars."[40]

Like Hubert, the priests are doing what others in the community probably would have done if they had the opportunity – settling in for a good time, basking in the envy of onlookers. If there is a more vigorous and less ceremonious representation of dining in Old English I am unaware of it. Nor, for that matter, is there a better representation of the way in which a food network can demystify the illusion of power that is preserved by the social pyramid. Passersby would be working at that hour, not drinking, and probably engaged in labor more tiring than saying Mass. The partying priests are underemployed. Their scandal is that they sit atop a food pyramid without having earned a place there. The pyramid is an illusion, and if we flatten it into a network, we can see that the priests offend their society as much their religion. All lines in food networks flow two ways. The priests seem connected to the network only as consumers, not producers, receiving without giving and collecting without contributing. Like Chaucer's Pardoner, they take something (offerings, including food) and give nothing (defective absolution).[41] It is clear to everybody that they are parasites.

"The Seasons for Fasting": art and politics

The workings of a local economy are visible in "The Seasons for Fasting." Over that material network lay another spun of laws and custom, some of them preserved in texts, including webs of the law, which specified the hours at which fasting began and ended. Penitential canons and pastoral letters directed the clergy's conduct, and so did other texts, all of them flouted by these men. Wulfstan, Ælfric, and others who sought to educate the clergy wanted priests to understand and honor their place

---

[39] Sauer, *Theodulfi Capitula in England*, ch. 34, pp. 370–71.
[40] Chaucer, "The General Prologue," *The Riverside Chaucer*, ed. Larry D. Benson, p. 27, ll. 240–43: "He knew the tavernes wel in every toun / And everich hostiler and tappestere / Bet than a lazar or a beggestere."
[41] Chaucer, "The Pardoner's Prologue," *The Riverside Chaucer*, p. 196, ll. 443–56.

in the Church's pyramid of power. It takes discipline to keep up appearances; lacking it, the priests lose prestige. They have long since forfeited their dignity. The food network exposes their dependence on others even as they create a network of their own, spreading corruption, persuading the tavern owner to serve wine or fish before the proper hour, and giving scandal. Where was the law when you needed it? To passersby both the merchant and his customers demonstrate that laws existed to be ignored and that the consequences of doing so were not serious.

Since they were written down and recopied, the texts, a thousand years later, are more visible and hence more real to us than the material networks they sought to regulate and the machinery of oxcarts and shallow-bottomed boats. It is not texts, however, but objects that offer the most information about food culture. Fish bones, repaired wooden bowls, knives, the odd spoon, and millions of sherds of pottery are vital witnesses to the food networks of the Anglo-Saxons, necessarily paired with patterns of land use, trade, and plant and animal remains. Countless fragments of the material record have been unearthed, cleaned, and catalogued. But their details are confined to appendices of site reports, translated into abstractions and diagrammed, or never published at all. The textual world that floats above them reaches to our own time and creates impressions of coherence and system. The material record has lost all semblance of its former unity and integrity, and hence its power to challenge the magnificence of the textual network. It is difficult to go from fragments of a pot to a kitchen, or even from a part of its bowl to an entire spoon. The material world was held together by the energy of the men and women who animated the objects that were used in everyday processes such as grinding grain or cutting up meat. We animate the words spoken in Old English texts; we cannot read them otherwise. Animating fish hooks, pieces of querns, and bits of glass and iron is far from an instinctive or automatic process.

Over the course of the Anglo-Saxon period, simple food objects changed less than the texts that governed the cultures in which they were used. Pots grew thinner, taller, their rims thicker or thinner, but quernstones changed hardly at all, and neither, it seems, did basic forms of wood or ironwork. There seems to be no need to read them, nothing to explain. I once discussed my interest in ordinary things and their power to communicate identity with colleagues. I showed them a drawing of a spoon. "I see that it's a spoon," one of them said, "but what did it mean?" They all wanted to know what it represented. I wanted to know why a spoon should have to mean something in order to mean something. Why must an object have symbolic value in order to communicate medieval experience and culture? Many objects did so, but most objects did not, and it seems wasteful and unwise to regard them as therefore useless to the study of identity. Real things are not knowable only from documents or from sign systems.[42]

---

[42] For similar views, see Peter Fowler, *Farming in the First Millennium AD*, pp. 29–30.

We logically associate the formation of identity with change. The slow-moving world of the material fares poorly compared to the speedy world of texts. Law codes in the early Old English period were accumulations of decrees that responded to events. By the eleventh century, law codes sounded like homilies, anxious to decree what ought to be rather than to adjudicate what had been. The *OE Handbook* manifests the same shift. It includes the shortest list of sins to be confessed (the law, so to speak) and the most extensive instructional material for the confessor of any penitential of its epoch anywhere.[43] Both forms say less about the past and more about the present. Within the estates genre, "The Seasons of Fasting" works against this pattern: most of the poem is concerned with the fasting laws of the past, and only at the end, for barely a quarter of its length, does the poet turn to the present – and then less to exhort in the manner of the laws or penitentials than to expose the gluttony of the priestly class, offering satire rather than inspiration. Long on politics and short on art, the satire offers a better view of food culture than *Beowulf* or any of its admired kin in the poetic corpus. To me, the very ordinariness of "The Seasons for Fasting" forces us to imagine the tables, benches, pots, and pans needed to enjoy food on a daily basis, the food objects the Anglo-Saxons rarely wrote about because such things were everywhere around them.

What texts reveal about food culture might not, in the end, be as useful as what food culture reveals about the limitations of texts to communicate material processes. Archaeology has embraced textuality, reading objects as if they embodied and exposed ideas about social identity in ways analogous to the written word. In such critical practice, ordinary objects that are devoid of decoration (which functions as writing) can seem mute. In part, there is a problem with identity. Just as material culture is more valued if it is symbolic than if it is simply functional, identity is prioritized if it resonates with modern categories of race and nation: the Dane, that is, not the dish-thegn. We readily think of Christian and Jewish foodways in conflict because both traditions are textual. Legislation from both sides is fictional: the imagined Christian in Jewish food law, the imagined Jew in Christian food law. This distinction is often drawn in a tendentious way by scholars who point out the bias of Christian commentators, but David M. Freidenreich has noted that Jewish laws also fictionalize Christians in biased ways.[44] In the Middle Ages, Jewish identity could be symbolic to Christians, and not attached to real Jews, and Christian identity could likewise be symbolic to Jews and equally remote from real Christians. Such references to social relations across confessional lines speak to the polarizing effect of lawmakers' ideas and fears, not to actual conditions.

Such axes or polarities correspond to modern oppositions and are reflected in scholarship. Materiality in Anglo-Saxon studies is inescapably

---

[43] See Chapter 8.
[44] See David M. Freidenreich, *Foreigners and Their Food: Constructing Otherness in Jewish, Christian, and Islamic Law*.

connected to the study of power, leading to a focus on the powerless, the marginalized, and the otherwise disadvantaged, as if the object of scholarship were to rescue the marginalized of the Middle Ages and recruit them to modern political ends. By this standard, which prizes politics over art, "The Seasons for Fasting" should have generated more comment than "The Dream of the Rood," which is not the case. In distinguishing politics from philosophy and art, the political theorist Michael Oakeshott writes that "Political action involves mental vulgarity, not merely because it entails the concurrence and support of those who are mentally vulgar, but because of the false simplification of human life implied in even the best of its purposes."[45]

Dividing the world into haves and have-nots is "false oversimplification." That makes sense for politicians in pursuit of power and for satirists in pursuit of limiting that power. But does it make sense for historians? Oakeshott draws a distinction between a political mentality and the mentality of art and philosophy. Of the latter two activities, he writes, "It is not their business to suggest a political remedy for political defects, but to provide an actual remedy for more fundamental defects by making a society conscious of its own character." "Their genius," he writes, "is to mitigate a little their society's ignorance of itself."[46] If that is the aim of art and philosophy, it is also the aim of history: to tell us what we do not know, to show us what we have not seen. The author of "The Seasons for Fasting" was an artist who sought to mitigate society's ignorance of properly observed Ember days and the clergy's indifference to its duties. As an artist he wanted to show the clergy reading or hearing the poem what they looked like to at least some of the laity they were supposed to teach – that, clearly, was something the clergy did not know and could not see. The poet was also a politician, however, exploiting a "false oversimplification" for the sake of satire. Incidental to either instructional or satiric purpose are the poem's glimpses of food culture and the working world. The poem's world is not summed up by its politicized and oversimplified axis of oppression, as if the clergy were the haves and everybody else the have-nots. That there are powerful people and the powerless, rich and poor, is something everybody knows or ought to know. Nor is that world captured by the art that Oakeshott sees as being "free from the world," for this poet had a bitter vision of the world with little finesse to elevate it to artful expression.

I suggest that the power of "The Seasons for Fasting" to make society "conscious of its own character" lies in the poem's objects, in the literal facts of the fish, oysters, and wine that are mentioned and the cooking pots, pitchers, benches, barrels, and numerous other objects whose presence is implied. Already simple, these things cannot be oversimplified, and the poet's indignation and anger precludes any attempt to complicate them.

---

[45] Michael Oakeshott, *Religion, Politics, and the Moral Life*, p. 93.
[46] Oakeshott, *Religion, Politics, and the Moral Life*, p. 96.

What these things have to say about their world can be learned only when we link them to each other and to networks that reached far and wide into the Anglo-Saxon landscape. Rather than impose modern ideas of justice on the early medieval evidence and oppose the pots of the rich to those of the poor, Hild's rich fare to Cædmon's simple supper – the polarized world of Robin Fleming's *Britain after Rome*, that is – I have looked for ways to see things in and of themselves.[47] The viewing conditions are compromised, for most food objects survive as fragments and have been recovered in contexts that have little to do with their function in the Anglo-Saxons' food world. Like words, objects are susceptible to discourse, but anyone who has spent time thinking about things from the early medieval world will probably agree that it is more difficult to speak for objects and about them than for and about texts. The less the object says, the more intently we must pursue its connections to other things and strive to create context for it: its century, for starters; the materials from which it was fashioned; and its trail of ownership.

We might echo Bjørnar Olsen and conclude that ordinary things resist being remembered in terms of cultural systems and symbolic worlds.[48] They remain remote from those rich nodes of meaning. But that does not mean we must forget them. Finding it difficult to get from the spoon to its meaning, we are tempted to exchange the spoon for an object that invites engagement with ideology and criticism – a brooch, a cross, a shield boss. In my view, we need to find more spoons, food for them to stir, and mouths for them to enter. Then we can say something about spoons and the social and situational identities of the people who used them. Eloquent in its silence, the spoon poses a riddle. "Say what I am," it commands. "Who made me? Who gave me to whom or traded me for what? How did I come to the place where I was found?" I cannot say what the spoon means, but I have tried to articulate a few of its questions. The one who in the future can answer them is one who will have learned much.

---

[47] Robin Fleming, *Britain after Rome*; see pp. xix–xx for her manifesto.
[48] Bjørnar Olsen, "Material Culture after Text," p. 90.

Works Cited

Abbo of St. Germain. *Bella Parisiacae Urbis III*. Ed. W. H. Stevenson and W. M. Lindsay. *Early Scholastic Colloquies*. Anecdota Oxoniensia, Mediaeval and Modern Series 15. Oxford: Clarendon, 1929.

Ackerman, James S. "Numbers." In Robert Alter and Frank Kermode, eds., *The Literary Guide to the Bible*. Cambridge, Mass.: Harvard University Press, 1987. 78–91.

Adomnan. *Life of Saint Columba*. Trans. Richard Sharpe. London: Penguin, 1995.

Æthelwulf. *De Abbatibus*. Ed. A. Campbell. Oxford: Clarendon, 1967.

Alexander, Magnus. *Mills*. Introduction to Heritage Assets (2011). Online resource: http://www.english-heritage.org.uk/publications/iha-mills/mills.pdf.

Amos, Ashley Crandell. *Linguistic Means of Determining the Dates of Old English Literary Texts*. Cambridge, Mass.: Medieval Academy of America, 1980.

Andrén, Anders. *Between Artifacts and Texts: Historical Archaeology in Global Perspective*. Trans. Alan Crozier. London: Plenum, 1998.

Andrews, P., ed. *Excavations at Hamwic: Volume II. Excavations at Six Dials*. Southampton Archaeological Monographs 6. CBA Research Report 109. York: CBA, 1997.

"Anglo-Saxon Watermill Found in Tyne." *British Archaeology*, no. 11, February 1996: News. Online resource: http://www.archaeologyuk.org/ba/ba11/BA11NEWS.HTML.

Anonymous. "Three Abbots of Evesham." Based on the work of Rev. W. G. Batt. In J. E. Clarke, ed., *Church Bells*. September 11, 1875. vol. 5, 483. London: W. Wells Gardner, 1875.

Appandurai, Arjun. *The Social Life of Things: Commodities in Cultural Perspective*. Cambridge: Cambridge University Press, 1986.

Arnold, C. J. "Early Pottery of the Illington-Lackford Type." *Oxford Journal of Archaeology* 7.3 (1988), 343–59.

Attenborough, F. L., ed. and trans. *The Laws of the Earliest English Kings*. Cambridge: Cambridge University Press, 1922; repr. New York: Russell and Russell, 1963.

Augustine of Hippo, St. *Concerning the City of God against the Pagans*. Ed. David Knowles and trans. Henry Bettenson. Harmondsworth: Penguin, 1972.

—. *St. Augustine on the Psalms*. Trans. Scholastica Hebgin and Felicitas Corrigan. 2 vols. Ancient Christian Writers, vols. 29–30. Westminster, Md.: The Newman Press, 1960–61.

Baker, Peter S., and Michael Lapidge, eds. *Byrhtferth's Enchiridion*. EETS, S.S. 15. Oxford: Oxford University Press, 1995.

Banham, Debby. *Food and Drink in Anglo-Saxon England*. Stroud: Tempus, 2004.

—. "'In the Sweat of Thy Brow Shalt Thou Eat Bread': Cereals and Cereal

Production in the Anglo-Saxon Landscape." In Higham and Ryan, eds., *Landscape Archaeology of Anglo-Saxon England*, 175–92.

—, ed. and trans. *Monasteriales Indicia: The Old English Monastic Sign Language*. Frithgarth, Norfolk: Anglo-Saxon Books, 1991.

Barrett, James C. "Aspects of the Iron Age in Atlantic Scotland: A Case Study in the Problems of Archaeological Interpretation." *Proceedings of the Society of Antiquaries of Scotland* 111 (1981), 205–19.

Barrett, James H., Alison M. Locker, and Callum M. Roberts. "'Dark Age Economics' Revisited: The English Fish-Bone Evidence, 600–1600." *Antiquity* 78 [301] (2004), 618–36. Repr. in Louis Sicking and Darlene Abreu-Ferreira, eds., *Beyond the Catch: Fisheries of the North Atlantic, the North Sea and the Baltic, 900–1850*. Leiden: Brill, 2009. 31–60.

Bately, Janet, ed. *The Old English Orosius*. EETS, S.S. 6. London: Oxford University Press, 1980.

Becker, C. J. "Viking Age Settlements in Western and Central Jutland: Recent Excavations." *Acta Archaeologica* 50 (1979), 89–208.

Bede. *Bede's Ecclesiastical History of the English People*. Ed. and trans. Bertram Colgrave and R. A. B. Mynors. Oxford: Clarendon, 1969.

—. *De Psalmorum libro exegesis*. In Migne, ed., *PL* 93: 524a–c.

—. *History of the Abbots of Wearmouth and Jarrow*. In D. H. Farmer, ed., and J. F. Webb, trans., *The Age of Bede*. London: Penguin, 1965; repr. 1998. 185–210.

Benedict, St. *The Rule of St. Benedict*. Trans. Leonard J. Boyle. Collegeville, Minn.: The Liturgical Press, 1948.

Beresford, Guy, et al. *Goltho: The Development of an Early Medieval Manor c. 850–1150*. English Heritage Archaeological Report no. 4. London: Historic Buildings and Monuments Commission for England, 1987.

Berger, John, *Ways of Seeing*. London: Penguin, 1972.

Bethurum, Dorothy, ed. *The Homilies of Wulfstan*. Oxford: Clarendon, 1957.

Biddle, Martin, and D. Smith. "The Querns." In Biddle, ed., *Object and Economy in Medieval Winchester*, Winchester Studies 7.ii. Oxford: Oxford University Press, 1990. 292–96, 881–90.

Bieler, Ludwig, ed. *The Irish Penitentials*. Dublin: Dublin Institute for Advanced Studies, 1963.

Blair, John. *The Church in Anglo-Saxon Society*. Oxford: Oxford University Press, 2005.

—. "Ecclesiastical Organization and Pastoral Care in Anglo-Saxon England." *Early Medieval Europe* 4 (1995), 193–212.

—. "Minster Churches in the Landscape." In Hooke, ed., *Anglo-Saxon Settlements*, 35–58.

—, ed. *Waterways and Canal-Building in Medieval England*. Oxford: Oxford University Press, 2007.

—, and Nigel Ramsay, eds. *English Medieval Industries: Craftsmen, Techniques, Products*. London: Hambledon, 1991.

Blake, Martin, ed. and trans., *Ælfric's De Temporibus Anni*. Cambridge: D. S. Brewer, 2009.

Blinkhorn, Paul. "Anglo-Saxon Pottery from Lake End Road West, Maidenhead." Online resource: http://independent.academia.edu/PaulBlinkhorn/Papers.

—. "Habitus, Social Identity and Anglo-Saxon Pottery." In Cumberpatch and Blinkhorn, eds., *Not So Much a Pot*, 113–24.

—. "Ipswich Ware." In Evans and Loveluck, eds., *Life and Economy*, 357–63.

—. "Of Cabbages and Kings: Production, Trade and Consumption in Middle Saxon England." In Mike Anderton, ed., *Anglo-Saxon Trading Places: Beyond the Emporia*. Glasgow: Cruithne, 1999. Online resource: http://independent. academia.edu/PaulBlinkhorn/Papers.

—. "Stranger in a Strange Land: Middle Saxon Ipswich Ware." Online resource: http://independent.academia.edu/PaulBlinkhorn/Papers.

Boswell, John. *Christianity, Social Tolerance, and Homosexuality: Gay People in Western Europe from the Beginning of the Christian Era to the Fourteenth Century.* Chicago: University of Chicago Press, 1980.

Bosworth, Joseph, and T. Northcote Toller. *An Anglo-Saxon Dictionary Based on the Manuscript Collections of the Late Joseph Bosworth, Edited and Enlarged by T. Northcote Toller.* Oxford: Oxford University Press, 1898; repr. 1954. Online resource: http://www.bosworthtoller.com/.

—, —, with Alistair Campbell, ed. *An Anglo-Saxon Dictionary Based on the Manuscript Collections of the Late Joseph Bosworth, Edited and Enlarged by T. Northcote Toller: Supplement.* Oxford: Oxford University Press, 1921; repr. 1955.

Bourdieu, Pierre. *Distinction: A Social Critique of the Judgement of Taste.* Trans. Richard Nice. Cambridge, Mass.: Harvard University Press, 1984.

—. *The Field of Cultural Production.* Ed. Randal Johnson. New York: Columbia University Press, 1993.

—. *The Logic of Practice.* Trans. Richard Nice. Stanford: Stanford University Press, 1990.

Bourdillon, Jennifer. "The Animal Provisioning of Saxon Southampton." In Rackham, ed., *Environment and Economy in Anglo-Saxon England*, 120–25.

Bouwsma, William J. *John Calvin: A Sixteenth-Century Portrait.* Oxford: Oxford University Press, 1988.

Boyle, Marjorie O'Rourke. "For Peasants, Psalms: Erasmus' *Editio Princeps* of Haymo (1533)." *Mediaeval Studies* 44 (1982), 444–69.

Brisbane, Mark. "Hamwic (Saxon Southampton): An 8th Century Port and Production Centre." In Rackham, ed., *Environment and Economy in Anglo-Saxon England*, 101–8.

Brodribb, A. C. C., A. R. Hands, and D. R. Walker. *Excavations at Shakenoak Farm, Near Wilcote, Oxfordshire.* Part III: Site F. Oxford: privately printed, 1972.

Brown, Bill. *A Sense of Things: The Object Matter of American Literature.* Chicago: University of Chicago Press, 2003.

—. "Thing Theory." *Critical Inquiry* 28 (2001), 1–22.

Brown, Duncan H. "The Social Significance of Imported Medieval Pottery." In Cumberpatch and Blinkhorn, eds., *Not So Much a Pot*, 95–112.

Brown, P. D. C. "The Ironwork." In Brodribb, Hands, and Walker, *Excavations at Shakenoak Farm*, 86–117.

Brueggemann, Walter. *The Message of the Psalms: A Theological Commentary.* Minneapolis: Augsburg Publishing, 1984.

Cadman, Graham, and Glenn Foard. "Raunds: Manorial and Village Origins." In Faull, ed., *Studies in Late Anglo-Saxon Settlement*, 81–100.

Calvin, John. *Commentary on the Book of Psalms.* Trans. James Anderson. *Calvin's Commentaries*, vol. 4. 22 vols. Edinburgh, 1844–57; repr. Grand Rapids, Mich.: Baker Book House, 1998.

Cameron, Angus, Ashley Crandell Amos, and Antonette diPaolo Healey, *et al.*, eds. *Dictionary of Old English: A to G Online.* Toronto: Dictionary of Old English Project, 2007.

Cameron, M. L. *Anglo-Saxon Medicine*. Cambridge: Cambridge University Press, 1993.

Campbell, A. P., ed. *The Tiberius Psalter: London, British Library, MS. Cotton Tiberius C.VI*. Ottawa: Ottawa University Press, 1974.

Campbell, Gill. "The Preliminary Archaeobotanical Results from Anglo-Saxon West Cotton and Raunds." In Rackham, ed., *Environment and Economy in Anglo-Saxon England*, 65–82.

Carnicelli, Thomas A., ed. *King Alfred's Version of St. Augustine's "Soliloquies."* Cambridge, Mass.: Harvard University Press, 1969.

Carver, Martin, ed. *The Age of Sutton Hoo: The Seventh Century in North-Western Europe*. Woodbridge: Boydell, 1992.

Cassian, John. *The Conferences of John Cassian*. Trans. C. S. Gibson. Library of Nicene and Post-Nicene Fathers of the Christian Church. Buffalo, NY: The Christian Literature Co., 1894; repr. Dublin: Veritas Splendor Publications, 2012.

Cassiodorus. *Cassiodorus: Explanation of the Psalms*. Trans. P. G. Walsh. 3 vols. Mahwah: Paulist Press, 1990–91.

Charles-Edwards, Thomas. "The Penitential of Theodore and the *Iudicia Theodori*." In Michael Lapidge, ed., *Archbishop Theodore: Commemorative Studies on his Life and Influence*. Cambridge: Cambridge University Press, 1995. 141–74.

Chaucer, Geoffrey. *The Canterbury Tales*. In Larry D. Benson, ed., *The Riverside Chaucer*. 3rd ed. Boston: Houghton Mifflin, 1987.

Clayton, Mary, and Hugh Magennis. *The Old English Lives of St. Margaret*. Cambridge: Cambridge University Press, 1994.

Cleere, H. "Anglo-Saxon Iron-Working Debris." In Brodribb, Hands, and Walker, *Excavations at Shakenoak Farm*, 117–18.

Clemoes, P. A. M., ed. *Ælfric's Catholic Homilies: The First Series, Text*. EETS, S.S. 17. Oxford: Oxford University Press, 1997.

Coatsworth, Elizabeth. "The Material Culture of the Anglo-Saxon Church." In Hamerow, Hinton, and Crawford, eds., *The Oxford Handbook of Anglo-Saxon Archaeology*, 779–96.

Cockayne, Rev. Oswald [Thomas O.], ed. *Leechdoms, Wortcunning and Starcraft of Early England*, Rolls Series 35, 3 vols. London, 1864; repr. London: Holland Press, 1961.

Cole, Ann. "The Place-Name Evidence for Water Transport in Medieval England." In Blair, ed., *Waterways*, 55–84.

Cool, H. E. M. *Eating and Drinking in Roman Britain*. Cambridge: Cambridge University Press, 2006.

Cooper, Alan. *Bridges, Law and Power in Medieval England, 700–1400*. Woodbridge: Boydell, 2006.

Crabtree, Pam J. "Animal Exploitation in East Anglian Villages." In Rackham, ed., *Environment and Economy in Anglo-Saxon England*, 40–54.

—. "Production and Consumption in an Early Complex Society: Animal Use in Middle Saxon East Anglia." *World Archaeology* 28 (1996), 58–75.

—. *West Stow, Suffolk: Early Anglo-Saxon Animal Husbandry*. East Anglian Archaeology, Report no. 47. Norfolk: Crowes, 1989.

Crawford, S. J., ed. *The Old English Version of the Heptateuch*. EETS, O.S. 160. 1922; repr. with additions by N.R. Ker, London: Oxford University Press, 1969.

Crawford, Sally. *Daily Life in Anglo-Saxon England*. Oxford: Greenwood World Publishing, 2009.

Cross, James. E., and Thomas D. Hill, eds. *The Prose Solomon and Saturn* and *Adrian and Ritheus*. Toronto: University of Toronto Press, 1982.

Cubitt, Catherine. "Bishops, Priests and Penance in Late Saxon England." *Early Medieval Europe* 14 (2006), 41–63.

Cunliffe, Barry. *Excavations at Portchester Castle*. Report of the Research Committee of the Society of Antiquaries of London, 33, vol. 2. London: Thames and Hudson, 1976.

Crummy, Nina. "Small Finds." In C. Gibson, with J. Murray, "An Anglo-Saxon Settlement at Godmanchester Cambridgeshire." In Griffiths, Reynolds, and Semple, eds., *Boundaries in Early Medieval Britain*, 183–90.

Cumberpatch, C. G. "Towards a Phenomenological Approach to the Study of Medieval Pottery." In Cumberpatch and Blinkhorn, eds., *Not So Much a Pot*, 125–51.

—, and P. W. Blinkhorn, eds. *Not So Much a Pot, More a Way of Life*. Oxford: Oxbow, 1997.

Davies, Gareth. *An Archaeological Evaluation of the Middle-Late Anglo-Saxon Settlement at Chalkpit Field*. Online resource: http://www.scribd.com/doc/3989245/CNEreport-draft.

Davies, John Reubin. "Ecclesiastical Organization: The Early Middle Ages." In Sean Duffy, Ailbhe MacShamhráin, and James Moynes, eds., *Medieval Ireland: An Encyclopedia*. New York: CRC Press, 2005. 241–47.

Dembinska, Maria. "Fasting and Working Monks: Regulations of the Fifth to Eleventh Centuries." In A. Fenton and Eszter Kisbán, eds., *Food in Change: Eating Habits from the Middle Ages to the Present Day*. Edinburgh: John Donald, 1986. 152–60.

Dobbie, Elliott van Kirk, ed. *The Anglo-Saxon Minor Poems*. ASPR 6. New York: Columbia University Press, 1942; repr. 1968.

Dobney, Keith, Allan Hall, and Harry Kenward. "The Bioarchaeology of Anglo-Saxon Yorkshire: Present and Future Perspectives." In Geake and Kenny, eds., *Early Deira*, 133–40.

—, Deborah Jacques, James Barrett, and Cluny Johnstone, eds. *Farmers, Monks and Aristocrats. The Environmental Archaeology of Anglo-Saxon Flixborough*. Excavations at Flixborough, vol. 3. Oxford: Oxbow, 2007.

—, —, —, and —. "Zooarchaeological Evidence for the Nature and Character of the Settlement." In Dobney, Jacques, Barrett, and Johnstone, eds., *Farmers, Monks and Aristocrats*, 217–45.

Douglas, Mary. *Leviticus as Literature*. Oxford: Oxford University Press, 2001.

—. *Purity and Danger: An Analysis of Concepts of Pollution and Taboo*. London: Routledge and Kegan Paul, 1966; repr. with a new preface, 2002.

Dunning, G. C. "The Imported Pottery." In West, ed., "Excavations at Cox Lane," 284.

—, J. G. Hurst, J. N. L. Myres, and F. Tischler. *Anglo-Saxon Pottery: A Symposium*. CBA Research Report 4. London: CBA, 1959.

Dyer, Christopher. "The Consumption of Freshwater Fish in Medieval England." In Michael Aston, ed., *Medieval Fish, Fisheries and Fishponds in England. Part I*. BAR, British Series 182. Oxford: BAR, 1988. 27–38.

—. "English Diet in the Later Middle Ages." In T. H. Ason, P. R. Coss, *et al.*, eds., *Social Relations and Ideas: Essays in Honour of R. H. Hilton*. Cambridge: Cambridge University Press, 1983. 191–216.

—. *Everyday Life in Medieval England*. London: Hambledon, 1994.

Emerton, Ephraim, trans. *The Letters of Saint Boniface*. New York: W. W. Norton, 1976.

Esmonde Cleary, Simon. "The Ending(s) of Roman Britain." In Hamerow, Hinton, and Crawford, eds., *The Oxford Handbook of Anglo-Saxon Archaeology*, 13–29.

Evans, D. H., and Christopher Loveluck, eds. *Life and Economy at Early Medieval Flixborough c. AD 600–1000: The Artefact Evidence*. Excavations at Flixborough, vol. 2. Oxford: Oxbow, 2009.

Evison, Vera I., Catherine Mortimer, Nicola Rogers, and Susan M. Youngs. "Consumption of Luxuries: The Glass and Copper Alloy Vessels." In Evans and Loveluck, eds., *Life and Economy*, 103–21.

Fagan, Brian. *Fish on Friday: Feasting, Fasting, and the Discovery of the New World*. New York: Basic Books, 2006.

Fairbrother, J. R. *Faccombe Netherton: Excavations of a Saxon and Medieval Manorial Complex*. Vol. 2. London: British Museum, 1990.

Faith, Rosamond. *The English Peasantry and the Growth of Lordship*. London: Leicester University Press, 1997.

Faull, Margaret L., ed. *Studies in Late Anglo-Saxon Settlement*. Oxford: Oxford University Department for External Studies, 1984.

Fell, Christine. "Some Domestic Problems." *Leeds Studies in English* NS 16 (1985), 59–82.

—. *Women in Anglo-Saxon England*. With Cecily Clark and Elizabeth Williams, *And the Impact of 1066*. Bloomington: Indiana University Press, 1984.

Finsterwalder, Paul Willem, ed. *Die Canones Theodori Cantuariensis und ihre Überlieferungsformen*. Weimar: H. Böhlaus, 1929.

Fleming, Robin. *Britain after Rome: The Fall and Rise, 400 to 1070*. London: Allen Lane, 2010.

—. "The New Wealth, the New Rich, and New Political Style in Anglo-Saxon England." *Anglo-Norman Studies* 23 (2001), 1–22.

—. "Rural Elites and Urban Communities in Late-Saxon England." *Past and Present* 141 (1993), 3–37.

Flynn, James R. *Are We Getting Smarter? Rising IQ in the Twenty-First Century*. Cambridge: Cambridge University Press, 2012.

Foot, Sarah. *Monastic Life in Anglo-Saxon England, c. 600–900*. Cambridge: Cambridge University Press, 2006.

Foreman, S., J. Hiller, and D. Petts. *Gathering the People, Settling the Land: The Archaeology of a Middle Thames Landscape, Anglo-Saxon to Post-Medieval*. Thames Valley Landscapes Monograph no. 14. Oxford: Oxbow, 2002.

Förster, Max. "Beiträge zur mittelalterlichen Volkskunde VIII." *Archiv* 129 (1912), 16–49.

Foucault, Michel. *The Order of Things: An Archaeology of the Human Sciences*. New York: Random House, 1970.

Fowler, Peter. *Farming in the First Millennium AD: British Agriculture between Julius Caesar and William the Conqueror*. Cambridge: Cambridge University Press, 2002.

Fowler, Roger. "A Late OE Handbook for the Use of a Confessor." *Anglia* 83 (1965), 1–34.

—, ed. *Wulfstan's Canons of Edgar*. EETS, O.S. 266. London: Oxford University Press, 1972.

Frantzen, Allen J. "All Created Things: Material Contexts for Bede's Story of Cædmon." In Frantzen and Hines, eds., *Cædmon's Hymn*, 111–49.

—. *Anglo-Saxon Keywords*. Malden, Mass.: Wiley-Blackwell, 2012.

—. "*Be mihtigum mannum*: Power, Penance, and Food in Late Anglo-Saxon England." In Stacy S. Klein, William Schipper, and Shannon Lewis-Simpson, eds., *The Maritime World of the Anglo-Saxons*. Tempe: Arizona Center for Medieval and Renaissance Studies, 2014. 157–85.

—. "Food Words in the Anglo-Saxon Penitentials." In Renate Bauer and Ulrike Krischke, eds., *Fact and Fiction: From the Middle Ages to Modern Times: Essays Presented to Hans Sauer on the Occasion of his 65th Birthday*. Frankfurt am Main: Lang, 2011. 83–99.

—. *The Literature of Penance in Anglo-Saxon England*. New Brunswick: Rutgers University Press, 1983.

—. "Making Sense: Translating the Anglo-Saxon Penitentials." In Antonette diPaolo Healey and Kevin Kiernan, eds., *Making Sense: Constructing Meaning in Early English*. University of Toronto Press, 2006. 40–71.

—, ed. *The Anglo-Saxon Penitentials: A Cultural Database*. Online resource: http://www.Anglo-Saxon.net.

—. and John Hines, eds. *Cædmon's Hymn and Material Culture in the World of Bede*. Morgantown: West Virginia University Press, 2007.

Frazer, William O. "Introduction." In Frazer and Tyrell, eds., *Social Identity in Early Medieval Britain*, 1–22.

—, and Andrew Tyrrell, eds. *Social Identity in Early Medieval Britain*. London: Leicester University Press, 2000.

Freidenreich, David M. *Foreigners and Their Food: Constructing Otherness in Jewish, Christian, and Islamic Law*. Berkeley: University of California Press, 2011.

Freshwater, Tom. "A Lava Quern Workshop in Late Saxon London." *London Archaeologist* 8.2 (1996), 39–45.

Fulk, R. D., Robert E. Bjork, and John D. Niles, eds. *Klaeber's* Beowulf. 4th ed. Toronto: University of Toronto Press, 2008.

—, and Christopher Cain. *A History of Old English Literature*. Malden, Mass.: Blackwell, 2003.

—, and Stefan Jurasinski, eds. *The Old English Canons of Theodore*. EETS, S.S. 25. Oxford: Oxford University Press, 2012.

Gardiner, Mark. "Hythes, Small Ports, and Other Landing Places in Later Medieval England." In Blair, ed., *Waterways*, 85–109.

—. "Implements and Utensils in *Gerefa* and the Organization of Seigneurial Farmsteads in the High Middle Ages." *Medieval Archaeology* 50 (2006), 260–67.

Garmonsway, G. N., ed. *Ælfric's Colloquy*. New York: Appleton-Century-Crofts, 1966.

Gaunt, G. D. "Comment on Sandstone Querns." In Rogers, *Anglian and Other Finds*, 1329.

Geake, Helen, and Jonathan Kenny, eds. *Early Deira: Archaeological Studies of the East Riding in the Fourth to Ninth Centuries AD*. Oxford: Oxbow, 2000.

Geddes, Jane. "Iron." In Blair and Ramsay, eds., *English Medieval Industries*, 167–88.

Gibson, C., with J. Murray. "An Anglo-Saxon Settlement at Godmanchester, Cambridgeshire." In Griffiths, Reynolds, and Semple, eds., *Boundaries in Early Medieval Britain*, 137–217.

Gneuss, Helmut. *Handlist of Anglo-Saxon Manuscripts*. Tempe: Arizona Center for Medieval and Renaissance Studies, 2001.

—. "A Preliminary List of Manuscripts Written or Owned in England up to 1100." *Anglo-Saxon England* 9 (1980), 1–60.

Godden, Malcolm, ed. *Ælfric's Catholic Homilies: The Second Series, Text.* EETS, S.S. 5. London: Oxford, 1979.

—. "Did King Alfred Write Anything?" *Medium Ævum* 76.1 (2007), 1–23.

—. "Money, Power and Morality in Late Anglo-Saxon England." *Anglo-Saxon England* 19 (1990), 41–65.

—, and Susan Irvine, eds. *The Old English Boethius: An Edition of the Old English Versions of Boethius's "De Consolatione Philosophiae."* 2 vols. Oxford: Oxford University Press, 2009.

Goodall, Ian H. "The Iron Objects." In Wade-Martins, ed., *Excavations in North Elmham Park,* 2: 509–16.

—, and E. A. Clark, with L. Webster and J. G. Watt. "Iron Objects." In Stamper and Croft, eds., *Wharram: A Study of Settlement on the Yorkshire Wolds,* 132–47.

—, with Blanche Ellis and Brian Gilmour. "Iron Objects." In Rogerson and Dallas, eds., *Excavations in Thetford,* 77–106.

Goossens, Louis, ed. *The Old English Glosses of MS. Brussels, Royal Library 1650.* Brussels: Paleis der Academiën, 1974.

Graham, Alan H., and Susan M. Davies. *Excavations in the Town Centre of Trowbridge, Wiltshire 1977 and 1986–1988. The Prehistoric and Saxon Settlements, and Saxo-Norman Manorial Settlement, and the Anarchy Period Castle.* Wessex Archaeology Report no. 2, Wessex Archaeology, 1993.

Graham-Campbell, James, and Magdalena Valor, eds. *The Archaeology of Medieval Europe, vol. 1: Eighth to Twelfth Centuries, AD.* Aarhus: Aarhus University Press, 2007.

Grattan, J. H. G., and Charles Singer. *Anglo-Saxon Magic and Medicine.* London: Oxford University Press, 1952.

Greef, Wulfert de. *The Writings of John Calvin: An Introductory Guide.* Trans. Lyle D. Bierma. Louisville: Westminster John Knox Press, 2008.

Green, Francis J. "Cereals and Plant Food: A Reassessment of the Saxon Economic Evidence from Wessex." In Rackham, ed., *Environment and Economy in Anglo-Saxon England,* 83–88.

Greene, J. Patrick, *Medieval Monasteries.* New York: Continuum, 1992.

Gretsch, Mechthild. "Glosses." In Lapidge *et al.*, eds., *BEASE*, 209–10.

—. *The Intellectual Foundations of the English Benedictine Reform.* Cambridge: Cambridge University Press, 1999.

Griffiths, David, Andrew Reynolds, and Sarah Semple, eds. *Boundaries in Early Medieval Britain,* Anglo-Saxon Studies in Archaeology and History 12. Oxford: Oxford University School of Archaeology, 2003.

Gurevich, Aron. *Medieval Popular Culture: Problems of Belief and Perception.* Trans. János M. Bak and Paul A. Hollingsworth. Cambridge: Cambridge University Press, 1988.

Gwara, Scott. *Latin Colloquies from Pre-Conquest Britain.* Toronto: Pontifical Institute for Mediaeval Studies, 1996.

—, and David W. Porter, eds. *Anglo-Saxon Conversations: The Colloquies of Ælfric Bata.* Woodbridge: Boydell, 1997.

Haddan, A. W., and W. Stubbs, eds. *Councils and Ecclesiastical Documents relating to Great Britain and Ireland.* 3 vols. Oxford: Clarendon, 1869–78.

Hagen, Ann. *A Handbook of Anglo-Saxon Food and Drink: Processing and Consumption.* Frithgarth, Norfolk: Anglo-Saxon Books, 1992.

----. *A Second Handbook of Anglo-Saxon Food and Drink: Production and Distribution.* Frithgarth, Norfolk, Anglo-Saxon Books, 1995.

Hall, David. "The Late Saxon Countryside: Villages and their Fields." In Hooke, ed., *Anglo-Saxon Settlements*, 99–122.

Hamerow, Helena. "Agrarian Production and the *Emporia* of mid Saxon England, c. AD 650–850." In Joachim Henning, ed., *Post-Roman Towns, Trade and Settlement in Europe and Byzantium, 1: The Heirs of the Roman West*. Berlin: Walter de Gruyter, 2007. 219–32.

—. "Communities of the Living and the Dead. The Relationship Between Anglo-Saxon Settlements and Cemeteries, c. 450–c. 850." In Martin Henig and Nigel Ramsay, eds., *The Archaeology and History of Christianity in England, 400–1200*. Oxford: BAR, 2010. 71–76.

—. *Early Medieval Settlements: The Archaeology of Rural Communities in North-West Europe 400–900*. Oxford: Oxford University Press, 2002.

—. "The Early to Middle Saxon Period." In Ann Clark, ed., *Excavations at Mucking. 1: The Site Atlas*. London: English Heritage in association with British Museum Press, 1993. 21.

—. *Excavations at Mucking. 2: The Anglo-Saxon Settlement*. London: British Museum Press, 1993.

—. "Settlement Mobility and the 'Middle Saxon Shift': Rural Settlements and Settlement Patterns in Anglo-Saxon England." *Anglo-Saxon England* 20 (1991), 1–17.

—, David A. Hinton, and Sally Crawford, eds. *The Oxford Handbook of Anglo-Saxon Archaeology*. Oxford: Oxford University Press, 2011.

—, and Arthur MacGregor, eds. *Image and Power in the Archaeology of Early Medieval Britain: Essays in Honour of Rosemary Cramp*. Oxford: Oxbow, 2001.

Hansen, Inge Lyse, and Chris Wickham, eds. *The Long Eighth Century*. Leiden: Brill, 2000.

Hardy, Thomas. *Far from the Madding Crowd*. New York: Harper and Brothers, 1918.

Härke, Heinrich. "Early Anglo-Saxon Social Structure." In Hines, ed., *The Anglo-Saxons*, 125–60.

—. "'Warrior Graves'?: The Background of the Anglo-Saxon Weapon Burial Rite." *Past and Present* 126 (1990), 22–43.

Harlsey, Fred, ed. *Eadwine's Canterbury Psalter*. EETS. O.S. 92. London: Trübner, 1889; repr. 1973.

Harmer, Florence E., ed. *Select English Historical Documents of the Ninth and Tenth Centuries*. Cambridge: Cambridge University Press, 1914.

Harris, Stephen J. *Race and Ethnicity in Anglo-Saxon Literature*. New York: Routledge, 2003.

Harrison, David. *The Bridges of Medieval England: Transport and Society 400–1800*. New York: Oxford University Press, 2004.

Harvey, P. D. A. "*Rectitudines Singularum Personarum* and *Gerefa*." *English Historical Review* 126 (1993), 1–22.

Healey, Antonette diPaolo, ed., with John Price Wilkin and Xin Xiang. *Dictionary of Old English Web Corpus*. Toronto: The Dictionary of Old English, 2009. Online resource: http://www.doe.utoronto.ca.

Hearne, Thomas, ed. *Hemingi Cartularium Ecclesiae Wigorniensis*. 2 vols. Oxford, 1723.

Hecht, Hans, ed. *Bischof Wærferths von Worcester Übersetzung der Dialoge Gregors des Grossen*. Bibliothek der angelsächsischen Prosa. Leipzig and Hamburg, 1900 and 1907; repr. Darmstadt: Wissenschaftliche Buchgesellschaft, 1965.

Heighway, Carolyn, A. P. Garrod, and A. G. Vince. "Excavations at 1 Westgate Street, Gloucester, 1975." *Medieval Archaeology* 23 (1979), 159–213.

Henel, Heinrich. ed., *Ælfric's De temporibus anni.* EETS, O.S. 213. London: Oxford University Press, 1942; repr. 1971.

Herlihy, David. *Medieval Households.* Cambridge, Mass.: Harvard University Press, 1985.

Hervey, Lord Francis. *Corolla Sancti Eadmundi.* London: John Murray, 1907.

Hessels, Jan Hendrik. *An Eighth-Century Latin-Anglo-Saxon Glossary.* Cambridge: Cambridge University Press, 1890.

Higham, Nicholas J., and Martin J. Ryan, eds. *Landscape Archaeology of Anglo-Saxon England.* Woodbridge: Boydell, 2010.

Hilton, Chadwick B. "The Old English *Season for Fasting*: Its Place in the Vernacular Complaint Tradition." *Neophilologus* 70:1 (1986), 155–59.

Hines, John, ed., *The Anglo-Saxons from the Migration Period to the Eighth Century: An Ethnographic Perspective.* Woodbridge: Boydell, 1997.

—. "Gerefa §§15 and 17: A Grammatical Analysis of the Lists of Nouns." *Medieval Archaeology* 50 (2006), 268–70.

—. "Literary Sources and Archaeology." In Hamerow, Hinton, and Crawford, eds., *The Oxford Handbook of Anglo-Saxon Archaeology,* 968–85.

—. *Voices in the Past: English Literature and Archaeology.* Cambridge: D. S. Brewer, 2004.

Hirst, Susan M. *An Anglo-Saxon Inhumation Cemetery at Sewerby, East Yorkshire.* York: York University Archaeological Publications, 1985.

—. "Mucking/East Tilbury: Lower Thames Meeting Place and Mart in the Early and Middle Saxon Periods?" In Jane Roberts and Leslie Webster, eds., *Anglo-Saxon Traces.* Tempe: Arizona Center for Medieval and Renaissance Studies, 2011. 101–15.

Hobley, Brian. "Lundenwic and Lundenburgh: Two Cities Rediscovered." In Hodges and Hobley, eds., *The Rebirth of Towns in the West,* 69–82.

Hodder, Ian, with Scott Hutson. *Reading the Past: Current Approaches to Interpretation in Archaeology.* 3rd ed. Cambridge: Cambridge University Press, 2003.

—, ed. *The Meanings of Things: Material Culture and Symbolic Expression.* London: Unwin Hyman, 1989.

Hodges, Richard. *The Anglo-Saxon Achievement: Archaeology and the Beginnings of English Society.* Ithaca: Cornell University Press, 1989.

—. "Characterisation and Discussion of Identified Imported Sherds." In Wade-Martins, ed., *Excavations in North Elmham Park,* 424–26.

—. *Dark Age Economics: The Origins of Towns and Trade A.D. 600–1000.* London: Duckworth, 1982.

—. *Goodbye to the Vikings? Re-reading Early Medieval Archaeology.* London: Duckworth, 2006.

—. *The Hamwih Pottery: The Local and Imported Wares from 30 Years' Excavations at Middle Saxon Southampton and their European Context.* London: CBA, 1981.

—, and Brian Hobley, eds. *The Rebirth of Towns in the West, AD 700–1050.* CBA Research Report 68. London: CBA, 1988.

Hooke, Della. "The Anglo-Saxons in England in the Seventh and Eighth Centuries: Aspects of Location in Space." In Hines, ed., *The Anglo-Saxons,* 65–85.

—. "Uses of Waterways in Anglo-Saxon England." In Blair, ed., *Waterways,* 37–54.

—, ed. *Anglo-Saxon Settlements.* Oxford: Blackwell, 1988.

—, ed. *Medieval Villages: A Review of Current Work.* Oxford: Oxford University Committee for Archaeology, 1985.

Hough, Carole."Penitential Literature and Secular Law in Anglo-Saxon England." In David Griffiths, ed., *Anglo-Saxon Studies in Archaeology and History* 11. Oxford: Oxford University School of Archaeology, 2000. 133–41.

—. "Place-name Evidence for an Anglo-Saxon Animal Name: OE **pohha* / **pocca* 'fallow deer.'" *Anglo-Saxon England* 30 (2001), 1–14.

Howe, Nicholas. *Migration and Mythmaking in Anglo-Saxon England.* New Haven: Yale University Press, 1989.

Hrabanus Maurus. *De universo libri viginti duo.* In Migne, ed., *PL* 111, col. 9a–614b.

Hughes, M. "Rural Settlement and Landscape in Late Saxon Hampshire." In Faull, ed., *Studies in Late Anglo-Saxon Settlement,* 65–80.

Hurst, J. G. "The Changing Medieval Village in England." In Peter J. Ucko, Ruth Tringham, and G. W. Dimbleby, eds., *Man, Settlement and Urbanism.* Cambridge, Mass.: Schenkman, 1972. 531–40.

—. "The Pottery." In Wilson, ed., *The Archaeology of Anglo-Saxon England,* 283–348.

Jankuhn, Herbert. *Die Ausgrabungen in Haithabu, (1937–1939): Vorläufiger Grabungsbericht.* Berlin: Ahnenerbe-Stiftung Verlag, 1943.

Jensen, Claus Kjeld, and Karen Høilund Nielsen. "Burial Data and Correspondence Analysis." In Jensen and Nielsen, eds., *Burial and Society: The Chronological and Social Analysis of Archaeological Burial Data.* Aarhus: Aarhus University Press, 1997. 29–61.

Johnson, Randal. "Editor's Introduction." In Bourdieu, *The Field of Cultural Production.* 1–25.

Jorvik Viking Centre. Online resource: http://www.jorvik-viking-centre.co.uk/.

Jost, Karl, ed. and trans. *Die "Institutes of Polity, Civil and Ecclesiastical."* Swiss Studies in English 47. Bern: Francke Verlag, 1959.

Jury, Louise. "Uncovered: Archaeologists Unearth Remnants of a Giant Medieval Watermill." Online resource: http://newsgroups.derkeiler.com/Archive/Soc/soc.history.medieval/2009-02/msg00131.html.

Keay, Simon. "The Amphora Project." Online resource: http://www.soton.ac.uk/archaeology/research/projects/amphora_project.page?

Kelly, Fergus. *Early Irish Farming: A Study Based Mainly on the Law-texts of the 7th and 8th Centuries AD.* Dublin: Dublin Institute for Advanced Studies, 1997.

Kelly, Susan. "Anglo-Saxon Lay Society and the Written Word." In Rosamond McKitterick, ed., *The Uses of Literacy in Early Medieval Europe.* Cambridge: Cambridge University Press, 1990, 36–62.

Kemp, Richard L. *Anglian Settlement at 46–54 Fishergate.* The Archaeology of York, Volume 7: Anglian York, Fasc. 1. York: CBA, 1996.

Ker, N. R. *Catalogue of Manuscripts Containing Anglo-Saxon.* Oxford: Oxford University Press, 1957.

—. "Three Old English Texts in a Salisbury Pontifical, Cotton Tiberius C.I." In Peter Clemoes, ed., *The Anglo-Saxons, Studies ... Presented to Bruce Dickins.* London, 1959. 262–79.

Keynes, Simon. "An Abbot, an Archbishop, and the Viking Raids of 1006–7 and 1009–12." *Anglo-Saxon England* 36 (2007), 151–220.

—, and Michael Lapidge, eds. and trans. *Alfred the Great.* Harmondsworth: Penguin, 1983.

Kindschi, L. "The Latin-Old English Glossaries in Plantin-Moretus MS. 32 and British Museum MS. Additional 32246." Stanford diss., 1955.

Kotzor, Günther, ed. *Das altenglische Martyrologium*, 2 vols. Munich: Bayerische Akademie der Wissenschaften, 1981.

Krapp, George Philip, ed. *The Junius Manuscript*. ASPR 1. New York: Columbia University Press, 1931; repr. 1969.

—, ed. *The Paris Psalter and the Meters of Boethius*. ASPR 5. New York: Columbia University Press, 1932; repr. 1970.

—, ed., *The Vercelli Book*. ASPR 2. New York: Columbia University Press, 1932; repr.1969.

—, and Elliott van Kirk Dobbie, eds. *The Exeter Book*. ASPR 3. New York: Columbia University Press, 1936, repr.1966.

Kurlansky, Mark. *Cod: A Biography of the Fish that Changed the World*. New York: Penguin, 1997.

Laing, Lloyd, and Jennifer Laing. *Anglo-Saxon England*. London: Routledge, 1979.

Lang, James. *Corpus of Anglo-Saxon Stone Sculpture, Volume 6: North Yorkshire*. London: Oxford University Press, 2002.

Lapidge, Michael. "Benedict Biscop." In Lapidge *et al.*, eds., *BEASE*, 60.

—. "Byrhtferth and the *Vita S. Ecgwini*." In Lapidge, *Anglo-Latin Literature 900–1066*. London: Hambledon, 1993. 293–315.

—, John Blair, Simon Keynes, and Donald Scragg, eds., *Blackwell Encyclopaedia of Anglo-Saxon England*. Oxford: Blackwell, 1999.

Latour, Bruno. *We Have Never Been Modern*. Cambridge, Mass.: Harvard University Press, 1993.

Leach, Edmund. *Culture and Communication: The Logic by Which Symbols are Connected*. Cambridge: Cambridge University Press, 1976.

Lee, Alvin A. *The Guest-Hall of Eden. Four Essays on the Design of Old English Poetry*. New Haven and London: Yale University Press, 1972.

Lee, Christina. *Feasting the Dead: Food and Drink in Anglo-Saxon Burial Rituals*. Woodbridge: Boydell, 2007.

Lees, Clare A. "The 'Sunday Letter' and the 'Sunday Lists.'" *Anglo-Saxon England* 14 (1985), 129–51.

Liebermann, F., ed. *Die Gesetze der Angelsachsen*. 3 vols. Halle, 1903–16; repr. Aalen: Scientia, 1960.

Lindelöf, U., *Der Lambeth-Psalter*. Acta societatis scientiarum Fennicae 35.1, 43.3. Helsinki: Acta societatis scientiarum Fennicae, 1909–14.

Little, Barbara J. "Texts, Images, Material Culture." In Little, ed., *Text-Aided Archaeology*, 217–21.

—, ed. *Text-Aided Archaeology*. Boca Raton: CRC Press, 1991.

Liuzza, R. M., ed. and trans. *Anglo-Saxon Prognostics: An Edition and Translation of Texts from London, British Library, MS Cotton Tiberius A.iii*. Cambridge: D. S. Brewer, 2011.

Lobell, Jarrett A. "Trash Talk: Sorting through a Mountain of Pottery to Track the Roman Old Trade." *Archaeology* (March–April 2009), 21–25.

Logeman, H., ed. *The Rule of St. Benet*. EETS, O.S. 90. London: Oxford University Press, 1888; repr. 1973.

Loveluck, Christopher. "Cædmon's World: Secular and Monastic Lifestyles and Estate Organization in Northern England, A.D. 650–900." In Frantzen and Hines, eds., *Cædmon's Hymn*, 150–90.

—. "Changing Lifestyles, Interpretation of Settlement Character and Wider Perspectives." In Loveluck, ed., *Rural Settlement*, 144–63.

—. "The Dynamics of Elite Lifestyles in the Rural World, AD 600–1150:

Archaeological Perspectives from Northwest Europe." In François Bougard, Régine Le Jan and Rosamond McKitterick, eds., *La Culture du haut Moyen Âge, Une Question d'Élites?* Haut Moyen Âge 7. Turnhout: Brepols, 2009. 139–70.

—. "A High-status Anglo-Saxon Settlement at Flixborough, Lincolnshire." *Antiquity* 72 (1998), 146–61.

—. "Wealth, Waste, and Conspicuous Consumption. Flixborough and its Importance for Middle and Late Saxon Rural Settlement Studies." In Hamerow and MacGregor, eds., *Image and Power*, 78–130.

—, ed. *Rural Settlement, Lifestyles and Social Change in the later First Millennium A.D.: Anglo-Saxon Flixborough in its Wider Context.* Excavations at Flixborough, vol. 4. Oxford: Oxbow, 2007.

— and David Atkinson, eds. *The Early Medieval Settlement Remains from Flixborough, Lincolnshire: The Occupation Sequence, c. A.D. 600–1000.* Excavations at Flixborough, vol. 1. Oxford: Oxbow, 2007.

—, Keith Dobney, and James Barrett. "Trade and Exchange – The Settlement and the Wider World." In Loveluck, ed., *Rural Settlement*, 112–29.

Loyn, H. R. *Anglo-Saxon England and the Norman Conquest.* London: Longman, 1962.

Macray, W. D., ed. *Chronicon Abbatiae de Evesham*, Rolls Series xxix. London, 1863.

Magennis, Hugh. *Anglo-Saxon Appetites: Food and Drink and Their Consumption in Old English and Related Literature.* Dublin: Four Courts, 1999.

—. *Images of Community in Old English Poetry.* Cambridge: Cambridge University Press, 1996.

Mainman, A. J. *Anglo-Scandinavian Pottery from 16–22 Coppergate.* The Archaeology of York, Volume 16: The Pottery, Fasc. 5. York: CBA, 1990.

—. *Pottery from 46–54 Fishergate.* The Archaeology of York, Volume 16: The Pottery, Fasc. 6. York: CBA, 1993.

Mann, Jill. *Chaucer and Medieval Estates Satire: The Literature of Social Classes and the General Prologue to the Canterbury Tales.* Cambridge: Cambridge University Press, 1973.

McDonnell, Gerry. "Slags and Ironworking Residues." In Hamerow, *Excavations at Mucking*, 82–83.

McKee, Larry, Victor P. Hood, and Sharon Macpherson, "Reinterpreting the Construction History of the Service Area of the Hermitage Mansion." In Little, ed., *Text-Aided Archaeology*, 161–76.

McNeill, John T., and Helena M. Gamer, trans. *Medieval Handbooks of Penance.* New York: Columbia University Press, 1938; repr. 1990.

Meadows, Karen I. "Much Ado about Nothing: The Social Context of Eating and Drinking in Early Roman Britain." In Cumberpatch and Blinkhorn, eds., *Not So Much a Pot*, 21–35.

Meens, R. M. J., "'A Relic of Superstition': Bodily Impurity and the Church from Gregory the Great to the Twelfth Century Decretists." In M. J. H. M. Poorthuis and J. Schwartz, eds., *Purity and Holiness. The Heritage of Leviticus.* Leiden: Brill, 1999. 281–93.

Meens, Rob. "Pollution in the Early Middle Ages: The Case of the Food Regulations in Penitentials." *Early Medieval Europe* 4 (1995), 3–19.

Mennell, Stephen. *All Manners of Food: Eating and Taste in England and France from the Middle Ages to the Present.* Oxford: Basil Blackwell, 1985.

Metzger, Bruce M. *The Complete Parallel Bible.* New York: Oxford University Press, 1994.

Meyvaert, Paul. "Bede and the Church Paintings at Wearmouth-Jarrow." *Anglo-Saxon England* 8 (1979), 63–77.

Migne, J.-P., ed. *Patrologiae cursus completus, series latina*. 221 vols. Paris, 1844–55.

Miller, Thomas, ed. *The Old English Version of Bede's Ecclesiastical History of the English People*. EETS, O.S. 95, 96, 110, 111. Oxford: Oxford University Press, 1890–98; repr. London, 1959–63.

Milne, Gustav, and Julian D. Richards. *Wharram: A Study of Settlement on the Yorkshire Wolds, VII. Two Anglo-Saxon Buildings and Associated Finds*. York University Archaeological Publications 9. York: University of York, Short Run Press, 1992.

Mitchell, W. J. T. *Iconology: Image, Text, Ideology*. Chicago: University of Chicago Press, 1986.

—. "What Is an Image?" *New Literary History* 15.3 (1984), 503–37.

Moffat, Douglas, ed. and trans. *The Old English "Soul and Body."* Cambridge: D. S. Brewer, 1990.

Moreland, John. "The Significance of Production in Eighth-Century England." In Hansen and Wickham, eds., *The Long Eighth Century*, 69–104.

Morris, Carole A. *Wood and Woodworking in Anglo-Scandinavian and Medieval York*. The Archaeology of York, Volume 17: The Small Finds, Fasc. 13. York: CBA, 2000.

—. "Wood Objects." In Carolyn Heighway, A. P. Garrod, and Alan G. Vince, "Excavations at 1 Westgate Street, Gloucester, 1975." *Medieval Archaeology* 23 (1979), 159–213 at 197–200.

Mostert, Marco. "St. Edmund, King of East Anglia." In Lapidge *et al.*, eds., *BEASE*, 160–61.

Mould, Quita, Ian Carlisle, and Esther Cameron. *Leather and Leatherworking in Anglo-Scandinavian and Medieval York*. The Archaeology of York, Volume 17: The Small Finds, Fasc. 16. York: CBA, 2003.

Munby, Julian. "Wood." In Blair and Ramsey, eds., *English Medieval Industries*, 379–405.

Myres, J. N. L. *Anglo-Saxon Pottery and the Settlement of England*. Oxford: Oxford University Press, 1969.

Napier, Arthur S. "Altenglische Miscellen." *Archiv* 84 (1890), 323–27.

—, ed. *The Old English Version of the Enlarged Rule of Chrodegang together with the Latin Original, An Old English Version of the Capitula of Theodulf together with the Latin Original, An Interlinear Old English Rendering of the Epitome of Benedict of Aniane*. EETS, O.S. 150. London: Oxford University Press, 1916; repr. 1971.

—, ed. *Wulfstan: Sammlung der ihm zugeschriebenen Homilien nebst untersuchungen über ihre echtheit*, Sammlung englischer Denkmäler 4. Berlin: Weidmann, 1883.

Näsman, Ulf. "Exchange and Politics: The Eighth-Early Ninth century in Denmark." In Hansen and Wickham, eds., *The Long Eighth Century*, 35–68.

Nielsen, Karen Høilund. "From Artefact to Interpretation Using Correspondence Analysis." In David Griffiths, ed. *Anglo-Saxon Studies in Archaeology and History* 8. Oxford: Oxford University School of Archaeology, 1995. 111–43.

Niles, John D., and Marijane Osborn, eds. *Beowulf and Lejre*. Tempe: Arizona Center for Medieval and Renaissance Studies, 2007.

Oakeshott, Michael. *Religion, Politics, and the Moral Life*. New Haven: Yale University Press, 1993.

Oakley, Thomas P. *English Penitential Discipline and Anglo-Saxon Law in their Joint Influence*. New York: Columbia University Press, 1923.

O'Connor, Terence. "8th–11th Century Economy and Environment in York." In Rackham, ed., *Environment and Economy in Anglo-Saxon England*, 136–47.

—. *Animal Bones from Flaxengate, Lincoln: c. 870–1500*. London: CBA, 1982.

—. *Bones from Anglo-Scandinavian Levels at 16–22 Coppergate*. The Archaeology of York, Volume 15: The Animal Bones, Fasc. 3. York: CBA, 1989.

—. *Bones from 46–54 Fishergate*. The Archaeology of York, Volume 15: The Animal Bones, Fasc. 4. York: CBA, 1991.

Oddy, W. A., and P. C. Van Geersdaele. "The Recovery of the Graveney Boat." *Studies in Conservation* 17 (1972), 30–38.

Oliver, Lisi. *The Beginnings of English Law*. Toronto: University of Toronto Press, 2002.

Olsen, Bjørnar. "Material Culture after Text: Re-Membering Things." *Norwegian Archaeological Review* 36 (2003), 87–104.

O'Neill, Patrick P., ed. *King Alfred's Old English Prose Translation of the First Fifty Psalms*. Cambridge: Medieval Academy, 2001.

Oosthuizen, Susan. "Medieval Field Systems and Settlement Nucleation: Common or Separate Origins?" In Higham and Ryan, eds., *Landscape Archaeology of Anglo-Saxon England*, 107–32.

Ordnance Survey: A Guide to Coordinate Systems in Great Britain, v 2.1. Southampton: Ordnance Survey, 2010. Online resource: www.ordnancesurvey.co.uk.

Ottaway, Patrick. *Anglo-Scandinavian Ironwork from 16–22 Coppergate*. The Archaeology of York, Volume 17: The Small Finds, Fasc. 6. York: CBA, 1992.

—. "The Products of the Blacksmith in Mid-Late Anglo-Saxon England." Online resource: http://www.pjoarchaeology.co.uk/academic-consultancy/anglosaxon-ironwork.html.

—, Lisa M. Wastling, Nicola Rogers, Martin Foreman, and David Surely. "Domestic Fittings and Implements." In Evans and Loveluck, eds., *Life and Economy*, 165–243.

—, et al. "Miscellaneous Iron Fixtures and Fittings: Knives." In Evans and Loveluck, eds., *Life and Economy*, 203–12.

Parkhouse, Jonathan. "The Distribution and Exchange of Mayen Lava Quernstones in Early Medieval Northwestern Europe." *Papers of the 'Medieval Europe Brugge 1997' Conference*, vol. 3, Exchange and Trade in Medieval Europe. Zellik: Instituut voor het Archeologisch Patrimunium, 1997. 97–106.

Parry, Stephen, ed. *Raunds Area Survey: An Archaeological Study of the Landscape of Raunds, Northamptonshire, 1985–94*. Oxford: Oxbow, 2006.

Payer, Pierre J. *Sex and the Penitentials: The Development of a Sexual Code 550–1150*. Toronto: University of Toronto Press, 1984.

Peers, Charles, and C. A. Ralegh Radford. "The Saxon Monastery of Whitby." *Archaeologica* 89 (1943), 27–88.

Pelteret, David A. E. *Slavery in Early Mediaeval England*. Woodbridge: Boydell, 1995.

Pestell, Tim. *Landscapes of Monastic Foundation: The Establishment of Religious Houses in East Anglia, c. 650–1200*. Woodbridge: Boydell, 2004.

—. "Writing and Literacy-Related Items: The Styli." In Evans and Loveluck, eds., *Life and Economy*, 123–38.

Pollington, Stephen. *The Mead-Hall: Feasting in Anglo-Saxon England*. Frithgarth, Norfolk: Anglo-Saxon Books, 2003.

Pope, John C., ed. *Homilies of Ælfric: A Supplementary Collection*. 2 vols. EETS, O.S. 259, 260. London: Oxford University Press, 1967–68.

Powell, H. P. "Geology of the Area around Shakenoak Farm." In Brodribb, Hands, and Walker, *Excavations at Shakenoak Farm*, 143–45.

Powlesland, Dominic. "Early Anglo-Saxon Settlements, Structures, Form and Layout." In Hines, ed., *The Anglo-Saxons from the Migration Period to the Eighth Century*, 101–24.

—. "West Heslerton Settlement Mobility: A Case of Static Development." In Geake and Kenny, eds., *Early Deira*, 19–26.

Pratt, David. *The Political Thought of King Alfred the Great.* Cambridge: Cambridge University Press, 2007.

Priebsch, Robert. "The Chief Sources of Some Anglo-Saxon Homilies." *Otia Merseiana* 1 (1899), 129–47.

Pringle, Heather. "Vikings and Native Americans." *National Geographic* (November 2012). Online resource: http://ngm.nationalgeographic.com/2012/11/vikings-and-indians/pringle-text.

Rackham, James, ed. *Environment and Economy in Anglo-Saxon England: A Review of Recent Work on the Environmental Archaeology of Rural and Urban Anglo-Saxon Settlements in England.* CBA, Research Report 89. York: CBA, 1994.

Raith, Josef, ed. *Die altenglische Version des Halitgar'schen Bussbuches (sog. Poenitentiale Pseudo-Ecgberti).* Bibliothek der angelsächsischen Prosa 13. Hamburg, 1933; repr. Darmstadt: Wissenschaftliche Buchgesellschaft, 1964.

Rahtz, Philip. "Buildings and Rural Settlements." In Wilson, ed., *The Archaeology of Anglo-Saxon England*, 49–98.

—. "Gazetteer of Anglo-Saxon Domestic Settlement Sites." In Wilson, ed., *The Archaeology of Anglo-Saxon England*, 405–52.

—. "Mills." In Lapidge *et al.*, eds., *BEASE*, 313–15.

—. "New Approaches to Medieval Archaeology, Part 1." In D. A. Hinton, ed., *25 Years of Medieval Archaeology*. Sheffield: University of Sheffield, 1983. 12–23.

—, and Donald Bullough. "The Parts of an Anglo-Saxon Mill." *Anglo-Saxon England* 6 (1977), 15–37.

—, and Robert Meeson. *An Anglo-Saxon Watermill at Tamworth: Excavations in the Bolebridge Street area of Tamworth, Staffordshire in 1971 and 1978.* BAR Research Report 83. London: CBA, 1992.

Reynolds, Andrew. *Anglo-Saxon Deviant Burial Customs.* Oxford: Oxford University Press, 2009.

Rhijn, Carine van, and Marjolijn Saan. "Correcting Sinners, Correcting Texts: A Context for the *Paenitentiale pseudo-Theodori.*" *Early Medieval Europe* 14 (2006), 23–40.

Richards, J. D. "Anglo-Saxon Settlement and Archaeological Visibility in the Yorkshire Wolds." In Geake and Kenny, eds., *Early Deira*, 27–41.

—. "Anglo-Saxon Symbolism." In Carver, ed., *The Age of Sutton Hoo*, 131–47.

—. *The Significance of Form and Decoration of Anglo-Saxon Cremation Urns.* BAR, British Series 166. Oxford: BAR, 1987.

Roberts, Jane. "Anglo-Saxon Vocabulary as a Reflection of Material Culture." In Carver, ed., *The Age of Sutton Hoo*, 185–202.

—, and Christian Kay, with Lynne Grundy, eds. *A Thesaurus of Old English: In Two Volumes.* London: King's College, 1995. Online resource: http://oldenglishthesaurus.arts.gla.ac.uk/.

Robertson, A. J., ed. *Anglo-Saxon Charters.* Cambridge: Cambridge University Press, 1956.

—, ed. and trans. *The Laws of the Kings of England from Edmund to Henry I.*

Works Cited

Cambridge: Cambridge University Press, 1925; repr. New York: AMS Press, 1974.

Rogers, Nicola S. H. *Anglian and Other Finds from 46–54 Fishergate*. The Archaeology of York, Volume 17: The Small Finds, Fasc. 9. York: CBA, 1993.

—, with Susan M. Youngs. "Copper-alloy Vessels and Container Mounts." In Evans and Loveluck, eds., *Life and Economy*, 115–21.

Rogers, Penelope Walton. *Textile Production at 16–22 Coppergate*. The Archaeology of York, Volume 17: The Small Finds, Fasc. 11. York: CBA, 1997.

Rogerson, Andrew, and Carolyn Dallas. *Excavations in Thetford 1948–59 and 1973–80*. East Anglian Archaeology, Report no. 22. Gressenhall: Norfolk Archaeological Unit, 1984.

Roesdahl, Else. *The Vikings*. Trans. Susan M. Margeson and Kirsten Williams. Rev. ed. London: Penguin, 1998.

—, Jean-Pierre Mohen, and François-Xavier Dillman, eds. *Les Vikings: Les Scandinaves et l'Europe 800–1200*. Paris: Association Française d'Action Artistique et auteurs, 1992.

Rosier, James L., ed. *The Vitellius Psalter*. Ithaca: Cornell University Press, 1962.

Rulon-Miller, Nina. "Sexual Humor and Fettered Desire in Exeter Book Riddle 12." In Jon Wilcox, ed., *Humor in Anglo-Saxon Literature*. Cambridge: D. S. Brewer, 2000. 99–126.

Samson, Ross. "Illusory Emporia and Mad Economic Theories." In Mike Anderton, ed., *Anglo-Saxon Trading Centres: Beyond the Emporia*. Glasgow: Cruithne, 1999. 76–90.

Sauer, Hans, ed. *Theodulfi Capitula in England: Die altenglischen Übersetzungen, zusammen mit dem lateinischen Text*. Munich: Wilhelm Fink, 1978.

—. "Zwei Spätaltenglishe Beichtermahnungen aus Hs. Cotton Tiberius A.iii." *Anglia* 98 (1980), 1–33.

Saunders, Tom. "Class, Space and 'Feudal' Identities in Early Medieval England." In Frazer and Tyrrell, eds., *Social Identity in Early Medieval Britain*, 209–32.

Sawyer, P. H. *Anglo-Saxon Charters, An Annotated List and Bibliography*. London: Royal Historical Society, 1968.

Scull, Christopher. "Urban Centres in Pre-Viking England?" In Hines, ed., *The Anglo-Saxons*, 269–98.

Schröer, Arnold, ed. *Die Winteney-Version der Regula S. Benedicti*. Halle, 1888; repr. with appendix by M. Gretsch. Tubingen: Max Niemeyer Verlag, 1978.

—, ed. *The Rule of St. Benedict*. In *Die angelsächsischen Prosabearbeitungen der Benediktinerregel*, with appendix by Helmut Gneuss. Bibliothek der angelsächsichen Prosa 2. Kassel, 1885–88; repr. Darmstadt: Wissenschaftliche Buchgesellschaft, 1964.

Schweitzer, Ilse. "The *Crux Gemmata* and Shifting Significances of the Cross in Insular Art." *Marginalia* 3 (2010). Online resource: http://www.marginalia.co.uk/journal/06illumination/schweitzer.php#54.

Serjeantson, Dale, and Christopher M. Woolgar. "Fish Consumption in Medieval England." In Woolgar, Serjeantson, and Waldron, eds., *Food in Medieval England*, 102–30.

Shanks, Michael, and Christopher Tilley. *Re-Constructing Archaeology: Theory and Practice*. Cambridge: Cambridge University Press, 1987.

Shillingsburg, Peter L. *From Gutenberg to Google: Electronic Representation of Literary Texts*. Cambridge: Cambridge University Press, 2006.

Shippey, T. A. "Old English Poetry: The Prospects for Literary History." In

275

Antonio Leon Sendra, ed., *Proceedings of the Second International Conference of SELIM (Spanish Society for English Medieval Language and Literature)*. Cordoba: SELIM, l993. 164–79.

Sisam, Kenneth. *Studies in the History of Old English Literature*. Oxford: Clarendon, 1953.

Skeat, Walter W., ed. *Ælfric's Lives of Saints*. 4 vols. EETS, O.S. 76, 82, 94, 114; repr. in 2 vols. London: Oxford University Press, 1966.

—, ed. *The Holy Gospels in Anglo-Saxon, Northumbrian, and Old Mercian Versions*. Cambridge: Cambridge University Press, 1871–87.

Slowikowski, A. M., and P. Blinkhorn, A. Mainman, A. Vince, and A. Wood. "The Anglo-Saxon and Medieval Pottery." In Stamper and Croft, eds., *Wharram: A Study of Settlement on the Yorkshire Wolds*, 60–100.

Somers, Margaret R., and Gloria D. Gibson. "Reclaiming the Epistemological 'Other': Narrative and the Social Construction of Identity." In Craig Calhon, ed., *Social Theory and the Politics of Identity*. Oxford: Wiley-Blackwell, 1994. 37–99.

Sorrell, Paul. "Like a Duck to Water: Representations of Aquatic Animals in Early Anglo-Saxon Literature and Art." *Leeds Studies in English*, n.s. 25 (1994), 29–68.

Stafford, Pauline. "Reeve." In Lapidge *et al.*, eds., *BEASE*, 386–87.

Stamper, P. A., and R. A. Croft, eds. *Wharram: A Study of Settlement on the Yorkshire Wolds, VIII. The South Manor Area*. York University Archaeological Publications 10. York: University of York, Short Run Press, 2000.

Stenton, Sir Frank. *Anglo-Saxon England*, 3rd ed. Oxford: Oxford University Press, 1971.

Storms, Godfried. *Anglo-Saxon Magic*. The Hague: Martinus, 1972.

Swanton, Michael, trans. *Anglo-Saxon Prose*. London: Dent, 1993.

Sweet, Henry, ed. *King Alfred's West-Saxon Version of Gregory's Pastoral Care*. EETS, O. S. 45, 50. London: Oxford University Press, 1871; repr. New York, 1973.

Sykes, N. J. "The Impact of the Normans on Hunting Practices in England." In Woolgar, Serjeantson, and Waldron, eds., *Food in Medieval England*, 162–75.

Thompson, Victoria. "The Pastoral Contract in Late Anglo-Saxon England: Priest and Parishioner in Oxford, Bodleian Library, MS Laud Miscellaneous 482." In Francesca Tinti, ed., *Pastoral Care in Late Anglo-Saxon England*. Woodbridge: Boydell, 2005. 106–20.

Thorpe, Benjamin, ed. *Diplomatarium Anglicum ævi Saxonici*. London: Macmillan, 1865.

Thrupp, John. *The Anglo-Saxon Home: A History of the Domestic Institutions and Customs of England from the Fifth to the Eleventh Century*. London: Longman, 1862.

Tilley, Christopher. *Reading Material Culture*. Oxford: Blackwell, 1990.

Timby, J., and P. Andrews. "The Pottery." In Andrews, ed., *Excavations at Hamwic*, 207–9.

Turner, Sharon. *The History of the Anglo-Saxons*. 3 vols. London: Longman, Hurst, Rees, Orme, and Brown, 1823.

Twiss, Katheryn C., ed. *The Archaeology of Food and Identity*. Center for Archaeological Investigations. Occasional Paper no. 34. Carbondale: Southern Illinois University, 2007.

Ulmschneider, Katharina. *Markets, Minsters, and Metal-Detectors: The Archaeology of Middle Saxon Lincolnshire and Hampshire Compared*. BAR, British Series 307. Oxford: Archaeopress, 2000.

United States Census Bureau. "Urban and Rural Population." (August 1995). Online resource: http://www.census.gov/population/censusdata/urpop 0090.txt.

Vangemeren, Willem A. *Psalms. The Expositor's Bible Commentary*, vol. 5. Rev. ed. Ed. Tremper Longman III and David E. Garland. 13 vols. Grand Rapids: Zondervan, 1991.

Veen, Marijke van der, Alexandra Livarda, and Alistair Hill. "New Plant Foods in Roman Britain – Dispersal and Social Access." *Environmental Archaeology* 13.1 (2008), 11–36.

Verhulst, Adriaan. *The Rise of Cities in North-West Europe.* Cambridge: Cambridge University Press, 1999.

Vince, Alan. "Saxon Urban Economies: An Archaeological Perspective." In Rackham, ed., *Environment and Economy in Anglo-Saxon England*, 108–19.

Vleeskruyer, R. *The Life of St. Chad: An Old English Homily.* Amsterdam: North Holland Publishing, 1953.

Vriend, Hubert Jan de, ed. *The Old English Herbarium and Medicina de Quadrupedibus.* EETS, O.S. 286. London: Oxford University Press, 1984.

Wade, Keith. "Ipswich." In Hodges and Hobley, eds., *The Rebirth of Towns in the West*, 93–100.

—. "A Settlement Site at Bonhunt Farm, Wicken Bonhunt, Essex." In D. G. Buckley, ed., *Archaeology in Essex to AD 1500.* London: CBA, 1980. 96–102.

Wade-Martins, Peter. *Excavations in North Elmham Park 1967–1972.* East Anglian Archaeology, Report no. 9. 2 vols. Gressenhall: Norfolk Archaeological Unit, 1980.

Walker, G. S. M., ed. *Sancti Columbani Opera.* Dublin: Dublin Institute for Advanced Studies, 1970.

Wastling, Lisa M., and Patrick Ottaway. "Cultivation, Crop Processing and Food Procurement." In Evans and Loveluck, eds., *Life and Economy*, 244–52.

Waterman, Dudley M. "Late Saxon, Viking and Early Medieval Finds from York." *Archaeologia*, 97 (1959), 59–106.

Webster, Leslie, and Janet Backhouse, eds. *The Making of England: Anglo-Saxon Art and Culture, A.D. 600–900.* London: The British Museum Press, 1991.

Wenisch, Franz. *Spezifisch anglisches Wortgut in den nordhumbrischen Interlinearglossierung des Lukasevangeliums.* Heidelberg: Carl Winter, 1979.

West, Stanley. *A Corpus of Anglo-Saxon Material from Suffolk.* East Anglian Archaeology, Report no. 84. Ipswich: Suffolk County Council, 1998.

—. "Excavations at Cox Lane (1958) and at the Town Defenses, Shire Hall Yard, Ipswich (1959)." *Proceedings of the Suffolk Institute of Archæology* 29.3 (1963), 233–303.

—. *West Stow Revisited.* Bury St. Edmunds: St. Edmundbury Borough Council, 2001.

—. *West Stow: The Anglo-Saxon Village.* 2 vols. East Anglian Archaeology, Report no. 24. Gressenhall: Norfolk Archaeological Unit, 1985.

Whitelock, Dorothy. *The Beginnings of English Society.* Pelican History of England 2. Harmondsworth: Penguin, 1952.

—, ed. *English Historical Documents. Vol. 1, c. 500–1042.* London: Eyre Methuen, 1979.

—, ed. and trans. with a note by N. R. Ker. *Anglo-Saxon Wills.* Cambridge: Cambridge University Press, 1930; repr. 2011.

—, ed. and trans. with Neil Ker and Lord Russell. *The Will of Æthelgifu: A Tenth-Century Anglo-Saxon Manuscript.* Oxford: The Roxburghe Club, 1968.

Wickham, Chris. *Framing the Early Middle Ages: Europe and the Mediterranean 400–800.* Oxford: Oxford University Press, 2005.

—. "The Other Transition: From the Ancient World to Feudalism." *Past and Present* 103 (1984), 3–36.

Wiessner, Polly, and Wulf Schiefenhövel. *Food and the Status Quest: An Interdisciplinary Perspective.* Providence: Berghahn Books, 1996.

Wildhagen, Karl, ed. *Der Cambridger Psalter.* Bibliothek der angelsächsischen Prosa 7. Hamburg, 1910; repr. Darmstadt: Wissenschaftliche Buchgesellschaft, 1964.

Williams, Ann. "A Bell-house and a *Burh-geat*: Lordly Residences in England before the Norman Conquest." In Christopher Harper-Bill and Ruth Harvey, eds., *Medieval Knighthood 4: Papers from the Fifth Strawberry Hill Conference.* Woodbridge: Boydell, 1992. 221–40.

Williams, Howard. *Death and Memory in Early Medieval Britain.* Cambridge: Cambridge University Press, 2006.

Williamson, Tom. *Shaping Medieval Landscapes: Settlement, Society, Environment.* Macclesfield: Windgather, 2003.

—. *Sutton Hoo and its Landscape: The Context of Monuments.* Oxford: Oxbow, 2008.

Wilson, David M. *The Anglo-Saxons.* Harmondsworth: Penguin, 1971.

—. "Craft and Industry." In Wilson, ed., *The Archaeology of Anglo-Saxon England,* 253–81.

—, ed. *The Archaeology of Anglo-Saxon England.* Cambridge: Cambridge University Press, 1981.

Windell, David, Andy Chapman, and Jo Woodiwiss. *From Barrow to Bypass: Excavations at West Cotton, Raunds, Northamptonshire 1985–1989.* Northampton: Northamptonshire County Council, 1990.

Withers, Benjamin C. *The Illustrated Old English Hexateuch, Cotton Claudius B.IV.* Toronto: University of Toronto Press, 2007.

Wolf, Kirsten. *Daily Life of the Vikings.* Westport, Conn.: Greenwood Press, 2004.

Wood, G. W. "The Vision of Eoves and What Came of It." In Rev. Benjamin Waugh, ed., *The Sunday Magazine.* London, 1892. 814–23.

Woolgar, C. M. "'Take this Penance Now, and Afterwards the Fare Will Improve': Seafood and Late Medieval Diet." In David J. Starkey, Chris Reid, and Neil Ashcroft, eds., *England's Sea Fisheries: The Commercial Sea Fisheries of England and Wales since 1300.* London: Chatham, 2000. 36–44, 247–48.

—, D. Serjeantson, and T. Waldron, eds. *Food in Medieval England: Diet and Nutrition.* London: Oxford University Press, 2006.

Wormald, Patrick. *Legal Culture in the Early Medieval West: Law as Text, Image and Experience.* London: Hambledon, 1999.

—. *The Making of English Law: King Alfred to the Twelfth Century.* Oxford: Blackwell, 1999.

Wright, Thomas. *The Homes of Other Days: A History of Domestic Manners and Sentiments in England from the Earliest Known Period to Modern Times.* London: Trübner, 1871.

Young, Jane, and Alan Vince. "The Anglo-Saxon Pottery." In Evans and Loveluck, eds., *Life and Economy,* 339–401.

Zupitza, Julius. *Ælfrics Grammatik und Glossar.* Sammlung englischer Denkmäler 1. Repr. with an introduction by Helmut Gneuss. Berlin: Weidmann, 1966.

Index

Gregory I (the Great, pope) 151, 212–13, 247
  Pastoral Care (in Old English), 10 n.2, 63, 96,
    97, 127, 128–9
Gregory III (pope) 193
Gurevich, Aron 28–29, 180

Habitus 16–17, 18, 92, 111, 158–9, 160, 164,
  174
Hagan, Ann 37, 42, 49, 50, 51–53, 99, 241
Haligar of Cambrai (Bishop) 181, 188
Hall
  as center of settlement 37, 54, 89
  as feasting site 43–44
  dimensions of 44
Hamerow, Helena 87
Hamwic (Hampshire)
  and *habitus* 119
  as urban 135
  ironwork at 137, 142
  market at 38, 52, 54, 88, 89–90
  plan of 89–90, 119
  pots and potters at 114, 118, 119–21
  querns at 90, 103, 104
  Six Dials 135, 158
  smithies at 134
  wood at 158
Hand-mills 101. *See also* Querns
Hardy, Thomas 35–36
Harke, Heinrich 18, 142
Harvey, P. D. A. 216
Hazan, Marcella 50
Hearths 44, 47, 93, 112, 136, 140
Hedeby (Denmark) 86, 143–4
Hellebore 66–7
Herlihy, David 58
Hermeneumata pseudo-Dositheana 70
Hild (abbess) 2, 35, 36, 37
Hillesley (Gloucester) 220
Hines, John 24–26, 56
Hirst, Susan 85
Hlothhere and Eadric (kings), laws of 42, 207
Hobley, Brian 137
Hodder, Ian 22
Hodges, Richard 50–54, 56, 90, 111, 116, 119,
  120, 234
Honey 177
Hooks, iron 137, 138, 140
  as instrument of torture 152
  for boats 143–4
  handles for 143, 144, 160
  See also Forks
Hooke, Della 53 n.67, 221, 237
Horsemeat, consumption of 186, 187, 193
Hospitality 206
Hrabanus Maurus (archbishop) 12
Humbert (bishop) 123
Hungate (York) 146
Hunters 193, 198. *See also* Colloquy
Hunting 4, 60, 61, 197, 212
  at Flixborough 121, 122
  by clergy 181, 198

tools for 141, 172
  See also Colloquy
Hurst, J. G. 107, 115, 118, 138
Hwit ("white foods") 243–4

Identity
  as dynamic 18–19
  of settlements 54, 91–2, 116–17, 120–1
  national 210
  personal 18, 105, 169, 173
  religious 256
  See also Situational Identity, Social Identity
Illington-Lackford ware 115
Images 23–24
Ine (king), laws of 42, 101, 208, 209, 210
Inland (area of estate) 39, 55, 99
Institutes of Polity 230, 249–50. *See also*
  Wulfstan
Ipswich (Suffolk)
  and habitus 119
  writing at 69
  trade networks of 38, 53, 116, 117. *See also*
  Ipswich ware
Ipswich ware 107, 111, 114, 115–16, 116–19, 143
Irish monasticism 38–39, 184, 186
  See also Columbanus, Cummean, Finnian
Iron, food objects made of
  and identity 135, 138, 141, 142, 154–5
  at early sites 136–7
  at later sites 137–41
  textual references to 148–53
  Sites where found
    Birka (Sweden) 143–4
    Cambridge, Downing Street 146
    Coppergate 135, 143–5
    Fishergate 144, 147
    Flixborough 44–5, 137–8, 139–40, 142,
      143, 144, 145
    Goltho 141
    Hamwic 137, 142
    Hedeby (Denmark) 143–4
    Jutland 148 n.90
    Lundenwic 137
    Mucking 136
    North Elmham 140, 143, 144
    Portchester Castle 136, 158
    Shakenoak 136–7
    Thetford 143, 144
    Wharram Percy 140–1
    Yelford 142
    York 136
    See also Buckets, Cauldrons, Chains,
      Fish hooks, Forks, Hooks, Knives,
      Ladles, Plowshare, Skewers,
      Spoons
Ironwork
  and identity 132, 138, 141–2, 154–5, 160
  and productive sites 69 n.146
  and wooden handles 135, 140, 143, 144,
    146, 155, 156, 160
  general characteristics of 132–6

ANGLO-SAXON STUDIES

Printed and bound by CPI Group (UK) Ltd, Croydon, CR0 4YY

09/06/2025

14685716-0005